D0457247

More Thoughts for Buffets

BY THE SAME AUTHORS

Thoughts for Food
Thoughts for Buffets
Thoughts for Festive Food
Thoughts for Good Eating

More Thoughts for Buffets

Houghton Mifflin Company   Boston   1984

Copyright © 1984 by Institute Publishing Company

All rights reserved. No part of this work may be reproduced
or transmitted in any form or by any means, electronic or
mechanical, including photocopying and recording, or by
any information storage or retrieval system, except as
may be expressly permitted by the 1976 Copyright Act or in
writing from the publisher. Requests for permission should be
addressed in writing to Houghton Mifflin Company,
2 Park Street, Boston, Massachusetts 02108.

Library of Congress Cataloging in Publication Data

Main entry under title:

More thoughts for buffets.

Includes index.
1. Buffets (Cookery). 2. Menus.
TX738.5.M67   1984   642'.4   84-12786
ISBN 0-395-35328-9

Printed in the United States of America

Q 10 9 8 7 6 5 4 3 2 1

Preface

Since the publication of *Thoughts for Buffets* in 1958, life-styles have changed dramatically. Women of the 1980s are active in the business world and have less time for cooking. More men are sharing and enjoying cooking tasks. Ease of air travel has made our palates more sophisticated. Food processors and microwave ovens have become essential aids in easing preparation. Ingredients from the world over, seasonal and fresh, are jetted to our neighborhood supermarkets. With a growing awareness of the fundamentals of sound nutrition, good health, and fitness, we have discovered that "less is more."

More Thoughts for Buffets is our response to these changes—a book for the eighties and beyond. It is our hope that this book will help busy hosts and hostesses entertain with style and ease and busy parents prepare family meals that are interesting and nutritious. Our theme is buffet service, a term that covers everything from elegant parties to pickup suppers before school activities and evening meetings.

We have included, once again, an advance preparation schedule for your convenience and have indicated the number of people a given menu will serve, if other than six. We present our book to you with pride and the hope that novices as well as seasoned cooks will enjoy using it for years to come.

Contrary to popular myth, too many cooks do *not* spoil the broth! We are deeply indebted to the many cooks, testers, editors, and contributors for the time, energy, talent, and caring they have put into this book.

Contents

Brunch Buffets

Each recipe serves six unless otherwise indicated.

A Sunday or holiday brunch is a warm and friendly way to entertain friends whose calendars are as crowded as our own. A well-planned brunch is also appropriate for those special times when the clan gathers. And brunch for your immediate family is a welcome way to vary the routine.

As coffee cakes are so often used in brunch menus, we offer a few suggestions for freezing them and thus facilitating your preparations.

To freeze coffee cakes: Cool, wrap in foil or freezer paper, freeze. If frosting is indicated, do it just before serving.

To serve: While still wrapped, let thaw several hours at room temperature. Then frost, if recipe so directs.

To heat: Wrap in foil (if not already wrapped) and heat in a 400° oven. Allow 15 minutes for individual rolls and 30 to 45 minutes for larger coffee cakes.

April Brunch   (Serves 12)

Fruit Mélange
Blintz Puff
Platter of Assorted Smoked Fish with Sliced Tomatoes and Scallions
Cauliflower Salad
Pecan Rolls
Sassy Prune Cake

PREVIOUS DAY	EARLY MORNING	FREEZER
Blintz Puff	*Cauliflower Salad*	*Cake*
Sassy Prune Cake		*Pecan Rolls*

Fruit Mélange

6 oranges, peeled and sliced
3 or 4 grapefruit, peeled and sectioned

2 quarts strawberries, cleaned and hulled
Sweetened, shredded coconut, to taste

Arrange orange slices and grapefruit sections alternately in a circle on a round platter. Mound strawberries in center. Sprinkle with coconut.

Blintz Puff

¼ pound butter or margarine, softened
⅓ cup sugar
6 eggs
1½ cups sour cream

½ cup orange juice
1 cup flour
2 teaspoons baking powder
½ teaspoon grated lemon rind (optional)

Filling:

8 ounces cream cheese, cut into pieces
2 cups small curd cottage cheese

2 egg yolks
1 tablespoon sugar
1 teaspoon vanilla extract

Butter a 13-by-9-inch pan. Beat the butter, sugar, eggs, sour cream, orange juice, flour, and baking powder until blended. Add lemon rind, if using. Pour half the batter into the greased pan. Cream the cream cheese with the other filling ingredients. Drop by spoonfuls over the batter in the baking dish. Gently spread the mixture with a knife to cover the surface. It will combine slightly with the batter in the dish. Pour the remaining batter over the filling. Bake in a preheated 350° oven, uncovered, 50 minutes to 1 hour. The blintz will be puffy and golden brown.

Note: The unbaked mixture can be refrigerated overnight. Bring back to room temperature before baking.

Platter of Assorted Smoked Fish with Sliced Tomatoes and Scallions

1 pound sliced, smoked salmon
½ pound peppered trout or peppered sable

1 large smoked white fish, boned and cut into small portions
3 large tomatoes

6 scallions

Arrange fish on glass platter and surround with sliced tomatoes and scallions.

Cauliflower Salad

2 small heads cauliflower
2 cups mayonnaise
½ cup chili sauce
2 tablespoons dill weed
4 tablespoons Italian dressing

2 tablespoons lemon juice
2 cups chopped celery
2 10-ounce packages frozen peas, defrosted

Break cauliflower into pieces and cook slightly. Cool. Mix mayonnaise and remaining 4 dressing ingredients. Combine vegetables and dressing and refrigerate.

Pecan Rolls
(Makes 1 dozen)

¼ teaspoon baking soda
¼ cup granulated sugar
1 teaspoon salt
1 package active dry yeast
2½ to 3 cups all-purpose flour
  (more if needed)
1 cup buttermilk

3 tablespoons salad oil
2 tablespoons water
4 tablespoons butter or
  margarine, melted
½ cup firmly packed brown
  sugar
½ cup pecan halves

1 teaspoon ground cinnamon

In large bowl, combine soda, granulated sugar, salt, yeast, and 1 cup of flour. Place buttermilk and oil in pan over medium-low heat until warm (120°); add to flour mixture and beat for 2 minutes. Stir in 1½ cups of remaining flour and beat until smooth. Turn dough out onto floured board and knead until smooth and elastic, about 10 minutes, adding more flour as needed. Let dough rest on board while preparing muffin cups.

Combine water, 2 tablespoons of the melted butter, and ¼ cup of the brown sugar. Distribute mixture equally among twelve 2½-inch muffin cups; top with pecan halves.

Roll dough into a 12-by-15-inch rectangle. Brush surface with remaining melted butter. Mix together remaining brown sugar and cinnamon; sprinkle evenly over buttered dough. Starting with a narrow end, roll lengthwise into a cylinder, cut into 12 slices, and place, cut side down, in muffin cups. Let rise, uncovered, in warm place until doubled in bulk (about 1½ hours). Bake in preheated 350° oven for about 25 minutes, until tops are golden. Invert immediately onto serving plate. Let pan rest briefly on rolls so syrup can drizzle down over them. Let rolls cool for 10 minutes before serving, as topping will be very hot. Freezes well.

Note: These rolls are not rich with butter and eggs but are delicious in an old-fashioned way.

Sassy Prune Cake

Cake:

2 cups flour	2 cups sugar
1 teaspoon baking soda	1 cup corn oil
½ teaspoon salt	3 eggs
1 teaspoon cinnamon	1 cup buttermilk
1 teaspoon allspice	1 cup cooked prunes, pitted and
½ teaspoon nutmeg	chopped

1 cup chopped pecans

Grease and flour a Bundt pan or 10-inch tube pan. Sift flour with baking soda and spices. Beat the sugar, oil, and eggs until very well combined, like a mayonnaise. Add dry ingredients alternately with buttermilk, blending after each addition. Stir in prunes, then nuts. Pour into prepared pan and bake in preheated 350° oven for 1 hour and 10 minutes.

Glaze:

1 cup sugar	½ cup buttermilk
¼ teaspoon salt	1 tablespoon light corn syrup
¼ teaspoon baking soda	1 teaspoon vanilla extract

Combine all ingredients in saucepan, bring to a boil, and stir for 5 minutes. While glaze is hot, carefully prick warm cake with a toothpick and pour half of the glaze on the cake while it is in the pan. Turn cake out on a rack and cool 10 minutes, keeping glaze warm. Place on cake plate and pour remaining glaze over top.

Note: Wax-paper strips placed under outer edges of cake will prevent the cake plate from collecting much of the glaze. Remove wax-paper strips before serving.

Spring Fantasy Brunch

Citrus Eye-Opener
Cottage Cheese Pancakes with Whipped Cinnamon Butter
and Hot Blueberry Syrup
Grilled Ham Steaks
Swiss Apple Salad
Cranberry Sour Cream Cake

PREVIOUS DAY	EARLY MORNING	FREEZER
Blueberry Syrup	*Citrus Juices*	*Cranberry Cake*
Apple Salad		
Whipped Butter		

Citrus Eye-Opener

Juice of 2 fresh grapefruit   6 ounces frozen orange juice
2¼ cups water

Early in day combine juices with water and chill.

Cottage Cheese Pancakes

6 eggs, separated   ½ teaspoon salt
1 cup cottage cheese   1 cup unsifted flour
1 cup milk

Beat egg yolks until thick and light colored, stir in cottage cheese, and beat until smooth. Sift in flour, add milk and salt, and blend until smooth. Beat egg whites until soft peaks form, fold into cheese mixture. Let stand for 5 minutes.

Grease griddle or skillet. Pour in ¼ cup batter at a time and cook until bubbly. Serve with Whipped Cinnamon Butter and Hot Blueberry Syrup.

Whipped Cinnamon Butter:
(Makes 1 cup)

½ pound butter   ½ teaspoon cinnamon
¼ teaspoon nutmeg

Beat butter and spices until light and fluffy. Spoon lightly into a serving dish.

Hot Blueberry Syrup:

3 cups fresh blueberries
1¼ cups water
2½ cups sugar

¼ cup light corn syrup
4 tablespoons fresh lemon juice
⅛ teaspoon nutmeg

2 teaspoons butter

Purée blueberries in processor, add ½ cup of the water and blend. Pour purée into saucepan and add sugar and remainder of the water. Cook over medium-high heat, stirring often. Lower heat and simmer for 10 minutes. Remove from heat and press mixture through sieve with a wooden spoon. Stir in corn syrup, lemon juice, and nutmeg. Additional nutmeg may be added to taste. Add butter and mix well. Cool and refrigerate. Reheat before serving.

Note: Can be made several days in advance.

Grilled Ham Steaks

2 ham steaks, ½-inch thick

Basting Sauce:

1 cup apricot jam
2 teaspoons prepared mustard
⅛ teaspoon ground cloves

Heat sauce ingredients in a small saucepan until blended and heated through. Broil or grill ham steaks, brushing with basting sauce. Cook for 6 minutes on each side, or until well browned.

Swiss Apple Salad

2 cups diced Swiss cheese
1 cup diced celery
¼ cup diced, peeled carrots

2 cups sour cream
Pinch of salt
4 medium unpared Granny Smith or other green apples

1 teaspoon Fruit Fresh (optional)

If making evening before serving, combine all ingredients except apples and chill. Add diced apples early in the morning. Fruit Fresh may be added in the morning to protect apples from discoloring.

Can be served as salad or dessert.

Cranberry Sour Cream Cake

1 cup sugar	1 teaspoon baking soda
8 tablespoons butter or margarine	¼ teaspoon salt
	1 cup sour cream
2 eggs	1 can whole berry cranberry sauce
2 cups flour	
1 teaspoon baking powder	½ cup nuts

Confectioners' sugar

Cream sugar and butter and add eggs one at a time, blending well. Mix flour, baking powder and soda, and salt. Alternately add flour mixture and sour cream to sugar mixture, ending with flour.

Grease 9-inch tube pan, dust lightly with flour. Add one-third of batter to tube pan, then spread with half of the cranberry sauce and nuts. Add another one-third of the batter and then the rest of the cranberry sauce and nuts. Top with the last one-third batter.

Bake for 55 minutes in preheated 350° oven. Cool in pan on rack. Remove from pan and finish cooling on rack. Dust with confectioners' sugar before serving. Freezes well.

Brunch on the Veranda

Spiced Iced Tea
Strawberry Cantaloupe Supreme
Puffed Shell with Chicken and Snow Pea Salad
or Egg and Spinach Salad
Blueberry Muffins
Crunchy Orange Muffins
Creamy Rice Pudding

PREVIOUS DAY	EARLY MORNING	FREEZER
Spiced Iced Tea	Salad fillings	Puffed Shell
Strawberry Cantaloupe Supreme		Blueberry Muffins
Rice Pudding		Orange Muffins

Spiced Iced Tea

8 tea bags (or 2 tablespoons
    black or orange pekoe tea)
2 cinnamon sticks
24 whole cloves

Rind and juice of 1 lemon
Rinds and juice of 2 oranges
8 cups boiling water
6 tablespoons sugar, or to taste

1 lemon, thinly sliced

Place the tea, cinnamon, and cloves in a heatproof pitcher or a large saucepan. Pour in juice and add the lemon and orange rinds. Pour boiling water over all and steep for 5 to 10 minutes. Strain and pour into serving pitcher. While tea is still hot add sugar to taste. Chill. Garnish with the sliced lemon when serving.

🌱 🌱 🌱

Strawberry Cantaloupe Supreme

Zest and juice (about 2 cups) of
    4 large oranges
2 cups water
1 cup sugar

¼ cup orange-flavored liqueur
    (optional)
1 quart strawberries
4 medium cantaloupes

With a vegetable peeler, remove zest (colored part of peel) from oranges. Cut into 1-inch-long thin strips. In saucepan, combine zest and water; simmer, covered, until tender, about 10 minutes. Drain and set aside.

Place the orange juice in another saucepan and add sugar. Boil, stirring frequently, until sauce is reduced to 1½ cups, about 15 minutes. Add orange zest and cook for 3 minutes longer. Cool. Add liqueur if desired, cover, and chill overnight.

Up to 4 hours before serving, wash, hull, and slice strawberries gently into syrup. Cover and chill. Just before serving, cut cantaloupes in half, making a plain or fancy edge. Scoop out and discard seeds. Evenly spoon strawberries and syrup into each melon half.

Puffed Shell with Salad Fillings

Shell:

⅔ cup water
5 tablespoons butter or
   margarine

¼ teaspoon salt
⅔ cup all-purpose flour
3 eggs

In a 2-quart pan over high heat, combine water, butter, and salt. Bring to a boil, stirring, and cook until butter is melted. Remove pan from heat and add flour all at once. Beat with a wire whisk until smooth. Reduce heat to medium and return pan to heat. Cook, stirring rapidly, until a ball forms in middle of pan and a film forms on the bottom (about 1 minute). Remove from heat and beat in eggs, one at a time, until batter is smooth and glossy. Spoon into a greased 9-inch spring-form pan. Spread evenly over bottom and up sides of pan.

Bake in preheated 400° oven for 40 minutes or until puffy and browned. Turn off oven. With a wooden pick, prick crust in ten to twelve places and let dry in closed oven for about 10 minutes. Remove from oven and let cool completely; remove from pan.

If making ahead, cover loosely with foil and store at room temperature until next day. Or wrap completely in foil and freeze. Bring crust to room temperature and recrisp, uncovered, in 400° oven for 10 minutes; let cool. Fill with salad and serve by cutting in wedges.

Chicken and Snow Pea Salad:

3 cups cooked chicken
1 8-ounce can water chestnuts
½ cup thin-sliced scallions,
   including tops
2 hard-cooked eggs, chopped
1 cup sour cream
1 teaspoon lime juice
2 teaspoons sugar

2 teaspoons curry powder
½ teaspoon ground ginger
Salt and freshly ground black
   pepper, to taste
¼ pound Chinese snow peas
Chopped fresh parsley or
   cilantro (optional)

Cut chicken into bite-sized pieces. Drain and slice water chestnuts. Combine both with sliced scallions and chopped eggs. In small bowl combine remaining ingredients, except snow peas, and stir into chicken mixture.

Clean and string the snow peas. Half-fill a 2-quart saucepan with water and bring to boil over high heat. Add snow peas and cook for 1½ minutes. Drain, rinse under cold water, and drain again. Pat dry.

To serve, line bottom and sides of pastry with snow peas. Pile chicken salad on top and sprinkle with parsley or cilantro.

Egg and Spinach Salad:

12 hard-cooked eggs, coarsely
    chopped
3 scallions, finely chopped,
    including tops
1 cup chopped celery
½ cup mayonnaise
1 teaspoon Dijon mustard

1 teaspoon mustard seeds
¼ teaspoon ground cumin
Salt and pepper, to taste
1½ cups small spinach leaves,
    or coarsely chopped large
    spinach leaves
Cherry tomatoes, halved

Combine eggs, scallions, and celery. In a small bowl, mix the next four ingredients, adding salt and pepper to taste. Stir into egg mixture. Can be refrigerated for up to 24 hours.

To serve, line bottom and sides of pastry with spinach leaves, pile egg salad over spinach, and garnish with halved cherry tomatoes.

Blueberry Muffins
(Makes 18)

¼ pound butter
1 cup sugar
2 eggs
1 teaspoon vanilla extract
2 cups flour

2 teaspoons baking powder
½ teaspoon salt
½ cup milk
2 cups blueberries
Sugar

Cream butter and sugar, add eggs, vanilla, flour, baking powder, salt, and milk. Fold in berries and mix quickly. Pour into buttered muffin tins, sprinkle sugar on top, and bake in preheated 375° oven for 25 to 30 minutes.

Crunchy Orange Muffins
(Makes 12)

6 tablespoons butter or
    margarine, softened
6 tablespoons honey
1 egg, lightly beaten
1 teaspoon grated orange peel

½ cup orange juice
1 cup all-purpose flour
1 teaspoon baking powder
½ teaspoon salt
¼ teaspoon baking soda

½ cup wheat germ

In a small bowl, blend butter and honey. Add egg, grated orange peel, and orange juice; blend thoroughly. In a separate bowl, stir together flour, baking powder, salt, baking soda, and wheat germ. Make a well in center of flour mixture; add liquid ingredients all at once, stir just enough to moisten thoroughly. Spoon batter into well-greased muffin cups, filling each two-thirds full. Bake in preheated 375° oven for 20 minutes or until browned and tops spring back when lightly touched.

Creamy Rice Pudding
(Serves 8)

6 cups milk
¾ cup long grain white rice
1 cup heavy cream
¾ cup sugar
3 egg yolks, beaten

Juice of 1 orange
2 teaspoons vanilla extract
¼ teaspoon salt
1 teaspoon grated nutmeg
½ cup raisins (optional)

Rinse out a medium saucepan with cold water. Drain but do not dry. Pour in milk and bring to a boil over medium heat. Stir in rice and return to boil. Reduce the heat and simmer, uncovered, until rice is tender, about 50 to 55 minutes. Mix cream, sugar, egg yolks, orange juice, vanilla, and salt. Set aside. When rice is tender, stir in cream mixture and raisins and mix until completely combined. Heat to a boil. Pour into 2-quart serving dish, sprinkle surface with nutmeg, and chill overnight.

Homecoming Brunch

Fruit Bowl
Frittata with Basil and Italian Sausages
Peasant Bread
Carrot Cake with Cream Cheese Frosting

PREVIOUS DAY	EARLY MORNING	FREEZER
Fruit Bowl	*Vegetables for Frittata*	*Carrot Cake*
Peasant Bread		

Fruit Bowl

2 cups water
1½ cups sugar, or to taste
3 tablespoons lemon juice
2 tablespoons aniseed
½ teaspoon salt

4½ cups fruit: pineapple, red apple slices, grapefruit sections, oranges, grapes, and kiwi

In 2-quart saucepan, over medium heat, cook water, sugar, lemon juice, aniseed, and salt until mixture makes a light syrup, about 15 minutes. Refrigerate until cool. Slice or dice all fruit except kiwi, and place in a large bowl. Strain chilled syrup over the fruit. Cover and refrigerate until well chilled, stirring occasionally. When ready to serve, slice kiwi and add to rest of fruit.

Frittata with Basil and Italian Sausages

Sausages in Pepper Sauce:

1¼ pounds mild Italian sausage, sliced in 2-inch pieces
4 tablespoons salad oil (approximately)
1 large onion, chopped
1 clove garlic, minced or crushed
4 medium-size red or green peppers, seeded and cut lengthwise into half-inch strips

2 1-pound cans tomatoes, with juice, chopped
⅓ cup finely chopped fresh basil (or 1½ tablespoons dried)
1¼ teaspoons salt
1 tablespoon sugar

In 12-inch frying pan cook sausages over medium heat until well browned; remove from pan, drain, and set aside. Measure drippings from sausage and add enough salad oil to make 4 tablespoons total. Cook onion and garlic, stirring frequently, until limp. Add peppers and cook, stirring, for 3 minutes. Add tomatoes, basil, salt, sugar. Bring to a boil, stirring constantly, until most of liquid has evaporated. Place sausages on sauce, cover, and keep warm while making frittata.

Frittata:

¾ cup sour cream	3 tablespoons butter
12 eggs	½ cup finely chopped scallions
¾ teaspoon salt	¾ cup freshly grated
¼ teaspoon pepper	Parmesan
2 tablespoons finely chopped fresh basil (or 2 teaspoons dried)	

Place sour cream in bowl; beat in eggs, one at a time. Stir in salt, pepper, and basil; set aside. In 10-inch frying pan with ovenproof handle, melt the butter over medium heat. Add scallions and cook, stirring, for 1 minute. Pour in egg mixture. Cook, lifting set portion of frittata with spatula to allow uncooked eggs to flow underneath. Continue cooking until eggs are softly set but top still looks moist and creamy. Remove from heat, sprinkle with cheese. Place under preheated broiler, about 6 inches from heat, just until cheese melts. Cut into wedges and serve warm with sausages and pepper sauce.

Peasant Bread
(Makes 2 loaves)

2 packages active dry yeast	2 teaspoons salt
2 cups lukewarm water	4½ to 6 cups flour

Dissolve yeast in water in a bowl. Add salt and gradually mix in enough flour to make a stiff dough. Turn dough out onto a floured surface; knead 10 minutes, adding more flour if necessary. Place dough in oiled bowl and cover with a slightly damp clean towel. Let rise in warm, draft-free place for about 1 hour or until doubled in bulk. Punch dough down, turn out, and shape into 2 round loaves. Place on an oiled baking sheet and make crisscross marks on top of the loaves with a sharp knife. Cover loaves with towel again and let rise about 1 hour until doubled in bulk. Brush loaves with water and bake in preheated 400° oven for 25 minutes. Reduce to 350° and bake 20 minutes longer, or until bread is golden and sounds hollow when tapped on the bottom.

Note: For a very crusty bread, brush loaves or spray several times during baking with water.

Carrot Cake

2 cups flour	1½ cups oil
2 tablespoons baking powder	2 cups grated carrots
½ teaspoon baking soda	1 8-ounce can crushed pineapple,
1 teaspoon salt	drained
2 teaspoons cinnamon	1 cup golden raisins
4 eggs	½ cup chopped pecans or
1½ cups sugar	walnuts

Sift together all dry ingredients except sugar. Beat eggs, add sugar, and mix well. Add oil to egg mixture and blend. Add egg mixture to flour, blend together. Add carrots, pineapple, raisins, and nuts and blend. Turn into 3 greased and floured 9-inch layer pans. Bake in preheated 350° oven for 35 to 45 minutes. Cool a few minutes in pans. Turn out and cool on racks.

Cream Cheese Frosting:

¼ pound butter	1 teaspoon vanilla extract
1 8-ounce package cream cheese	2 cups confectioners' sugar,
	sifted
¼ cup milk (optional)	

Combine butter, cream cheese, and vanilla. Cream well. Add sugar slowly, beating well. If too thick, add a little milk. Recipe will frost a three-layer cake.

Note: If cake is frozen, defrost overnight.

Tyrolean Brunch

Mimosa
Baked Maple French Toast
Sausages
Italian Plums in Wine
Walnut Coffee Cake

PREVIOUS DAY	EARLY MORNING	FREEZER
Italian Plums		*Coffee Cake*

Mimosa
(Serves 12)

1 bottle champagne	12 strawberries
3 cups orange juice	12 orange slices

Mix champagne and orange juice just before serving. Place a strawberry and an orange slice in each glass and add juice mixture. Serve in champagne glasses if possible.

Baked Maple French Toast

1 dozen eggs	¾ cup heavy cream
1½ cups maple syrup	12 slices (5-by-4-by-1-inch)
¼ teaspoon salt	Vienna bread
1½ teaspoons baking powder	1 cup clarified butter
Freshly grated nutmeg	

Whisk eggs and maple syrup. Dissolve salt and baking powder in cream, whisk into egg mixture. Spread bread slices, in one layer, in a large baking dish. Pour egg mixture over. Let bread soak 30 minutes, turning twice.

Place oven rack in top of oven. Heat a jelly-roll pan in oven for 3 minutes. Put 3 tablespoons clarified butter (see Additional Thoughts) in pan. Arrange soaked bread in pan, leaving an inch between slices. Sprinkle with nutmeg. Repeat until all bread is ready to bake. Bake 8 minutes in preheated 450° oven, then brush tops with remaining clarified butter and bake until puffed and browned, about 8 minutes more. If toast is browning too quickly, reduce heat to 425°.

Italian Plums in Wine
(Serves 12)

4 pounds fresh Italian prune
  plums
3 cups dry white wine

1 cup sugar
2 cinnamon sticks
2 3-inch strips lemon zest

2 cups water

Rinse plums thoroughly. Place remaining ingredients into large saucepan and bring to a boil. Reduce heat and simmer 5 minutes, stirring occasionally to dissolve sugar. Add plums and simmer 10 to 15 minutes longer or until plums are tender but still hold their shape. Remove plums with slotted spoon to a serving bowl. Continue to boil liquid until reduced to about 4 cups. Pour syrup over plums, cover, and refrigerate several hours or overnight.

Walnut Coffee Cake

½ cup milk
1 tablespoon sugar
1 package active dry yeast
3¾ cups flour
Pinch of salt

20 tablespoons butter (2½
  sticks)
2 whole eggs
2 egg yolks
2 tablespoons sour cream

2 tablespoons wine

Warm milk to 105° to 115°, add sugar and yeast, set aside to proof until foamy, about 10 minutes. Mix flour and salt in large bowl of electric mixer, or manually with wooden spoon. Add remaining ingredients all at once with yeast mixture and mix until well blended. Cover and set in a warm spot for 1 hour or until doubled.

Filling:

1⅓ cups sugar
Lemon zest
12 ounces walnuts, finely
  chopped

3 tablespoons milk
½ cup raisins

Combine all ingredients and mix well. For processor: Blend sugar and lemon zest with steel blade. Add nuts and process with 8 on-off pulses. Scrape down sides, add milk and raisins and process 4 to 6 pulses to blend.

Divide dough into 4 equal parts (it will be sticky). Place one part on well-floured board, turn to coat lightly, and roll to approximately a 6-by-18-inch strip. Spread with one-quarter of the filling, leaving a ⅓-inch margin uncovered on the long sides. Roll up, pinch long side well to seal, pinch and fold short sides under. Lay seam-side down on a cookie sheet, cover with a clean tea towel, and allow to rest for 30 minutes. Repeat with other 3 parts of dough. Bake 2 rolls on each cookie sheet.

Bake cake in preheated 400° oven for 10 minutes. Reduce heat to 350° and continue baking for another 30 minutes. For shiny finish, brush dough with egg yolk just before baking and again halfway through baking time.

Brunch Olé

Sangria
Spicy Egg and Cheese Soufflé
Layered Salad
Walnut-Corn-Bran Muffins
Tangy Lemon Tea Cake
Fresh Pears and Grapes

PREVIOUS DAY	EARLY MORNING	FREEZER
Layered Salad	*Sangria (except club*	*Muffins*
Spicy Soufflé	*soda)*	*Tangy Tea Cake*

Sangria

1 bottle red wine, chilled	**2 ounces cognac**
½ orange, thinly sliced	**8 teaspoons sugar**
½ lemon, thinly sliced	**½ cup fresh blackberries**
1 kiwi, peeled and sliced	**Club soda, to taste**

Pour wine into glass pitcher and add fruit slices, cognac, and sugar. Stir until sugar dissolves. Add blackberries. Chill several hours. Add ice cubes and club soda to taste.

🐚 🐚 🐚

Spicy Egg and Cheese Soufflé

1 pound Cheddar cheese	½ teaspoon salt (optional)
1 pound Monterey Jack cheese with chilies	½ teaspoon pepper (optional)
	1 tablespoon flour
4 eggs, separated	1 large tomato, sliced
¾ cup evaporated milk	1 large onion, sliced

Grate or dice cheeses and mix together. Put into buttered 9-by-12-inch baking dish or 2-quart casserole. Mix egg yolks, evaporated milk, salt, pepper, and flour together well. Beat egg whites until stiff. Gently fold beaten egg whites into egg yolk mixture. Pour over cheese mixture and poke cheese with fork or toothpick to allow liquid to "soak in."

Bake 30 minutes in preheated 325° oven. Remove from oven, place sliced tomatoes and onions on top, and bake for additional 30 minutes or until knife comes out clean.

Layered Salad

1 quart shredded iceberg lettuce (about 1 big head)	1 large red pepper, chopped
	1½ cups mayonnaise
1 large cucumber, halved lengthwise, thinly sliced	1 4-ounce can chopped green chilies with liquid
3 medium tomatoes, chopped	2 teaspoons chili powder
2 medium avocados, sliced	½ teaspoon onion powder
1 large green pepper, chopped	¼ teaspoon salt

Layer lettuce, cucumber, tomatoes, avocados, and peppers in 2½-quart container, preferably a glass bowl. Combine remaining ingredients and spread over salad. Cover and refrigerate overnight. Toss slightly when ready to serve.

Walnut-Corn-Bran Muffins
(Makes 12)

1 cup milk	1 cup flour
½ cup All-Bran	½ cup cornmeal
4 tablespoons unsalted butter	½ cup toasted chopped
3 tablespoons dark brown sugar	walnuts
1 egg	2 teaspoons baking powder
1 teaspoon walnut oil (optional)	¼ teaspoon salt

Walnut oil, to coat pan

Mix milk and bran in medium-size bowl. Let stand at room temperature for 8 hours.

Cream butter and sugar; stir in egg and oil. Blend in dry ingredients and bran mixture until moistened throughout. Fill muffin cups coated with walnut oil. Bake in preheated 400° oven for 20 to 25 minutes. Cool in pans for 7 minutes before serving.

Tangy Lemon Tea Cake

1½ cups flour	2 eggs
1 teaspoon baking powder	1 tablespoon grated lemon rind
¼ teaspoon salt	½ cup milk
8 tablespoons unsalted butter	¼ cup lemon juice
1 cup sugar	⅓ cup sugar

Sift first three ingredients together. Cream butter and sugar until light and fluffy. Add eggs one at a time, then add grated lemon rind, beating well after each addition. Beat in flour mixture alternately with milk. Pour into a well-greased and floured 8½-by-4½-by-2¾-inch loaf pan. Bake in preheated 350° oven for 50 minutes or until cake tester comes out clean.

Cool in pan for 5 minutes. Turn out on rack over wax paper. Combine lemon juice and sugar and spoon mixture over bread. Serve with fresh pears and grapes.

Windy City Brunch

Blintz Appetizers
Bing Cherry and Grapefruit Salad
Tuna Egg Pie
Blueberry Brunch Cake
Spiced Nuts

PREVIOUS DAY	EARLY MORNING	FREEZER
Cherry and Grapefruit Salad *Spiced Nuts*	*Tuna Egg Pie* *Blueberry Brunch Cake*	*Blintz Appetizers*

Blintz Appetizers

2 pounds white bread, thinly
   sliced, crusts removed
2 8-ounce packages cream cheese
½ cup sugar

2 egg yolks
½ pound butter
Cinnamon
1 pint sour cream

1½ cups strawberry preserves

Roll bread with rolling pin. Mix cream cheese, sugar, and egg yolks until smooth. Spread mix in bread and roll up jelly-roll style. Melt butter and dip each roll quickly and completely into it, and place on flat cookie sheet. Sprinkle tops with cinnamon. (Can be frozen at this point.) Bake in preheated 400° oven for 10 minutes (15 minutes if frozen), or until tops are brown and crisp. Serve with bowls of sour cream and strawberry preserves.

Bing Cherry and Grapefruit Salad
(Serves 10)

1 16-ounce can pitted Bing
   cherries, drained; reserve juice
2 3-ounce packages lemon
   gelatin
½ cup cold water
½ cup red port

2 16-ounce jars or cans
   grapefruit sections; reserve
   juice
½ cup slivered almonds,
   toasted

Measure cherry juice and add enough water to equal 1 cup. Heat the liquid and dissolve one package of lemon gelatin, stirring the mixture. Add ½ cup of cold water and the port. Chill until slightly thickened; fold in the cherries. Fill an 8- to 10-cup mold halfway with this mixture and refrigerate until chilled and set.

Measure the grapefruit juice and add water to equal 2 cups. Heat the juice and stir in the remaining package of lemon gelatin until it is dissolved. Chill until thickened; fold in the grapefruit sections and almonds. Pour this mixture over the set cherry layer. Refrigerate until well set.

Tuna Egg Pie
(Serves 8)

2 packages crescent rolls	6 eggs, separated
2 small cans tuna, drained	1½ cups flour
2 large tomatoes, sliced	1½ teaspoons salt
12 to 16 ounces shredded	¾ teaspoon pepper
Cheddar cheese (or Swiss or	2 cups plain yogurt (or sour
American)	cream)

Paprika

Layer rolls lightly (do not pat down) in bottom of two greased 9-inch pie plates. Spread tuna over rolls, then tomato slices, then cheese. Mix together egg yolks, flour, salt, pepper, and yogurt. Beat egg whites until stiff, add to yolk mixture, pour over cheese, dividing mixture between two pans. Sprinkle paprika over all. Bake in preheated 350° oven, uncovered, for ½ hour or until top browns. Cool 5 minutes before slicing and serve immediately.

Note: Tuna, tomato, and cheddar can be changed to:
1. Sliced onions, mushrooms, and Swiss cheese (mushrooms should be as dry as possible)
2. Zucchini, tomatoes, and mozzarella cheese
3. 1 pound crumbled bacon, tomatoes, and cheese

Blueberry Brunch Cake

2 cups sifted flour	1 egg
4 teaspoons baking powder	½ cup milk (approximately)
½ teaspoon salt	2 cups fresh blueberries
1½ tablespoons butter	3 tablespoons sugar
¾ cup sugar	1 teaspoon cinnamon

Combine the flour, baking powder, and salt. Cut in the butter and sugar. Beat the egg in a glass measuring cup, adding enough milk to bring the level of liquid in the cup to ¾ cup, plus two tablespoons. Beat the liquid into the dry ingredients. Carefully fold in the fresh blueberries. Pour the batter into a greased 9-inch-square pan. Combine the 3 tablespoons sugar and the cinnamon and sprinkle over the cake. Bake in preheated 350° oven for 40 minutes.

Note: To prevent berries from sinking, reserve 1 tablespoon of the flour and sprinkle over them before adding to batter.

Spiced Nuts
(Makes 2 cups)

1 egg white	1 tablespoon cinnamon
1 tablespoon water	½ teaspoon salt
2 cups walnut or pecan halves	½ teaspoon nutmeg
½ cup sugar	Dash of ground cloves

Beat egg white and water until frothy. Stir in nuts. Mix together sugar and spices. Toss coated nuts in spice mixture, spread on buttered cookie sheet. Bake 30 minutes in preheated 300° oven. Stir three or four times while baking. Nuts will be sticky when you take them from oven. Cool. Pack in airtight container.

Winter Welcome Brunch

Fruit Smoothie Punch
Smoked Salmon Mousse
Grapefruit Relish Salad
Apple Pancakes
Carrot-Walnut Cupcakes
Shellbinders

PREVIOUS DAY	EARLY MORNING	FREEZER
Smoked Salmon Mousse	*Fruit Punch*	*Cupcakes*
Pancake batter	*Grapefruit Salad*	*Shellbinders*

Fruit Smoothie Punch

1 quart fresh or frozen
strawberries or boysenberries,
or canned pears, apricots, or
peaches

½ to 1 cup cognac or
naturally flavored brandy
3 bottles sparkling white wine or
champagne

Combine fruit in blender with brandy. Blend until smooth; refrigerate. Just before serving pour mixture over ice mold in punch bowl. Add champagne or sparkling wine.

Smoked Salmon Mousse

¼ pound smoked salmon,
finely chopped
1 8-ounce package cream cheese
at room temperature
¼ cup chopped scallions

1 6-ounce package green onion
dip mix
½ cup sour cream
1 teaspoon dried dill weed

Blend all ingredients in a mixer, then pack into a crock or small mold sprayed with vegetable shortening spray. Chill overnight or up to two days ahead. Unmold on serving plate and garnish with dill. Serve with cocktail bread or cucumber rounds.

Grapefruit Relish Salad

3 small green peppers, cut in
rings and seeded
3 pink grapefruit, peeled and
sectioned
¾ pound fresh mushrooms,
sliced

1 cup red wine vinegar
¾ cup water
1½ tablespoons sugar
¾ teaspoon dried thyme
½ cup vegetable oil
Salad greens

Place pepper rings, grapefruit sections, and mushrooms in medium-size nonmetallic bowl. Mix remaining ingredients, except salad greens, and pour over grapefruit mixture. Let stand for 30 minutes; stir occasionally. Serve at room temperature or chilled. When ready to serve, pour off dressing and serve relish on salad greens.

Apple Pancakes
(Serves 2)

Batter:

½ cup milk	3 eggs
½ cup flour	1 teaspoon sugar
	Pinch of salt

Topping:

¼ cup sugar	1 teaspoon cinnamon

Apples:

5 tablespoons butter or margarine	1 or 2 apples, sliced

In medium bowl, mix all batter ingredients with whisk or mixer; set aside. In small bowl combine topping ingredients. In a 10-inch skillet with an oven-safe handle or a porcelain pie tin, melt butter and sauté apples for about 3 minutes, until soft and glazed. Spread apples evenly around pan; pour batter over apples and bake in preheated 500° oven for 3 minutes. While batter is still runny, sprinkle topping over pancake and bake for 7 to 10 minutes more. Spread topping to taste. The pancake is done when topping has melted and caramelized.

Note: Recipe is enough for two. If serving more, repeat for every two people and bake each recipe in separate skillet or pie tin.

Carrot-Walnut Cupcakes
(Makes 18)

1½ cups whole wheat flour	½ cup honey
1½ teaspoons baking soda	2 eggs
½ teaspoon salt	1 teaspoon vanilla extract
1 teaspoon ground cinnamon	2 to 3 carrots, finely shredded
½ teaspoon ground nutmeg	(about 1½ cups)
1 cup vegetable oil	1 cup finely chopped walnuts

Line 18 medium-size muffin pan cups with paper baking cups or grease well.

Sift flour, soda, salt, cinnamon, and nutmeg onto wax paper. Combine oil, honey, eggs, and vanilla in large mixing bowl; beat until creamy and thick. Stir in flour mixture until batter is smooth. Add carrots and walnuts and mix well. Spoon batter into prepared muffin tins, filling halfway. Bake in preheated 350° oven for 20 minutes or until tops spring back when lightly pressed with fingertip. Cool cupcakes in pan on wire rack for 5 minutes. Remove from cups, cool completely.

Honey—Cream Cheese Frosting:

1 8-ounce package cream cheese, softened	2 tablespoons honey
	½ cup chopped walnuts

Whip cream cheese with honey in medium-size bowl. Frost muffins and sprinkle with chopped nuts.

Shellbinders

1 cup firmly packed dark brown sugar	1 teaspoon baking soda
½ pound butter or margarine	1½ teaspoons baking powder
1 egg	1 cup quick oatmeal
1 teaspoon vanilla extract	1 cup flaked sweetened coconut
1½ cups flour	1 cup crushed Raisin Bran
	Extra raisins (optional)

Cream brown sugar and butter until light and fluffy, then add egg, vanilla, flour, baking soda, baking powder, and oatmeal one at a time, beating well after each addition. Stir in coconut and raisin bran and extra raisins if desired. Flatten batter onto ungreased jelly-roll pan with sides, and bake in preheated 350° oven for 12 to 15 minutes.

Icing:

1 tablespoon melted butter	1 or more tablespoons hot water
1 or more cups confectioners' sugar	1 teaspoon vanilla extract

Mix all ingredients, adding sugar and water until good spreading consistency is achieved. Spread over cake when it is completely cooled. Cut into squares and serve.

First Snowfall Brunch

Orange Marmalade Grapefruit
Baked Egg Soufflé
Sautéed Chicken Livers Normandy
Parmesan Pita Wedges
Cranberry Sorbet
Oatmeal Lace Cookies

PREVIOUS DAY	EARLY MORNING	FREEZER
Oatmeal Cookies	*Fruit*	*Cranberry Sorbet*
Pita Wedges		

Orange Marmalade Grapefruit

**4 grapefruit, cut in half, room
   temperature
½ cup orange marmalade**

**1 tablespoon Grand Marnier
   (optional)**

Slice a bit of rind off the bottom of each grapefruit half, to prevent rolling, and place on rimmed cookie sheet. Mix marmalade with liqueur and spread on grapefruit halves. Broil until bubbly and browned. Watch carefully to avoid burning.

Baked Egg Soufflé

**6 eggs
⅓ cup milk
½ teaspoon salt
⅛ teaspoon pepper (optional)**

**⅛ teaspoon dry mustard
¼ pound processed American
   cheese, cubed**

Beat eggs, milk, and seasonings until bubbly. Stir in cubed cheese. Pour into greased 1-quart casserole and bake in preheated 350° oven until brown and puffy, about 30 minutes.

Note: For 25 minutes nothing happens and in the last 5 minutes it puffs up into a beautiful soufflé. Do not overbake.

This is a perfect brunch dish. Anything can be added to it: chopped chicken, tuna, ham, etc. A cream or tomato sauce poured over it when served is delicious.

Recipe can be doubled with an increase in cooking time to 40 to 45 minutes.

Sautéed Chicken Livers Normandy

3 thick slices bacon, diced
3 tablespoons butter
1 tart green apple, peeled and thinly sliced
¾ to 1 pound whole chicken livers

3 tablespoons all-purpose flour
2 tablespoons dry Marsala
1 small onion, chopped
Salt and freshly ground black pepper, to taste

Fry bacon pieces in skillet until crisp. Drain on a paper towel and dispose of bacon grease. Add 1 tablespoon of the butter to the skillet and sauté apple slices until soft; set aside. Lightly dredge chicken livers in flour. Melt the remaining butter in the skillet and sauté chicken livers for about 5 minutes. Add apples, bacon, Marsala, onion, and seasoning; cook for a few more minutes to blend.

Parmesan Pita Wedges

2 to 3 large pitas

Cut pita in quarters. Brush with melted butter and sprinkle with dill and Parmesan cheese. Place in preheated 350° oven for 10 minutes, or until toasted.

Cranberry Sorbet

4 cups fresh cranberries
3 cups boiling water
2¼ cups sugar, or less, to taste

1 cup orange juice
Juice of 1 lemon

Cook cranberries in water until soft. Press through a strainer or food mill. Heat again and stir in sugar until dissolved. Remove from heat and add juices. Freeze for several hours or overnight (should be firm). Remove from freezer and beat in processor or mixer. Return to freezer in suitable serving dish and cover tightly. Let soften slightly before serving.

Oatmeal Lace Cookies
(Makes 5 dozen)

1 cup quick oatmeal
1 cup sugar
2 tablespoons flour

¼ teaspoon baking powder
Pinch of salt
¼ pound butter, melted

1 egg, beaten

Mix dry ingredients in bowl; add butter and egg and mix well. Drop by half-teaspoonfuls on foil-covered baking sheets, at least 2 inches apart. Bake in preheated 400° oven for 5 to 8 minutes. Begin checking color at 5 minutes. Cookies are done when golden or darker. Let cool on foil for several minutes after slipping off cookie sheet. Peel from foil when cool.

Paul Bunyan Brunch

Grapefruit Appetizer
Scrambled Eggs in the French Manner
Banana Pancakes with Syrup
Glazed Canadian Bacon
Sausage Links
Chipper Brunch Cake

PREVIOUS DAY	EARLY MORNING	FREEZER
Fruit Sauce	*Pancake batter*	*Chipper Cake*
Grapefruit Appetizer		

Grapefruit Appetizer

5 fresh medium grapefruit
½ cup water
¼ cup honey
1 tablespoon fresh ginger, pared
  and cut into ¾-by-¹⁄₁₆-inch
  julienne strips

1½ pints fresh ripe
  strawberries
½ ripe medium avocado

Pare grapefruit, removing all white pith. Over large bowl, cut grapefruit sections away from membranes. Place sections in medium bowl. Squeeze any juice from membranes into large bowl. Measure out ½ cup juice for use in sauce, reserve remainder for other use.

Put the ½ cup grapefruit juice, water, honey, and ginger in small saucepan and heat to boiling. Reduce heat and simmer, covered, until ginger is tender, about 20 to 25 minutes. Remove from heat and cool completely. Add honey mixture to grapefruit, toss to combine. Cover and refrigerate, 4 hours or overnight.

An hour before serving, rinse, drain, and hull strawberries. Cut lengthwise into ¼-inch slices. Pare and pit avocado half, cut into ¾-inch dice. Remove grapefruit from refrigerator and add strawberries and avocado, tossing lightly to combine. Allow to stand at room temperature until serving time.

Scrambled Eggs in the French Manner
(Serves 8)

16 eggs	2 tablespoons butter
2 3-ounce packages cream cheese with chives	Salt and freshly ground black pepper, to taste
Parsley	

Beat eggs well. Cut cream cheese into small cubes. Melt butter over low heat in a large, heavy skillet. Add the well-beaten eggs and cream cheese to butter in the skillet. Cook, stirring with a fork, until eggs set into soft curds. Season with salt and pepper, garnish with parsley.

Banana Pancakes

1 cup packed cottage cheese	1 cup sifted all-purpose flour
1 cup sour cream	1 teaspoon baking powder
1 cup plus 2 tablespoons honey	2 small, firm bananas, peeled and cut into ⅛-inch slices
½ teaspoon vanilla extract	Vegetable oil
½ teaspoon salt	¼ cup fresh lemon juice
4 eggs, at room temperature	

Blend cottage cheese, sour cream, 2 tablespoons honey, vanilla, and salt until very smooth. Beat eggs in medium bowl until frothy; beat in the cheese mixture. Sift together flour and baking powder in a small bowl and stir gradually into cheese and egg mixture. Do not overmix.

Lightly dust banana slices with flour. Brush griddle or large, heavy skillet with thin film of oil, heat over low, then medium, heat until a few drops of water splashed on hot surface continue to sizzle for several seconds. Drop batter by tablespoonfuls onto griddle. Top each with 1 banana slice. Spoon ½ teaspoon batter on top of each banana slice. Cook until bubbles form over entire surface of each pancake, about 2 minutes. Turn with spatula. Cook until undersides are golden brown and pancakes are puffed, about 1 minute. Remove pancakes to ovenproof platter and keep warm in oven set at lowest setting. Lightly oil griddle again, if necessary, and continue to cook pancakes, storing in oven until all batter and banana slices are used.

Heat 1 cup honey and the lemon juice in small heavy saucepan over low heat until hot, about 2 minutes. Serve with pancakes.

Glazed Canadian Bacon
(Serves 6 to 10)

1 3- to 5-pound whole Canadian bacon	1 tablespoon prepared mustard
Whole cloves	½ to 1 cup pineapple, apple, or orange juice
½ cup maple syrup	

Preheat oven to 325°. Place bacon in a shallow nonstick baking pan or spray pan with nonstick vegetable spray. Score bacon and stud with cloves. Spread mustard over cut surface. Pour fruit juice over bacon and roast 14 minutes per pound, basting frequently with pan juices. Twenty minutes before end of roasting time, pour maple syrup over meat, baste, and bake until meat is well glazed.

Sausage Links
2 or 3 small sausage links per person

Place links on a cold rack in a pan with sides. Bake, uncovered and without turning, in a preheated 400° oven for 20 to 25 minutes or until links are no longer pink when slashed. Do not pierce the links before or during cooking but only to check at end of baking time.

Chipper Brunch Cake

1 cup brown sugar	½ teaspoon cinnamon
1 cup cake flour	1 cup sour cream
8 tablespoons butter	½ teaspoon baking soda
1 cup granulated sugar	2 eggs
1 cup all-purpose flour	1 teaspoon vanilla extract

1 cup mini chocolate chips

Combine first 5 ingredients. Remove ½ cup, add cinnamon, and set aside for streusel topping.

Combine sour cream and baking soda and set aside for a few minutes, then add eggs and vanilla. Add sour cream mixture to combined flour mixture. Pour half of batter into greased 9-inch-square cake pan. Sprinkle some of the reserved streusel mixture over batter. Pour remaining batter over streusel, sprinkle remaining streusel mixture on top. Sprinkle mini chocolate chips over all. Bake in preheated 350° oven for 45 minutes.

Luncheon Buffets

Each recipe serves six unless otherwise indicated.

Though luncheons are no longer a mainstay of the social calendar, there are still times when you want to invite people in to meet a visiting friend or guest, when you need to host a committee meeting, or when, serendipitously, you have time for a rare afternoon of bridge or conversation.

We have included menus for both warm and cool weather, using produce that is available during different seasons. Many of these menus are also appropriate for family occasions.

V.I.P. Luncheon

Hot Shot Tomato Soup
Easy Crabmeat Soufflé
Green Bean and Walnut Salad
Onion Kichel
Cold Fruit Compote
Chocolate Pound Cake

PREVIOUS DAY	EARLY MORNING	FREEZER
Crabmeat Soufflé	*Hot Shot Tomato Soup*	*Onion Kichel*
Cook beans and chill	*Green Bean Salad*	
Cold Fruit Compote		
Chocolate Pound Cake		

Hot Shot Tomato Soup

2 10½-ounce cans beef bouillon	1 teaspoon grated lemon rind
2 6-ounce cans tomato-vegetable juice	1 teaspoon Worcestershire sauce
	1 bay leaf
	1 lemon, sliced paper thin

Combine all ingredients except lemon slices. Bring to a boil and simmer for 5 minutes. Remove bay leaf. Serve soup in mugs and garnish each with lemon slice.

Easy Crabmeat Soufflé

Butter, for bread and casserole	1 6-ounce package frozen crabmeat, thawed and well drained
1 10½-ounce can condensed cream of shrimp soup	4 eggs, well beaten
⅓ soup can milk	9 slices white bread (crust removed, buttered and quartered)
1 jigger dry sherry wine	
½ teaspoon salt	
1 tablespoon dry mustard	

10 ounces grated Cheddar cheese

Butter a 1½- to 2-quart soufflé dish. Combine soup, milk, wine, seasonings, crabmeat, and eggs, blending well. Layer one-third of the bread, one-third of the soup mixture, and one-third of the cheese, and continue, finishing with a layer of cheese. Refrigerate overnight, covered with plastic wrap. Preheat oven to 350°. Bake for 1 hour and 15 minutes, until puffed and golden.

Green Bean and Walnut Salad

2 pounds fresh green beans
½ cup water chestnuts or
  jicama, diced
White wine vinegar, to taste
¼ cup dried herbs: parsley,
  chives, and thyme, combined

¼ cup walnut or olive oil
Salt and freshly ground black
  pepper, to taste
½ cup chopped walnuts

Cook beans in large pot of boiling water until tender, about 6 to 7 minutes. Drain, rinse in cold water, and drain again. (Beans can be cooked the day before and chilled.) Put beans in large salad bowl and mix with water chestnuts or jicama. Blend vinegar, herbs, oil, salt, and pepper. Coat salad, toss well, and chill. Toast walnuts in 325° oven for 5 to 8 minutes. Toss with beans and serve.

Onion Kichel (Crackers)

2½ cups flour
2 teaspoons baking powder
¼ cup oil
1 large onion, diced

½ teaspoon salt
2 eggs
1 tablespoon water
2 tablespoons poppy seeds

Onion salt or seasoning salt

Blend all ingredients except onion salt or seasoning salt. (Can be mixed in a processor. If so, blend everything except onion and salts. Then blend in onion so it does not liquefy.) Roll out dough on floured board very thin. Cut into diamond shapes. Sprinkle with onion or seasoning salt. Bake on cookie sheets until brown in preheated 350° oven about 5 to 10 minutes. If prepared in advance and not frozen, store in airtight container. If frozen, crisp in oven before serving. Freezes well.

Cold Fruit Compote

1 pound assorted dried fruits
1 5-ounce can pineapple chunks
  in own juice
1 9-ounce can pineapple juice,
  no sugar added

2 teaspoons rum extract
1 teaspoon orange extract
1 teaspoon vanilla extract
3 packets sugar substitute
  (approximately 1 teaspoon)

Mix all ingredients together. Cover and refrigerate overnight.

Chocolate Pound Cake

2 cups flour	2 eggs
1 teaspoon baking soda	1 cup sour cream, at room
½ cup butter or margarine,	temperature
softened	1 teaspoon vanilla extract
1½ cups tightly packed brown	2 ounces unsweetened chocolate,
sugar	melted and cooled

Grease 9-by-5-by-3-inch loaf pan. Mix flour and baking soda, set aside. In large bowl cream butter until fluffy, add brown sugar, and beat until blended. Add eggs one at a time, beating thoroughly after each addition. Gradually beat in flour mixture just until blended and smooth. Beat in sour cream and vanilla until blended. Add chocolate and beat until well blended. Pour into greased loaf pan and bake in a preheated 325° oven for 60 to 70 minutes or until top springs back when lightly pressed. Cool on rack in pan for 20 minutes; carefully remove from pan and cool completely on rack.

Note: Should be made a day in advance for easier slicing.

Cool Weather Luncheon

Mountain Greenery Soup
Torta Rustica
Tossed Green Salad with Balsamic Vinaigrette
Fresh Fruit
Triple Chocolate Cake

PREVIOUS DAY	EARLY MORNING	FREEZER
Balsamic Vinaigrette	*Torta dough*	*Triple Chocolate Cake*
Begin Mountain		
Greenery Soup		

Mountain Greenery Soup

6 scallions with tops, chopped	1 cup spinach leaves
3 tablespoons unsalted butter	1 tablespoon salt
3 tablespoons flour	¼ teaspoon white pepper
4 cups fresh or frozen peas	6 cups chicken stock
1 head Boston lettuce, shredded	1 cup whipping cream

3 egg yolks

In large pot, sauté scallions in butter until soft. Stir in flour and stir for 2 minutes. Add 3 cups of the peas, lettuce, spinach, salt, pepper, and stock. Bring to a boil, turn down flame to simmer, cover, and simmer 40 to 45 minutes. Set aside to cool. Soup may be prepared ahead to this stage. Refrigerate until just before serving, then purée cooled soup in a blender or processor until smooth. Beat cream and egg yolks together. Return soup to pot and add cream and egg mixture. Cook over low heat, stirring constantly, for 5 minutes. Add last cup of peas. Do not boil.

Torta Rustica

Dough:

1 package active dry yeast	6 eggs, beaten
¼ cup lukewarm water	4 cups all-purpose flour
1 cup unsalted butter, melted	½ teaspoon salt

Dissolve yeast in warm water. In large bowl, beat butter into the eggs. Whisk in the yeast, 2 cups of the flour, and salt. Let mix stand for 10 minutes or until bubbles form. Stir in remaining flour with a wooden spoon. When well blended, place the dough in a warm spot for 1 hour or until it doubles in bulk. Punch dough down, cover with plastic wrap, and refrigerate overnight or a minimum of 6 hours. Remove dough from refrigerator 30 minutes before use.

Filling:

5 eggs
1 teaspoon thyme, fresh or dried, or to taste
2 10-ounce packages chopped frozen spinach, defrosted and drained, or 2 pounds cooked fresh spinach, drained and chopped
¾ cup ricotta cheese

1 teaspoon basil
1 teaspoon nutmeg
1 teaspoon salt
½ teaspoon cayenne pepper
¼ teaspoon freshly ground black pepper
1 pound mozzarella, thinly sliced
12 ounces crabmeat
2 tablespoons small capers

1 tablespoon milk

In a bowl, beat 4 of the eggs and season with thyme to taste. Make 2 omelets of 2 eggs each in a 7-inch crepe pan. Set aside. In another bowl, combine spinach, ricotta, and basil and other seasonings. Set aside.

Roll out three-fourths of dough to ½-inch thickness. Lay dough inside a 9-inch springform pan, cutting away excess dough. Layer in the following order: ⅓ pound of the mozzarella, 1 omelet, one-half of the spinach mixture, 4 ounces of the crab, and all the capers. Then repeat layers: ⅓ pound mozzarella, 1 omelet, remaining spinach, remaining crab, and end with remaining ⅓ pound of the cheese.

Roll out remaining dough to fit over the top of mold. Tuck dough inside to overlap edges, releasing springform if necessary to get dough tucked in, completely surrounding filling.

Combine remaining egg with milk and brush the top of dough. Bake in preheated 350° oven for 35 to 45 minutes or until top is golden brown. Cool on rack for 15 minutes before unmolding. Run knife around sides before releasing the spring.

Balsamic Vinaigrette

1 medium clove garlic, peeled
4½ tablespoons balsamic vinegar

¼ teaspoon salt, or to taste
Freshly ground pepper, to taste
¾ cup olive or vegetable oil

Process garlic in food processor. Add vinegar while machine is running; then run 15 seconds. Scrape down container sides. Add salt and pepper. With machine running add oil through chute in steady stream within

40 seconds. Process 5 seconds. Store in tightly sealed jar at room temperature. Reprocess before using if dressing separates. Toss over 2 heads of Boston lettuce.

Triple Chocolate Cake

Unsweetened cocoa (enough to dust greased 10-inch Bundt pan)
1 18½-ounce box deep chocolate or devil's food cake mix (without pudding)
1 4-ounce box *instant* chocolate pudding
¾ cup sour cream
½ cup vegetable oil
¼ cup mayonnaise
½ cup toasted and chopped almonds
3 tablespoons almond liqueur (Amaretto or similar)
1 teaspoon almond extract
1 cup chocolate chips (miniature preferred)

Grease 10-inch Bundt pan and dust with cocoa. Place all ingredients except chocolate chips in large bowl and beat 2 minutes with electric mixer on medium speed. Mix in chocolate chips. Pour into prepared pan and bake in preheated 350° oven for 50 to 55 minutes, or until cake tests done. Cool on rack for 10 minutes before removing from pan. Place slightly warm cake on serving platter.

Glaze:

1 cup confectioners' sugar
3 tablespoons milk
1 teaspoon almond extract

Combine the 3 ingredients and drizzle over warm cake immediately. If freezing cake, add glaze after defrosting. Freezes well.

Grecian Luncheon

Hot Mushroom Spread
Stuffed Grape Leaves
Meat, Spinach, and Cheese Pie
Greek Salad and Dressing
Apricot Torte

Hot Mushroom Spread
(Makes about 2½ cups)

4 slices bacon
½ pound fresh mushrooms, chopped
1 onion, chopped fine
1 clove garlic, minced
2 tablespoons flour
⅛ teaspoon white pepper
8 ounces cream cheese, cubed

2 teaspoons Worcestershire sauce
1 teaspoon soy sauce
½ cup sour cream
1 teaspoon fresh lemon juice
Paprika
¼ cup chopped nuts
½ loaf each cocktail rye and pumpernickel breads

Cook bacon until crisp. Crumble and set aside. Pour out all but 2 tablespoons drippings and sauté mushrooms, onion, and garlic until liquid evaporates. Whisk in flour. Add pepper, cream cheese, Worcestershire sauce, and soy sauce and cook until cheese is melted. Blend in sour cream, lemon juice, and bacon and warm slowly until heated through. Do not boil. Sprinkle with paprika and chopped nuts. Serve warm with breads.

Stuffed Grape Leaves

2 pounds onions, chopped
1 cup oil
1 tablespoon salt
¼ to ½ cup chopped dill
Juice of 1 lemon
1 cup tomato sauce

1½ cups water
1 cup uncooked white rice
¼ pound pine nuts
1 jar grape leaves (approximately 1 pound)

Sauté onions in oil, about 15 minutes. Add salt and chopped dill, and cook 15 minutes. Add half of lemon juice and the tomato sauce, cook 15 minutes. Add water and rice, and cook according to instructions on box. Add pine nuts when rice is half done. Cook until rice is almost done. Rinse grape leaves in cold water. Save ripped leaves for bottom of pot. You will need a Dutch oven or similar type of pot. Roll about

1 tablespoon rice mixture in each grape leaf. Line pot with ripped leaves. Closely arrange stuffed leaves in a stack, add ½ cup water, and remaining half of the lemon juice, plus remaining juice from pot.

Cover rolled leaves with any extra leaves and place a small plate over them to keep leaves compact. Cover pot and bring to a boil. Simmer for 1 hour.

Note: Cannot be frozen successfully.

Meat, Spinach, and Cheese Pie

Meat Mixture:

1¼ cups chopped onions	¾ teaspoon freshly ground
Oil	black pepper
1 pound ground beef	¾ teaspoon oregano
¾ teaspoon salt	½ cup grated Parmesan
	2 eggs, beaten

Sauté onions in oil until tender. Add ground beef and cook until brown. Drain excess fat, add remaining ingredients to meat mixture, mix well, and set aside.

Spinach and Cheese Filling:

5 or 6 scallions, including tops, chopped	1 teaspoon salt
Oil	1½ teaspoons pepper
1½ pounds spinach, cooked and squeezed dry	3 eggs, beaten
½ cup chopped parsley	⅓ pound feta cheese, crumbled
¾ cup chopped dill	⅓ pound cottage cheese or ricotta
1½ tablespoons dried mint	

Sauté scallions in oil until tender. Add spinach and cook a few more minutes. Add parsley, dill, mint, salt, and pepper. Add eggs and cheeses and mix well.

Pastry:

½ pound commercial phyllo leaves	½ pound butter, melted

Line two buttered 9-inch pie plates with phyllo leaves, brushing each sheet with butter. There should be about 6 sheets in each tin.

Put meat mixture in lined pie plates and spread evenly. Spread spinach and cheese filling over meat. Cover pies with remaining pastry, buttering each sheet and tucking the sheets in neatly. Butter top and cut through the top of pastry into six serving portions. Bake in preheated 350° oven for 55 minutes. If frozen, defrost in refrigerator for 6 hours.

Greek Salad

1 small head romaine or Boston lettuce
¼ cup chopped scallions
2 medium-size potatoes, cooked, peeled, and sliced (approximately 2 cups)
2 cups cherry tomatoes, sliced

2 2-ounce cans flat anchovy fillets
¼ cup coarsely chopped parsley
1 bunch radishes, trimmed and sliced
¼ cup crumbled feta cheese

1 cup black olives, or 1 cup pitted ripe olives, halved

Line large, deep platter or shallow bowl with lettuce leaves. Tear remainder of lettuce into bite-size pieces and place in center. Sprinkle scallions over lettuce. Layer potatoes, tomatoes, anchovies, parsley, radishes, and cheese on top. Place olives in a ring around outer edge.

For a lighter salad, omit potatoes and add another head romaine or Boston lettuce torn into bite-size pieces.

Greek Salad Dressing:

2 tablespoons lemon juice
½ teaspoon oregano, crumbled

½ teaspoon salt
Freshly ground black pepper, to taste

¼ cup olive or vegetable oil

Combine dressing ingredients in a jar with a tight lid. Shake well to mix. Just before serving, drizzle dressing over vegetable mixture.

Apricot Torte

2 6-ounce packages dried
   apricots
¾ cup granulated sugar, plus
   2 tablespoons
6 tablespoons melted butter
2 cups graham cracker crumbs
6 tablespoons chopped walnuts
1 teaspoon cinnamon

6 tablespoons softened butter
3 cups sifted confectioners' sugar
2 eggs
1 teaspoon vanilla extract
1 cup heavy cream, sweetened to
   taste
2 teaspoons kirsch
Chopped unsalted pistachios or
   shaved semisweet chocolate

Cover apricots with water in 3-quart pot and cook until tender. Add ¾ cup granulated sugar and purée in food processor. Set aside to cool. Mix melted butter with cracker crumbs, nuts, remaining 2 tablespoons sugar, and cinnamon, press into bottom of a buttered 10-inch springform pan. Bake at 350° for 8 to 10 minutes. Cream softened butter and confectioners' sugar. Beat in eggs, one at a time, blending until mixture is smooth. Add vanilla extract. Spread over baked crust and even off top. Torte can be refrigerated at this point. When ready to serve, spoon the apricot purée over the buttercream and top with cream whipped with kirsch. Sprinkle with chopped pistachio nuts or shaved chocolate curls.

Note: Can be prepared a day in advance up to whipped cream and assembly.

Confirmation Luncheon

Shrimp Antipasto
Vegetable Strudel
Winter Fruit Salad
Vanilla-Chocolate Chunk Mousse

PREVIOUS DAY	EARLY MORNING	FREEZER
Shrimp Antipasto		*Vegetable Strudel*
Winter Fruit Salad		*Vanilla-Chocolate*
		Chunk Mousse

Shrimp Antipasto

Marinade:

1 clove garlic
½ cup olive oil
4 tablespoons lemon juice
3 tablespoons rice wine vinegar
   or red wine vinegar

1 tablespoon leek soup mix
1 tablespoon chopped parsley
1 tablespoon sugar
¼ cup dill

Tabasco, Worcestershire sauce, salt,
and freshly ground black pepper to taste

Process all marinade ingredients.

Antipasto:

1 pound cooked, cleaned shrimp
1 9-ounce package frozen
   artichoke hearts, cooked and
   drained
1 3¼-ounce can pitted black
   olives

5 ounces baby Swiss cheese, cut
   in cubes
1 avocado, cut in cubes
1 red pepper, cut in strips
Salad greens

Pour marinade over shrimp, artichokes, and olives. Marinate overnight. Just before serving, add cheese, avocado, and red pepper. Drain and serve on bed of salad greens.

Vegetable Strudel

2 cups chopped fresh broccoli
2 cups chopped fresh cauliflower
1 cup chopped carrots
2 eggs
1 tablespoon chopped fresh
   parsley
1 teaspoon dried basil
½ teaspoon dried tarragon

1 teaspoon salt
Freshly ground black pepper, to
   taste
½ pound Cheddar cheese,
   grated
½ box phyllo pastry (about
   10 to 12 sheets)
6 tablespoons butter, melted

Combine broccoli, cauliflower, and carrots in a steamer and cook until slightly tender. Set aside.

Combine eggs, parsley, and seasonings, beating well. Add steamed vegetables and cheese. Mix well, but gently. The filling can be prepared ahead of time and refrigerated until ready to use.

Prepare a baking sheet with oil or parchment paper and set aside. Place 1 phyllo sheet on work surface, keeping other sheets covered with a damp cloth. Brush first sheet with butter and continue brushing each sheet and stacking. Leaving a 2-inch border on short end, put filling across the long way about 2 or 3 inches wide. Fold in short ends, then roll dough into a strudel type roll. Place seam on bottom and transfer to baking sheet. Brush butter on ends to make sure it is sealed tightly. Bake about 30 minutes in preheated 375° oven until golden brown. Wait about 5 minutes before cutting. Freezes well.

Note: Strudel can be prepared and frozen, then baked an extra 10 minutes directly from the freezer. It may need some extra butter. It is easy to double the recipe, then bake one strudel and freeze one.

Winter Fruit Salad

1 pineapple	¼ cup sugar, or to taste
2 bananas	2 tablespoons lime or lemon
2 red Delicious apples	juice
1 papaya	

Peel, core, and quarter the pineapple. Slice bananas and three-quarters of the pineapple into ¼- to ½-inch slices. Quarter and core the apples, but do not peel them. Peel and remove seeds from the papaya. Cut apples and papaya into small rectangles. Place the remaining one-quarter pineapple, cut into pieces, in a blender or processor. Add sugar and juice and blend until it forms a smooth sauce. Pour over cut-up fruit in serving bowl. Refrigerate for at least 2 or 3 hours.

Vanilla-Chocolate Chunk Mousse

Crust:

20 chocolate wafers, crushed	2 tablespoons sugar
3½ tablespoons butter, melted	

Mix wafers, sugar, and melted butter, press into bottom of springform pan, and refrigerate while preparing the filling.

Filling:

4 egg whites, at room
  temperature
¼ teaspoon salt
Dash of cream of tartar
¼ cup sugar
2 cups whipping cream

4 teaspoons vanilla extract
7 ounces semisweet chocolate
½ cup almonds, chopped
  coarsely and toasted until
  golden

Beat whites until foamy. Add salt, cream of tartar, and beat to soft peaks. Add sugar, 1 tablespoon at a time, beating well after each addition. Beat until smooth and shiny and stiff peaks form. Beat whipping cream and vanilla until stiff, fold into egg whites. Place in freezer-safe bowl, uncovered, in the freezer. Freeze until the top is very icy and almost solid. The bottom layer will be very cold but not frozen. This will take approximately 45 to 50 minutes.

Melt chocolate over hot water. Add almonds. Quickly fold chocolate into very cold cream mixture. Shards of chocolate will form when hot meets cold. Fold in well and pour into the chilled crust. Wrap very well in plastic wrap and foil. To freeze for a long period, put wrapped mousse in an airtight plastic bag.

Sauce:

2 5-ounce milk chocolate bars
  with hazelnuts, *or* 2 semisweet
  chocolate bars, chopped

¾ to 1 cup half-and-half

When ready to serve, make sauce by melting candy bars with ½ cup of half-and-half in a double boiler or microwave. Stir in additional cream to thin for desired consistency.

Refrigerate and warm before serving.

Note: Mousse should sit at room temperature for 30 to 40 minutes before cutting.

Marvelous March Luncheon

Hearty Consommé
Ham and Asparagus Sandwich Supreme
Hot Chicken Salad Pie with Curry Crust
Fruit Clouds
Chocolate Streusel Coffee Cake

PREVIOUS DAY	EARLY MORNING	FREEZER
Hearty Consommé	Curry Crust	Chocolate Streusel Cake
Prepare asparagus		
Chicken Salad filling		
Fruit Clouds		

Hearty Consommé

5 cups beef bouillon	½ cup cooked rice
1 large tomato, peeled and diced	Rye crisps

Heat bouillon. Add chopped tomatoes and rice. Serve very hot in bouillon cups, accompanied by toasted rye crisps.

Ham and Asparagus Sandwich Supreme

Prepared mustard	Mayonnaise
6 slices white bread	24 cooked or canned asparagus
6 slices ham	tips
6 slices sharp Cheddar cheese	

Spread mustard on bread, top with ham. Spread mayonnaise on ham; top with asparagus tips and 1 slice cheese. Broil until cheese melts. Slice in quarters diagonally and serve immediately.

Hot Chicken Salad Pie with Curry Crust

Curry Crust:

½ cup chicken broth	½ cup flour
4 tablespoons butter or	1 teaspoon curry powder
margarine	2 eggs

Bring broth and butter to a boil, stir in flour and curry powder all at once. Stir vigorously over low heat until mixture leaves sides of pan and forms a ball. Cool slightly. Add one egg at a time, beating until smooth each time. Spread batter evenly in bottom of 9-inch glass pie plate. Bake 45 minutes in preheated 400° oven. Cool.

Filling:

2 cups cut up cooked chicken	2 tablespoons lemon juice
1 cup finely chopped celery	½ cup slivered almonds
2 tablespoons minced onion	¾ cup mayonnaise
3 tablespoons chopped chutney	1 cup sliced almonds

Mix first 6 ingredients with mayonnaise and toss. Pile on top of Curry Crust. Sprinkle top with almonds. Bake for 30 to 45 minutes in preheated 350° oven. Slice into wedges and serve.

Note: Can be frozen before adding almonds. Defrost at room temperature for 1 hour, add nuts, and proceed as above.

Fruit Clouds

2 3-ounce packages strawberry gelatin	2 10-ounce packages frozen strawberries
2 cups boiling water	1 cup sour cream
2 navel oranges, peeled and diced	

Dissolve gelatin in water. Add the frozen berries and stir until they separate; add sour cream and beat with hand beater for 1 to 2 minutes. Fold in orange; spoon at once into tall dessert glasses and chill until firm.

Chocolate Streusel Coffee Cake

Dough:

1 package active dry yeast	¾ cup scalded milk, cooled
¼ cup warm water	¼ teaspoon salt
⅓ cup sugar (plus a pinch)	¼ teaspoon cardomom or lemon rind
¼ pound soft butter	
3 egg yolks	3 cups flour

Dissolve yeast in warm water (with pinch of sugar, only if it foams). Combine ⅓ cup sugar and butter in food processor with steel blade or in a bowl. Add egg yolks one at a time, mixing well after each addition. Add milk, then salt and cardamom or lemon rind, then flour, and finally, the yeast. Mix well after each addition. Dough may be thick and sticky and it may be necessary to add a little extra flour. Add just enough for dough to form a ball and leave the sides of the bowl. Knead until smooth and elastic. Place dough into a well-oiled bowl, turning so that entire surface is coated with oil. Cover and let rise for 1 hour and 15 minutes in a warm, draft-free place.

Filling:

½ cup sugar
¼ cup flour
2 tablespoons butter
1½ teaspoons unsweetened
    cocoa

½ teaspoon cinnamon
¾ cup coarsely chopped
    pecans

Combine all ingredients and set aside.

Glaze:

1 cup confectioners' sugar   4 teaspoons milk
            ½ teaspoon vanilla extract

Mix all ingredients and set aside.

When dough has risen, roll out to 8-by-20-by-½-inch rectangle. Spread filling over rolled dough. Roll up dough lengthwise over the filling, pressing ends to seal. Place on cookie sheet in a figure 8 shape. Bake at 325° for 30 to 35 minutes or until lightly brown. Spread glaze on top while cake is still warm. Freezes well.

Note: If frozen before baking, place foil-wrapped cake in preheated 375° oven and bake for 40 minutes, then glaze. If frozen after baking, defrost at 350° for 20 minutes, then glaze.

Luncheon for House Guests

Caviar Mold
Pasta Primavera
Apple Butter Bread
Individual Fruit Salads with Paprika French Dressing
Super Mocha Cake

PREVIOUS DAY	EARLY MORNING	FREEZER
Caviar Mold	Fruit Salads	Apple Butter Bread
French Dressing	Frosting	Cake layers
Custard Filling		

Caviar Mold
(Serves 6)

6 to 8 hard-cooked eggs,
  chopped
1 to 2 teaspoons mayonnaise
Salt and freshly ground black
  pepper, to taste

½ cup sour cream
8 ounces cream cheese, softened
2 to 4 ounces lumpfish caviar
  (black or white)

8 scallions, chopped fine

Mix eggs, mayonnaise, salt, and pepper together to blend into an egg salad with good spreading consistency (*not* too runny). Spread egg salad evenly on bottom of serving dish. Spread sour cream for next layer. Chill for 30 minutes at this point to set. Spread softened cream cheese for next layer. Lightly drop or spread caviar over surface for next layer. Sprinkle chopped scallions over top.

Chill mold for at least 1 hour. Serve with firm, unsalted crackers. *Note:* Use glass loaf pan, quiche dish, or glass pie dish.

Pasta Primavera

1 bunch broccoli, cleaned and
  cut into bite-size pieces
4 asparagus spears, cut into
  thirds

1½ cups green beans, trimmed
  and cut into 1-inch pieces
½ cup peas, fresh or frozen
½ cup pea pods

7 tablespoons peanut or olive oil
2 cups fresh mushrooms, thinly
   sliced
Salt and freshly ground black
   pepper, to taste
1 teaspoon hot, fresh red or
   green chili peppers (or ½
   teaspoon dried red pepper
   flakes)

¼ cup finely chopped parsley
1 teaspoon finely chopped garlic
3 cups ripe tomatoes, cubed
6 chopped fresh basil leaves (or
   1 teaspoon dried)
1 pound spaghetti or spaghettini
5 quarts boiling salted water
4 tablespoons butter
2 tablespoons chicken broth

½ cup heavy cream, or more
⅔ cup grated Parmesan
⅓ cup toasted pine nuts

Cook the broccoli, asparagus, and beans separately in boiling salted water until tender but crisp, about five minutes. Drain well, run them under cold water, and drain again. Reserve. Cook peas and pea pods for 1 minute if fresh, or 30 seconds if frozen. Drain, chill with cold water, drain again. Combine all vegetables. Heat 1 tablespoon oil in a skillet, add mushrooms and salt and pepper to taste. Shaking in skillet, cook for about 2 minutes. Combine mushrooms with the chopped chilies and parsley. Heat 3 tablespoons oil in saucepan, add the mushroom mixture and half the garlic, add the tomatoes and salt and pepper to taste. Cook about 4 minutes, stirring gently so as not to break up the tomatoes. Add the basil, stir, and set aside.

Put remaining 3 tablespoons of oil in large skillet. Add remaining garlic and the vegetable mixture and cook, stirring gently, just to heat through. Drop spaghetti into boiling salted water; cook al dente. Drain and return to kettle to keep warm.

Melt the butter in a pan large enough to hold spaghetti and all vegetables and add the chicken broth, cream, and cheese, stirring constantly. Cook gently, on and off the heat, until smooth. Add the spaghetti and toss quickly to coat. Add half the vegetables and pour in the liquid from the tomatoes, tossing and stirring over very low heat.

Add the remaining vegetables. If the sauce seems dry, add about ¼ cup more cream. Sauce should not be soupy. Add the pine nuts and give mixture one final toss. Serve in heated bowls, spooning the tomatoes over each serving.

Apple Butter Bread

2 packages active dry yeast
1 teaspoon sugar
2 cups warm water
½ cup apple butter
¼ cup butter, melted
2 tablespoons honey
1½ tablespoons salt
3½ cups stone-ground whole
   wheat flour

1 cup dried apples, coarsely
   chopped
2 to 2½ cups bread flour or
   half bread, half cake flour
1 to 2 tablespoons cornmeal
1 egg, beaten with 1 teaspoon
   water

In large bowl of electric mixer, dissolve yeast and sugar in ½ cup of the water. Let it proof until it bubbles, about 10 minutes. Mix in remaining water, apple butter, butter, honey, and salt. Gradually beat in whole wheat flour until smooth. Stir in dried apples until well distributed. With the dough hook, beat in enough white flour to form a stiff dough. Add cornmeal and knead until smooth and elastic, adding more flour if necessary. Place in large, greased bowl, turning to coat all sides of dough. Cover with a damp towel and let rise 1½ to 2 hours in a warm place until doubled in bulk. (An oven heated to 250° and then turned off will work fine.)

Punch down dough and divide in half. Put each half into a 9-by-5-inch loaf pan; or use two greased heart-shaped clay pots. Cover with damp towel and let rise in warm place for about 1 hour. Brush loaves with beaten egg mixture and sprinkle lightly with water.

In preheated 425° oven, bake for 10 minutes; then lower heat to 375° and bake 25 minutes longer, until loaves turn brown and sound hollow when tapped. Cool on wire racks.

Individual Fruit Salads

8 heads Belgian endive
1 small cantaloupe, peeled and
   cut into thin wedges
1 large grapefruit, peeled and
   sectioned

1 avocado, peeled, halved, and
   cut into slices
6 sprigs watercress

Arrange the endive on 6 salad plates. Place alternating wedges of melon and grapefruit sections on endive. Top with slices of avocado, decorate with watercress, and serve with Paprika French Dressing in a separate dish.

Paprika French Dressing:

¾ teaspoon salt
⅛ teaspoon pepper
½ teaspoon sweet paprika

1 teaspoon sugar
3 tablespoons tarragon vinegar
½ cup salad oil

¼ cup olive oil

Stir dry ingredients with the vinegar until salt and sugar are dissolved. Beat in the oil and serve very cold. Chill, and shake well before serving. Recipe makes 1 cup.

Super Mocha Cake

3 cups sifted cake flour
¾ teaspoon baking soda
¾ teaspoon salt
¾ cup unsweetened Dutch cocoa
1⅛ cups strong coffee, hot

12 tablespoons butter (1½ sticks)
2¾ cups sugar
¾ cup thick sour cream
5 egg whites
1½ teaspoons vanilla extract

Resift cake flour three times with baking soda and salt. Set aside. Mix cocoa and hot coffee. Cool. Cream butter until soft. Add sugar gradually, beating until mixture is light and fluffy. Add cocoa mixture, sour cream, and flour alternately, ending with flour. Mix well after each addition. Beat egg whites until stiff but not dry and fold into mixture, along with vanilla. Turn batter into 3 well-greased 9-inch pans and bake in preheated 350° oven about 30 minutes, or until done. Invert on racks to cool. When cool, spread custard cream filling between layers. Spread frosting on top and sides. Drizzle warm glaze over frosting and around edge of cake; let it drip down the sides.

Custard Cream Filling:

⅓ cup flour
Dash of salt
½ cup sugar

1⅓ cups hot milk
2 egg yolks
⅓ cup heavy cream, whipped

1 teaspoon vanilla extract

Mix flour, salt, and ¼ cup of the sugar. Then stir in hot milk. Cook in double boiler until smooth and thickened, stirring constantly. Combine yolks with remaining sugar. Then combine with hot milk mixture and cook, stirring, 2 to 3 minutes longer. Cool, until bottom of pan is cool. Fold in whipped cream and vanilla.

Frosting:

1 cup sugar	½ teaspoon cream of tartar
1 egg white	½ cup boiling water

Beat all ingredients at high speed in electric mixer for 20 minutes.

Chocolate Drip Glaze:

2 squares unsweetened chocolate	½ cup sugar
2 tablespoons dark corn syrup	4 tablespoons cream
2 teaspoons butter	

Place ingredients in a skillet and cook until thick. Cool slightly until not burning hot, but still warm.

April Shower Luncheon

Lemon Frost
Broiled Mushroom Puffs
Spicy Asparagus Vinaigrette
Caraway Puffs
Fruited Chicken Salad
Chocolate Date Cake

PREVIOUS DAY	EARLY MORNING	FREEZER
Chicken for salad	Chicken Salad	Mushroom Puffs
Vinaigrette		Caraway Puffs
Date Cake		

Lemon Frost

Finely grated peel of ½ lemon	1 tablespoon egg white
1 pint lemon ice or sherbet	3 ounces Benedictine
1 cup lemon juice	6 ounces vodka
¼ cup superfine sugar	2 cups crushed ice
Kiwi slices or fresh violets, for garnish	

Blend all ingredients except ice and garnish in a blender or food processor for 30 seconds. Add 1 cup ice and blend another 30 seconds. Pour ingredients into a glass pitcher. Blend remaining cup of ice in blender or processor for 15 seconds. Add to lemon mixture. Stir until well mixed. Serve in chilled wine glasses. Garnish as desired.

Broiled Mushroom Puffs
(Makes 36)

1 pound mushrooms	2 tablespoons Worcestershire
4 tablespoons butter	sauce
8 ounces cream cheese	1 teaspoon curry powder
2 tablespoons grated onion	2 egg yolks
Salt and freshly ground black	36 slices white bread, cut into
pepper, to taste	rounds
1 tablespoon finely chopped	Mayonnaise
parsley	

Chop mushrooms and sauté in butter. Mash cream cheese until very soft and season with onion, salt, pepper, parsley, Worcestershire sauce, and curry. Add egg yolks and beat until smooth. Toast one side of bread rounds. Spread untoasted side with mayonnaise and heap mushrooms on top. Cover with cheese mixture and place rounds under hot broiler until cheese puffs up and browns lightly. Freezes well (before broiling).

Spicy Asparagus Vinaigrette

48 small fresh asparagus spears	1 head red or any loose-leaf
	lettuce
6 strips pimento	

Trim asparagus into pieces about 6 inches long and scrape each spear with a vegetable peeler. Lay asparagus into large skillet. Cover with boiling salted water and cook until tender-crisp, about 5 to 7 minutes. Drain and chill. Arrange asparagus in 6 separate bunches, spoke fashion, on a lettuce-covered platter and "tie" each bunch with a strip of pimento. Cover and return to refrigerator. Just before serving, pour Spicy Vinaigrette over asparagus.

Spicy Vinaigrette:

½ cup red wine vinegar	1 teaspoon finely chopped chives
¾ teaspoon salt	1 teaspoon finely chopped green
¼ teaspoon freshly ground	olives
black pepper	1 teaspoon finely chopped
1½ cups olive oil	parsley
1 teaspoon capers	1 hard-cooked egg, chopped

Combine all ingredients and mix well. Chill.

Caraway Puffs
(Makes 24)

2 packages active dry yeast	2 teaspoons salt
½ cup warm water	½ teaspoon baking soda
¼ cup sugar	2 eggs, slightly beaten
2 tablespoons caraway seeds	4⅔ cups all-purpose flour
2 cups creamed cottage cheese	Butter or margarine

In mixing bowl, dissolve yeast in water with sugar. Add caraway seeds. Heat cheese just until lukewarm. Mix cheese, salt, soda, and eggs into yeast mixture. Add flour gradually, mixing until dough cleans the bowl. This can be done in electric mixer.

Let rise in warm place until doubled, 45 to 60 minutes. Stir dough down. Divide among 24 large, well-greased muffin cups. Cover and let rise again until doubled, about 45 minutes. Bake in preheated 350° oven for about 25 minutes, until puffs are golden and sound hollow when tapped. Remove from tins and brush with butter. Bake 1 tin at a time, as they rise very high. Use buttered spoon when filling muffin cups, as dough is very sticky.

Fruited Chicken Salad

4 whole chicken breasts	½ cup cashews, toasted
2 ribs celery, chopped	¾ cup mayonnaise
¼ cup scallions, chopped	1 tablespoon lemon juice
1 13-ounce can crushed	½ teaspoon each salt and
pineapple, drained well	pepper

½ cup pitted, halved dark
cherries, either fresh or canned
(drained)

Combine all ingredients except cherries. Toss, adjust seasoning, and add cherries right before serving.

Chocolate Date Cake

1 cup chopped dates	1 cup granulated sugar
1 cup boiling water	½ pound butter
1 cup flour	2 eggs
½ teaspoon salt	1 teaspoon vanilla extract
1 teaspoon baking soda	1 cup chocolate chips
1 heaping tablespoon	Confectioners' sugar
unsweetened cocoa	

Grease and flour 9-by-12-inch pan. Pour boiling water over chopped dates. Set aside. Sift together flour, salt, baking soda, and cocoa. Set aside. Cream sugar and butter. Add eggs and vanilla. Add date mixture, then flour mixture. Stir in ½ cup of the chocolate chips. Pour into prepared pan. Add remaining ½ cup chocolate chips on top. Bake in preheated 350° oven for 30 to 35 minutes. Sprinkle with confectioners' sugar while hot.

🌿 🌿 🌿

Luncheon in Tuscany

Tuna Antipasto
Instant Vegetarian Minestrone
Easy Italian Bread
Tater Crisp Chicken
Strawberries with Raspberry Sauce

PREVIOUS DAY	EARLY MORNING	FREEZER
Tuna Antipasto	*Instant Minestrone*	*Easy Italian Bread*
	Raspberry Sauce	

Tuna Antipasto
(Serves up to 12)

½ cup vinegar
1 cup ketchup
½ cup chili sauce, or more, to taste
¼ cup oil
Garlic salt, to taste
2 6- to 7-ounce cans white meat tuna, in water
1 8-ounce jar small carrots
1 4½-ounce jar button mushrooms

1 3-ounce jar pearl onions
1 14-ounce can black olives, drained
1 8-ounce jar green olives, drained
1 8-ounce jar gherkin pickles, drained
1 16-ounce can chick peas, drained

Boil vinegar, ketchup, chili sauce, oil, and garlic salt for 1 minute. Add drained tuna and vegetables, and boil for 1 more minute. Refrigerate. Serve in large glass bowl.

Instant Vegetarian Minestrone

2 16-ounce cans vegetarian baked beans
2 15-ounce cans mini-ravioli
1 1-pound, 13-ounce can tomatoes, crushed (use liquid)
1 10-ounce package frozen carrots, in butter sauce
1 10-ounce package frozen lima beans, in butter sauce
1 to 2 10-ounce packages frozen green beans, crosscut

1 to 2 10-ounce packages frozen chopped spinach
1 cup freeze-dried green pepper
1 cup freeze-dried onions
1 16-ounce jar spaghetti sauce
Salt and freshly ground black pepper, to taste
Dash of Worcestershire sauce
Grated Parmesan cheese

Put everything into a large pot with enough water to just cover all ingredients and bring to boil. Ready in minutes. Serve with grated Parmesan and Easy Italian Bread (see Index). Flavor even improves if made a day in advance.

Tater Crisp Chicken

1 2- to 3-pound frying chicken, boned

¼ cup melted butter
1 cup instant potato flakes
Salt and pepper

Grease 13-by-9-inch baking dish. Cut chicken into bite-size pieces with or without skin. Dip pieces into melted butter; roll in potato flakes. Place in buttered dish. Season to taste. Bake in preheated 400° oven for 50 to 60 minutes, or until done.

Note: Can also be put on toothpicks and served with a sweet-and-sour dip as an appetizer.

Strawberries with Raspberry Sauce

2 packages, 6 to 7 ounces each, frozen raspberries
½ cup kirsch or curaçao
6 tablespoons orange juice

2 quarts fresh strawberries
Whipped cream, or vanilla ice cream

Purée partially thawed raspberries in processor. Add liqueur and juice and process a few seconds. Refrigerate. A few hours before serving, pour sauce over cleaned and hulled berries in individual bowls. Serve with whipped cream or vanilla ice cream.

🌿 🌿 🌿

Cool Summer Luncheon

Cold Potato-Basil Soup
Shrimp and Scallop Salad
Sesame Seed Nibbles
Raspberry-Lemonade Ring
Pecan Torte

PREVIOUS DAY	EARLY MORNING	FREEZER
Potato-Basil Soup	*Shrimp and Scallop*	
Sesame Seed Nibbles	*Salad*	
Raspberry-Lemonade	*Pecan Torte*	
Ring		

Cold Potato-Basil Soup

6 tablespoons unsalted butter
4 cups chopped yellow onions
3 cups firmly packed fresh basil
  leaves, minced
2 cups strong chicken stock
1 pound new potatoes, peeled,
  cut into pieces, and cooked

2 teaspoons salt
½ teaspoon pepper
3 to 4 dashes of hot pepper
  sauce
2 cups whipping cream

Melt butter in large saucepan and sauté onions until soft. Do not brown. Add minced basil and sauté for 1 minute. Add stock, cooked potatoes, salt, pepper, and pepper sauce. Pureé all in food processor until smooth. Stir in cream and chill. Adjust seasonings to taste. Flavor improves if made at least one day in advance.

Shrimp and Scallop Salad

3 dozen large shrimp, shelled
  and deveined
2 pounds scallops

¾ pound snow peas
3 cucumbers, peeled, seeded, and
  sliced

6 celery ribs, thinly sliced

Cook shrimp in boiling water until just pink. Drain well and transfer to bowl. Cook scallops in boiling water until translucent. Drain well and add to shrimp. Place snow peas in colander and pour boiling water over them. Drain well. Transfer to another bowl, add cucumbers, and toss lightly; let cool.

Add celery to seafood mixture and blend well. Add half of dressing and toss to coat. Add remaining dressing to vegetable mix and toss well. Mound seafood on serving platter and surround with snow-pea mixture, or serve on platter arranged in rows. Chill slightly before serving.

Dressing:

½ cup water
½ cup white vinegar
½ scant cup vegetable oil

4 tablespoons light soy sauce
3 tablespoons dry mustard
3 tablespoons dry sherry

1½ tablespoons sugar

Combine all ingredients and blend well.

Sesame Seed Nibbles
(Makes 5 dozen)

¾ cup sesame seed
1 cup flour
1 teaspoon salt

Dash of cayenne pepper
5 tablespoons butter
2 tablespoons ice water

Mix together ½ cup of the sesame seed, flour, ½ teaspoon of the salt, and cayenne. Cut in the cold butter and add the ice water to make a dough the consistency of pie crust. Roll out ⅛-inch thick and cut into small rounds with a 1½-inch cookie cutter. Place on greased baking sheet. Pat remaining sesame seeds on top of rounds. Bake in preheated 350° oven for 20 minutes, until light tan. Before removing from sheet and while still hot, sprinkle lightly with remaining salt.

Note: Sesame Seed Nibbles can be kept in a covered tin or cracker jar and reheated before serving.

Raspberry-Lemonade Ring

1 10-ounce package frozen
   raspberries
1 6-ounce package raspberry
   gelatin

1 pint vanilla ice cream, softened
1 6-ounce can lemonade
   concentrate, thawed

Drain raspberries. Save juice. Dissolve gelatin in 2 cups boiling water. Add ice cream and stir until melted. Add lemonade and berry juice. Chill until partially set, then stir in berries and pour into 6-cup ring mold. Chill until set.

Pecan Torte

Torte:

4 eggs
1 pound light brown sugar
1 cup flour

1½ teaspoons baking powder
½ pound pecans, chopped
1 teaspoon vanilla extract

Beat eggs and sugar together. Mix remaining torte ingredients into creamed eggs and sugar, then press mixture into 2 greased 9-inch layer pans. Bake in preheated 350° oven for 25 to 30 minutes, on low shelf.

Filling:

1 tablespoon butter	1 cup heavy cream
1 tablespoon flour	5 tablespoons powdered sugar
2 egg yolks	5 ounces pecans, chopped

1 cup whipping cream

Melt butter and add flour. Beat egg yolks and add cream. Add egg mixture to flour mixture and cook until very thick in double boiler. It will be like a light pudding or custard.

When cool, add sugar and chopped pecans to filling. Put filling between layers and cover top with whipped cream several hours before serving. If you prefer not to use whipped cream, double the filling.

Bridal Luncheon   (Serves 8)

Almond-Orange Punch
Poached Salmon with Mayonnaise Verte
Rice Wimbledon with Courtside Dressing
Arranged Salad with Lemon French Dressing
Flourless Chocolate Cake

PREVIOUS DAY	EARLY MORNING	FREEZER
Courside Dressing	*Rice Wimbledon*	*Ice Ring for punch*
Mayonnaise Verte	*Arrange salad*	
Lemon French Dressing		
Flourless Chocolate Cake		

Almond-Orange Punch
(Serves 10)

2½ quarts freshly squeezed
    orange juice
1¼ cups Grand Marnier
⅓ cup orgeat syrup
⅓ cup Amaretto or other
    almond-flavored liqueur

Whole blanched almonds
Mint leaves
Orange slices
1 bottle Riesling or champagne,
    or about ½ cup rum, to
    taste

Mix together the juice, Grand Marnier, syrup, and almond liqueur in punch bowl. Freeze almonds, mint leaves, and orange slices in Ice Ring (see Index) and float in punch.

Add Riesling or champagne for light, fruity punch. For punch with more kick, add rum to taste.

Poached Salmon

1 6- to 7-pound fresh salmon (wrapped in cheesecloth)

Court Bouillon #1:

2 quarts water
2 cups dry white wine
1 rib celery
1 small onion, stuck with 1
    whole clove

1 tablespoon salt
3 bruised peppercorns
Pinch of thyme
1 bay leaf
3 sprigs parsley

Combine ingredients in a fish poacher and bring to a boil; reduce heat and place fish into poacher. Simmer for 8 to 10 minutes per pound. Let salmon cool in the stock, then chill. Carefully remove skin, fin bones, and center bones if possible, leaving fish as whole as possible. Chill. Serve with Mayonnaise Verte.

Mayonnaise Verte:

½ cup watercress or spinach
¼ cup fresh parsley
¼ cup fresh dill weed or fresh
    tarragon (or 1 tablespoon of
    either dried)

2 scallions, white and green
    parts, sliced thin
2 cups mayonnaise

Mince the greens and herbs and blend into mayonnaise. Chill several hours or overnight to blend flavors.

Rice Wimbledon

4 cups hot cooked rice
2 tablespoons vegetable oil
2 oranges, sectioned

½ cup pineapple chunks
2 ripe kiwi, sliced
½ cup pecan halves, toasted

Combine all ingredients except kiwi and pecans. When ready to serve, garnish with pecans and kiwi and serve with a bowl of Courtside Dressing.

Courtside Dressing:

¾ cup sugar
1 teaspoon dry mustard
1 teaspoon salt

⅓ cup pear or other white
   vinegar
1 cup vegetable oil

1 tablespoon celery seed

Combine ingredients and chill overnight to enhance flavor.

🦪 🦪 🦪

Arranged Salad

1 bunch broccoli
1 head cauliflower
3 medium summer squash
4 carrots (any other fresh
   vegetables can be substituted)
Coarse salt and freshly ground
   black pepper, to taste

Dried oregano
Fresh basil
Olive oil
Lemon wedges

Steam the vegetables separately until cooked but still crisp. Blanch with cold water. Arrange on platter. Sprinkle with coarse salt, pepper, and herbs, and serve with Lemon French Dressing. Surround with lemon wedges. Serve at room temperature.

Lemon French Dressing:

1 cup olive or vegetable oil (or
  combination)
⅓ cup lemon juice
½ teaspoon dry mustard
½ teaspoon paprika
1 teaspoon sugar
1 teaspoon salt
¼ teaspoon freshly ground
  black pepper

2 tablespoons finely snipped
  fresh herbs: basil, dill,
  marjoram, oregano, thyme; or
2½ teaspoons dried herbs
  (½ teaspoon each of the
  above)

Put oil and next 6 ingredients in a medium-size jar with a tight-fitting lid and shake. Add herbs and shake again. Refrigerate. Before serving, shake again.

Flourless Chocolate Cake

14 ounces good quality
  semisweet baking chocolate
⅞ pound unsalted butter
1½ cups sugar

10 eggs, separated
1 tablespoon cognac
1 teaspoon vanilla extract
½ pint whipping cream

Butter and lightly flour a 12-inch springform pan. Place chocolate chunks and butter in top of a double boiler and melt slowly, stirring constantly. Add 1¼ cups of the sugar to the chocolate mixture. Continue to stir until chocolate is dissolved. Beat the egg yolks separately. Add some of the chocolate mixture to egg yolks and return all to the saucepan. Cook until slightly thickened (stirring constantly). Add cognac and vanilla. Beat egg whites into soft peaks, add the remaining ¼ cup sugar, and beat until peaks are stiff. Fold into chocolate mixture. Pour into prepared pan. Bake 3 hours in preheated 250° oven. Remove from oven, cool to room temperature, and chill in refrigerator. Serve with dollops of whipped cream.

Poolside Luncheon

Quick Vichyssoise Florentine
Santa Fe Sandwiches
Two-Way Easy Cranberry Mold
Melt-in-Your-Mouth Angel Food Cake with Chocolate Filling

PREVIOUS DAY   EARLY MORNING   FREEZER
Cranberry Mold   *Vichyssoise*   *Angel Food Cake*
Chocolate Filling

Quick Vichyssoise Florentine

2 10¾-ounce cans condensed
   cream of potato soup
2 soup cans milk
1 10-ounce package frozen
   chopped spinach

2 tablespoons minced chives
1 teaspoon basil
¼ teaspoon white pepper
1 cup sour cream or sour half-
   and-half

In saucepan, combine all ingredients except sour cream. Heat until
spinach is thawed, bring to boiling point, reduce heat, simmer 1 minute. Pour half of mixture into blender or processor and purée. Repeat
with second half. Stir in sour cream. May be reheated to serve, or
chilled. Freezes well.

Santa Fe Sandwiches

6 large pitas, split to form 12
   pockets
1 pound sliced Monterey Jack
   cheese
2 cups alfalfa sprouts

3 large tomatoes, diced
1 pound bacon, cooked and
   crumbled
2 avocados, sliced and sprinkled
   with lemon juice

Arrange ingredients on large platter and allow guests to fix their own
sandwiches.

Two-Way Easy Cranberry Mold

Basic Mixture:

2 packages unflavored gelatin
½ cup cold water
2 16-ounce cans cranberry jelly

1 cup pineapple juice
¼ teaspoon salt

Dissolve gelatin in water, then melt over low heat. Stir in cranberry
jelly to liquefy. Add juice and salt. Cool.

Grapefruit-Cranberry Salad:

3 grapefruit, peeled, seeds
  removed, and sectioned

½ cup chopped walnuts

Pour a thin layer of the cranberry mixture into the bottom of a 9-cup mold. Arrange the grapefruit sections attractively around the mold. Sprinkle nuts over the fruit. Slowly pour in the rest of the cranberry mixture. Chill until set.

Cranberry-Fruit Salad:

Make cranberry base above, chill to thicken, then fold in:

1 cup chopped walnuts
1 cup seedless white grapes,
  halved

1 cup canned pineapple tidbits,
  drained

Chill until set.

Melt-in-Your-Mouth Angel Food Cake

1 cup sifted cake flour
1¼ cups confectioners' sugar
1½ cups egg whites
  (approximately 12)

1½ teaspoons cream of tartar
1½ teaspoons vanilla extract
½ teaspoon almond extract
1 cup granulated sugar

Sift flour with confectioners' sugar three times. Beat egg whites with cream of tartar and vanilla and almond extracts until mixture makes soft peaks; then beat in granulated sugar, 2 tablespoons at a time, until well blended. Fold in one-quarter of the dry ingredients at a time.

Pour batter into *ungreased* 10-inch tube pan and bake in preheated 375° oven for 30 minutes. Remove from oven and turn upside down to cool. Either place tube of cake pan onto top of bottle neck, or, if pan has legs, turn it up on them.

Chocolate Filling:

½ pound unsalted butter
1 cup confectioners' sugar
2 ounces unsweetened chocolate,
  melted

5 egg yolks
1 teaspoon vanilla extract
5 egg whites, stiffly beaten
½ pound pecans, chopped

Slice angel food cake into 3 horizontal layers. (If toothpicks are inserted into cake at desired levels, the slicing can be done more easily with serrated knife.) Cream butter and sugar. Add melted chocolate. Beat in 1 egg yolk at a time. Add vanilla. Beat thoroughly. Fold in beaten egg whites and nuts. Spread frosting between layers and on top and sides of cake. Chill for 24 hours.

Note: Cake must be cold when served.

Summer's Best Luncheon

Cold Peach Soup
Curried Shrimp in Puff Pastry
Steamed Asparagus
Marinated Carrots
Peppersnaps
Fresh Apple Cake

PREVIOUS DAY	EARLY MORNING	FREEZER
Peach Soup	*Puff Pastry*	*Peppersnaps*
Marinated Carrots	*Steam asparagus*	
Apple Cake		

Cold Peach Soup
(Serves 5)

2 cups puréed peaches (16-ounce can drained peach halves or slices, or 3 cups fresh peaches, peeled and sliced)
2 tablespoons confectioners' sugar
2 tablespoons lemon juice
3 cups dry white wine
1 small bay leaf
1 whole clove
1 small cinnamon stick
½ cup sour cream (or ½ cup heavy cream, whipped)

In medium bowl, mix peaches, sugar, and lemon juice. Let stand 20 minutes. In saucepan bring wine and spices to boil. Reduce heat and simmer 1 minute. Strain and cool. Stir wine into peaches. Chill. Serve topped with dollop of sour or whipped cream.

Curried Shrimp in Puff Pastry
(Makes 24)

Puff Pastry:

1 cup water	Salt (optional)
¼ pound butter	1 cup flour
	4 large eggs

Butter a jelly-roll pan, sprinkle with flour, then shake out excess. Put water into large saucepan with butter and salt, and heat to boil. Add flour all at once, stirring vigorously and thoroughly until a ball is formed and mixture cleans sides of the saucepan. Add one egg at a time, beating thoroughly with spoon until each is well blended into the mixture. When all eggs are added, spoon mixture into a pastry bag fitted with a #6 round tip. Hold the bag straight up with tip close to the surface of jelly-roll pan and squeeze, making 24 mounds of pastry all over pan. Or place mixture in mounds on pan with a medium-size serving spoon.

Bake in preheated 425° oven for 30 minutes, or until golden brown and cooked through. Remove from pan. Cool on wire rack.

Curried Shrimp:

1½ pounds fresh shrimp, shelled and deveined	2 tablespoons curry powder
2 tablespoons butter	2 cups whipping cream
6 tablespoons finely chopped onion	6 tablespoons chutney
	Salt and pepper, to taste

Cut shrimp into ½-inch pieces or smaller. Should be about 2½ to 3 cups. Melt butter in saucepan, add onion, and cook, stirring, until wilted. Add curry powder, blend. Add cream and chutney, cook down to about 1 cup. Add salt and pepper. Add shrimp and cook, stirring, about 2 minutes, until they lose their raw look completely.

Slice tops off of all puffs. Spoon an equal portion of the shrimp mixture into each bottom. Replace tops and serve.

Steamed Asparagus

2 pounds fresh asparagus   ⅓ cup melted butter
2 lemons, cut into wedges

Place asparagus in steamer or large skillet, add barely enough water to cover bottom of pan, and steam approximately 10 minutes, or until tender. Serve with melted butter and lemon wedges.

Marinated Carrots

2 pounds carrots, sliced thin at   1 medium onion, sliced thin and
   at angle   quartered
1 green pepper, sliced thin and quartered

Cook carrots until just tender (still crisp). Mix the vegetables together, pour marinade over, and refrigerate overnight. Drain well.

Marinade:

1 10½-ounce can tomato   1 teaspoon dry mustard
   soup, undiluted   1 teaspoon Worcestershire sauce
⅔ cup sugar   1 teaspoon salt
½ cup cooking oil   ¾ teaspoon pepper
¾ cup vinegar

Combine all ingredients. Mix well.

Peppersnaps
(Makes 8 dozen)

2 cups unsifted flour   ½ teaspoon salt
2 teaspoons cinnamon   ½ teaspoon baking soda
2 teaspoons freshly ground black   6 tablespoons butter, softened
   pepper   2 cups confectioners' sugar
2 eggs

In small bowl combine flour, cinnamon, black pepper, salt, and baking soda. Set aside. In medium bowl, cream butter and sugar. Add eggs and mix well. Gradually add reserved flour mixture, stirring just until blended. Wrap in wax paper or clear plastic wrap and refrigerate several hours or overnight.

Form ½-teaspoon balls of dough. Place on greased baking sheets 2 inches apart. Bake at 350° about 10 minutes, or until lightly browned. Cool on wire racks.

Fresh Apple Cake

6 medium cooking apples	1 teaspoon baking soda
Lemon juice	½ teaspoon salt
¼ pound butter	1 cup sour cream
1¼ cups granulated sugar	½ cup vanilla cookie crumbs
2 eggs	¼ cup brown sugar
1 teaspoon orange extract	1 teaspoon cinnamon
2 cups sifted flour	½ teaspoon nutmeg
1 teaspoon baking powder	⅛ teaspoon allspice

¼ cup melted butter, cooled

Pare and slice apples, sprinkle with lemon juice, and set aside. Cream ¼ pound of butter and 1 cup of the sugar until light and fluffy. Add eggs and beat thoroughly. Add extract. Sift flour with baking powder, baking soda, and salt. Add flour in thirds to creamed mixture alternately with sour cream. Spread batter in greased 13-by-9-inch pan. Sprinkle with cookie crumbs. Arrange apple slices in rows on batter. Top with mixture of remaining white sugar, brown sugar, and spices. Drizzle with ¼ cup melted butter. Bake in preheated 400° oven for 30 minutes.

August Luncheon

Cold Avocado Soup
California Tuna Plate
Zucchini Bread
Bean Sprout Salad
Hot Milk Cake
Chocolate-Dipped Fruit

PREVIOUS DAY	EARLY MORNING	FREEZER
Begin Tuna Plate preparation	*Cold Avocado Soup*	*Zucchini Bread*
Chocolate-Dipped Fruit	*Hot Milk Cake*	

Cold Avocado Soup

2 large avocados, peeled and cut
   in large pieces
2 cloves garlic
2 10½-ounce cans chicken
   broth

2 cans water
Juice of 1 lemon
1 pint heavy cream
Salt and freshly ground black
   pepper, to taste

Blend all ingredients except cream, salt, and pepper at high speed. Pour into large bowl and stir in cream, and chill. Add salt and pepper to taste. Serve in small glass bowls or cups.

California Tuna Plate

2 15-ounce cans tuna
1 10-ounce package frozen peas
1 cup thinly sliced celery
¾ cup mayonnaise
1 tablespoon lemon juice

½ to 1 teaspoon curry powder
⅛ teaspoon garlic salt
1 cup chow mein noodles
Salad greens
½ cup toasted nuts

Drain tuna and break into chunks. Cook and drain peas; or defrost without cooking, drain well, and dry before adding. Combine tuna, peas, and celery, cover lightly, and chill well. Combine mayonnaise, lemon juice, curry powder, and garlic salt. Chill well. Shortly before serving add noodles and toss lightly; add mayonnaise mixture and toss again. Serve on a bed of crisp salad greens and sprinkle with toasted nuts.

Note: For variety, drain 2 3-ounce jars of cocktail onions and toss with the tuna; add sliced radishes or stuffed olives.

Zucchini Bread

3 eggs
1 cup oil
2 cups sugar
2 teaspoons vanilla extract
2 cups shredded unpeeled
  zucchini
1 8-ounce can crushed pineapple,
  drained
3 cups flour

2 teaspoons baking soda
½ teaspoon baking powder
1 teaspoon salt
1½ teaspoons cinnamon
¾ teaspoon nutmeg
1 cup each chopped pecans and
  dates, *or* 2 additional cups
  zucchini

Beat first 4 ingredients together. Add rest of ingredients and mix well. Preheat oven to 350°. Pour mixture into two greased 9-by-5-inch loaf pans. Bake 1 hour. Freezes well.
  Note: Will defrost at room temperature in 2 hours.

Bean Sprout Salad

6 tablespoons sesame oil
3 tablespoons dry sherry
1½ pints bean sprouts,
  washed and picked over
¼ cup olive oil
3 tablespoons soy sauce
3 tablespoons lemon juice

Freshly ground black pepper, to
  taste
3 cups shredded Chinese cabbage
2¼ cups canned bamboo
  shoots, drained, cut into long
  spears

2 heads Boston lettuce

Combine sesame oil and sherry and mix with bean sprouts. Combine next 4 ingredients into a dressing and pour half over the combined cabbage and bamboo shoots. Arrange lettuce leaves on serving plates and arrange bean sprouts and cabbage mixtures on the plates. Serve with remaining dressing.

Hot Milk Cake

3 eggs
1½ cups sugar
1½ cups flour

3 teaspoons baking powder
¾ cup milk
1 tablespoon butter

Grease two 9-inch cake pans and line with wax paper. Beat eggs and sugar. Add flour and baking powder. Add scalding milk to which has been added butter. Bake in preheated 350° oven for 25 minutes.

Caramel Icing:

12 tablespoons butter (1½ sticks)

2 cups sugar

1 cup cream (room temperature)

Pecans, halved

Cook butter and sugar slowly for about 45 minutes or until caramel browns. Add cream and cook until icing boils. Cool by placing saucepan in bowl of ice. Beat icing (which usually doesn't get very stiff— it is runny when spread on cake). Decorate top of cake with pecan halves.

Chocolate-Dipped Fruit

4 ounces semisweet chocolate

4 ounces bitter chocolate

¼ cup butter

¼ cup light corn syrup

Fresh strawberries or assorted dried fruits

Combine first 4 ingredients in a 1-quart saucepan over very low heat. Stir until melted and smooth. Remove from heat and beat with a wooden spoon until cool but still pourable. Using two forks, dip fruit halfway into chocolate. Cool on wax paper and refrigerate overnight, uncovered. Remove fruit from paper and store in one layer in tightly covered container in refrigerator.

September Leaves

Light Wine Refresher

Ceviche

Apricot Melba Mold

Onions Stuffed with Wild Rice and Sausage

Broccoli and Tomato Salad with Raspberry–Walnut Oil Dressing

Failproof Popovers

Honeydew Basket

Crunchy Brownie Bars

Light Wine Refresher
(Makes about 7 cups)

3 cups Catawba or other white grape juice, or 3 cups chilled light white wine: Chablis or Sauterne

½ cup lemon juice, fresh or from concentrate
½ cup sugar
1 quart club soda, chilled

Seedless white grapes, orange slices, or strawberries, for garnish

In pitcher, combine first 3 ingredients, stir until sugar dissolves. Just before serving, add club soda. Garnish as desired. Serve over ice.

Ceviche
(Serves 12)

1 pound raw bay scallops
6 ounces mushrooms, sliced
4 ounces raw salmon, sliced
2 ounces red bell peppers, julienned

1 teaspoon chopped cilantro
½ cup lime juice
½ cup lemon juice
2 ounces diced tomatoes
2 teaspoons salt

Mix all ingredients together. Chill for 12 hours.

Apricot Melba Mold

Apricot Layer (first layer):

½ envelope unflavored gelatin
⅓ cup orange juice

1 17-ounce can apricots, with juice
1 3-ounce package lemon gelatin

2 tablespoons lemon juice

Soften gelatin in orange juice. Purée apricots and juice in a blender, then heat to a boil. Add lemon gelatin mix and plain gelatin mixture and stir until dissolved. Add lemon juice. Pour into 6-cup mold, or individual molds, and refrigerate until set.

Cheese Layer (second layer):

1 3-ounce package softened
    cream cheese
2 tablespoons mayonnaise

2 tablespoons milk
2 tablespoons chopped pecans

Combine ingredients and spread over set apricot layer. Leave a narrow border around the outside edges so top and bottom layers will be sealed.

Raspberry Layer (third layer):

1 10-ounce package frozen
    raspberries, thawed
2 tablespoons lemon juice
1 3-ounce package raspberry
    gelatin

½ envelope plain gelatin,
    softened in ¼ cup cold
    water
1 cup boiling water

Drain the raspberries and reserve the juice. Combine juice, lemon juice, and enough cold water to make 1 cup. Dissolve raspberry gelatin and gelatin mixture in the boiling water. Combine with the juices and berries; cool. Spoon over the cheese layer. Chill and unmold for serving.

Onions Stuffed with Wild Rice and Sausage

¾ cup wild rice
1 teaspoon salt
3 cups boiling water
6 large yellow onions
¼ pound butter
1 cup chopped mushrooms
½ cup bulk sausage

2 tablespoons minced fresh
    parsley
½ teaspoon dried sage,
    crumbled
Salt and freshly ground black
    pepper
Beef or chicken broth

Wash rice in cold water and remove any foreign particles. Add salt to 3 cups boiling water. Gradually pour in rice so water does not stop boiling. Reduce heat, cover, and simmer until rice is tender and all water is absorbed—30 to 45 minutes. Set aside.

Remove loose outer skins of onions without cutting off either end. Add onions to large pot of boiling water. Reduce heat and simmer 10 minutes. Drain and cool. Generously butter a deep baking dish. With sharp knife, cut out stems (tops) of onions, leaving roots intact. Remove any remaining skin from outside. Cut out center, leaving ½-inch-thick shell. Set shells in dish. Chop scooped-out onion. Melt butter in large skillet over medium-high heat. Add ⅓ cup chopped onion (save balance for other recipes) and mushrooms and sauté until golden. Crumble sausage and add to skillet. Continue cooking until sausage is browned, about 3 minutes. Drain off fat, transfer mixture to bowl, and add rice, parsley, sage, salt, and pepper. Fill onion shells with this mixture. Add enough broth to pan to come halfway up sides of onions. Bake in preheated 450° oven for 20 minutes. Spoon some broth over onions before serving.

Broccoli and Tomato Salad

2 pounds broccoli	4 large shallots, thinly sliced
Salt	1 teaspoon dried basil
Raspberry–Walnut Oil Dressing (see Index)	2 large tomatoes, peeled, seeded, and coarsely chopped

Boil cleaned and trimmed broccoli in enough lightly salted water to cover, about 12 to 15 minutes, until tender but still crisp. Drain broccoli in a colander, transfer to a large bowl, and, while still hot, mix with the dressing, shallots, and basil. Turn broccoli several items as it cools. Add the tomatoes, cover with plastic wrap, and refrigerate. Remove from refrigerator several hours before serving.

Failproof Popovers
(Makes 6)

1 cup milk	2 eggs
1 cup flour	½ teaspoon salt
	6 cold, greased popover tins

Stir ingredients until blended. Disregard lumps. Fill tins one-half full. Place in cold oven. Set to 450°, and bake 30 minutes. Do not peek.

Honeydew Basket

1 very large ripe honeydew
   melon
1 pint strawberries, cleaned and
   halved
2 large peaches, sliced

1 cup seedless grapes
1 cup blueberries
Vanilla, to taste
Sugar, to taste
Kirsch or fruit-flavored liqueur
   (optional)

Using a scallop or zigzag pattern, cut a lid off the stem end of the melon, about 4 inches in diameter. Carefully remove seeds from lid and cavity. With a melon ball cutter, remove honeydew flesh, but do not cut too close to the rind. Use as much honeydew as desired; add listed fruits or other summer fruits of your choice. Sweeten with vanilla, sugar, and/or liqueur. Fill melon with fruits and replace lid. Chill 2 hours before serving.

Serving suggestion: Place melon on platter lined with shiny green leaves. A few fresh flowers add to this presentation.

Crunchy Brownie Bars

½ pound butter or margarine,
   melted
2 cups sugar
6 tablespoons unsweetened cocoa
2 teaspoons vanilla extract

4 eggs
1 cup flour
½ teaspoon salt
1 7-ounce jar marshmallow
   cream

Grease a 15-by-10½-by-1-inch pan. Cream the butter, sugar, and cocoa until fluffy. Beat in vanilla and eggs. Combine dry ingredients and stir into creamed mixture. Spread in prepared pan. Bake in preheated 350° oven for 25 minutes. Remove pan from oven, spread with marshmallow cream and topping, then cool and cut into bars.

Topping:

1 cup crunchy peanut butter
6 ounces chocolate chips

6 ounces butterscotch chips (or
   use 12 ounces chocolate chips)
3 cups Rice Krispies

Combine and melt over low heat. Set aside.

Committee Luncheon

Liptauer Dip with Crudités
Crème Calalou
Exotic Turkey Salad
Banana Bread
Chocolate Mousse Pie
Assorted Melon Slices

PREVIOUS DAY	EARLY MORNING	FREEZER
Liptauer Dip	*Crème Calalou*	*Chocolate Mousse Pie*
Turkey for salad	*Turkey Salad*	*Banana Bread*

Liptauer Dip

½ cup cottage cheese
½ cup sour cream
1 tablespoon caraway seeds
2 teaspoons grated onion

2 teaspoons prepared mustard
2 teaspoons capers, chopped
Salt and freshly ground black
   pepper, to taste

Crudités

Beat together cheese and sour cream until smooth. Add remaining ingredients. Season with salt and pepper to taste. Serve cold surrounded by Crudités (see Index).

Crème Calalou (Fresh Spinach and Coconut Soup)

1 pound fresh spinach, including
   the stems, roots trimmed
2 tablespoons unsalted butter
2 medium-size onions, peeled
   and thinly sliced (about 1 cup)
2 ounces fresh or canned
   sweetened coconut

4½ cups chicken broth
Salt and freshly ground black
   pepper, to taste
½ teaspoon grated nutmeg
1 medium-size firm lemon, thinly
   sliced

Cook the spinach with the water that is still clinging to leaves after rinsing. When the spinach is wilted, place in a colander under cold running water until it is completely cold. Melt the butter in a 3-quart saucepan and sauté the sliced onions for 10 minutes, until soft. Shred the coconut and add to the onions with 4 cups of the chicken broth. Simmer covered for 20 minutes.

Strain the onions and coconut and reserve the liquid. Place mixture in food processor and process 15 seconds. Add the spinach and remaining ½ cup of the broth and process 1 minute. Mix this into the chicken broth and heat thoroughly. Adjust seasonings. Garnish with lemon slices.

Note: To open a fresh coconut, punch out the 3 eyes with a hammer and nail. Drain the milk into a dish and save for another use. Place coconut in 400° oven for 20 minutes, then wrap coconut in a towel and hit with a hammer to crack it open. Separate the white meat from the shell and remove the brown skin with a vegetable peeler.

Exotic Turkey Salad

1 teaspoon curry powder
1 teaspoon butter
⅓ cup mayonnaise
⅓ cup plain yogurt or sour cream
2 tablespoons chutney
1 teaspoon lemon juice

1 quart diced cooked turkey
1 cup sliced celery
2 cups seedless grapes
6 fresh or canned pineapple slices
Salad greens
½ cup macadamia nuts

Sauté curry powder a few minutes in butter. Combine mayonnaise, yogurt or sour cream, chutney, and lemon juice, and blend in curry. Mix turkey, celery, grapes, and curry dressing together in a bowl. Place pineapple rings on greens on large platter or individual plates, and spoon a mound of the salad on each ring. Sprinkle with nuts.

Banana Bread

¼ pound butter, cut into 6 to 8 pieces
1 cup sugar
2 eggs
4 bananas, very ripe, cut into thirds

2 cups all-purpose flour
1 teaspoon baking powder
1 teaspoon baking soda
¼ teaspoon salt

Place butter, sugar, and eggs into bowl of food processor and, using steel blade, process until blended. Add bananas and process until well blended. Combine flour, baking powder, baking soda, and salt and gradually add to processor. Turn machine on-off, pushing mixture from sides of bowl. Process until flour disappears into other ingredients. Spoon into greased and floured 9-inch loaf pan and bake in preheated 350° oven for 1 hour.

Chocolate Mousse Pie

Crust:

3 cups chocolate wafer crumbs   ¼ cup unsalted butter, melted

Combine crumbs and butter, and press on bottom and sides of 10-inch springform pan. Refrigerate 30 minutes.

Filling:

1 pound semisweet chocolate   6 tablespoons confectioners'
2 whole eggs   sugar
4 egg yolks   4 egg whites
2 cups whipping cream

Melt chocolate in top of double boiler over simmering water. Let cool to lukewarm (95° F). Add 2 whole eggs and mix well. Add 4 yolks and mix until thoroughly blended.

Whip 1 cup cream with confectioners' sugar until soft peaks form. Beat 4 egg whites until stiff but not dry. Stir a little of the cream and whites into chocolate mixture to lighten. Fold in remaining cream and whites until completely incorporated. Turn into crust and chill at least 6 hours, preferably overnight.

Whip remaining 1 cup cream with sugar to taste until quite stiff.

Loosen crust on all sides using sharp knife and remove springform. Spread all but about ½ cup cream over top of mousse. Pipe remaining cream into rosettes in center and around edge of pie. Freezes well. Thaw overnight in the refrigerator.

Chinese Luncheon

Pineapple Lichee Cup
Cold Chinese Beef Salad
Chinese Chicken Vegetable Pasta
Butterball Cookies
Oriental Oranges

PREVIOUS DAY	EARLY MORNING	FREEZER
Butterball Cookies	*Vegetables for Beef Salad and Pasta* *Oriental Oranges*	*Beef Salad meat* *Butterball Cookies*

Pineapple Lichee Cup

Juice of 2 limes
1 pint pineapple sherbet
6 ounces green crème de menthe

1½ ounces Cointreau
1 cup crushed ice
Lichee nuts

Nutmeg

Whirl first 5 ingredients in blender. Pour into large champagne glasses or double old-fashioned glasses. Top with a lichee nut and a sprinkling of nutmeg.

Cold Chinese Beef Salad

2 pounds flank steak
Teriyaki sauce
1 pound snow peas

1 10-ounce bag baby spinach leaves
1 pint cherry tomatoes

Fried noodles

Brush steak with teriyaki sauce. Broil 3 to 4 minutes per side. Let stand until cooled, slice into thin strips. Twenty minutes before serving, shake salad dressing well and mix with snow peas and meat. Line large tray with baby spinach leaves. Place mixture in mound in middle of tray and surround with cherry tomatoes. Scatter canned fried noodles on top of salad and serve additional fried noodles in a bowl.

Note: Can be prepared early in day and assembled when ready to serve. Meat can be cooked and frozen until ready to serve.

Dressing:

½ cup lemon juice
6 tablespoons light soy sauce
¼ cup vegetable oil
2 tablespoons Oriental sesame
  oil

4 thin slices fresh ginger root,
  peeled and shredded
1½ teaspoons sugar
⅓ teaspoon white pepper

Combine in jar and shake well.

Chinese Chicken Vegetable Pasta

4 tablespoons peanut oil
1 peeled garlic clove (on
  toothpick)
½ teaspoon crushed dry red
  chili peppers
2 chicken breasts, boned and
  skinned, cut in ½-inch
  cubes
2 teaspoons chili paste and garlic
2 cups cauliflower, cut in
  flowerets
2 cups broccoli, cut in 2-inch
  julienne
4 carrots, cut in ¼-inch
  rounds

1 red pepper, cut in 1-inch
  squares
1 green pepper, cut in 1-inch
  squares
1 8-ounce can sliced water
  chestnuts, drained
1 cup scallions, cut in 1-inch
  lengths
13 ounces chicken stock or broth
1 pound egg noodles or thin
  spaghetti
2 tablespoons cornstarch
¼ cup water

Preheat wok to high heat; add 2 tablespoons of the oil. When oil is medium hot, add garlic and crushed chili peppers, and stir-fry until golden. Remove garlic. Add chicken pieces, stir-fry 1 minute. Add 1 teaspoon of the chili paste and garlic and stir-fry 2 minutes. Remove chicken and reserve. Add remaining 2 tablespoons oil to pan and swirl. When oil is hot, add all vegetables at once except scallions. Toss and flip for 1 minute. Add remaining teaspoon chili paste and flip for 2 minutes.

Return chicken to wok, stir well. Add scallions, stir well. Add chicken stock, cover wok. Bring to a boil, lower heat, simmer 15 minutes.

Meanwhile, cook pasta and drain; keep hot. Mix cornstarch and water together, stir well, add to wok. Toss to coat, stir well. Serve chicken-vegetable mixture on top of hot pasta.

Note: Chili paste and garlic can be purchased in Oriental food specialty shops or in large supermarkets.

Butterball Cookies
(Makes about 4 dozen)

¾ pound butter, room temperature
3 cups flour

1 cup sugar
2 egg yolks
Jelly

Combine all ingredients except jelly in a bowl and blend well. Chill 2 to 3 hours. Break off small pieces of dough and roll into balls. Place on greased cookie sheet and make indentation with finger in center of each. Fill with ½ teaspoon of jelly of your choice. Bake in preheated 375° oven for 12 to 15 minutes or until lightly browned. Let cool on rack. Store in airtight container.

Oriental Oranges

4 or 5 large seedless oranges
2½ cups orange liqueur

½ cup water
¾ cup sugar
Juice of 1 lemon

With a potato peeler or zester, remove outer skin of oranges and reserve. Peel remaining skin and all of the pith from the oranges. Slice each orange in 3 even crosswise slices and layer on bottom of attractive bowl with sides at least 1 inch high. (A white quiche dish works well.)

Combine remaining ingredients in a saucepan and bring slowly to a boil, stirring occasionally. Add orange strips and simmer until syrup is reduced by about one-third. Cool. Pour syrup over sliced oranges and chill.

Ethnic Buffets

Each recipe serves six unless otherwise indicated.

America has the advantage of being a "melting pot," and we are richer for having such a wealth of ethnic backgrounds. These days a trip down supermarket aisles can transport one around the world. We don't pretend to be experts in all culinary disciplines but do offer a sampling of international menus and recipes to inspire your gustatory experiments.

MEXICAN

Mexican Buffet (Serves 12)

Tex-Mex Dip with Chips
Spicy Vegetable Dip with Crudités
Chicken Olé
Enchiladas
Taco Pie
Refried Bean Casserole
Fiesta Rice
Refreshing Fruit Tart
Ice Cream Balls with Assorted Toppings

PREVIOUS DAY	EARLY MORNING	FREEZER
Tex-Mex Dip	*Spicy Vegetable Dip*	*Ice Cream*
Enchiladas		
Refried Bean Casserole		
Fruit Tart crust		

Tex-Mex Dip

3 medium-size ripe avocados
2 tablespoons lemon juice
½ teaspoon salt
½ teaspoon freshly ground
  black pepper
1 cup sour cream
1 1¼-ounce package taco
  seasoning
2 10½-ounce cans jalapeño
  pepper bean dip or 1 1-pound
  can refried beans with 1
  4-ounce can chopped chili
  peppers added

8 ounces shredded Cheddar
  cheese
3 medium tomatoes, chopped
1 4-ounce can pitted black
  olives, sliced
1 bunch scallions, chopped, tops
  included
2 16-ounce bags nacho or taco
  chips

Crush avocados and mix with lemon juice, salt, and pepper and set aside. Mix together sour cream and taco seasoning. Spread bean dip evenly on a large round dish with at least 1-inch sides and cover with avocado mixture, then sour cream, and sprinkle cheese on the top. Chill. Immediately before serving, garnish top with chopped tomatoes, sliced olives, and scallions. Serve with nacho or taco chips.

Note: Does not freeze successfully.

Spicy Vegetable Dip

1 cup mayonnaise
½ cup ketchup
2 teaspoons grated fresh
  horseradish

1 teaspoon tarragon vinegar
Lemon juice, to taste
Freshly ground black pepper, to
  taste

Combine all ingredients, season to taste, and chill before serving. Serve with Crudités (see Index).

Chicken Olé

1 3- to 4-pound chicken boiled
  until meat can be easily

deboned, or 3 pounds chicken
breasts poached until just
cooked

1 24-ounce can tomatoes
1 onion, chopped
1 4-ounce can chopped green
   chilies, hot or mild

1 or 2 cloves garlic
1 cup vegetable oil
1 dozen tortillas
1 pound Monterey Jack cheese,
   shredded

While chicken is cooking, combine tomatoes, onion, chilies, and garlic in saucepan and simmer approximately 30 minutes.

In hot cooking oil, fry tortillas until crisp, a few at a time. Drain on paper towels and break into several pieces each. Place a layer of tortillas on bottom of a greased 9-by-13-inch casserole, then a layer of chicken pieces, and cover with ½ of the tomato sauce. Sprinkle on half of the cheese and then repeat to make another layer. Bake uncovered in preheated 350° oven for 30 minutes, until cheese is bubbly. Cut into squares to serve.

Enchiladas

8 ounces Monterey Jack cheese,
   grated
1 4-ounce can chopped green
   chilies, mild or hot

12 6-inch flour tortillas
¾ to 1 cup vegetable oil
1 2-ounce can enchilada sauce or
   Mexican salsa

Combine cheese and chilies. Very quickly fry tortillas, one at a time, in hot cooking oil, not more than 10 seconds per side. Place each tortilla on a paper towel and put about ¼ to ⅓ cup of cheese mixture along one side. Roll up tortilla, folding sides in to hold cheese. Place close together in a 9-by-13-inch casserole. Can be made ahead to this stage and refrigerated. Before serving, drizzle salsa or enchilada sauce over top of tortillas and bake 12 to 15 minutes at 350°, uncovered, until cheese is bubbly.

Taco Pie

1¼ pounds ground beef,
   browned and drained
1 package taco seasoning mix
½ cup water
⅓ cup pitted black olives,
   sliced
1 8-ounce package crescent-type
   dinner rolls

1½ cups crushed corn chips
1 cup sour cream or unflavored
   yogurt
1 cup shredded Cheddar cheese
Lettuce, for garnish
Avocado slices, for garnish

Mix browned meat in large frying pan with seasoning mix, water, and olives. Simmer about 5 minutes. Separate crescent dough into triangles and place in greased 10-inch pie pan, pressing gently to form a crust. Spoon meat mix over crust, then 1 cup of the corn chips, then sour cream, and cover with cheese. Sprinkle remaining corn chips on top. Bake at 375° for 25 minutes, watching crust to make sure it does not get too brown. Let pie stand several minutes before cutting. Serve in wedges, garnished with shredded lettuce and avocado slices.

Refried Bean Casserole

1 1-pound, 4-ounce can refried beans	¼ cup water
	1 cup grated Cheddar cheese
½ cup taco sauce	¼ cup chopped onion

Combine all ingredients in a greased 1½-quart casserole. Bake 15 minutes at 350° or until beans are hot and cheese is bubbly.

Fiesta Rice

1 large green pepper, chopped	1 large can tomatoes, drained well and chopped, liquid reserved
1 large red pepper, chopped	
1 large onion, chopped	
2 to 3 cloves garlic, minced	½ teaspoon salt
2 tablespoons butter or margarine	¼ teaspoon cayenne pepper
	4 cups cooked white rice
1 2½-ounce jar pimentos, chopped	

Sauté peppers, onion, and garlic in butter. Mix in pimentos, tomatoes, salt, and cayenne and add cooked rice. Heat gently before serving. If mixture becomes too dry, add reserved tomato liquid as needed.

Refreshing Fruit Tart

Crust:

1¼ cups flour	2 tablespoons sour cream
¼ pound chilled butter or margarine, cut into chunks	

With steel blade, process flour, butter chunks and sour cream, using on-off technique until mixture appears crumbly. Do not overprocess to form a ball. Pat crumbly mixture into a 10-inch tart pan, pressing to form crust. Bake in preheated 375° oven for 10 minutes or until golden. Cool. Crust can be made a day in advance.

Filling:

6 peaches, nectarines, plums, *or*	⅓ cup sour cream
3 peeled apples or pears, sliced	¾ cup sugar
3 egg yolks	¼ cup flour
	1 teaspoon vanilla

Slice fruits and arrange in crust. Mix rest of filling ingredients in processor until blended, pour over fruit, and bake at 350° for 1 hour and 10 minutes.

Ice Cream Toppings

Apricot-Orange Sauce:

1 pound apricot preserves	⅓ cup orange juice

In a small pan, combine the preserves and juice. Cook over medium heat until the preserves are melted. Stir occasionally. Serve over assorted ice cream balls.

Caramel Sauce:

1½ cups sugar	⅛ teaspoon salt
1 tablespoon butter or margarine	½ teaspoon vanilla extract

Heat sugar over very low heat in a heavy skillet, stirring or shaking constantly until it melts and forms a golden sauce. Remove from heat and gradually stir in 1 cup hot water. Return to heat and bring to a boil. Simmer slowly until thick. Remove from heat and add the butter, salt, and vanilla extract. Serve over ice cream balls.

South of the Border Dinner

Gazpacho
Fresh Broccoli Salad
Chicken Mexicali
Callavacitos
Mexican Corn Bread
Acapulco Chocolate Mousse

PREVIOUS DAY	EARLY MORNING	FREEZER
Gazpacho	*Broccoli Salad*	*Corn Bread*
Chicken Mexicali		
Callavacitos		
Mousse (3 days ahead)		

Gazpacho

3 10-ounce cans spiced tomato juice
1 cucumber, peeled and chopped
2 medium tomatoes
1 tablespoon sugar
¼ cup cider vinegar
¼ cup salad oil
1 small onion

Combine 1 can tomato juice, ½ cucumber, 1 tomato, and sugar, vinegar, and oil in a blender or food processor. Blend for a few minutes and add remaining 2 cans tomato juice, ½ cucumber, tomato, and onion. Blend thoroughly and chill overnight.

Fresh Broccoli Salad

4 cups broccoli, sliced crosswise
½ cup chopped green pepper
¼ cup chopped onion
⅔ cup sour cream
3 tablespoons mayonnaise
1 teaspoon dry mustard
1 teaspoon sugar
1 tablespoon fresh dill (or 1 teaspoon dried)
Few dashes of bottled hot pepper sauce
Salt and freshly ground black pepper, to taste
2 medium tomatoes, seeded, chopped, and very well chilled

In a large bowl, combine broccoli, green pepper, and onion. In a smaller bowl combine sour cream, mayonnaise, mustard, sugar, dill, and hot pepper sauce. Season to taste with salt and pepper. Gently stir dressing into vegetable mixture. Cover and chill several hours. Just before serving, carefully stir tomatoes into salad.

Chicken Mexicali

1 1-pound, 4-ounce can chunk pineapple (juice reserved)	½ cup sliced black olives
3 pounds frying chicken pieces	½ cup sliced olives stuffed with pimento
1 tablespoon butter or margarine	½ cup water
1 medium onion, chopped	1 teaspoon salt
1 clove garlic, pressed	1 teaspoon coriander
1 1-pound can whole tomatoes, undrained	1 teaspoon ground cumin or chili powder
1 cup white rice	

Drain pineapple, reserving juice. In large skillet, brown chicken in butter. Remove from skillet. Sauté onion and garlic in pan drippings, draining excess. Stir in reserved pineapple juice, tomatoes, rice, olives, water, and seasonings. Return chicken to skillet.

Cover and simmer 25 minutes longer. Add pineapple and cover until pineapple is heated through.

Note: Can be prepared one day in advance, adding pineapple when reheating.

Callavacitos (New Mexico Zucchini)

4 to 5 6- to-7-inch medium zucchini	1 4-ounce can green chilies, diced
1 small yellow onion, chopped	1 7-ounce can whole kernel corn
1 to 3 tablespoons butter	Freshly ground black pepper
3 to 4 ounces sharp Cheddar cheese, grated	

Bring water to boil and parboil zucchini for 5 minutes. Meanwhile, sauté onion in butter until transparent. Drain zucchini well and dice. Add onion, other vegetables, and seasonings. Stir in sharp cheese. Refrigerate until ready to cook. Bake in preheated 350° oven for 45 minutes.

Mexican Corn Bread

2 eggs
1 cup sour cream
1 cup cream-style corn
⅔ cup salad oil
1½ cups cornmeal
3 teaspoons baking powder

½ to 1 teaspoon seeded and
  chopped green jalapeño
  pepper
2 tablespoons chopped green
  pepper

1 cup grated Cheddar cheese

Mix all ingredients except cheese, and blend. Grease and heat a 10-inch iron skillet or a 9-by-13-inch rectangular pan. Pour half of batter into the skillet or pan, sprinkle with half the cheese. Repeat layering, finish with balance of cheese. Bake in preheated 350° oven for 1 hour. Serve hot with butter.

Acapulco Chocolate Mousse

8 ounces semisweet chocolate
1 cup unsalted butter
½ cup boiling water
2 teaspoons cinnamon
1 cup granulated sugar, plus 2
  tablespoons

4 large eggs
1 tablespoon coffee liqueur
1 cup whipping cream
Grated semisweet chocolate, for
  garnish

Line a 5-cup charlotte or soufflé dish with double thickness of foil, making sure that foil is smooth. Leave enough foil over the edge of the dish to be able to cover top of mold for wrapping later.

In top of double boiler, melt chocolate and butter; remove from heat, add water, cinnamon, and sugar. Mix well. Beat eggs well and add a small amount of chocolate mixture to eggs, beating well. Add egg mixture to chocolate and combine thoroughly. Add liqueur and mix well.

Pour into foil-lined mold and bake in preheated 350° oven for 40 minutes or until thick crust forms on the top. Remove from oven. Mixture will wiggle, and falls and cracks as it cools. Cool. Wrap and refrigerate at least 3 days.

To serve, turn upside down on platter, peel off foil. Mixture will be sticky. Whip cream and add remaining 2 tablespoons sugar. Spread whipped cream over mousse and sprinkle with grated semisweet chocolate.

ITALIAN

Venetian Variety

Bagna Cauda with Crudités
Breadsticks
Italian Salad Bowl
Boneless Lemon Chicken
Linguini di Lido
Mediterranean Cheesecake

PREVIOUS DAY	EARLY MORNING	FREEZER
Cheesecake	*Bagna Cauda*	*Bread Sticks*
	Italian Salad Bowl	
	Boneless Lemon	
	Chicken	

Bagna Cauda (Hot Anchovy Dip) with Crudités

6 to 8 garlic cloves, peeled and
   slightly crushed
¼ pound butter

¼ cup olive oil
½ cup well-drained, finely
   chopped anchovy fillets

In small saucepan, heat garlic cloves in butter and oil without boiling.
Let steep in a warm place for 15 minutes. Discard the garlic and reheat
mixture without letting it boil. Add anchovies and stir until dissolved.
Stir sauce vigorously until thoroughly blended. Do not let boil! If made
early in the day, reheat thoroughly, stirring constantly. Serve in heated
bowl, or over a candle warmer. Serve with Crudités (see Index).

Breadsticks

1 envelope active dry yeast
¾ cup warm water

1½ teaspoons sugar
¼ teaspoon salt
2½ cups all-purpose flour (approximately)

In large bowl, sprinkle yeast into water; stir in sugar and let stand 5 minutes. With electric mixer, add salt and 1¼ cups flour. Beat until elastic. Add ¾ cup more flour, knead with dough hook or on floured board until smooth.

Cut dough into 20 equal pieces and roll each into smooth ball. Cover with plastic wrap and let rest for 10 minutes. Roll each piece into a rope about 15 inches long and set ½-inch apart on greased baking sheets, turning to grease all sides. Cover and let rise until puffy, about 15 minutes.

In preheated 375° oven, bake until golden, approximately 15 minutes; cool on wire racks. Wrap airtight overnight and recrisp in 375° oven for 5 minutes, or freeze.

Italian Salad Bowl

1 head lettuce	8 ounces mozzarella
1 green pepper	8 ounces pepperoni
1 8-ounce jar sweet red peppers	½ cup seasoned croutons
1 4-ounce jar mild peppers	1 tomato, or 10 cherry tomatoes
1 3-ounce can pitted green olives	4 scallions
1 4-ounce can pitted black olives	4 hard-cooked eggs, quartered
1 8-ounce can garbanzo beans, drained	Italian dressing

Tear lettuce into bite-size pieces. Cut green pepper into squares or strips and add to lettuce. Drain and rinse peppers, olives, and garbanzo beans, and add to salad vegetables. Slice cheese and sausage into bite-size pieces and add to salad. Add croutons, tomatoes, thinly sliced scallions, and quartered eggs. Toss with Italian dressing immediately before serving.

Boneless Lemon Chicken

2 to 3 pounds skinned, boned chicken breasts	¼ cup peanut or olive oil
½ cup flour	½ pound or more thick-sliced fresh mushrooms
1 teaspoon salt	¼ to ½ cup dry Madeira
¼ teaspoon paprika	Juice of 1 lemon
¼ teaspoon white pepper	1 tablespoon capers (optional)
4 tablespoons butter	1 lemon, sliced thin
	Parsley

Note: It is most important that the chicken not be overcooked. This dish can be assembled earlier in the day and warmed in a low oven if the chicken is undercooked the first time. Fillet of sole can be substituted for chicken, but the fish cannot be prepared in advance.

Place chicken breasts between two sheets of wax paper and pound them until approximately ⅜-inch thick. Combine flour, salt, paprika, and pepper in a bag. Add the breasts and coat well. Shake off excess. Heat butter and oil in a large skillet and sauté chicken breasts, a few at a time, no more than 2 minutes per side. Drain on paper towels. Add mushrooms, sauté for several minutes. Add Madeira and lemon juice. If there is not enough liquid add more wine. Return chicken to skillet and spoon sauce over it. Sprinkle with capers, lemon slices, and parsley. Cook covered for about 2 or 3 more minutes. Sauce should thicken.

Linguini di Lido

3 tablespoons light olive oil
1 large onion, minced
2 cloves garlic, minced
½ cup dry white wine
1½ tablespoons fresh basil (or 1½ teaspoons dried)
1 tablespoon fresh marjoram (or 1 teaspoon dried)
1½ cups canned tomatoes, well drained

1½ pounds mussels, scrubbed and debearded, *or* 2 pounds small clams, scrubbed
1 pound sea scallops, halved
1 pound large shrimp, peeled, deveined, and butterflied
Salt and freshly ground pepper
1 pound linguini, cooked al dente

In 4- or 5-quart saucepan, heat oil, add onion, and sauté until lightly golden. Add garlic and sauté another 30 seconds. Stir in wine, basil, marjoram, and cook 1 minute. Add tomatoes, increase heat, and boil 5 minutes. Reduce heat, add mussels or clams. Cover and cook until shells open about ½ inch, approximately 5 minutes. Add scallops and shrimp. Cover and cook 2 to 3 minutes, until scallops and shrimp are barely firm. Season to taste with salt and pepper. Add linguini and toss gently to mix.

Mediterranean Cheesecake

⅔ cup cornflakes
¼ cup Grape-Nuts
2 teaspoons butter
2 teaspoons brown sugar
2 teaspoons grated orange rind
2 envelopes unflavored gelatin
¾ cup sugar

3 eggs, separated
1½ cups nonfat milk
3 cups ricotta
1 tablespoon orange juice
1 tablespoon lemon juice
1 teaspoon grated lemon rind
1 teaspoon vanilla extract

2 kiwi, peeled, for garnish

Combine cornflakes and Grape-Nuts in blender or food processor and process to form fine crumbs. Add butter, brown sugar, 1 teaspoon of the orange rind; blend well. Press crumbs evenly onto bottom of 8-inch springform pan. Bake 5 minutes. Cool.

In top of double boiler combine gelatin and ¼ cup of the sugar. Beat in egg yolks and milk. Cook, stirring frequently, over boiling water until gelatin dissolves and mixture coats spoon. Remove from heat. Chill until it thickens but does not set.

Whip cheese in blender or processor until thick and smooth. Stir in juices, remaining orange and lemon rind, and vanilla. Beat egg whites with remaining ½ cup of sugar to form soft peaks. Stir gelatin mixture into cheese mixture. Fold in egg whites. Spoon gently into springform pan and refrigerate at least 6 hours. Garnish with sliced kiwi.

Italian Dinner

Zucchini Pizza
Spicy Marinated Shrimp
Lemon Veal Scaloppini with Artichoke Hearts
Hay and Straw Pasta
Italian Salad
Biscuit Tortoni
Chocolate Krisp Cookies

PREVIOUS DAY	EARLY MORNING	FREEZER
Spicy Shrimp	*Zucchini Pizza*	*Biscuit Tortoni*
Italian Salad		*Chocolate Krisp*
Cook pasta		*Cookies*

Zucchini Pizza

1 medium onion, chopped	4 cups shredded zucchini,
1 tablespoon butter	squeezed dry
8 ounces tomato sauce	2 cups shredded mozzarella and
Dash of basil and dill, or	Cheddar
oregano	2 eggs, slightly beaten
¼ teaspoon salt	½ pound mushrooms, sliced
¼ teaspoon garlic powder	

Grated Parmesan (optional)

Sauté onion in butter until soft. Add tomato sauce and seasonings. Simmer 10 minutes. Mix zucchini with 1 cup of the cheese mixture and the eggs. Press mixture into 10-by-15-inch oiled jelly-roll pan and bake in preheated 400° oven for 10 minutes. Spoon sauce over zucchini, arrange mushrooms on top, and sprinkle with remaining cheese, adding Parmesan, if desired. Bake for 25 to 30 minutes longer, until crisp and bubbly. Cut into squares and serve warm.

Spicy Marinated Shrimp

1 clove garlic, halved	3 tablespoons horseradish
¼ cup chopped celery	1 tablespoon mustard
4 tablespoons chopped green	¼ teaspoon paprika
pepper	¼ teaspoon each salt and
4 scallions, chopped	pepper
3 tablespoons salad oil	½ cup chili sauce
1½ tablespoons lemon juice	2 pounds shrimp, cooked and
4 tablespoons chopped parsley	shelled
2 dashes of Tabasco sauce	

Rub bowl with garlic. Add all ingredients except shrimp and chili sauce and mix well. Blend in chili sauce thoroughly, add shrimp, and marinate overnight.

Lemon Veal Scaloppini with Artichoke Hearts

2 to 3 pounds veal for scaloppini
Salt and pepper, to taste
1 cup flour
6 tablespoons butter or
  margarine
3 cups chicken broth
¾ cup dry vermouth
1½ tablespoons Worcester-
  shire sauce

1 teaspoon marjoram
¾ teaspoon garlic powder
3 12- to-16-ounce cans artichoke
  hearts, drained
2 lemons, sliced thin
2 teaspoons dill weed
Lemon slices, for garnish
Fresh dill, for garnish

Salt and pepper veal lightly and dredge in flour. Brown in butter in large skillet. Remove veal from pan, add 1 cup of the chicken broth, and deglaze pan. Place veal back in pan. (It may be necessary to use two skillets at this stage.) Add all remaining ingredients except dill. Simmer for 10 to 15 minutes, covered. Discard lemons. Serve on green noodles or Hay and Straw Pasta. Garnish with fresh sliced lemon. Sprinkle with dill.

Note: Sliced fresh turkey breast can be substituted for veal.

Hay and Straw Pasta

½ pound ⅛-inch green
  noodles
½ pound ⅛-inch yellow
  pasta
¼ pound butter
¼ pound prosciutto, minced,
  or ½ pound sliced
  mushrooms

1 10-ounce package tiny peas,
  thawed but not cooked
1½ cups half-and-half
½ egg yolk, slightly beaten
1 cup freshly grated Parmesan
  cheese
¼ teaspoon freshly grated
  nutmeg

Cook noodles in salted water until al dente and drain very well. Melt butter in medium-size saucepan over medium heat. Add prosciutto or mushrooms and sauté for 2 minutes. Lower heat and add peas, half-and-half, egg yolk, ¾ cup of the cheese, and nutmeg. Blend, and toss with the noodles. Put the mixture into a 2-quart flat, rectangular baking dish. Sprinkle with remaining cheese and bake until top turns golden, about 8 to 10 minutes.

This dish does not have to be baked. Just toss the noodles with all ingredients and serve with extra grated cheese. If pasta absorbs a lot of liquid, more half-and-half can be added to avoid dryness.

Pasta can be cooked and drained the day before serving, and stored in refrigerator in a plastic bag. Before using, drop into pot of boiling water to heat very briefly and proceed with recipe. Do not assemble dish until serving time or the result will be dry.

Italian Salad

3 green peppers
3 ripe tomatoes
1 large red onion
1 7- or 8-ounce can pitted black
  olives
½ cup sliced celery

¼ cup oil
1½ tablespoons dried oregano
¼ teaspoon freshly ground
  black pepper
¼ cup vinegar
1 teaspoon salt

Slice peppers into thin strips. Cut tomatoes into wedges. Slice the red onion and separate into rings. Slice the olives into halves. Combine the remaining ingredients and pour over the vegetables. Marinate all day or overnight in the refrigerator, in a 3-quart glass or enamel bowl.

Note: Vegetables can be prepared the day before; dressing can be prepared several days in advance.

Biscuit Tortoni

¼ cup Amaretto liqueur
1 teaspoon unflavored gelatin
4 egg yolks
¼ cup water
½ cup sugar
1 cup whipping cream

½ cup chopped toasted
  almonds
¼ cup crushed almond
  macaroons
Candied fruit or sliced toasted
  almonds, for garnish

Combine liqueur and gelatin in heat-resistant cup and mix until gelatin is softened. Place cup in a pot of simmering water to dissolve and liquefy gelatin. Beat egg yolks until light and lemon colored. In medium-size pan, over medium heat, bring water and sugar to a boil, and stir until sugar is completely dissolved. Cook until syrup spins a thread, 230° on candy thermometer, about 5 minutes.

Turn mixer to low speed, slowly pour sugar syrup into beaten yolks.

Beat until well blended. Add the gelatin and beat until thickened, about 6 minutes. Let mixture cool. Whip the cream and fold it with the almonds and macaroon crumbs into the egg and gelatin mixture.

Place 12 foil-lined paper cups into a muffin tin. Tin will help support the desserts until they are frozen. Carefully spoon the mixture into the cups and chill. Before serving, garnish with candied fruits and/or almonds.

Note: Can be made and frozen up to three weeks in advance. Be sure to wrap tightly in foil after first freezing. Transfer to refrigerator about 3 hours before serving.

Chocolate Krisp Cookies
(Makes about 40)

3 ounces semisweet chocolate	⅓ cup firmly packed brown
1 ounce unsweetened chocolate	sugar
1 tablespoon butter	2 tablespoons sifted flour
1 teaspoon vanilla extract	⅛ teaspoon baking powder
1 tablespoon water	1 cup semisweet chocolate chips
1 egg	1 cup Rice Krispies

Pecan halves, to top cookies

Melt chocolate (except chips) with butter in top of double boiler. Stir until smooth and thoroughly mixed. Remove from heat and let cool to the touch. Stir in vanilla, water, egg, sugar, flour, and baking powder. Mix in chocolate chips and Rice Krispies. Drop by tablespoons onto non-stick cookie sheets, about 2 inches apart. Press pecan halves into centers of cookies. Bake in preheated 350° oven for 12 minutes.

Florentina

Minestrone
Marinated Tomato Salad
Breast of Chicken Florentine
Risotto
Easy Italian Bread
Crème Caramel

PREVIOUS DAY	EARLY MORNING	FREEZER
Crème Caramel	*Marinate tomatoes*	*Minestrone*
		Italian Bread

Minestrone

1 pound dry pinto beans	3 medium potatoes, sliced
3 heaping tablespoons beef base	4 small zucchini, sliced
2 large onions, chopped	1 pound cabbage, shredded
3 tablespoons olive oil	½ cup macaroni
6 medium carrots, sliced	1 10-ounce package frozen green
7 ribs celery, sliced	beans
3 medium leeks, sliced	2 tablespoons basil
1 1-pound can tomatoes	1 clove garlic, minced
Salt	½ cup chopped parsley

Grated Parmesan

Rinse pinto beans well, cover with 4 quarts cold water, and bring to boil. Boil for 2 minutes, then let stand in covered pot for 1 hour. Add beef base and simmer for 1 hour or until beans are tender. In another large pan, sauté onions in 2 tablespoons of the olive oil for 5 minutes. Add carrots, celery, and leeks, and cook another 5 minutes. Cut up tomatoes, add them, and simmer all rapidly for 10 minutes, until most of the liquid has been evaporated. Add to the bean mixture and simmer for 30 minutes. Taste and season with salt.

Add potatoes, zucchini, cabbage, macaroni, and frozen beans and simmer for 15 minutes, uncovered. In small frying pan, sauté basil, garlic, and parsley in the remaining 1 tablespoon olive oil until parsley is bright green. Mix into soup and serve with grated Parmesan cheese. Freezes well.

Note: Two pounds of beef shanks and soup bones can be used in place of beef base. If this is preferred, cooking time at the beginning should be 2½ hours instead of 1.

Marinated Tomato Salad

3 medium tomatoes, cut in wedges	1 cup corn oil
1 large zucchini, sliced thin	½ cup white wine vinegar
1 medium yellow squash, sliced thin	1½ tablespoons chopped fresh mint leaves (or 1½ teaspoons dried)
2 medium onions, sliced thin	1½ teaspoons sugar (optional)

Toss together tomatoes, zucchini, squash, and onion in large, shallow dish. In small bowl, stir together corn oil and remaining ingredients. Pour dressing over vegetables, tossing to coat well. Cover and refrigerate several hours, stirring occasionally.

Breast of Chicken Florentine

½ cup flour
Salt and pepper
3 whole chicken breasts, split, skinned, and boned
2 eggs, lightly beaten
1 tablespoon water
¼ cup grated Parmesan

½ cup bread crumbs
2 pounds fresh spinach
12 tablespoons butter (1½ sticks)
½ pound mushrooms, sliced thin
1 tablespoon lemon juice

¼ teaspoon nutmeg, to taste

Combine flour with salt and pepper. First coat chicken with seasoned flour, then dip it into beaten egg and water. Lastly, coat chicken with cheese and bread crumbs combined. Set chicken aside for a moment. Wash spinach, shake off excess water, and place in saucepan and cook, covered, until done, about 10 minutes. Melt 8 tablespoons of butter in large skillet and cook chicken until nicely brown. Turn and cook other side. While chicken is cooking, cook mushrooms in half of remaining butter. When all is done, drain spinach and toss with remaining butter and lemon juice. Add salt and nutmeg to taste.

Spoon spinach onto 6 plates, top with piece of chicken, and cover with mushrooms.

Risotto

½ cup finely minced onion
4 tablespoons unsalted butter
1½ cups Italian short grain rice
4 to 5 cups chicken stock

¾ cup heavy cream
Salt and white pepper, to taste
½ cup fresh peas
⅓ cup freshly grated Parmesan

In a heavy saucepan, sauté the onion in butter until transparent. Do not brown. Slowly add the rice and 1½ cups of the stock. Let it boil, uncovered, until the stock is absorbed by the rice. Add another cup of stock and cook until absorbed. Add a third cup of stock and cook until rice is not quite tender. Add the cream; salt and pepper to taste. If dry, add remaining stock and cook until all liquid is absorbed. Add fresh peas and Parmesan and serve immediately.

Easy Italian Bread

1 package active dry yeast
1½ cups warm water
3½ cups flour, or more

2¼ teaspoons coarse salt
1 scant teaspoon sugar
1 egg white, beaten

Dissolve yeast and sugar in 1½ cups warm water and allow the mixture to foam. Put 3½ cups flour and salt into mixer with a dough hook. Add yeast mixture and knead for about 10 minutes, until dough is smooth and elastic. Add more flour as needed. Cover and let rise in warm place for 1 hour. Knead again for 5 minutes. Divide into 3 long loaves. Place on buttered baking sheet that has cornmeal scattered over it. Brush top with egg white and bake in preheated 350° oven for 30 minutes.

Crème Caramel

⅚ cup sugar
2 tablespoons boiling water
3 eggs

¼ teaspoon salt
2 cups milk, scalded
½ teaspoon vanilla extract

Caramelize ½ cup sugar in heavy pan over low heat, shaking pan so sugar melts. When sugar becomes golden syrup, stir in 2 tablespoons boiling water. Pour a little caramel mixture into custard cups, one at a time, placing pan on low heat in between. Swirl in cup to coat bottom and sides. Set cups aside as caramel hardens.

In large bowl, beat eggs, remaining sugar, and salt to blend. Stir in scalded milk, add vanilla extract. Pour or ladle into 6 prepared custard cups. Place cups in pan holding 1 inch hot water. Place pan (with cups) into preheated 350° oven and bake for 45 to 50 minutes, until custard is set. (A knife inserted comes out clean.) Remove from oven and cool or refrigerate.

To serve, loosen edge of custard around cup and invert onto individual serving dishes as caramel drips over top.

CHINESE

Peking Party

Puffed Butterfly Shrimp
Orange Teriyaki Chicken
Scallops Oriental
Stir-fried Pork and Snow Peas
Chinese Salad
Tea Freeze
Lime Wafers

PREVIOUS DAY	EARLY MORNING	FREEZER
Teriyaki Chicken	*Butterfly Shrimp*	*Tea Freeze*
Chinese Salad		
Lime Wafers		

Puffed Butterfly Shrimp

Batter:

1 cup flour   ⅔ cup cold water
1 tablespoon baking powder   4 teaspoons white sesame seeds
¼ teaspoon salt   3 tablespoons minced scallions,
5 tablespoons oil   including green part

Mix the flour, baking powder, and salt in a bowl. Add 5 tablespoons of oil gradually as you stir. Mix very well. The dough should look like pie dough. Stir in the water a little at a time to form a thick batter. Stir in the sesame seeds and scallions.

Shrimp:

4 cups oil for frying (approximate)
1 pound (15 to 20) fresh shrimp, shelled, deveined, and butterflied

Heat oil to deep-frying temperature, 375°. Holding each shrimp by the tail, dip it into the batter and put immediately into the hot oil. Cook only a few at a time. If the oil is the proper temperature, the shrimp will puff and immediately pop to the surface. When the batter on the top side looks set, turn the shrimp and brown the other side until golden. Place on paper towels to drain. Serve piping hot. Does not freeze successfully.

Shrimp can be prepared for frying, and batter mixed, early in the morning. Fried shrimp will keep in a warm oven for 30 to 40 minutes.

Note: To butterfly shrimp, peel off shell, except for the last section and the tail. Remove the back vein and split the shrimp on the belly side, being careful not to go all the way through.

Orange Teriyaki Chicken

2 cloves garlic, minced
1 medium-size chopped onion
2 teaspoons minced fresh ginger
  root
1 orange, chopped fine
1 lemon or lime, chopped fine
¼ cup ketchup
½ cup teriyaki sauce
½ cup orange juice
¾ cup white wine
⅓ cup safflower or corn oil
Freshly ground black pepper, to
  taste
32 small chicken pieces, wings or
  thighs
1 cup sesame seeds

Mix all ingredients except chicken and sesame seeds in a large, flat, nonaluminum pan. Add chicken and toss to coat each piece well. Marinate at least 6 hours or overnight.

Drain chicken. Reserve marinade. Arrange chicken on baking sheets. Bake in preheated 350° oven about 20 minutes. Sprinkle sesame seeds all over chicken and grill or broil for 5 minutes on each side, basting well with marinade until crisp.

Scallops Oriental

2 pounds bay scallops
Flour
1 pound mushrooms, halved
Oil
2 small onions, minced
2 tablespoons dry sherry or
  vermouth
2 teaspoons soy sauce
2 teaspoons sesame oil
2 tablespoons oyster sauce
2 slices ginger root, minced

Dust scallops with flour. Sauté scallops and mushrooms in small amount of oil. Add onions and all other ingredients. Cook 2 to 3 minutes. Decorate with 1 scallion, sliced thin, lengthwise.

Stir-fried Pork and Snow Peas

1½ pounds pork tenderloin	4 egg whites, lightly beaten
2 teaspoons light soy sauce	3 tablespoons cornstarch
¼ teaspoon pepper	Peanut oil
2 cloves garlic, minced	¼ pound snow peas

Hoisin sauce (May be bought in specialty stores or in supermarket.)

Cut meat diagonally into thin 2-inch slices. Mix soy sauce, pepper, and garlic. Marinate pork in soy sauce mixture for 15 minutes. Mix egg whites and cornstarch together into gummy batter. Fill wok up to 3 to 4 inches from bottom with peanut oil and heat to 375°. Coat pork quickly with egg mixture and deep-fry until golden; takes about 6 to 8 minutes. Drain pork slices on paper towel. Drain oil (can be saved for future use), wipe pan, and reheat with 2 tablespoons oil. Quickly stir-fry snow peas and serve with pork slices. Serve Hoisin sauce on side or use light soy sauce for milder dip.

Note: Two-inch lengths of scallions can be used instead of snow peas.

Chinese Salad

4 cups shredded Chinese cabbage	¼ pound fresh snow peas
2 cups baby spinach leaves, wash, dried well, stems removed	1 cup canned water chestnuts, sliced and drained
1 cup cherry tomatoes	1½ tablespoons toasted sesame seeds

Combine vegetables and water chestnuts and toss well. Toast sesame seeds. When ready to serve, pour dressing over salad ingredients, stir well. Place on serving platter and sprinkle with sesame seeds.

Note: Ingredients can be prepared a day ahead. Do not combine until ready to serve.

Dressing:

3 tablespoons vegetable oil	2 tablespoons light soy sauce
3 tablespoons fresh lemon juice	½ teaspoon salt (optional)

Combine ingredients in a jar and shake well.

Tea Freeze

1⅓ cups boiling water	1 cup cream
⅓ cup loose tea	1½ cups sugar
1 teaspoon dried mint	1 tablespoon grated orange rind
1 cup ginger ale	½ cup lemon juice
2 cups milk	⅛ teaspoon salt

Pour boiling water over tea and mint; brew 5 minutes and strain. Add ginger ale, milk, and cream. Mix together sugar, orange rind, lemon juice, and salt. Slowly add to tea mixture. Pour into refrigerator trays or 6-cup mold. Freeze until firm, stirring 2 or 3 times during freezing period.

Lime Wafers
(Makes 8 dozen)

½ pound butter or margarine	3 tablespoons unstrained lime
2 cups sugar	juice
3 eggs	½ teaspoon salt
1 teaspoon grated lime rind	¼ teaspoon ground ginger
5 cups sifted all-purpose flour	

Cream butter until light. Gradually add sugar and beat until light and fluffy. Add eggs, lime rind and juice, salt, and ginger. Blend well. Add enough sifted flour to make soft dough that can be rolled out. Roll on lightly floured board to ⅛-inch thickness. Cut cookies with 2-inch circular cutter. Place on greased baking sheet. Bake in preheated 375° oven for 12 to 15 minutes.

Teahouse Dinner

Oriental Shrimp and Scallop Salad
Won Ton Crisps
Chinese Pepper Steak
Chicken with Hot Pepper
White Rice
Ginger Ice Cream
Tea Wafers

PREVIOUS DAY	EARLY MORNING	FREEZER
Prepare Oriental Salad ingredients	*Marinate steak*	*Ginger Ice Cream*
Marinate chicken		*Tea Wafers*

Oriental Shrimp and Scallop Salad

2 pounds shrimp, shelled, deveined, cooked, and chilled
1 pound scallops, cooked, sliced in half horizontally
½ pound snow peas, blanched quickly and chilled
1 cup sliced celery, chilled

⅔ cup sliced scallions, chilled
1 16-ounce can Chinese vegetables, drained and chilled
2 11-ounce cans mandarin oranges, drained
2 tablespoons sliced almonds
Bibb lettuce

Whole almonds, for garnish

Reserve some shrimp and scallops for top of salad. Trim ends and remove strings from snow peas. In bowl, mix all vegetables, oranges, seafood, and sliced almonds. When ready to serve, pour dressing over salad. Line glass platter or bowl with lettuce leaves; spoon salad over lettuce. Garnish with remaining shrimp and scallop slices. Scatter whole almonds over top and serve.

Note: Individual ingredients can be prepared a day in advance for assembling at time of serving. Taste to adjust seasonings.

Dressing:

2 tablespoons light soy sauce
⅓ cup white wine

½ cup vegetable oil
3 cloves garlic, mashed

3 thin slices ginger root, peeled

Mix soy sauce, wine, oil, garlic, and ginger root in jar. Shake well. When ready to use, remove garlic and ginger.

Won Ton Crisps

20 won ton (or 5 egg roll) skins
4 tablespoons butter, melted
½ cup grated Parmesan

Instant minced onion, or dry herb of choice

Cut won ton skins in half or cut egg roll skins into eighths. Brush some butter on a large, rimmed cookie sheet. Arrange skins so they touch, but do not overlap. Brush with butter; sprinkle with cheese and onion or other herb. Bake 5 or 6 minutes or until golden brown in preheated 375° oven.

Chinese Pepper Steak

3 pounds flank steak
5 tablespoons soy sauce
2 tablespoons sherry
1 teaspoon sugar
1½ teaspoons cornstarch
¾ teaspoon salt

3 green peppers
5 tablespoons oil
1 cup sliced mushrooms
1 tomato or 12 cherry tomatoes
   (optional)

Cut flank steak across grain and diagonally into ⅛-by-4-by-1-inch strips. Pound lightly with a knife. Combine soy sauce, sherry, sugar, cornstarch, and salt, and spread over meat. Let stand until ready to cook.

Cut seeded green peppers into strips 1 inch wide. Heat oil at 350° in electric frying pan or on top of stove in regular frying pan. When oil is hot, add green pepper strips. Cook for 3 minutes, stirring occasionally. Add mushrooms and cook for 2 minutes more. Push vegetables to sides of pan and add meat. Cook for 2 minutes more. Meat should be rare and the green pepper crisp. Serve over cooked rice. Wedges of tomato or cherry tomatoes may also be added during last minute of cooking in place of 1 green pepper.

Chicken with Hot Pepper

3 tablespoons soy sauce
1 tablespoon cornstarch
2 large chicken breasts, boned,
   skinned, and cut into ½-
   inch cubes
1 tablespoon sherry

2 teaspoons sugar
1 teaspoon white vinegar
¼ cup peanut oil
1 teaspoon crushed red pepper
⅓ cup sliced scallions
½ teaspoon ground ginger

½ cup peanuts or cashews

Blend 1 tablespoon of the soy sauce with cornstarch in a bowl. Mix in chicken and set aside. Combine remaining 2 tablespoons soy sauce with sherry, sugar, and vinegar in another bowl. Heat oil in wok over high heat. Add red pepper and cook until pepper turns black. Add chicken and stir-fry for 2 minutes.

Remove chicken from wok and stir-fry scallions and ginger for 1 minute. Return chicken to wok and cook for 2 minutes. Add soy mixture and cook 1 or 2 minutes, stirring constantly. Add nuts, mix well, and serve with rice. This is a very "hot" dish.

Note: Chicken can be marinated overnight or early in morning.

Ginger Ice Cream

2¼ teaspoons ground ginger	2 cups milk
¼ teaspoon salt	2 cups heavy cream
1¼ cups sugar	3 teaspoons vanilla extract

Combine first 3 ingredients. Add milk and stir until sugar is dissolved. Stir in cream and vanilla. Turn into 2 ice-cube trays or an 8-by-8-by-2-inch baking dish. Freeze until almost firm. Remove from freezer and place in large bowl of electric mixer. Beat until fluffy, starting at low speed and increasing to highest as mixture softens. Do not beat enough to melt. Return to trays or baking dish and freeze until firm, stirring once before completely frozen.

Tea Wafers

⅓ cup butter or margarine	1⅓ cups sifted all-purpose
⅔ cup sugar	flour
¼ teaspoon salt	¼ teaspoon baking powder
1 egg	Lemon juice
2 to 3 tablespoons instant tea	1 cup confectioners' sugar

Cream together butter, sugar, and salt. In separate bowl beat egg and tea together until tea is dissolved; stir into creamed mixture. Sift together flour and baking powder, add half the tea mixture, stir until well blended, blend in remaining tea mixture.

Refrigerate 3 to 4 hours. Divide dough in half, return one-half to refrigerator. Roll other half out to ⅛-inch thickness. Cut with cookie cutter into desired shapes. Bake on ungreased baking sheet in preheated

350° oven for 8 to 10 minutes. Repeat with remaining dough.

When cool, frost with lemon glaze made by blending enough lemon juice into confectioners' sugar to make it of spreadable consistency.

Oriental Buffet

Shanghai Shrimp
Beef and Broccoli with Oyster Sauce
Game Hens Chinese Style
Stir-fried Chinese Vegetable Medley
Oriental Salad with Lorenzo Dressing
Fresh Pineapple Sorbet
Almond Cookies

PREVIOUS DAY	EARLY MORNING	FREEZER
Game Hens	*Beef marinade*	*Pineapple Sorbet*
Prepare vegetables	*Vegetable sauce*	
Salad dressing	*Salad vegetables*	
Almond Cookies		

Shanghai Shrimp

2 pounds fresh shrimp, rinsed, shelled, deveined, and dried well (or defrosted frozen shrimp)
8 drops ginger juice (squeeze ginger root in garlic press)
2 teaspoons dry sherry
2 teaspoons cornstarch
4 scallions, cut into 2-inch lengths
1½ cups cooking oil
4 slices fresh peeled ginger root, about ¼-inch thick

Slice shrimp in half lengthwise. Mix ginger juice, sherry, cornstarch, and scallions. Add shrimp to this mixture. Heat wok until hot. Add oil and heat to 375°. Add the ginger slices (on toothpicks) to oil. Add shrimp and stir constantly, about 2 minutes, until all shrimp are pink. Drain in colander. Remove ginger and serve at once.

Note: Delicious with black Chinese vinegar and light soy sauce, served in cruets, mixed individually by guests for dip.

Beef and Broccoli with Oyster Sauce

Sauce:

2 tablespoons oyster sauce   1 tablespoon dry sherry
                1 teaspoon sugar

Combine ingredients and set aside.

Beef and Broccoli:

2 pounds sliced flank steak	1½ cups peanut oil
1 tablespoon wine	1 scallion, cut into 1-inch slices
1 tablespoon cornstarch	1 clove garlic, minced
2 tablespoons oyster sauce	2 slices ginger, minced
1 tablespoon soy sauce	8 sliced water chestnuts
1 tablespoon oil	1 teaspoon cornstarch, dissolved
2 cups broccoli flowerets	in ¼ cup water

1 teaspoon sesame oil

Slice flank steak against the grain and marinate for 1 hour or more in the wine, cornstarch, and oyster and soy sauces. Heat 1 tablespoon oil in wok, stir in broccoli, and set aside. Heat 1½ cups oil in wok or large skillet. Quickly cook beef in oil. Strain, and return 2 tablespoons oil to the wok. Stir in scallion, garlic, and ginger. Return beef and broccoli to wok and add water chestnuts. Stir in cornstarch dissolved in water and heat until sauce boils and thickens. Add sesame oil and serve.

Game Hens Chinese Style

4 fresh game hens	¼ cup maple syrup and dark
1 tablespoon Hoisin sauce	soy sauce combined (2
1 tablespoon yellow bean paste	tablespoons of each)
2 teaspoons plum sauce	2 teaspoons 5-spice seasoning
2 teaspoons rice wine or dry sherry	

Clean, wash, and dry hens well. Mix next 5 ingredients together. Season hens inside and out with 5-spice seasoning. Rub in well. Rub half of sauce mixture into cavities of hens. Rub outsides of hens with remaining sauce mixture.

Cover birds tightly with plastic wrap and refrigerate overnight.

Place hens in shallow casserole and roast in preheated 375° oven, backs up, for 35 minutes, basting twice. Turn hens over, baste well, and roast 40 minutes longer, basting 3 times. Hens are cooked when golden brown. Serve immediately as hot dish or serve at room temperature as part of a cold Chinese buffet.

Hens can be fully cooked, then wrapped airtight and frozen for up to a month. Thaw hens at room temperature, and reheat for about 20 minutes at 350° if they are to be served hot.

To serve Chinese style, slice in half vertically and arrange on platter with thin scallion strips between the halves.

Note: Hoisin sauce, bean paste, and plum sauce are available in Oriental food stores or in large supermarkets.

Stir-fried Chinese Vegetable Medley

Sauce:

1 tablespoon soy sauce	1 teaspoon pale dry sherry
1 tablespoon Chinese oyster sauce	½ teaspoon sugar
	½ teaspoon salt

Mix the 5 sauce ingredients in a bowl and set aside.

Vegetable Medley:

2 tablespoons oil, for frying	¼ cup fresh sliced bamboo shoots
2 scallions, cut into 1-inch rings	
4 Chinese dried mushrooms, soaked until spongy, stems removed	¼ cup sliced fresh water chestnuts (or canned water chestnuts, well rinsed)
½ pound fresh snow peas	1 tablespoon sesame oil

Heat a wok or frying pan over high heat. Swirl in the oil for frying. When the oil is hot, add the scallions, then the mushrooms. Stir-fry for 10 seconds. Add the snow peas, bamboo shoots, and water chestnuts, cooking and stirring just until the pea pods turn a very bright green. Pour in the sauce mixture and stir and cook about 20 seconds. Stir in sesame oil and serve hot.

Note: Can be doubled *once*—but be sure to use a very large wok or skillet so some vegetables do not get mushy before others are cooked. Vegetables will lose their crispness and color if cooked even 15 minutes before serving. Vegetables and sauce can be prepared the day before. Do *not* use frozen vegetables!

Oriental Salad

2 pounds fresh spinach, chopped	2 tomatoes
1 cup bean sprouts	7 ounces Enoki mushrooms
40 pea pods	

Arrange spinach as base of salad. Top with bean sprouts and pea pods, garnish with chopped tomatoes and Enoki mushrooms, and serve with Lorenzo Dressing.

Lorenzo Dressing:

4 tablespoons pear vinegar or white wine vinegar	¼ teaspoon walnut oil
	1 cup olive oil
¾ teaspoon salt	1¼ cups chopped watercress
⅛ teaspoon pepper	6 to 8 ounces chili sauce

Combine vinegar, salt, pepper, and walnut oil, and mix well. Add remaining ingredients and mix well.

Fresh Pineapple Sorbet

2 pounds, or more, pineapple in season

Cut fruit and freeze on cookie sheets in individual, separated pieces. Shortly before serving, place in food processor and process with metal blade until smooth.

Fruit can be frozen several days in advance and stored in plastic freezer bags until needed. Process right before serving.

Note: Can also use strawberries, raspberries, or peaches.

Almond Cookies
(Makes about 48)

½ pound butter
¾ cup sugar
1 teaspoon almond extract
2 cups sifted all-purpose flour

½ teaspoon baking powder
½ cup blanched almonds,
   ground
Extra sugar to roll cookies in

48 whole blanched almonds

Cream butter in large bowl. Gradually add sugar, beating until mixture is light and fluffy. Beat in almond extract. Sift flour and baking powder together and add gradually to butter mixture. Blend in ground almonds by hand. Using 1 level tablespoon per cookie, shape dough into 48 cookies. Roll cookie balls in sugar. Place on parchment sheet on cookie sheet and press flat with bottom of glass. Place 1 whole almond on top of each cookie. Bake in preheated 375° oven about 10 to 12 minutes. Cool cookies on rack.

Moon Gate Evening

Rumaki
Szechwan Cucumber, Carrot, and Noodle Salad
Stir-fried Chicken and Green Peppers in Basic Dark Sauce
Sweet-and-Sour Scallops
Crunchy Chinese Celery
Pears in Orange Juice

PREVIOUS DAY	EARLY MORNING	FREEZER
	Salad vegetables	*Rumaki*
	Salad dressing	
	Celery ingredients	
	Pears in Orange Juice	

Rumaki
(Makes 24)

½ pound chicken livers
½ cup apple juice
3 tablespoons soy sauce
1 tablespoon honey

½ pound bacon slices
1 Granny Smith apple, cut into
   24 pieces

Cut livers into 2 or 3 pieces, depending on size. Mix juice, soy sauce, and honey. Add livers and refrigerate several hours. Drain liver and reserve marinade. Cut bacon slices in half crosswise. Wrap a piece of liver and an apple piece in one-half slice of bacon. Secure with wooden picks. Place rumaki on a rack in broiler pan and brush with marinade. Bake in preheated 400° oven until bacon is crisp and livers are cooked.

Note: Can be assembled early in day, and can be frozen before broiling.

Szechwan Cucumber, Carrot, and Noodle Salad

2 to 3 cucumbers, peeled and
   shredded
1 teaspoon salt
1 package cellophane noodles,
   soaked and cut
2 large carrots, shredded
2 scallions, shredded (add pinch
   of sugar)
2 tablespoons soy sauce

1 tablespoon sesame oil
1 tablespoon white vinegar
½ teaspoon ground roast
   Szechwan peppercorns
1 tablespoon chili oil, or less (to
   taste)
1 tablespoon minced garlic, or to
   taste

Sprinkle cucumber shreds with 1 teaspoon salt. Let stand 10 minutes and then squeeze out water. Mix with noodles, carrots, and scallions. Combine dressing ingredients separately. Serve salad at room temperature or chilled; add dressing just before serving.

Stir-fried Chicken and Green Peppers in Basic Dark Sauce

Basic Dark Sauce:

1 clove garlic, minced
3 tablespoons peanut oil
2½ tablespoons light soy
  sauce
2½ tablespoons dry sherry
1 tablespoon rice or white
  vinegar

1 tablespoon minced scallions
1 to 2 teaspoons fresh ginger
  root, minced
1 teaspoon cornstarch
⅛ teaspoon hot pepper sauce
Freshly ground black pepper, to
  taste

Combine all ingredients and shake well in covered jar.

Chicken and Green Peppers:

3 whole chicken breasts, boned,
  skinned, and cubed
Basic Dark Sauce

1 tablespoon oil
1 green pepper, seeded and
  cubed

½ cup pecans

Toss chicken in Basic Dark Sauce. Let stand 10 minutes. Drain and reserve marinade.

Heat oil in wok or large skillet. Add chicken. Stir-fry for 2 to 4 minutes until opaque. Stir in green pepper and pecans. Stir-fry for 2 minutes. Stir in reserved marinade. Cook and stir for 3 minutes, or until sauce thickens. Serve over rice.

Sweet-and-Sour Scallops

¾ pound bay scallops
½ teaspoon minced ginger
1 tablespoon chopped scallion
1 teaspoon light soy sauce
1 teaspoon wine
1 egg white

2 tablespoons cornstarch
Oil, for deep frying
1 cup unsweetened pineapple
  chunks (reserve juice)
Salt, to taste

Marinate scallops in mixture of next six ingredients. Marinate for 30 minutes. Do not overmarinate.

Deep-fry scallops for 1 minute. Drain.

Sweet-and-Sour Sauce:

1 tablespoon light soy sauce
1 tablespoon white vinegar
2 teaspoons sugar
1 tablespoon cornstarch

¾ cup reserved pineapple juice
   (may need to add water)
1 green pepper, cut into 1-inch
   pieces

In saucepan heat all sauce ingredients except pepper, stirring until it thickens. Add green pepper and stir 1 minute.

Stir scallops and pineapple into sauce, and salt to taste.

Crunchy Chinese Celery

2 tablespoons oil
1 cup sliced onions
1 clove garlic, minced
6 cups thinly sliced (crosswise)
   celery
½ cup water chestnuts

2 tablespoons soy sauce
1 teaspoon sugar
⅛ teaspoon black pepper
1 tablespoon toasted sesame
   seeds

Heat oil until hot in large skillet or wok. Sauté onions and garlic for 1 minute. Add celery, and stir for 5 minutes. Stir in water chestnuts, soy sauce, sugar, and pepper. Cook and stir until celery is crisp tender, about 3 minutes. Sprinkle with sesame seeds just before serving.

Pears in Orange Juice

6 firm, ripe Bartlett pears
⅓ cup sugar
1 cup fresh orange juice
1 tablespoon fresh lemon juice

1 2-inch cinnamon stick
4 whole cloves
⅛ teaspoon ground nutmeg
Dash of salt

Peel, core, and quarter pears. Place in a baking dish. Mix remaining ingredients in saucepan. Bring to boiling point and pour over pears. Cover and bake 30 minutes in 350° oven. Remove cover and bake 10 minutes more, or until pears are tender. Cool in pan. Serve at room temperature.

MEDITERRANEAN

Adriatic Riches

Pita Appetizer
Cucumber Soup
Onion, Avocado, and Orange Salad
with Honey and Poppy Seed Dressing
Seafood Brochette
Parmesan Green Beans
Lemon Rice
Rosemary Bread
Circe's Chocolate Cake

PREVIOUS DAY	EARLY MORNING	FREEZER
Salad dressing	*Cucumber Soup*	*Rosemary Bread*
Seafood marinade		
Circe's Chocolate Cake		

Pita Appetizer

3 8-inch pita breads
1½ to 2 cups shredded
   Cheddar cheese
½ cup mayonnaise
½ cup chopped scallions
½ cup chopped black olives
¼ teaspoon curry powder

Cut pita into fourths. Cut off outer edge. Cut quarters once again and separate. You should have 16 small triangles from each pita, 48 in all. Combine remaining ingredients and spread on pita pieces. Toast under broiler until cheese bubbles. Serve immediately.

Cucumber Soup

2 medium-size cucumbers, cut
   paper thin, then in quarters
Pinch of salt
Dash of Tabasco sauce
1½ cups strong chicken stock
1 cup condensed tomato soup
   (tomato juice can be used for
   a thinner soup)

2 cups plain yogurt
½ pint light cream
Milk, to taste (optional)
2 boiled potatoes, riced
   (optional)

Place cucumber pieces in bowl and salt them. Mix Tabasco, chicken stock, tomato soup, yogurt, and cream together with rotary beater until quite smooth. Press moisture out of cucumber slices. Purée half the cucumber and add the rest directly to mixture. Combine cucumber purée with the rest of soup. Add milk if you wish. For sturdier soup, add the riced potatoes.

Onion, Avocado, and Orange Salad

2 heads Boston lettuce
1 medium red onion, sliced thin,
   separated into rings

1 large avocado, peeled and
   sliced into thin wedges
2 oranges, peeled and sectioned

On individual salad plates, arrange a bed of the lettuce, a few onion rings, and alternate wedges of avocado and orange sections. Serve with Honey and Poppy Seed Dressing.

Honey and Poppy Seed Dressing:
(Makes 1 pint)

⅔ cup sugar
1 teaspoon dry mustard
1 teaspoon paprika
½ teaspoon salt
⅓ cup honey

3 tablespoons lemon juice
3 tablespoons vinegar
2 teaspoons grated onion
1 cup salad oil
1 tablespoon poppy seeds

Mix the first 4 ingredients in blender or processor. Add honey, lemon juice, vinegar, and onion, and blend for 1 minute. With machine running, pour oil in through opening in cover or feed tube. Pour dressing into a jar and stir in the poppy seeds.

Seafood Brochette

Marinade:

½ cup olive oil
¼ cup chili sauce
4 tablespoons fresh lemon juice
2 tablespoons Worcestershire
   sauce

2 cloves garlic, minced
½ teaspoon salt
Cayenne pepper, to taste

Combine and set aside.

Brochette:

6 wooden skewers
16 large shrimp, shelled and
   deveined

16 cubes of swordfish (½ inch
   by 1 inch)
16 scallops (large type)

Soak skewers in water for 5 minutes. Skewer seafood, alternating shrimp, swordfish, and scallops. Place filled skewers in a large, flat glass dish that has a rim. Marinate for 30 minutes at room temperature, turning after 15 minutes.

Broil or grill over charcoal until fish turns brown and shrimp pink, about 10 minutes or longer. Serve with lemon wedges.

Note: Marinade can be mixed and refrigerated several days ahead, tightly covered. Seafood is highly perishable and should be cooked no later than one day after purchase. Be sure to keep it well refrigerated until just before cooking.

Parmesan Green Beans

4 quarts boiling water
1½ pounds green beans

1 tablespoon butter
¼ cup grated Parmesan

¼ teaspoon dried oregano

Bring water to a boil, add beans, and boil, uncovered, for 6 to 10 minutes. Taste for tenderness. Drain and toss with remaining ingredients.

Lemon Rice

¼ pound butter or margarine
2 cups long grain white rice
Grated peel of 1 lemon
3 cups boiling water
½ teaspoon salt

3 tablespoons lemon juice
1 cup cream
Freshly ground white pepper, to taste

Melt butter in saucepan over low heat. Add the rice and grated lemon peel. Stir for 3 minutes until rice is opaque. Add the boiling water and salt, and simmer, covered, for 18 minutes or until water is absorbed. Add lemon juice to taste. Slowly add the cream and stir constantly for 3 to 4 minutes. Add pepper and taste for seasoning adjustments.

Rosemary Bread

1½ cups warm water
1 tablespoon sugar
1 package active dry yeast
4 cups flour (or more)

½ cup chopped onion
2 teaspoons salt
Oil
1 teaspoon coarse salt

Dried rosemary

Combine the water, sugar, and yeast until yeast is dissolved and mixture begins to foam. Stir in 2 cups of the flour and blend well. Add remaining 2 cups of flour, the onion, and 2 teaspoons salt. Knead until smooth, adding more flour if the mixture is too sticky. Oil a large bowl and turn dough over to lightly coat the top. Cover dough in bowl with a towel and let rise until doubled (about 1 hour). Shape dough into a round loaf and place on an oiled cookie sheet. Let rise until doubled (about 30 minutes).

Brush the top of the loaf lightly with oil, sprinkle with coarse salt and rosemary, and bake in preheated 400° oven about 25 minutes or until the bottom sounds hollow when tapped. Serve warm.

Note: This is a coarse bread, excellent with peasant soups or stews.

Circe's Chocolate Cake

3 squares unsweetened chocolate
¼ pound butter or margarine
½ cup salad oil
1 cup water
2 cups all-purpose flour
1 teaspoon baking soda

Dash of salt
2 cups sugar
2 eggs
½ cup sour milk (or ½ cup
    milk plus 1 teaspoon lemon
    juice or vinegar)

1 teaspoon vanilla extract

Put chocolate, butter, and oil in saucepan. Melt over low heat. Add water, cool 15 minutes. Sift together flour, soda, and salt. Add sugar, eggs, sour milk, and vanilla. Mix well with wooden spoon. Stir in cooled chocolate. Quickly turn into 2 greased and floured 8-inch-square cake pans. Bake in preheated 350° oven for 30 to 35 minutes. Cool in pans for 5 minutes. Turn out on rack.

Filling:

1 6½-ounce can evaporated
    milk
¾ cup sugar
¼ cup water

½ cup chopped dates
1 teaspoon vanilla extract
½ cup chopped walnuts or
    pecans

½ cup heavy cream

Combine milk, sugar, and ¼ cup water in saucepan. Cook until sugar is dissolved. Add dates. Cook until thick, about 5 minutes. Add vanilla and nuts and cook completely. Whip cream. Spread filling on 1 layer of cake, top with whipped cream, then add second layer of cake. Refrigerate while making frosting.

Frosting:

1 small package semisweet
    chocolate chips

½ cup sour cream
Dash of salt

Melt chocolate pieces in top of double boiler. Remove from heat. Stir in sour cream and dash of salt. Beat until smooth. Cool. Spread on top and sides of cake. Refrigerate cake until ready to serve.

Mediterranean Dinner (Serves 8)

Sardine Mold
Spinach-Cheese Pie
Riviera Salad with Zesty Garlic-Parsley Vinaigrette
Mediterranean Chicken
Risotto with Asparagus and Pine Nuts
Coconut Ice Cream with Citrus Ambrosia
Minichip Kisses

PREVIOUS DAY	EARLY MORNING	FREEZER
Minichip Kisses	*Sardine Mold*	*Spinach Pie*
	Chicken	*Coconut Ice Cream*
	Ambrosia	
	Zesty Vinaigrette	

Sardine Mold

2 3-ounce packages cream cheese
2 3¾-ounce cans Portuguese
  skinless and boneless sardines,
  drained
½ teaspoon grated onion
  (optional)

½ teaspoon lemon juice
Dash of Worcestershire sauce
½ teaspoon A-1 Sauce
1 4-ounce bottle stuffed olives
Pineapple leaves, as garnish

In small bowl, soften cream cheese to room temperature and mash
sardines into cheese. Add rest of ingredients except olives. Chill and
mold into cone-shaped mound. Cover mound with sliced olives. Garnish with several small leaves from pineapple at top. Serve with rye
rounds or crackers.

Spinach-Cheese Pie
(Makes 32 squares)

1 pint small curd cottage cheese
6 eggs
1 10-ounce package frozen
  chopped spinach, thawed and
  drained
6 tablespoons flour

½ cup melted butter
1 pound Cheddar cheese, grated
2 tablespoons chopped scallions
Salt and freshly ground black
  pepper, to taste

Put cottage cheese into bowl and add eggs one at a time. Add well-drained spinach, blend in flour, and add remaining ingredients. Spread into 2 9-inch-square pans. Can be frozen at this stage. If frozen, bring to room temperature before baking in preheated 350° oven for 45 to 50 minutes. Cut into 2-inch squares and serve.

Riviera Salad

3 cups bite-size pieces romaine
3 cups bite-size pieces Boston lettuce
3 cups bite-size pieces curly endive
1 cup fine crosswise slices celery
3 tomatoes, quartered
3 hard-cooked eggs, chopped
½ cup julienne slices beets
¼ cup chopped watercress

Combine the greens and vegetables in large salad bowl. Mix with Zesty Garlic-Parsley Vinaigrette.

Zesty Garlic-Parsley Vinaigrette:

½ cup vinegar
1½ cups oil
¾ teaspoon salt
1 clove garlic, crushed
¼ teaspoon freshly ground black pepper
1 tablespoon finely chopped capers
1 tablespoon finely chopped chives
1 tablespoon finely chopped parsley
1 tablespoon finely chopped gherkins

Combine all ingredients thoroughly. Combine with salad immediately before serving.

Mediterranean Chicken

¾ cup all-purpose flour
1 teaspoon salt
¼ teaspoon pepper
8 whole chicken breasts, skinned, boned, and halved
2 tablespoons butter, melted
2 tablespoons olive oil
1 teaspoon oregano
1 large clove garlic, minced
2 cups dry red wine
1 12-ounce can frozen orange juice concentrate, thawed
8 large mushrooms, sliced
2 large red onions, sliced in ½-inch slices, made into rings
2 large green peppers, sliced into ½-inch rings
1 cup coarsely chopped black Greek olives

Combine flour, salt, and pepper. Dust chicken pieces lightly with mixture. Heat half the butter and oil in large skillet over medium heat. Stir in oregano and garlic. Add chicken in batches and sauté until golden on both sides. Transfer chicken pieces to 4-quart ovenproof container and set aside.

Combine wine and orange juice in medium bowl and pour into skillet in which chicken was cooked. Bring to boil and simmer uncovered for 4 to 5 minutes, scraping bottom of pan to deglaze. Pour sauce over chicken breasts. Cover loosely with foil and bake in preheated 375° oven for 20 minutes. If baked without foil top, bake for 15 to 20 minutes.

Heat remaining butter and oil in same skillet, add mushrooms, onions, and green peppers. Sauté over medium heat for 3 or 4 minutes, only until slightly softened. Spoon over chicken and top with olives. Return to oven uncovered for an additional 30 minutes, basting every 10 minutes until chicken is tender and well glazed.

Risotto with Asparagus and Pine Nuts

½ cup pine nuts
1 pound fresh asparagus
4 cups chicken stock
1 cup dry white wine
4 tablespoons butter
1 medium onion, finely chopped

1½ cups Italian short grain rice
½ cup freshly grated Parmesan
Salt and freshly ground black pepper, to taste

Toast nuts in 325° oven until light brown and reserve. Peel asparagus and cut into ½-inch pieces. Leave tips whole. Heat 4 cups of stock and the wine in saucepan until simmering. Melt butter in a heavy saucepan, add onion, and sauté until light brown. Add rice and stir to coat with butter. Add enough of the simmering stock to just cover the rice. Gently simmer, uncovered, until liquid is almost evaporated and mixture is thick. Stir frequently. This will take about 4 minutes. Repeat the procedure, adding only enough liquid to barely cover the rice each time. Cook until rice is tender but firm and mixture is thick and creamy, about 25 minutes. Add asparagus stems, and 5 minutes later add the tips. When rice is cooked, remove from heat. Add the cheese and pine nuts and season to taste. Serve immediately.

Citrus Ambrosia
(Makes 1 quart)

½ cup sugar
2 tablespoons cornstarch
1 cup fresh orange juice
1 cup fresh grapefruit juice
½ cup Amaretto or other
  almond liqueur

2 tablespoons butter or
  margarine
1 cup fresh orange sections
1 cup fresh grapefruit sections
1 cup diced fresh pineapple

Combine sugar and cornstarch in medium saucepan. Stir in juices. Over medium heat, stir until mixture thickens and boils. Cook 1 minute. Add liqueur and butter, heat, and stir until butter melts. Just before serving, fold in fruit and heat only until heated through. Serve warm over coconut ice cream.

Minichip Kisses
(Makes about 42)

4 large eggs, whites only
¼ teaspoon salt
½ teaspoon white vinegar
1 cup granulated sugar

2 teaspoons orange-flavored
  liqueur
¾ cup mini chocolate chips
1 tablespoon confectioners' sugar

Place the egg whites and salt in a large bowl, bring to room temperature, and beat until frothy. Add vinegar and beat until soft peaks form. Gradually add the granulated sugar and beat the mixture until stiff, glossy peaks are formed. Beat in the liqueur. Gently fold in the minichips.

Line baking sheets with foil, placed shiny side down. Drop meringue in level tablespoonfuls, 2 inches apart, onto prepared sheets. Sift confectioners' sugar over the cookies and bake in preheated 275° oven for 35 to 45 minutes or until they are firm and lightly colored. Cool the cookies on a rack and store in airtight container.

Turkish Delight

Mock Boursin au Poivre
Cold Crabmeat Dip
Caesar Salad
Shish Kebab with Barbecue Marinade
Rice and Noodle Casserole
Refrigerated Raspberry Cake
Toffee

PREVIOUS DAY	EARLY MORNING	FREEZER
Mock Boursin	*Dressing for salad*	*Rice and Noodle*
Cold Crabmeat Dip	*Marinade*	*Casserole*
Raspberry Cake		
Toffee		

Mock Boursin au Poivre

8 ounces cream cheese, softened
1 clove garlic, minced
1 teaspoon caraway seed
1 teaspoon dried basil
1 teaspoon dill weed
1 teaspoon chopped chives
Lemon pepper

Combine first six ingredients. Form into a flattened ball. Roll in lemon pepper. Cover and chill for several days. Serve as a spread with crackers.

Cold Crabmeat Dip

1 7-ounce package frozen crabmeat, defrosted and drained
½ cup chili sauce
½ cup mayonnaise
1 tablespoon horseradish
1 teaspoon dry mustard
1 tablespoon Worcestershire sauce
Dash of Tabasco sauce
Dash of celery salt
2 hard-cooked eggs, chopped fine
2 scallions, chopped

Combine all ingredients and chill for several hours or overnight. Serve with crackers or Crudités (see Index) for dipping.

Caesar Salad

2 heads romaine lettuce
2 2-ounce cans flat fillets of
  anchovies, cut up (reserve oil)
1 large clove garlic, pressed
⅓ cup wine vinegar
Salt and freshly ground black
  pepper, to taste
⅔ cup olive oil

1 tablespoon prepared mustard
1 tablespoon tangy mustard-
  mayonnaise dressing (Durkee's
  Famous Sauce)
1 teaspoon Worcestershire sauce
1 to 3 drops hot pepper sauce
2 coddled eggs, beaten
⅓ cup croutons

½ cup grated Parmesan

Break up greens into salad bowl. Mix together all other ingredients, up to the eggs. Beat well and pour over greens. Add eggs and croutons. Toss well with freshly grated Parmesan cheese on the top. Serve at once.

Shish Kebab with Barbecue Marinade

3 pounds boneless sirloin of beef
  or leg of lamb, cut in cubes
3 tomatoes, quartered

2 green peppers, cut into 1½-
  inch squares
2 zucchini, cut in 1-inch rounds

2 medium onions, quartered

Marinade:

1½ cups salad oil
¾ cup soy sauce
¼ cup Worcestershire sauce
2 tablespoons dry mustard
2¼ teaspoons salt
1 tablespoon freshly ground
  black pepper

½ cup wine vinegar
1½ teaspoons dried parsley
  flakes
3 cloves garlic, crushed
⅓ cup fresh lemon juice

Marinate cubed beef or lamb and vegetables 5 hours at room temperature before barbecuing. Pour off excess marinade and store in refrigerator for up to a week for other use. String meat and vegetables on skewers and barbecue on grill as desired.

Rice and Noodle Casserole

¼ pound butter or margarine	1 10-ounce can undiluted
¼ pound fine noodles	condensed chicken soup
1 cup long grain brown rice	1 cube chicken bouillon
1 10-ounce can undiluted	dissolved in 1 cup hot water
condensed onion soup	2 tablespoons soy sauce

Melt butter in skillet. Add noodles and brown slightly. Add rice, soups, bouillon. Cover. Simmer until almost all liquid is absorbed. Mix in soy sauce and bake 45 minutes to 1 hour in preheated 375° oven. Remove cover near end of cooking time to brown top. May be frozen before the baking step.

Refrigerated Raspberry Cake

2 pints fresh raspberries	1 teaspoon vanilla extract
½ cup sugar	2 cups whipping cream
	3 packages ladyfingers

Rinse and drain raspberries thoroughly. Reserve a few berries for garnish. Add sugar and vanilla to cream and beat until it stands in soft peaks. Fill an 8-inch springform pan with alternating layers of ladyfingers, raspberries, and sweetened whipped cream, beginning with ladyfingers and ending with cream. Chill 10 to 12 hours or overnight.

Just before serving, remove sides from springform pan and place on serving plate. Stand remaining ladyfingers upright around sides of mold and press firmly. Garnish with reserved raspberries.

Toffee
(Makes about 3 pounds)

1 pound butter	1 11.7-ounce bag milk chocolate
1¼ cups sugar	chips
½ teaspoon vanilla extract	1 cup finely chopped walnuts or
2 cups sliced almonds (optional)	pecans

In heavy saucepan, melt butter. Add sugar and cook over medium heat, stirring constantly with wooden spoon, until thick and caramel colored, to 300° on candy thermometer; approximately 30 minutes.

Add vanilla and almonds and pour into 10-by-15-inch pan and smooth out. Sprinkle chocolate chips over hot toffee and allow to melt 1 or 2 minutes. Spread chocolate evenly with a knife over toffee and press nuts into chocolate. Cool. When cool, either cut or break into pieces. Store in refrigerator.

Dinner on Olympus

Shrimp Mousse with Cucumber and Sour Cream Dressing
Greek Vegetable Salad with Anchovies
Athenian Fish
Lemon Chicken
Wild Rice Casserole
Royal Almond Cake

PREVIOUS DAY	EARLY MORNING	FREEZER
Wild Rice Casserole	*Vegetable Salad*	
Shrimp Mousse	*Cucumber Dressing*	

Shrimp Mousse

1 10¾-ounce can condensed tomato soup
1 envelope unflavored gelatin, dissolved in ¼ cup water
8 ounces cream cheese, room temperature
1 cup mayonnaise
1 cup finely chopped celery
1 cup finely chopped onion
1 pound cooked shrimp, cut into small pieces

Heat tomato soup to a boil, add gelatin and water mixture, and stir until dissolved. Beat cream cheese until creamy. Add tomato soup, mayonnaise, and rest of ingredients. Fill a 6-cup ring mold that has been coated with oil and chilled in freezer. Serve with Cucumber and Sour Cream Dressing.

Cucumber and Sour Cream Dressing:

1 cup sour cream

1 tablespoon mayonnaise

2 tablespoons fresh lemon juice

1 cup grated, drained cucumber

1 teaspoon salt

Dash of cayenne

Mix all ingredients and chill at least 1 hour.

Greek Vegetable Salad with Anchovies

½ cup olive oil

12 medium mushrooms, quartered

1 teaspoon leaf oregano

2 medium-size onions, chopped fine

4 medium-size tomatoes, peeled, seeded, and chopped

1 medium-size eggplant, peeled and diced

2 cooked artichoke hearts, cut in quarters, or 1 10-ounce package frozen artichoke hearts

3 cloves garlic, chopped fine

Juice of 3 lemons

½ teaspoon salt

12 anchovy fillets

12 black olives, pitted

Pour the oil into a large saucepan. Add the mushrooms and sauté over medium heat for 3 minutes. Add the oregano, onions, tomatoes, eggplant, artichokes (if you use frozen artichokes, add anchovies and olives before chilling), garlic, lemon juice, salt, and cook for 10 minutes. Allow the salad mixture to cool, then transfer to a salad bowl. Add the anchovy fillets and olives and chill well before serving.

Athenian Fish

4 medium onions, chopped

3 cloves garlic, minced

¼ cup olive oil

1 16-ounce can chopped tomatoes, well drained

2 tablespoons raisins

2 tablespoons chopped parsley

2 tablespoons fresh lemon juice

½ cup chopped green olives

Salt and freshly ground pepper, to taste

2 pounds scrod or haddock fillets

Spray 9-by-13-inch casserole with noncaloric shortening. In frying pan, sauté onions and garlic until soft in hot oil. Do not brown. Add tomatoes, raisins, parsley, lemon juice, olives, salt, and pepper. Put fish into prepared casserole. Spoon sauce over fish and refrigerate. Remove from refrigerator 20 minutes before baking and bake in preheated 325° oven for 40 minutes.

Lemon Chicken

3 whole chicken breasts, skinned
   and boned
3 tablespoons lemon juice
2 tablespoons soy sauce
4 tablespoons peanut oil

2 teaspoons minced ginger root
2 cloves garlic, minced
½ teaspoon salt
¼ teaspoon ground turmeric
¼ teaspoon white pepper

2 teaspoons Oriental sesame oil

Cut chicken into bite-size pieces. Whisk together lemon juice, soy sauce, 1 tablespoon of the peanut oil, ginger, garlic, salt, turmeric, and pepper. Pour over chicken and toss. Let stand at room temperature for 1 hour, covered. Remove chicken with slotted spoon, pat dry, and reserve marinade. Sauté in 3 remaining tablespoons peanut oil until tender (2 minutes). Stir in sesame oil and marinade. Simmer 1 minute at lower heat.

Wild Rice Casserole

½ pound sliced mushrooms
2 tablespoons minced onion
2 tablespoons minced green
   pepper
1 clove garlic, minced
1 cup chopped pecans (optional)

¼ pound butter
2 cups cooked wild rice
4 cups cooked white rice
   (prepared in chicken broth)

Sauté mushrooms, onion, green pepper, garlic, and nuts in butter until all are tender. Mix in rice and put into a buttered casserole. Refrigerate until serving time. Bring to room temperature and bake in preheated 325° oven until heated through.

Royal Almond Cake

14 tablespoons butter (1¾ sticks)
¾ cup sliced almonds
1½ cups plus 1 tablespoon sugar
3 eggs, separated

1½ teaspoons vanilla extract
¼ teaspoon almond extract
2½ cups cake flour
3 teaspoons baking powder
1 teaspoon salt
1 cup milk

1 teaspoon grated lemon rind

Butter sides and bottom of 10-inch tube or Bundt pan heavily with 2 to 3 tablespoons butter. Sprinkle sides and bottom of pan with ¾ cup sliced almonds and 1 tablespoon sugar.

Cream butter, 1 cup of the sugar, and 3 egg yolks until light and fluffy, and stir in vanilla and almond extracts. Add dry ingredients alternately with milk and grated lemon. Beat egg whites until stiff, adding remaining ½ cup sugar a little at a time. Fold egg whites into batter; pour into prepared pan. Bake 1 hour in preheated 350° oven.

Party Buffets

Each recipe serves six unless otherwise indicated.

When entertaining a group, select a menu that suits the season, lends itself to attractive presentation, and requires a minimum of last-minute work. Plan your buffet traffic pattern to flow naturally. Wrapping silverware in napkins makes it easier to pick up and hold on to, and having a separate setup for desserts and coffee and tea decreases congestion.

Gala Dinner

Crudités with Horseradish Mayonnaise Dip
Egg Mousse with Crabmeat Sauce
Sole in Beer Batter
Brandied Carrots
Spinach Pasta with Gorgonzola Sauce
Best Lemon Pie with Neverfail Meringue

PREVIOUS DAY	EARLY MORNING	FREEZER
Horseradish Dip	*Brandied Carrots*	
Egg Mousse		
Lemon Pie		

Crudités

Radishes	Broccoli
Celery	Green peppers
Fennel hearts	Carrots
Cherry tomatoes	Zucchini
Asparagus	Cucumbers
Scallions	Kohlrabi
Cauliflower	Turnips

Clean, trim, and cut into appropriate pieces any or all of the raw vegetables listed above. Arrange attractively on a large platter.

Horseradish Mayonnaise Dip

1 cup mayonnaise	1 teaspoon tarragon vinegar
½ cup ketchup	Lemon juice, to taste
2 teaspoons grated fresh horseradish	Freshly ground black pepper, to taste

Combine first 4 ingredients. Season to taste with lemon juice and pepper. Chill before serving with Crudités.

Egg Mousse with Crabmeat Sauce
(Serves 12 as appetizer)

1 package unflavored gelatin (add more, if desired)	Salt and freshly ground black pepper, to taste
½ cup cold water	½ teaspoon curry powder
1 scant cup chicken broth	12 hard-cooked eggs, chopped fine
1 cup mayonnaise	1 cup sour cream, for topping
1 teaspoon lemon juice	Crumbled bacon (optional)
1 teaspoon grated onion	Red or black caviar (optional)
1 teaspoon chopped parsley or chives	

Dissolve gelatin in ½ cup cold water. Add to boiling chicken broth. Mix in rest of ingredients, adding eggs last and omitting sour cream and garnishes. Pour into 6-cup oiled (or sprayed with noncaloric shortening) ring mold. Refrigerate overnight.

Remove from mold to serving platter. Frost with sour cream and top with crumbled bacon *or* red or black caviar. Serve with Crabmeat Sauce and crackers or cocktail rye.

Crabmeat Sauce:

1 7-ounce can crabmeat	⅓ cup sour cream
⅓ cup mayonnaise	⅓ cup chili sauce

Combine all ingredients and chill. Serve in center of ring mold.

Sole in Beer Batter

5½ cups oil	2 egg whites
2½ cups flour	¼ tablespoon salt
1 quart light beer	6 to 8 6-ounce Atlantic sole fillets
	½ cup all-purpose flour

Mix 2½ cups of the oil and flour, using wire whisk. Add beer to mixture until it is smooth. In separate bowl, whip egg whites with salt until they become fluffy. Then add to batter.

Dip sole in flour, then drop each fillet into beer batter. Deep fry in remaining hot oil until golden, about 2½ minutes per side. Serve immediately.

Brandied Carrots

2 pounds carrots	⅔ cup brandy (or unsweetened orange juice or pineapple juice)
3 tablespoons butter, melted	
	1½ teaspoons sugar
	Salt, to taste

Cut carrots into 2-inch-long julienne strips and place in 9-inch-square baking dish. Mix remaining ingredients and pour over carrots. Bake in preheated 375° oven for 30 to 40 minutes or until carrots are tender. Stir once during baking period.

Spinach Pasta with Gorgonzola Sauce

¼ pound Gorgonzola,
  crumbled
½ cup milk
3 tablespoons butter
⅓ cup whipping cream

1 pound spinach pasta, cooked
  al dente
⅓ cup freshly grated
  Parmesan

Combine Gorgonzola, milk, and butter in large nonaluminum skillet. Over low heat, stir until smooth. Add cream and blend well. Add pasta and Parmesan and toss until noodles are coated.

Note: Can be prepared about 1 hour in advance and gently reheated.

Best Lemon Pie with Neverfail Meringue

1¼ cups sugar
6 tablespoons cornstarch
2 cups water
3 egg yolks

⅓ cup lemon juice
1½ teaspoons lemon extract
3 tablespoons butter
2 teaspoons vinegar

1 baked 9-inch pie shell

Mix sugar and cornstarch in top of double boiler. Add water. Combine yolks with lemon juice and beat; add to cornstarch mix. Cook over hot (not boiling) water until thick, about 25 minutes. Add extract, butter, and vinegar, stirring thoroughly. Pour into deep 9-inch pie shell and cool.

Meringue:

1 tablespoon cornstarch
2 tablespoons cold water
½ cup boiling water

3 egg whites
6 tablespoons sugar
Pinch of salt

1 teaspoon vanilla extract

Blend cornstarch and cold water in saucepan. Add boiling water and cook, stirring constantly, until clear and thickened. Let stand until completely cold. In electric mixer beat egg whites until foamy. Gradually add sugar and beat until stiff, but not dry. Turn mixer to low speed, add salt and vanilla. Gradually beat in cold cornstarch mixture. Turn mixture to high speed and beat well. Spread meringue over cooled pie filling. Bake in preheated 350° oven for 10 minutes.

Ides of March Dinner

Herring Antipasto
Mushroom Sesame Crescents
Marinated String Bean Salad
Chicken Artichoke Cacciatore
Rice Pilaf
Spinach and Tomato Casserole
Chocolate Mousse Cake

PREVIOUS DAY	EARLY MORNING	FREEZER
Herring Antipasto	Spinach and Tomato	Mushroom Crescents
String Bean Salad	Casserole	
Chocolate Mousse Cake		

Herring Antipasto

1 large jar herring, in wine sauce, drained and rinsed
1 green pepper, diced
1 4½-ounce jar marinated artichokes, drained and sliced
1 12-ounce bottle chili sauce
½ red onion, chopped
1 2½-ounce jar pitted black olives, sliced

Mix together all ingredients and marinate for 24 hours. Serve on rye rounds.

Mushroom Sesame Crescents
(Makes approximately 200 small pieces)

Filling:

2 pounds mushrooms
1 medium onion
¼ pound butter
2 cloves garlic, minced
Salt and freshly ground black pepper, to taste
1 tablespoon flour (or more)
1 tablespoon half-and-half

In processor, finely chop mushrooms and onion. Sauté in butter with garlic, salt, and pepper, until all liquid is absorbed. Stir in flour, add half-and-half, and let cool.

Dough:

¾ pound butter
1½ cups creamed cottage
    cheese, small curd

3 cups flour, or more
1 egg, beaten
Sesame seeds

In food processor, cream butter, add cheese, then flour. Do one-half at a time, unless you have a *large* processor. If dough is refrigerated, bring to room temperature before using.

To assemble crescents, roll out one-quarter of pastry at a time on a floured cutting board until about ⅛-inch thick. Cut into 2-inch rounds. Put ¼ teaspoon of filling in the center of each. Fold over and seal edges so that each is shaped like a crescent. These can be frozen on cookie sheets and transferred to plastic bags for storage when frozen solid. Defrost before baking; takes about 3 to 4 hours.

Just before baking, brush with beaten egg and sprinkle with sesame seeds. Bake at 400° for 10 minutes. They should be lightly browned.

Marinated String Bean Salad

1½ pounds fresh string beans
    (or 2 10-ounce packages
    frozen)
2 16-ounce bottles Italian
    dressing

1 2-ounce jar pimentos
¼ pound mushrooms, thinly
    sliced (optional)
1 medium-size red onion, sliced
    very thin

Put fresh beans in boiling water for 1 to 2 minutes, until they turn emerald green. Drain. If using frozen beans, thaw and drain. Combine beans with remaining ingredients and marinate for 1 to 2 days before serving. Stir every few hours. Drain marinade before serving beans.

Chicken Artichoke Cacciatore

2 6-ounce jars marinated
    artichoke hearts
2 tablespoons olive oil
1 3-pound broiler-fryer chicken,
    cut up and skin removed
Flour, for dredging
1 no. 2 can tomatoes or 12-
    ounce can tomato paste
2 cloves garlic, minced

½ pound fresh mushrooms,
    sliced
1¼ teaspoons salt
½ teaspoon oregano
½ teaspoon freshly ground
    pepper
½ teaspoon basil
¼ cup sherry
Chopped parsley, for garnish

Drain marinade from artichokes into large skillet and add olive oil. Dredge chicken in flour, then brown in oil until golden. Transfer chicken pieces from skillet to large casserole. Combine tomatoes, artichoke hearts, garlic, mushrooms, and all spices in the hot skillet and stir. When thoroughly mixed, pour over chicken. Cover and bake in preheated 350° oven for 1 hour, or until tender. During last few minutes, add sherry. Serve garnished with chopped parsley.

Rice Pilaf
(Serves 10 to 12)

4 tablespoons butter
½ cup finely chopped onion
2 cups long grain rice
4 cups chicken broth, fresh or
  canned

⅓ cup unsalted pistachio or
  pine nuts
Freshly ground pepper, to taste
2 tablespoons finely chopped
  parsley

Heat butter in a 3- or 4-quart casserole, add the onion, and cook until it is lightly browned. Add the rice and stir until all grains are evenly coated with butter. Pour in the chicken broth and bring it to a boil. Reduce the heat as low as possible, cover the casserole, and cook the rice for about 20 minutes or until all liquid has been absorbed. Remove the pan from the heat and let the rice stand, still covered, for 10 minutes before serving. Just before serving, using a fork, stir in the nuts, pepper, and parsley.

Spinach and Tomato Casserole

2 packages frozen spinach
  soufflé, defrosted
2 tomatoes, cut into ¼-inch
  slices

1 cup sour cream chive croutons,
  any other flavor croutons, or
  seasoned bread crumbs
1 or 2 tablespoons butter

Spray oval or rectangular 1½-quart casserole with noncaloric shortening. Spoon spinach soufflé into casserole. Place tomatoes over top. Crush croutons or use bread crumbs and spread on tomatoes. Dot with butter. Bake in preheated 350° oven for 40 to 50 minutes.

Chocolate Mousse Cake

Cake and Filling:

7 ounces semisweet chocolate	1 cup sugar
¼ pound unsalted butter	1 teaspoon vanilla extract
7 eggs, separated	⅛ teaspoon cream of tartar

Use an ungreased 9-inch springform pan. Melt the chocolate and butter over low heat or in the microwave oven. In a large bowl, beat the egg yolks and ¾ cup of the sugar until light and fluffy. Slowly beat in the melted chocolate, butter, and vanilla. Beat egg whites until foamy, add cream of tartar, and beat to soft peaks. Add the remaining ¼ cup sugar gradually, beating the whites to stiff peaks. Fold the whites into the chocolate mixture. Pour three-fourths of the batter into the springform pan. Cover the remaining batter and store in the refrigerator. Bake the batter in the springform pan for 35 minutes in preheated 325° oven. Remove from oven and cool. The center will sink as it cools. Spread the refrigerated batter on top of the cooled, baked cake. Refrigerate several hours or overnight to firm the top.

Frosting:

1 cup whipping cream	⅓ cup confectioners' sugar
1 teaspoon vanilla extract	

Beat cream until soft peaks form, add sugar and vanilla, and beat until stiff. Frost the top and sides of the cake. This can be done several hours before serving.

Elegant Spring Dinner

Mini Potato Pancakes
Cascadilla
Roman Lamb Chops
Spinach Soufflé with Phyllo Dough
Frozen Fruit Mold
Hot Fudge Sundae Pie

Mini Potato Pancakes

1 medium onion	1 to 2 teaspoons salt
2 eggs, beaten	½ teaspoon white pepper
6 medium white potatoes, peeled	3 tablespoons oil
1 tablespoon matzo meal or flour	Sour cream and caviar, for dipping
⅛ teaspoon baking powder	

Chop onion in processor and add to beaten eggs in large mixing bowl. Grate potatoes in processor. Add potatoes to egg mixture. Add matzo meal, baking powder, salt, and pepper to egg mixture and combine. Heat oil in large skillet, drop in potato mixture by tablespoons, brown on both sides, and drain on paper toweling. Serve warm. Freezes well.

These can be frozen on cookie sheets in freezer and then placed into plastic bags for storage. To reheat, line jelly-roll pan with brown paper, place frozen pancakes on paper, and bake in preheated 400° oven for 8 to 10 minutes.

Serve with bowls of sour cream and caviar for dipping.

Cascadilla (Cold Creamy Tomato Soup)

2 small green peppers	¾ teaspoon dill weed
2 small cucumbers	6 cups tomato juice
2 scallions	1½ cups plain yogurt
1 large clove garlic, crushed	Mushrooms, for garnish
1½ tablespoons honey	Croutons, for garnish

Chop green peppers, cucumbers, and scallions finely (or process, with garlic, with several on-off pulses of food processor). Combine chopped vegetables with remaining ingredients. Chill and garnish, when serving, with sliced mushrooms and croutons.

Roman Lamb Chops

6 shoulder lamb chops
4½ tablespoons fresh lemon
juice

Salt and pepper, to taste
3 tablespoons butter
1½ teaspoons oregano

2 small cloves garlic, minced

Place chops in foil-lined broiler rack. Combine remaining ingredients in small saucepan and heat until butter is melted. Brush on chops. Broil about 5 minutes, turn, brush with sauce, and continue broiling, approximately 8 to 10 minutes.

Spinach Soufflé with Phyllo Dough

2 bunches scallions, chopped
¼ cup finely chopped onion
2 tablespoons butter
1 10-ounce package frozen
spinach, cooked and well
drained
½ teaspoon each salt, freshly
ground black pepper, and
nutmeg

¼ pound feta cheese
¼ pound Swiss cheese, grated
8 ounces dry cottage cheese
3 eggs, slightly beaten
Phyllo leaves
3 tablespoons melted butter

Sauté scallions and onions in the 2 tablespoons butter. Add to cooked spinach, along with spices. Blend cheeses with beater until lumpy. Add eggs. Oil bottom of 9-by-13-inch glass baking dish. Place 1 phyllo leaf on bottom and brush lightly with melted butter. Place another leaf and brush again. Spread layer of spinach and onion mixture, then add 3 phyllo leaves, lightly buttered. Add a layer of cheese-and-egg mixture, then 3 more buttered phyllo leaves. Repeat layers, lightly buttering leaves each time. You should have 4 or 5 layers. Top the last with 5 phyllo leaves, also buttered lightly. (Can be prepared in morning to this stage and covered with damp towel.) Bake in preheated 350° oven for 40 minutes. Does not freeze successfully.

Frozen Fruit Mold

1 envelope unflavored gelatin
¼ cup warm water
1 1-pound, 4-ounce can crushed
 pineapple
1 cup sugar
2 3-ounce packages softened
 cream cheese

1 8-ounce bottle maraschino
 cherries, sliced, with juice
1 1-pound, 13-ounce can fruit
 cocktail, drained
1 cup whipping cream, whipped

Dissolve gelatin in warm water. Place pineapple and sugar in medium-size pot and bring to boil. Add dissolved gelatin and allow to thicken in refrigerator for 1½ hours. Beat cream cheese and cherry juice in large bowl. Fold in fruit cocktail and sliced cherries. Add thickened pineapple mixture and fold in the whipped cream. Spoon into 1½-quart ring mold and freeze.

Note: Remove from freezer 1½ hours before serving.

Hot Fudge Sundae Pie

Crust:

1¼ cups chocolate wafer
 crumbs
¼ cup finely ground toasted
 nuts (almonds, hazelnuts, or
 walnuts)

3 tablespoons sugar
6 tablespoons unsalted butter,
 melted

Combine crust ingredients and press into a 9-inch or 10-inch pie pan. Cover with plastic wrap and chill 30 minutes.

Sauce:

1 cup sugar
¾ cup unsweetened cocoa
4 tablespoons unsalted butter

1 teaspoon instant coffee
1 cup whipping cream

Combine sugar, cocoa, and coffee in medium saucepan. Add ½ cup of the whipping cream, blending well. Add remaining cream, blending well. Cook over medium heat, stirring constantly until sugar is dissolved. Add butter and cook until smooth and thickened, about 5 to 8 minutes. Keep warm.

Filling:

1 quart vanilla ice cream, softened	½ cup whipping cream, whipped
1 quart chocolate ice cream, frozen	Coarsely chopped toasted nuts, for garnish

Maraschino cherries, with stems, for garnish

Spread half of softened vanilla ice cream in the pie shell; freeze. Drizzle half of fudge sauce on vanilla ice cream; it will firm enough to spread remaining vanilla ice cream over it. Return to freezer. Scoop balls of chocolate ice cream and arrange on top, then pour on the remaining fudge sauce. Decorate pie with remaining whipped cream, nuts, and cherries.

Note: Crust and vanilla ice cream layers can be prepared weeks ahead if well wrapped for freezer. Fudge sauce can be prepared several days ahead and refrigerated. Warm before using.

Formal Anniversary Party

Artichoke Quichettes
Caviar Supreme
Asparagus in Prosciutto
Fillet of Sole Bienville
Basil Rice
Garden Green Beans
Brownie Tart
Charlotte Russe with Raspberry Sauce

PREVIOUS DAY	EARLY MORNING	FREEZER
Sauce Bienville	*Caviar Supreme*	*Artichoke Quichettes*
Brownie Tart	*Asparagus*	
Charlotte Russe	*Green Beans*	
Raspberry Sauce		

Artichoke Quichettes

Pastry:

¼ pound butter   3 ounces cream cheese
1 cup flour

Beat together butter and cream cheese until smooth. Add flour and mix until dough forms a ball (do not use processor). Wrap in wax paper and chill for at least 30 minutes, or overnight. Roll dough to ¼-inch thickness on floured surface, adding more flour if necessary. Cut out dough and press lightly into individual lightly floured tartlet pans about 1½ inches in diameter.

Filling:

1 4½-ounce jar marinated   1 cup grated Swiss cheese
    artichokes, well drained and   2 eggs, lightly beaten
    chopped   ½ cup milk
1 medium onion, chopped and   ½ teaspoon nutmeg
    lightly sautéed   1 or 2 dashes of Tabasco sauce
Freshly ground white pepper

Mix artichokes, onion, and cheese together and put about 1 teaspoon of the mixture into each individual quiche. Mix remaining ingredients and spoon into each quiche. Bake in preheated 450° oven for 10 minutes. Reduce heat to 350° and bake another 15 minutes. These can be served immediately or frozen at this point. If frozen, reheat directly from freezer at 450° for 10 minutes.

Note: It is sometimes easier to remove quiches from pans if they are slightly frozen. Place pans in freezer for 15 to 20 minutes. Quiche should pop right out of pan.

Caviar Supreme

1 package unflavored gelatin   ¼ cup cold water

Use an 8-inch or 9-inch springform or quiche pan with removable sides. Soften gelatin in cold water. You may have to reliquefy by placing it in a pan of hot water or in microwave.

Homemade Mayonnaise:
(Makes 1¾ cups)

1 egg
1 tablespoon fresh lemon juice
1 tablespoon red wine vinegar
1 teaspoon Dijon mustard

1 teaspoon salt
1½ cups oil (vegetable with 3
   tablespoons olive oil mixed)

In processor or blender, combine first 5 ingredients and 3 tablespoons of the oil, mixing for 5 seconds. With machine running, slowly add remaining oil in steady stream until mayonnaise thickens.

Egg Layer:

6 hard-cooked eggs
½ cup plus 1 tablespoon
   Homemade Mayonnaise

¼ cup minced fresh parsley
1 large scallion, minced
½ teaspoon salt
Dash or two of Tabasco sauce

Combine all ingredients and 1 tablespoon liquid gelatin. Adjust seasoning and spread mixture on bottom of pan. Cover and refrigerate about 20 to 30 minutes until slightly set.

Avocado Layer:

2 large or 3 medium avocados,
   puréed
1 large shallot, minced
2 tablespoons fresh lemon juice
2 heaping tablespoons
   Homemade Mayonnaise

¼ teaspoon salt
Dash of Tabasco sauce
1½ cups sour cream
6 to 8 ounces red or black caviar

Combine first 6 ingredients with 1 tablespoon dissolved gelatin. Adjust seasoning and gently spread on top of egg layer. Refrigerate 20 or 30 minutes.

When ready to serve, spread sour cream on top of avocado layer, gently spoon on caviar, and serve garnished with lemon slices and with thin slices of pumpernickel or rye bread.

Asparagus in Prosciutto

30 spears fresh asparagus,
uniform size, stalks trimmed
6 large slices prosciutto
½ cup freshly grated
Parmesan cheese

½ cup bread crumbs
½ cup melted butter
Freshly ground pepper, to taste
Paprika

Steam asparagus for 5 minutes or until just tender. (Do not overcook!) Wrap 5 stalks in each slice of prosciutto, leaving the tips showing. Place individual bundles in buttered shallow baking dish and sprinkle with cheese and bread crumbs. Drizzle melted butter over all and season. Asparagus can be prepared to this point, refrigerated, and brought to room temperature before heating. When ready to serve, bake uncovered in preheated 350° oven for 10 minutes.

Fillet of Sole Bienville

6 fillets of sole, about 8 ounces
each

Lemon pepper
Garlic salt
Parsley

Use fillets approximately 8 ounces each, or two 3- to 4-ounce fillets per person. Season each fillet with remaining ingredients. Roll fillet and secure with picks. Right before serving, poach each fillet in Court Bouillon #2 for about 7 to 8 minutes, until fish flakes easily. Be careful not to overcook as fish will fall apart.

Court Bouillon #2:

4 cups chicken broth
2 cups dry white wine
Several stalks celery

Several carrots
Fresh parsley
1 whole onion

Bring all ingredients to boil. (It is not necessary to cook bouillon ahead of time.) Add rolled fish filets and cook on medium heat for 7 to 8 minutes.

Sauce Bienville:

16 scallions, chopped, tops
  included
½ pound mushrooms,
  chopped
4 tablespoons flour
1½ cups chicken broth
3 egg yolks
¾ cup dry white wine
1 to 2 teaspoons salt
½ teaspoon freshly ground
  black pepper
¼ to ½ teaspoon cayenne
2 cups cooked shrimp, chopped
  (use shrimp that is as fresh as
  possible, not bagged, frozen,
  cooked type)
Bread crumbs
Paprika
Lemon slices, for garnish
Cherry tomatoes *or* whole
  baked, seasoned tomatoes, for
  garnish

Sauté scallions and mushrooms lightly in butter. Blend in flour and gradually add broth. Beat egg yolks with wine and add to mix, stirring constantly until thickened. Add seasonings and combine. Sauce may be made to this point and then refrigerated up to a day. When ready to serve, bring to room temperature, add cooked shrimp, and reheat gently.

Pour over poached fillets and sprinkle with bread crumbs and a little paprika. Garnish with lemon slices and cherry tomatoes or whole baked, seasoned tomatoes.

Basil Rice

¼ pound butter
1 large onion, chopped
½ pound mushrooms, sliced
1 cup brown rice
1 cup white rice
1½ cups dry white wine, plus
  more if needed
2½ cups chicken broth
½ cup grated Parmesan cheese
¼ cup heavy cream
2 tablespoons chopped fresh
  basil
¼ teaspoon dried sage
1 tablespoon dried oregano
¼ cup chopped fresh parsley
2 tablespoons bread crumbs
Salt and freshly ground black
  pepper, to taste
Tomatoes (optional)

Melt butter and sauté onion and mushrooms until tender. Add both rices, wine, and broth and bring to boil. Cover and simmer about 45 minutes or until rice is tender and most of liquid is absorbed. Add cheese, cream, herbs, bread crumbs, salt, and pepper. This dish is also good stuffed into baked seasoned tomatoes.

Garden Green Beans

1½ pounds fresh green beans, trimmed and uniform size
½ cup chopped scallions, tops included
6 tablespoons butter

2 cloves garlic, minced
½ cup minced celery
½ cup minced fresh parsley
½ teaspoon dried rosemary
1 teaspoon dried basil

¾ teaspoon salt, or to taste

Steam green beans until barely tender, drain, and return to pan. Slightly sauté scallions in butter, then combine all other ingredients and add to green beans. They can be prepared to this point and then reheated gently for a few minutes when ready to serve.

Brownie Tart

Crust:

1 cup all-purpose flour
¼ cup firmly packed brown sugar
1 ounce unsweetened chocolate, grated

¼ pound well-chilled butter, cut into ½-inch pieces
2 tablespoons milk
1 teaspoon vanilla extract

Combine flour, sugar, and grated chocolate in large bowl. Cut in butter with a fork until mixture resembles coarse meal. Mix in milk and vanilla until blended. Pat pastry onto bottom and sides of a 10-inch tart pan.

Note: Can be refrigerated overnight.

Filling:

3 ounces unsweetened chocolate
3 ounces semisweet chocolate
¼ pound butter, cut into tablespoon-size pieces, room temperature

1⅓ cups sugar
3 eggs, beaten to blend
2 teaspoons vanilla extract
¾ cup all-purpose flour

Melt chocolate in top of double boiler over hot water. Remove from heat, stir in butter, one piece at a time. Transfer to large bowl. Add sugar and blend well. Cool. Add beaten egg, ⅓ at a time, blending well after each addition. Mix in vanilla extract. Gradually add flour, blending well. Pour into pastry shell and bake for 20 to 25 minutes in preheated 350° oven. Cool.

Icing:

2 ounces semisweet chocolate, melted

2 tablespoons butter, at room temperature

1 teaspoon vegetable oil

Melt chocolate, butter, and oil together and spread over tart after it is slightly cooled. Confectioners' sugar and chopped walnuts may be substituted for icing.

Charlotte Russe with Raspberry Sauce

Raspberry Sauce:
(Makes 2½ cups)

2 10-ounce packages frozen raspberries
3 tablespoons sugar

1 tablespoon lemon juice
¼ cup water
1 teaspoon cornstarch

Defrost raspberries and purée in processor. Add sugar and lemon juice to purée. Place in medium-large saucepan over medium-high heat. Blend water and cornstarch. Stir into berry mixture and bring to a boil, stirring constantly. Reduce heat and stir until slightly thickened (about 5 minutes). Strain sauce through fine sieve and let cool.

Charlotte Russe:

8 eggs, room temperature, separated
¾ cup sugar
2 envelopes unflavored gelatin
¼ cup cold water
3 teaspoons lemon juice
½ cup Raspberry Sauce

¼ cup dry sherry
Pinch of cream of tartar
2 cups whipping cream
1½ to 2 packs ladyfingers
1 10-ounce package frozen raspberries (or 1 cup fresh)

Beat the yolks with sugar in a large bowl until pale yellow, about 7 minutes. Sprinkle gelatin over cold water and let stand for 5 minutes in small pan of hot water or microwave to dissolve. Stir lemon juice into the ½ cup of Raspberry Sauce. Stir sherry into yolks and blend in the lemon juice and raspberry mixture. Stir in gelatin in thin steady stream. In another bowl, beat egg whites with cream of tartar until stiff. Gently fold into berry mixture. Whip cream until soft peaks form and fold into berry mixture.

Lightly grease bottom and sides of 9-inch springform pan. Line bottom and sides with ladyfingers, rounded side out. Pour filling into pan, smoothing top. Cover surface with wax paper and foil and refrigerate overnight.

In morning, defrost frozen raspberries. To serve, remove sides of springform pan, place Charlotte on a large, rimmed platter, pour remaining Raspberry Sauce over top, and garnish with fresh or defrosted whole berries.

Maypole Plenty

Scallops with Tomato and Garlic
Avocado Soup
Roast Lamb with Rosemary
Saucy Carrots
Tabouleh
Crisp-fried Pastry
Gourmet Strawberry
Dip

PREVIOUS DAY	EARLY MORNING	FREEZER
Avocado Soup	Roast Lamb	
Tabouleh	Gourmet Strawberry	
Crisp-fried Pastry	Dip	

Scallops with Tomato and Garlic

1½ pounds sea scallops
¼ cup milk
Salt and freshly ground pepper, to taste
½ cup flour
2 tablespoons olive oil
2 cups Italian tomatoes, drained and coarsely chopped

2 tablespoons chopped fresh basil (or 3 teaspoons dried)
6 tablespoons corn oil
3 tablespoons butter
1 tablespoon finely chopped garlic
2 tablespoons finely chopped parsley

Put scallops in mixing bowl and add milk, salt, and pepper. Put flour in a flat dish. Heat olive oil in heavy skillet. Add tomatoes, salt, and pepper. Heat to boil, and cook 5 minutes. Add basil and remove from heat. Heat corn oil in large skillet that will hold scallops in a single layer. Drain scallops but do not pat dry. Dredge scallops in flour and shake off excess. Cook scallops in hot oil about 3 minutes or until golden brown on one side. Turn, cook 3 to 5 minutes on second side.

Pour heated tomato sauce into fairly wide serving dish. As scallops are cooked, place them on top of sauce. Pour off fat from skillet and wipe skillet out. Add butter to skillet and cook, swirling, until it starts to brown. Add garlic and pour over scallops immediately. Sprinkle with chopped parsley and serve.

Avocado Soup

4 ripe avocados
2 cups milk
2½ cups canned condensed chicken broth

¾ teaspoon celery salt
Salt and pepper, to taste
Snipped chives, for garnish

Peel avocados, remove pits, and blend in a food processor until smooth. Pour milk through feed tube and blend until smooth. Pour into a bowl, stir in chicken broth and seasonings, and mix well. Chill several hours. Serve cold with snipped chives as garnish.

Roast Lamb with Rosemary

1 8- to 9-pound leg of lamb
1 clove garlic, slivered
3 or 4 sprigs fresh rosemary (or
  1½ teaspoons dried)
3 to 4 tablespoons olive oil
Salt and freshly ground black
  pepper

Instant flour, to thicken gravy
1 10-ounce can condensed beef
  broth
4 tablespoons red wine
Parsley sprigs, for garnish

With sharp knife, remove *all* fat from top, underside, and between muscles and near bone of lamb, cutting away as little meat as possible. Insert peeled garlic slivers into crevices between muscles. Do same with rosemary, reserving ½ teaspoon or a sprig for roasting pan. Pour oil into roasting pan and heat for 10 minutes in preheated 400° oven. When oil is crackling, place lamb meaty side down in pan and roast for 10 minutes. Turn meaty side up and season with salt and pepper. Reduce heat to 350° and cook 45 to 50 minutes for rare roast. Add 20 minutes for pink lamb and 45 for well done. Remove roast to warmed platter, allow to set 5 minutes, then carve. Slice very thin. Make gravy by adding fine ground instant flour to pan drippings and stir over high heat on top of stove, using wire whisk. Add heated beef broth, stir, allow to rethicken, and check seasoning. Add wine and any juice from carved lamb to mixture. Serve gravy with carved lamb.

Note: Lamb can be roasted in morning and reheated in 275° oven before serving. Garnish platter with fresh parsley.

Saucy Carrots

4 cups carrots, cut into 1-inch
  pieces
¾ cup scallions, cut into 1-
  inch pieces

4 tablespoons butter or
  margarine
2 tablespoons honey
1½ teaspoons salt

Fresh watercress, for garnish

Cook carrots in boiling water until tender. Add scallions and cook 2 minutes. Drain well. Stir in the butter, honey, and salt, and heat well. Before serving, garnish with watercress.

Tabouleh

1 1-pound box rice or wheat
  pilaf
1 to 3 tomatoes, cut in small
  pieces
8 scallions, chopped
1 green bell pepper, chopped
Chopped parsley

Chopped mint leaves
Salt and freshly ground black
  pepper, to taste
Lemon juice, to taste
3 tablespoons bottled Italian
  dressing
Romaine lettuce (optional)

Cook pilaf according to directions on box. Add other ingredients. Cover and refrigerate at least 24 hours. Serve with crackers. Can also be served as a salad, on romaine leaves.

Crisp-fried Pastry
(Makes 3 to 4 dozen)

2¼ cups flour
2 large eggs
2 egg yolks
2 tablespoons dark rum

1 tablespoon superfine sugar
⅛ teaspoon salt
Oil, for deep frying
Confectioners' sugar, to taste

Place flour, eggs, egg yolks, rum, 1 tablespoon sugar, and salt in food processor with metal blade, and knead until a ball forms, then refrigerate for 1 to 2 hours. Use a pasta machine to produce paper-thin dough and cut with a sharp knife into 7-inch strips. If not using pasta machine, roll out on floured board to a ⅛-inch thickness and then cut into strips. Tie strips loosely in knots. Deep fry 4 or 5 at a time until lightly browned. Remove with slotted spoon, drain, and sprinkle with confectioners' sugar.

Store in an airtight container.

Gourmet Strawberry Dip

4 tablespoons sour cream
4 tablespoons frozen whipped
  topping
2 tablespoons brown sugar

1 tablespoon Grand Marnier
2 tablespoons orange curaçao
½ tablespoon dark rum
1½ quarts large strawberries

Fold first 2 ingredients together and add remaining ingredients one at a time, whisking gently. Serve in individual small bowls. Wash and hull strawberries and serve in a big bowl.

Dinner Printemps

Salmon Tartare
Cream of Watercress Soup
Endive Mimosa with Mustard Vinaigrette
Grilled Beef Tenderloin
Vegetables with Lemon-Shallot Butter
Gumbo Rice
Broiled Tomatoes
Baked Brie with Apples
Meringue Torte

PREVIOUS DAY	EARLY MORNING	FREEZER
Mustard Vinaigrette	*Watercress Soup*	
Shallot Butter	*Prepare vegetables*	
Meringue Torte	*Tomato-cheese mix*	

Salmon Tartare

1½ pounds fresh salmon
   fillets, skinned
3 scallions, minced
⅓ teaspoon minced garlic
3 teaspoons each cognac, lemon
   juice, and minced parsley

1½ teaspoons capers
¾ teaspoon Dijon mustard
⅓ teaspoon each coarse salt
   and freshly ground pepper
Lettuce, for garnish
Thin toast or melba toast

Trim all fat, skin, and membranes from salmon. Remove all bones
with tweezer. Coarsely chop salmon, add scallions and garlic, and
chop together. Transfer mixture to a medium bowl. Stir in remaining
ingredients through pepper. Taste and adjust seasonings. Refrigerate,
covered, for 1 hour. Put on platter lined with lettuce leaves and serve
with toast. Should be prepared only 1 hour before serving.

Cream of Watercress Soup

7 shallots, chopped	3 chicken bouillon cubes
2 tablespoons butter	3 cups boiling water
3 large bunches watercress, finely	Salt and freshly ground black
chopped	pepper, to taste
3 tablespoons flour	2 egg yolks
5 cups chicken broth	¾ cup cream

Cook shallots in butter for 5 minutes. Do not allow to brown. Add watercress and cook slowly 10 to 15 minutes. Sprinkle in flour and mix well. Add broth, cubes, and water and simmer for 15 minutes. Season to taste.

Just before serving, heat soup, combine egg yolks with cream, pour into soup and serve. If serving cold, omit the egg yolks. Decorate with whole pieces of watercress.

Endive Mimosa with Mustard Vinaigrette

2 heads endive	8 radishes
	6 hard-cooked eggs

On individual salad plates, arrange well-cleaned crisp endive. Slice radishes and arrange on endive. Coarsely chop hard-cooked eggs and sprinkle over radishes and endive. Serve with Mustard Vinaigrette.

Mustard Vinaigrette:

2 tablespoons Dijon mustard	1 shallot, diced
1 cup olive oil	1 teaspoon salt
½ cup wine vinegar	½ teaspoon oregano
1 clove garlic, diced	¼ teaspoon pepper
1 stalk hearts of palm, sliced very thin	

Combine all ingredients and refrigerate several days (at least 2) to develop flavor before serving.

Grilled Beef Tenderloin

¼ pound butter	1 whole, trimmed beef
3 cloves garlic, minced	tenderloin, 4 to 5 pounds
	Salt and pepper

Melt butter and add minced garlic. Brush butter mixture on meat. Sprinkle with salt and pepper. Grill for 25 minutes (for rare meat) on covered grill. Baste and turn twice or more during cooking.

Vegetables with Lemon-Shallot Butter

1½ tablespoons minced shallots	3 tablespoons chopped parsley (optional)
2 lemons, including zest and juice	2 pounds small red potatoes, scrubbed
½ pound unsalted butter	2 12-ounce packages fresh baby carrots, peeled and trimmed
Salt and freshly ground black pepper, to taste	2 pounds snow peas, trimmed

In small bowl, place shallots, lemon zest and juice, butter, salt, pepper, and parsley and mix until well combined. Set aside. Cook vegetables in separate pots of boiling water until just tender. Potatoes will cook in 15 to 20 minutes, carrots in 5 to 10 minutes, and snow peas in 1 to 3 minutes. While vegetables are cooking, heat lemon-shallot butter in a saucepan over medium heat until bubbly. Pour into sauceboat and keep warm. Drain vegetables and arrange on platter or around roast. Pass lemon-shallot butter separately.

Gumbo Rice

1 10½-ounce can condensed chicken gumbo soup	1½ cups long grain white rice
1½ 10½-ounce cans condensed consommé	6 tablespoons butter or margarine
	1 tablespoon seasoned salt

Put all ingredients together in casserole. Cover and bake 1 hour in preheated 350° oven. To microwave, cook on high for 15 to 17 minutes, stir.

Broiled Tomatoes

8 ounces cream cheese	½ teaspoon grated onion
4 ounces blue cheese	2 drops Worcestershire sauce
1 tablespoon sherry	Salt, to taste
1 tablespoon cream	6 tomatoes
2 tablespoons chopped parsley	Fine dry bread crumbs
Paprika	

Mix first 8 ingredients together. Cut tomatoes in half and spread cut sides with cheese mix. Sprinkle with bread crumbs and dust with paprika. Broil slowly until crumbs are nicely browned.

Baked Brie with Apples

1 6- to 8-inch Brie at room temperature	1 tablespoon butter
3 ounces sliced almonds, lightly toasted	3 to 4 Granny Smith apples
	Lemon juice

Place Brie in 10-inch quiche pan. Spread almonds and butter on cheese and bake in preheated 350° oven for 15 minutes. Let stand for 10 minutes. Slice apples with apple cutter so slices will be uniform and dip into lemon juice to prevent discoloration. Arrange apples around Brie and serve.

Meringue Torte

6 egg whites	1½ pints whipping cream
1½ teaspoons vinegar	4 tablespoons confectioners' sugar
1½ cups granulated sugar	
1½ teaspoons vanilla extract	1½ teaspoons vanilla extract
Pinch of salt	1 pound Heath bars, crushed

On the day prior to serving, beat egg whites until almost stiff. Add vinegar, sugar, vanilla, and salt. Draw three 9-inch circles on wax paper. Place wax paper on cookie sheet. Fill each circle with meringue mix. Bake at 275° for one hour, or until firm, crisp, and lightly browned. Leave meringue out overnight.

In the morning, beat together whipping cream, confectioners' sugar, and vanilla until stiff. Fold in crushed candy bars. Reserve ¼ cup candy to decorate top. Spread cream mixture between the 3 meringue layers. Refrigerate.

Louisiana Delight

Piquant Almond Spread
Asparagus and Celery Française with Garlic French Dressing
Shrimp Creole with White Rice
Marinated Vegetables
Processor French Bread
Bananas Foster, Louisianne

PREVIOUS DAY	EARLY MORNING	FREEZER
Asparagus and Celery marinade *Marinate vegetables* *French Bread*	*Almond Spread*	

Piquant Almond Spread

¼ cup blanched almonds, chopped and roasted
3 ounces cream cheese
¼ cup sweet pickle relish, drained

Dash of pepper sauce
Salt, to taste
½ teaspoon horseradish
Mayonnaise (enough to make spreading consistency)
Crackers
Paprika, for garnish

Combine first 7 ingredients and mix well. Spread on crackers. Sprinkle with paprika.

Asparagus and Celery Française

2 celery hearts
Chicken broth or consommé
¾ cup Garlic French Dressing
1 10-ounce package frozen asparagus
2 cups salad greens

2 hard-cooked eggs, chopped or grated
Freshly ground black pepper, to taste
12 cherry tomatoes or 2 medium tomatoes, cut into wedges

Remove outer ribs from celery and cut off most of the leaves. Simmer in broth or consommé to cover, until just tender. Cool in the broth. Split the celery in half lengthwise. Marinate in Garlic French Dressing overnight in refrigerator. Cook asparagus according to package directions, drain, and cool. Marinate with celery for 1 hour. When ready to serve, arrange on salad greens. Sprinkle a little dressing on the greens. Top with chopped eggs down center of asparagus, sprinkle with pepper, and arrange tomatoes around outer edge.

Garlic French Dressing:
(Makes 4 cups)

1 cup sugar	½ cup grated onion
1 cup ketchup	1 clove garlic, minced
2 cups corn oil	1 teaspoon salt
	1½ tablespoons paprika

Combine all ingredients in a jar and shake well. May be mixed in an electric blender. Place in refrigerator for 2 days before serving.

Shrimp Creole

4½ tablespoons butter or margarine	Salt and freshly ground black pepper, to taste
3 tablespoons flour	1 to 1½ teaspoons dried basil
3 garlic cloves, minced	4 teaspoons sugar
1½ cups chopped onions	3 pounds raw, shelled shrimp, frozen or fresh
1 cup chopped green pepper	
¾ cup sliced mushrooms	1½ tablespoons chopped parsley
2 15-ounce cans tomato sauce with tomato bits	Hot pepper sauce, to taste

Melt butter in large skillet. Add flour and brown to make a roux. Add garlic, onions, and green pepper, and cook until onions are transparent. Add mushrooms, tomato sauce, salt, pepper, basil, and sugar. Simmer, covered, for 15 minutes to blend flavors, stirring occasionally. If too thick, add up to 1 cup water before adding shrimp. Add shrimp and simmer, covered, until they turn pink. Add parsley and hot pepper sauce and keep warm until ready to serve with white rice, prepared according to the directions on the package.

Marinated Vegetables

1 pound summer squash
½ pound cauliflower, cut into
   small pieces
3 cups artichoke hearts (*not*
   marinated), drained and rinsed
1 small can sliced black olives

2 pounds fresh mushrooms,
   whole
½ red onion, sliced
1 8-ounce bottle Italian dressing
3 teaspoons Dijon mustard
2 avocados

Juice of 1 lemon

Cut squash into ½-inch slices. Parboil squash and cauliflower. (Can be blanched in microwave.) Cut artichokes into three pieces each. Drain olives. Mix all ingredients except avocados and lemon juice, and marinate overnight. Slice avocado an hour before serving and mix with lemon juice. Add to mixture and combine well.

Processor French Bread

2 to 2½ cups flour, combined
   with
1½ cups cake flour
1 package active dry yeast

1 cup warm water
2 teaspoons salt
1 egg white
2 tablespoons water

Grease cookie sheet and sprinkle with corn meal.

Place ½ of flour in processor bowl. Dissolve yeast in water and add ½ cup of mixture to flour. Using steel knife, turn machine on-off 4 times. Add rest of liquid. Turn machine on and off. Add ¾ of remaining flour and 1 teaspoon salt. Turn on-off 4 times. Turn on and leave running until dough forms a ball. Place in oiled bowl, cover with damp cloth. Let rise until doubled, about 1½ hours. Pummel dough flat on floured board and roll up into a cigar shape. Place diagonally on cookie sheet with seam on bottom. Let rise again until double. Cut slits across top. Using a fork, mix egg white, 2 tablespoons water, and remaining salt in a small bowl; brush bread with glaze. Bake in preheated 400° oven for approximately 30 minutes with a pan of hot water on the shelf underneath.

Note: Can be prepared in morning or frozen after baking.

Bananas Foster, Louisianne

12 tablespoons butter (1½ sticks)	6 bananas, halved lengthwise, then quartered
1½ cups dark brown sugar	2 ounces banana liqueur
1½ teaspoons cinnamon	1 cup dark rum, warmed
1 quart French vanilla ice cream	

In a flat skillet or flambé pan, melt and stir together butter, sugar, and cinnamon over low heat. When blended, add bananas and liqueur. Cook just to coat bananas, stirring gently. Add rum, making sure all rum is in pan, and then ignite. Baste fruit with sauce until flame dies. Serve over ice cream.

Around-the-World Dinner

Peppy Shrimp Spread
Cho-Cho Beef Sticks
Honey and Curry Glazed Chicken
Turban of Wild Rice
Cold Broccoli with Cashews
Sesame Ring
Oranges Mexicano
Peanut Bar Cookies

PREVIOUS DAY	EARLY MORNING	FREEZER
Peppy Shrimp Spread	Oranges Mexicano	Cho-Cho Beef
Chicken sauce		Cookies
Wild Rice		

Peppy Shrimp Spread

1 8-ounce package cream cheese	Garlic salt
3 tablespoons sour cream	Onion salt
2 tablespoons horseradish	6 ounces cooked shrimp, finely chopped
5 drops Worcestershire sauce	Melba rounds
5 drops Tabasco sauce	

Mix cream cheese, sour cream, and seasonings in processor until creamy. Stir in shrimp. Refrigerate several hours or overnight. Serve with melba rounds.

Cho-Cho Beef Sticks

½ cup soy sauce
1 cup dry sherry
1 cup chopped fresh ginger
1½ cups honey

½ cup oyster sauce
2 cloves garlic, chopped
⅓ cup brown sugar
1½ pounds flank steak

Combine all ingredients except beef. Heat on low flame for 5 to 7 minutes. Set aside. Slice flank steak into paper-thin slices and put on individual 5-inch bamboo sticks that have been soaked in water for 30 minutes. (Soaking skewers prevents splintering and burning.) Pour sauce over skewered steak and marinate for 1 hour.

Place skewers in foil broiling pans and broil approximately 5 minutes until done. Turn once during cooking. Freezes well.

Honey and Curry Glazed Chicken

3 pounds boned chicken breasts,
    washed, skinned, and dried
4 tablespoons butter, melted
½ cup honey

¼ cup prepared mustard
½ to 1 teaspoon curry
    powder, to taste

Breasts can be whole or split. Combine butter and all other ingredients. Roll chicken in mixture to coat. Arrange in a single layer in a baking dish. Pour remaining sauce over chicken. Bake in preheated 375° oven, 40 minutes to 1 hour for whole breasts or 30 to 40 minutes for halves.

Note: Sauce can be prepared a day in advance and refrigerated.

Turban of Wild Rice

1 cup chopped celery
1 medium onion, chopped
1 pound fresh mushrooms, sliced
½ cup raisins

½ cup slivered almonds
12 tablespoons butter (not
    margarine!) (1½ sticks)
3 cups wild rice

6 cups chicken broth

Sauté vegetables, raisins, and almonds in butter and set aside. Cook rice in chicken broth according to package directions. Combine vegetables and rice and place mixture in lightly greased 2-quart casserole. Bake in preheated 350° oven approximately 30 minutes.

Cold Broccoli with Cashews

2 pounds fresh broccoli	Salt and freshly ground black
½ cup olive oil	pepper, to taste
¼ cup lemon juice	1 teaspoon dried chervil

½ cup salted cashews, coarsely broken

Cook broccoli until just tender. Place in serving dish. Combine oil, juice, and seasonings and pour over broccoli. Refrigerate until chilled (2 to 3 hours). Just before serving sprinkle with cashews.

Sesame Ring

1 package active dry yeast	2 teaspoons salt
1¼ cups lukewarm water	2 tablespoons melted butter
4 to 4½ cups all-purpose flour	1 egg yolk
1 egg	4 tablespoons sesame seeds

Dissolve yeast in ¼ cup of the water and let proof for about 10 minutes. Pour 4 cups of flour into large electric mixing bowl with dough hook. Add the egg, yeast, remaining water, salt, and butter, and knead until dough is smooth and elastic. A little more flour can be added to make a stiff dough. Form dough into ball and put into large oiled bowl, turning to coat on all sides. Cover with towel and let rise until doubled, about an hour. Punch down, knead a few turns, and form into as smooth a ball as possible. Pull dough carefully into an even doughnut shape, pulling up dough from the sides into a pinched circular seam on top. Place in a buttered, 10-inch metal pie pan or on a buttered cookie sheet. Cover with towel and let rise until nearly double. Brush top with beaten egg yolk and sprinkle liberally with sesame seeds. Bake in preheated 375° oven for about 50 minutes.

Oranges Mexicano

3 large seedless oranges	2 tablespoons freshly squeezed
2 tablespoons confectioners'	lime juice
sugar	1½ ounces tequila

¾ ounce Cointreau or Triple Sec

Peel oranges and slice into rounds. If membranes are not tender, section them and remove membranes. Sprinkle with sugar, add the lime juice, and gently mix. Marinate in the refrigerator. Just before serving, add the liqueurs and stir together. Serve in stemmed glasses.

Peanut Bar Cookies
(Makes 48)

1½ cups brown sugar	2 cups dry roasted peanuts
½ pound butter (2 sticks)	½ cup light corn syrup
3 cups flour	2 tablespoons butter
1 teaspoon salt	1 tablespoon water

1 cup butterscotch chips

Blend sugar and ½ pound butter until well combined. Slowly add combined flour and salt. Mixture will appear grainy. Press into an ungreased 15-by-10-inch jelly-roll pan. Bake in preheated 350° oven for 10 to 12 minutes, remove from oven, and sprinkle with nuts. Combine corn syrup, 2 tablespoons butter, water, and chips and boil for 2 minutes, stirring constantly. Pour over batter and bake an additional 10 to 12 minutes. Cool before cutting into bars.

Summer Company

Honeydew Drink
Coconut Chicken with Plum Sauce
Russian Spinach Salad
Salmon Steak Teriyaki
Stuffed Snow Peas
Nutty Pasta
Parmesan Triangles
Cold Raspberry Soufflé
Graham Wafers

PREVIOUS DAY	EARLY MORNING	FREEZER
Salad dressing	*Snow Peas*	*Coconut Chicken*
Raspberry Soufflé	*Pasta sauce*	
Graham Wafers	*Pasta vegetables*	

Honeydew Drink
(Serves 4)

1 ripe honeydew melon, halved and seeded	1 egg white
Juice of 5 limes	1½ cups crushed ice
2 tablespoons sugar	3 ounces Midori melon liqueur
	3 ounces light rum

Scoop out flesh and discard the rind from half the melon. Dice the flesh and put it into a blender or processor with lime juice, sugar, and egg white. Blend until smooth. Add ice, liqueur, and rum and blend for 1 minute. Pour into chilled, stemmed glasses. Garnish with thin slice of honeydew.

Coconut Chicken with Plum Sauce
(Makes about 60 strips)

6 whole chicken breasts, skinned and boned, cut into strips	¼ teaspoon ground ginger
1 teaspoon onion powder	2 cups sifted flour
⅓ cup lemon juice	2 teaspoons baking powder
1 teaspoon salt	1½ cups milk
1 teaspoon curry powder, or to taste	2 7-ounce packages unsweetened coconut
	3 cups vegetable oil

Pound chicken. Combine next 5 ingredients. Add chicken and stir to coat well. Marinate 30 minutes. Combine flour, baking powder, and milk. Beat until smooth (batter will be very thick). Drain excess marinade into batter. Dredge the chicken with flour, dip in batter, and roll in coconut. Heat oil to 375°. Fry chicken until golden brown. Serve with Oriental plum sauce or Sweet-and-Sour sauce (see Index). Freezes well (freeze and thaw in a single layer).

Russian Spinach Salad

2 pounds fresh spinach
1 cup salad oil
¼ cup sugar
⅓ cup ketchup
¼ cup vinegar
½ cup mayonnaise
1 tablespoon Worcestershire
  sauce

1 medium onion, chopped
Salt, to taste
½ pound mushrooms, cleaned
  and sliced (optional)
6 strips bacon, cooked until crisp
2 hard-cooked eggs, chopped

Wash spinach, dry thoroughly, and refrigerate in plastic bag until just before serving. Make dressing with next 8 ingredients. Mix well and store in refrigerator. To assemble salad, put spinach in salad bowl, add mushrooms, crumbled bacon, and chopped eggs. Add dressing to taste (one-half may be sufficient).

Salmon Steak Teriyaki

6 salmon steaks
⅓ cup cooking oil
3 tablespoons lemon juice

3 tablespoons soy sauce
¾ teaspoon dry mustard
¾ teaspoon ground ginger

1 teaspoon garlic powder

Place salmon steaks in shallow pan. Combine oil, lemon juice, soy sauce, mustard, ginger, and garlic powder. Pour over steaks. Let stand at room temperature for 1 hour, turning once. Drain. Reserve marinade. Place steaks on broiler pan, broil 3 inches from heat, turn, brush with marinade, and broil 5 minutes more.

Note: Can also be grilled on barbecue.

Stuffed Snow Peas

50 snow peas

½ pound Boursin

Remove stems from peas and string them. Blanch in boiling water for 30 seconds. Plunge into cold water and then drain. Using a small, sharp knife, slit the seam of each pod. Spread softened cheese into each pea pod and arrange on a platter.

Nutty Pasta

½ cup part-skim ricotta
1½ tablespoons Dijon
   mustard
½ teaspoon salt
¼ teaspoon freshly ground
   black pepper
8 ounces plain low-fat yogurt
1 pound pasta wheels

1 tablespoon vegetable oil
½ cup grated Parmesan
2 small zucchini, diced
2 large ripe tomatoes, diced
¼ cup finely chopped scallions
   or chives
¼ cup fresh mixed herbs
   (chervil, parsley, thyme)

½ cup shelled unsalted pistachios

Blend ricotta in food processor until very smooth. Blend in mustard, salt, and pepper. Add yogurt and process briefly. Empty into bowl, cover, and refrigerate. Sauce should be texture of mayonnaise. Cook pasta in boiling water until al dente. Drain and toss with oil and cheese in a large bowl. Add zucchini, tomatoes, scallions, and herbs. Just before serving, toss with sauce and sprinkle on pistachios.

Parmesan Triangles
(Makes 120)

2 cups all-purpose biscuit mix
⅓ cup butter or margarine,
   melted

1 cup grated Parmesan

Prepare biscuit mix as for rolled biscuits. On lightly floured surface, knead dough ten times. Roll out to a 10-by-6-inch rectangle. Cut into 1-inch squares and then cut each square in half diagonally. Dip triangles into melted butter and coat with cheese. Place on greased cookie sheet. Bake in preheated 450° oven for 6 to 8 minutes or until lightly browned. Serve warm.

Cold Raspberry Soufflé

3 tablespoons plain gelatin
   softened in ¾ cup cold
   water
3 10-ounce packages frozen
   raspberries
9 tablespoons sugar

1½ tablespoons fresh lemon
   juice
¼ cup kirsch
6 egg whites
¼ teaspoon salt
1½ cups whipping cream

Combine raspberries, 3 tablespoons of the sugar, lemon juice, and softened gelatin in a saucepan. Cook slowly until gelatin is dissolved. Cool the mixture, add kirsch, and chill until partially set, stirring every ten minutes. (This will take at least 1 hour.)

Beat the egg whites with the salt until soft peaks form, add the remaining sugar, and beat until smooth and glossy. Beat the whipping cream until stiff. Fold berries, cream, and whites together. Pour into a prepared soufflé dish, cover with plastic wrap, and refrigerate.

To prepare soufflé dish, take a 24-by-12-inch piece of foil and fold to form a 24-by-4-inch piece. Wrap the foil around the top edge of a 1½-quart soufflé dish and tape to fasten. The collar should extend about 2½ to 3 inches above the dish.

Note: Pretty served with fresh blueberries.

Graham Wafers

15 graham crackers, separated at perforations into 45 pieces
½ pound butter (no substitutions!)
½ cup sugar
1 4-ounce package sliced almonds

Butter cookie sheet and spread graham crackers to cover surface in a solid sheet. In a saucepan, melt butter and sugar. Bring to a boil and boil for 3 minutes exactly. Pour mixture over graham crackers and spread with a spatula. Sprinkle almonds over top. Bake in a preheated 325° oven for exactly 10 minutes. Remove from pan and cool on rack, making sure they do not touch. Cookies will become crisp. Store in an airtight container with wax paper or foil between layers.

Commencement Dinner

Onion Rounds
Zesty Shrimp
Salad with Blue Cheese Dressing
Rack of Lamb
Stuffed Eggplant Provençal
Tangy Rice
Pavlova with Raspberry Sauce

PREVIOUS DAY	EARLY MORNING	FREEZER
Zesty Shrimp	*Onion Rounds*	
Tangy Rice	*Rack of Lamb*	
Raspberry Sauce	*Stuffed Eggplant*	
Salad dressing		

Onion Rounds
(Serves 6 to 8)

1 2.8-ounce can French-fried onions	Worcestershire sauce, to taste
½ cup mayonnaise	Ritz crackers or melba rounds
	Grated Parmesan

Crush onions and mix with mayonnaise and Worcestershire. Spread on crackers or melba rounds. Sprinkle with Parmesan. Broil for 2 minutes. Serve warm. Can be prepared early in the day, put on flat pans, and broiled just before serving.

Zesty Shrimp

2 pounds fresh or frozen large shrimp, shelled and deveined	1 clove garlic, minced
½ cup cooking oil	1½ teaspoons salt
½ cup lime juice	½ teaspoon dried dill weed
3 tablespoons dry white wine	⅛ teaspoon bottled hot
1 tablespoon chopped chives	pepper sauce

Thaw shrimp if using frozen. Place in shallow baking dish. Mix cooking oil, lime juice, wine, chives, garlic, salt, dill weed, and hot pepper sauce. Pour this mixture over shrimp. Cover. Refrigerate 4 to 6 hours or overnight.

Remove shrimp, reserving the marinade, and put in a wire grill basket. Grill over high heat 8 minutes or until cooked, turning and brushing with reserved marinade often. Serve on wooden picks.

Note: Can also be served as a main dish. Can be cooked on barbecue grill.

Salad with Blue Cheese Dressing

3 quarts mixed greens: romaine, escarole, endive, Boston, or iceberg lettuce	1 cucumber, thinly sliced 2 large tomatoes, cut in thin wedges

Greens may be washed and prepared in bite-size pieces early in day. Be sure greens are dry before arranging in salad bowl. Arrange cucumber and tomato on top. Serve with Blue Cheese Dressing.

Blue Cheese Dressing:

¾ cup sour cream	⅓ teaspoon garlic powder
½ teaspoon each dry mustard, salt, and freshly ground black pepper	1 teaspoon Worcestershire sauce
	1⅓ cups mayonnaise
	4 ounces Danish blue cheese

Combine first 6 ingredients in mixing bowl; blend at low speed for 2 minutes. Add mayonnaise, blend ½ minute at low speed, then 2 minutes at medium speed. By hand, crumble cheese into small pieces and add. Blend at low speed no longer than 4 minutes. Chill overnight in refrigerator before serving.

Rack of Lamb

2 racks of lamb	¼ teaspoon salt
2 tablespoons chopped fresh parsley	4 tablespoons Dijon mustard
2 cloves garlic, minced	¼ teaspoon paprika
1 teaspoon dried thyme	4 tablespoons peanut oil
	½ cup bread crumbs
3 tablespoons melted butter	

Trim racks well and cover bones with foil. Score the tops. Whip parsley, garlic, thyme, salt, mustard, paprika, and oil in food processor and brush top of racks with this mixture. Can be done to this stage in the morning.

Heat oven to 500°, roast lamb for 10 minutes, remove from oven, and reduce heat to 400°. Sprinkle bread crumbs over tops of lamb and dribble with melted butter. Return to oven and roast for additional 15 minutes. Lamb will be pink on the inside.

Stuffed Eggplant Provençal

3 eggplants
2 medium onions, chopped (1 to 1½ cups)
2 cloves garlic, minced
4 to 6 tablespoons vegetable oil
12 ounces tomato sauce
1½ cups ripe olives, quartered
1 tablespoon thyme

1 tablespoon basil
¾ teaspoon salt
12 ounces Monterey Jack cheese, sliced
½ cup grated Parmesan
3 medium tomatoes, cut into wedges

Trim off stems and cut eggplants in half lengthwise. Prebake eggplants for 5 to 10 minutes, until soft enough to scoop out the pulp from the center of each half, leaving ½-inch shell. Cube the pulp and combine with onions, garlic, and oil in large skillet. Sauté, stirring, over medium-high heat for 10 minutes or until very tender. Eggplant will be soft and moist-looking when it is done. Mix in tomato sauce, olives, thyme, basil, and salt. Heat through. Spoon one-sixth the mixture into each shell and top with two slices Monterey Jack, sprinkled with Parmesan. Put tomato wedges on top and sprinkle with extra Parmesan. Oil the cut edges of the eggplant, if exposed. Place in baking pan and bake in preheated 400° oven for 20 to 25 minutes, until hot and bubbly.

Tangy Rice
(Serves 4)

3 cups hot or cold cooked rice
¾ cup raisins
¾ cup chopped nuts
¾ cup chopped ripe olives
3 tablespoons oil

Grated peel from 1 medium lemon
¾ teaspoon salt
½ teaspoon cinnamon
¼ teaspoon nutmeg

Mix all ingredients in order given, serve hot or cold.

Pavlova with Raspberry Sauce
(Serves 10 to 12)

4 egg whites at room temperature
⅛ teaspoon salt
1 cup sugar
1 tablespoon cornstarch

1 teaspoon white wine vinegar
1 teaspoon vanilla extract
1 pint heavy cream, whipped
Fresh fruit: apricots, nectarines, kiwi, peaches, etc., for garnish

Beat egg whites and salt until frothy on high speed of electric mixer. Add sugar, 1 tablespoon at a time. Mix last tablespoon of sugar with cornstarch and add to egg whites with vinegar and vanilla. Beat until very stiff peaks form. Cover a baking sheet with parchment paper or brown paper. Shape meringue into a 9- to 10-inch circle, mounding slightly. Place in preheated 400° oven. Immediately reduce temperature to 250°. Bake 1½ hours or until lightly brown and dry on surface. Remove from oven. Meringue will crack. This meringue is not solid and crisp all the way through. It has a semisoft center.

Cool completely. If desired, wrap airtight and store up to 24 hours at room temperature. Before serving, swirl whipped cream over meringue, covering it completely. Garnish with fruit. Accompany with Raspberry Sauce to be spooned over each serving.

Raspberry Sauce:

1 tablespoon cornstarch	¼ teaspoon vanilla extract
½ cup sugar	1 10-ounce package frozen
Salt	raspberries or 1½ to 2 cups
½ cup water	slightly crushed fresh
2 teaspoons lemon juice	raspberries

In a saucepan, blend together first 3 ingredients. Add water, lemon juice, and vanilla and stir well. Add berries. Cook, stirring, until sauce thickens. Cool, cover, and chill overnight, if desired.

Welcome to Biloxi

Artichoke Appetizer
Spicy Salmon Spread
Red Lettuce Salad with Basil Dressing
Veal Nancy
Spinach Dumplings with Italian Tomato Sauce
Miss Ruth's Praline Cookies
Lemon Angel Soufflé with Brandied Fluff Sauce

PREVIOUS DAY	EARLY MORNING	FREEZER
Basil Dressing	Spicy Salmon Spread	
Tomato Sauce	Spinach Dumplings	
Praline Cookies		
Lemon Soufflé		

Artichoke Appetizer

1 6-ounce jar marinated artichoke hearts (drained)	½ cup grated Parmesan
	¼ cup chopped onion
Dash of Worcestershire sauce	½ cup salad dressing

Coarsely chop artichokes and mix with remaining ingredients. Heat in preheated 350° oven for 15 to 20 minutes, until bubbly. Serve with fresh vegetables or crackers.

Spicy Salmon Spread

1 15½-ounce can salmon	2 teaspoons prepared horseradish
8 ounces cream cheese, softened	¼ teaspoon salt
1 tablespoon lemon juice	2 medium cucumbers, scrubbed
1 tablespoon chopped onion	and sliced in ¼-inch slices

Pinch of dill

Drain salmon, remove skin and bones. Stir in cheese, juice, onion, horseradish, and salt. Spread on cucumber slices and sprinkle with pinch of dill. Chill 4 hours or more.

Red Lettuce Salad with Basil Dressing

1 large head red leaf lettuce	6 slices bacon, cooked and
½ pint cherry tomatoes	crumbled
1 medium red onion, sliced thin	1 cup croutons

Wash lettuce and tear into bite-size pieces. Combine with rest of salad ingredients. Pour Basil Dressing over salad and serve immediately.

Basil Dressing:

½ cup mayonnaise	1 tablespoon sugar
2 tablespoons wine vinegar	1 tablespoon dried basil

Combine all dressing ingredients. If made in advance, store in airtight container.

Veal Nancy

½ teaspoon each dill weed,
celery salt, Italian herb
seasoning, and paprika
1 teaspoon garlic powder or
granules
1 4- to 5-pound veal shoulder
roast, boned and rolled
Flour, for dredging

Oil, for browning
3 to 4 carrots, cut in cubes
3 ribs celery, sliced
1 large onion, minced
2 tablespoons chopped fresh
parsley (or 1 tablespoon dried)
1 can tomato sauce with tomato
bits
1 bay leaf

Combine seasonings, dill weed through garlic powder. Roll the roast
in flour and then in combined seasonings. Sauté in oil in Dutch oven.
Brown on all sides. Remove from pan, add more oil if necessary, and
place vegetables and parsley in same pan. Sauté for about 2 minutes.
Place roast over the vegetables, pour tomato sauce over all. Add bay
leaf. Cover and roast in preheated 350° oven for 2½ to 3 hours.

Note: Vegetables can be pureéd to make a thicker gravy, or served
with the roast as is.

Spinach Dumplings

2 10-ounce packages frozen
spinach, defrosted and drained
1 pound ricotta
1 egg yolk
¾ cup flour
2 teaspoons dried oregano

2 teaspoons dried parsley
Salt and freshly ground black
pepper, to taste
1 tablespoon dried shallots (or 1
teaspoon onion powder)
½ cup grated Parmesan

Blend all ingredients except Parmesan in a food processor. Bring salted
water to a boil in a 6-quart pot. Form balls the size of walnuts from
the spinach mixture. Drop in boiling water about 10 at a time. If
mixture is sticky, chill it, uncovered (it also helps to use wet hands).
When dumplings rise to the top, remove with slotted spoon and put
in shallow greased baking dish. (Can be refrigerated at this time to
be baked before serving.) Pour Italian Tomato Sauce over, sprinkle
with Parmesan cheese, and bake for 15 minutes in preheated 325°
oven.

Variation: Good baked with the Parmesan alone, too.

Italian Tomato Sauce:

1 medium onion, chopped
½ green pepper, chopped
2 cloves garlic
2 tablespoons olive oil

6 ounces tomato paste
¼ cup minced fresh parsley
1 tablespoon oregano
1 bay leaf

¼ teaspoon salt

Cook onion, pepper, and garlic in olive oil for 5 minutes. Add the rest of the ingredients and simmer for 20 minutes. Discard bay leaf before using sauce.

Miss Ruth's Praline Cookies
(Makes 24 cookies)

1 cup firmly packed light brown
   sugar
1 tablespoon flour
¼ teaspoon salt

1 egg white
1 teaspoon vanilla extract
1½ cups pecan halves or large
   pieces of pecans

Sift brown sugar, flour, and salt together. With rotary beater, beat egg white in a small bowl just until stiff but not dry. With rubber spatula, fold in sugar mixture and vanilla. Gently fold together mixture and pecans, to coat pecans completely. Drop by spoonfuls on prepared greased cookie sheets. Bake in preheated 275° oven for 25 to 30 minutes, or until lightly browned. With spatula, remove cookies at once to wire rack to cool.

Lemon Angel Soufflé

2 envelopes unflavored gelatin
½ cup cold water
3 teaspoons grated lemon rind
8 eggs, separated

1 cup lemon juice
1 teaspoon salt
2 cups sugar
2 cups heavy cream

Fold a 30-inch piece of aluminum foil in half lengthwise and tie around outside of a 1½-quart soufflé dish as a collar. Sprinkle gelatin over cold water to soften. Grate lemon rind, then extract juice.

Combine egg yolks, lemon juice, salt, and 1 cup of the sugar in top of double boiler. Cook over boiling water, stirring constantly until slightly thickened and custardy. Remove from heat and add gelatin and lemon rind. Mix well. Turn into 3-quart bowl and let cool. Beat egg whites until they hold a shape and gradually beat in remaining cup sugar. Continue to beat until mixture holds peaks.

Whip cream until stiff. On top of lemon mixture pile stiffly beaten egg whites and whipped cream. Fold mixtures together gently. Pour into soufflé dish. Refrigerate at least 6 hours or overnight. Serve with Brandied Fluff Sauce.

Brandied Fluff Sauce:

1⅓ cups sifted confectioners' sugar	1 large egg, separated
¼ pound soft butter or margarine	2 tablespoons brandy
Salt	½ cup heavy cream, whipped
	Ground nutmeg, for garnish

In mixer, gradually cream sugar into butter. Beat salt into egg yolk and add to butter mixture. Stir all and cook over hot water 6 to 7 minutes or until mixture is light and fluffy. Add brandy. Beat egg white until it stands in soft, stiff peaks. Fold into the sauce along with whipped cream. Garnish with nutmeg.

Note: Also good on hot steamed puddings, plain cake, etc.

Company Chicken Dinner (Serves 10)

Bourbon Pâté with Homemade Melba Toast
Red Snapper Soup
Garlic Roast Chicken
Green Noodle Casserole
Grilled Vegetables
Trifle

PREVIOUS DAY	EARLY MORNING	FREEZER
Bourbon Pâté	*Snapper Soup*	*Green Noodle Casserole*
	Trifle	

Bourbon Pâté
(Makes 1½ to 2 cups)

½ pound butter
1 small onion, minced
1 pound chicken livers
1½ cups rich chicken broth,
   divided
2 tablespoons sherry
½ teaspoon paprika

⅛ teaspoon ground allspice
½ teaspoon salt
⅛ teaspoon liquid hot pepper
   sauce
1 clove garlic, minced
½ cup bourbon
1 cup chopped walnuts

1 envelope unflavored gelatin

Sauté first 3 ingredients for 5 to 7 minutes, add ¾ cup of the broth, sherry, paprika, allspice, salt, pepper sauce, garlic, whiskey, and nuts. Soften gelatin in additional ¾ cup broth and cook until dissolved. Put all ingredients into a blender and blend to desired smoothness. Chill in a crock for 12 hours. Serve with Homemade Melba Toast.

Homemade Melba Toast:
(Serves 10)

½ loaf thin-sliced home-style white bread

Trim sides of bread and slice in half diagonally. Spread pieces on cookie sheet, using as many as necessary. Bake in preheated 300° oven until light brown in color. Turn each piece over and brown on other side. Watch carefully so toast doesn't burn.

Red Snapper Soup
(Serves 10)

2 cups diced celery
2 cups diced onions
2 cloves garlic, crushed
6 tablespoons butter
1 cup tomato purée
2 teaspoons tomato paste

½ gallon fish stock
2 bay leaves
⅓ cup roux
1½ pounds fresh red snapper
   fillets, cubed
½ cup dry sherry

Salt and freshly ground black pepper, to taste

Using large soup pot, sauté the vegetables in butter until golden brown.

Add tomato purée and paste. Sauté with vegetables. Add fish stock and bay leaves. Bind soup with roux and cook for 45 minutes; add cubed red snapper and sherry and cook 15 to 20 minutes longer. Adjust seasoning. Does not freeze successfully.

Roux:

4 tablespoons butter   4 tablespoons flour

Melt butter in small frying pan. Add flour a tablespoon at a time, whisking to blend. Cook, stirring constantly, until thickened and reduced, 5 to 10 minutes.

Garlic Roast Chicken
(Serves 10)

4 broiler-fryers, cut into quarters   9 garlic cloves, crushed
½ pound parve margarine, or   2 teaspoons salt
   butter, softened and divided   1 teaspoon ground black pepper
½ cup olive oil

Rinse chicken and pat dry with paper towels. Combine ¼ pound of the margarine, all of the garlic, salt, and pepper, and mix in small bowl. Rub the entire chicken with this mixture.

Heat the remaining ¼ pound margarine with oil. Brush chicken with part of this mixture and place chicken in shallow pan in preheated 400° oven for 25 minutes. Remove from oven and turn, brushing again with oil mixture. Continue roasting for another 25 minutes, turning occasionally and brushing with pan drippings.

Green Noodle Casserole
(Serves 12)

8 ounces green spinach noodles,   8 ounces Cheddar, shredded
   cooked al dente   2 10-ounce packages frozen
6 eggs, beaten   chopped spinach, defrosted
2 pounds creamed cottage cheese   and squeezed dry
¼ pound butter, in chunks   2 tablespoons onions, minced
4 ounces mozzarella, shredded   Salt and garlic powder, to taste
½ cup buttered bread crumbs (optional)

Mix all ingredients and put into greased 9-by-12-inch glass dish. Cover with bread crumbs and bake in preheated 350° oven for 1 hour. Freezes well unbaked. If frozen, bake in preheated 350° oven for an additional 20 minutes.

Grilled Vegetables
(Serves 10)

½ pound whole medium-size mushrooms
½ pound pearl or small white onions
3 green peppers, halved, seeded, and quartered
¾ cup olive oil
¾ cup vegetable oil
½ cup red wine vinegar
3 tablespoons fresh lemon juice
1 teaspoon Dijon mustard
1 teaspoon dried oregano
½ teaspoon dried tarragon
¾ teaspoon salt
¼ teaspoon freshly ground black pepper

Wipe mushrooms clean with cloth and remove ¼ inch of stem. Place mushrooms, onions, and peppers in medium-size bowl and set aside. Combine remaining ingredients in bowl and pour over vegetables. Refrigerate 6 hours or overnight, turning occasionally. Soak bamboo skewers in water for approximately 30 minutes to soften. Spear vegetable chunks onto skewers and grill for 10 minutes, brushing occasionally with reserved marinade. Can also be broiled.

Trifle
(Serves 10)

1 sponge cake or angel food cake (9-inch tube pan size)
½ to ¾ cup sherry or Grand Marnier
1 3-ounce package instant vanilla pudding, made with ½ cup more milk than package directions call for
8 ounces raspberry jam or preserves
3 cups fruit (approximately): bananas, strawberries, blueberries, raspberries
1 cup whipping cream
3 tablespoons sugar
Fruit *or* grated semisweet chocolate, for garnish

In a 2-quart glass bowl arrange a layer of cake pieces torn into chunks.

Sprinkle with ¼ cup liqueur. Be sure each piece is moistened but not soaked. Pour 1 cup of pudding over this. Dot with half of the raspberry jam, cover with a layer of fruit, and repeat layers, reserving ½ cup of pudding to cover top layer of fruit.

This can be made in morning to this point. Three hours before serving, whip cream with sugar, spread over top of pudding, and refrigerate. Just before serving, garnish with fruit or grated chocolate.

Seaside Cuisine

Miniature Parmesan Tortes
Avocado Ring
Bibb Lettuce with Creamy Dressing
Island Grilled Halibut
Ginger-Glazed Carrots
Pilaf Italienne
Peach-Pear Pie
Chocolate Chip Pie

PREVIOUS DAY	EARLY MORNING	FREEZER
Avocado Ring	*Parmesan Tortes*	
Salad dressing	*Chocolate Chip Pie*	
Peach-Pear Pie		

Miniature Parmesan Tortes

½ cup ketchup
½ cup Worcestershire sauce
1 large loaf white bread, cut into
  small rounds

¼ cup mayonnaise
½ cup grated Parmesan

Combine first 2 ingredients and spread on half of the bread rounds. Combine remaining ingredients and spread on the rest of the bread rounds. Place mayonnaise rounds on top of ketchup rounds and brown under broiler.

Note: Rounds can be made with cookie cutter or small shot glass, refrigerated on cookie sheets after stacking, and broiled right before serving.

Avocado Ring

1½ tablespoons plain gelatin
¼ cup cold water
1 cup boiling water
1¼ teaspoons salt
1 teaspoon grated onion
Dash of Tabasco sauce
2 tablespoons fresh lemon juice
2½ cups sieved or mashed
  avocado (6 to 8 avocados)

1 cup sour cream
1 cup mayonnaise
Few drops green food coloring
  (optional)
Salad greens, for garnish
Fruit, for garnish

Soften gelatin in cold water and dissolve in boiling water. Blend in salt, onion, Tabasco, and lemon juice. Cool to room temperature. Add avocado, sour cream, and mayonnaise to cooled gelatin, and food coloring if desired. Turn into an 8-inch ring mold and chill until firm.

Unmold on serving plate and garnish with salad greens and fruit such as pineapple chunks and grapefruit and orange sections.

Bibb Lettuce Salad

2 or 3 heads Bibb lettuce   1 large red onion, sliced thin

Arrange lettuce on individual salad plates. Separate onion slices into rings and arrange on lettuce. Serve with Creamy Dressing.

Creamy Dressing:

⅓ cup red wine vinegar
⅓ cup half-and-half or light
  cream
¼ cup imported olive oil

1 heaping teaspoon salt
1 teaspoon freshly ground
  pepper
1 teaspoon minced garlic

Combine all ingredients and shake very well to mix. Refrigerate overnight to blend flavors.

Island Grilled Halibut

2 cloves garlic
¼ teaspoon freshly ground
   black pepper
4 tablespoons sugar

⅓ cup soy sauce
6 tablespoons sesame oil
2 bunches scallions, chopped
Sesame seeds

6 thick halibut steaks

Mix marinade ingredients and marinate steaks for several hours. Place steaks on grill and cook for 7 minutes on each side or until fish flakes easily.

Note: This marinade can also be used for shrimp.

Ginger-Glazed Carrots

1 pound fresh carrots, peeled
   and cut into 2- or 3-inch strips
1½ cups orange juice
½ cup light brown sugar

1½ tablespoons butter or
   margarine
1 tablespoon cornstarch
¼ cup cold water

½ teaspoon ground ginger

Steam carrots until tender but still crisp. Place in serving bowl and keep warm. Combine orange juice, sugar, and butter in saucepan. Heat almost until boiling. Dissolve cornstarch in water and add to orange-juice mixture. Stir and cook until clear and thick. Add ginger and pour over carrots, and toss.

Pilaf Italienne

4 tablespoons unsalted butter
1 medium onion, chopped
1 medium clove garlic, crushed

2 cups orzo (rice-shaped pasta)
2½ cups chicken stock, heated
   to a boil

½ cup grated Gruyère

Melt butter in skillet over low heat. Add onion and garlic. Cover and cook 10 minutes. Add orzo and stock. Cover and cook over low heat until liquid is absorbed. This may take from 25 to 40 minutes. Stir in cheese until melted. Serve hot.

Peach-Pear Pie

Pastry:

1 cup flour	1 egg yolk
Salt	1 tablespoon sugar
¼ pound butter or margarine, softened and cut in small pieces	Ice water

Mix flour and salt in a large bowl. Make a well in center. Place butter, yolk, and sugar in well. With fingers, mix until blended. Gradually work in flour, adding water if necessary, until dough is smooth and holds together. Shape into ball, wrap tightly, and chill at least 1 hour or until firm enough to roll. On well-floured surface, roll pastry into 11-inch circle. Carefully place in 9-inch quiche pan, flan ring, or pie plate. (If dough should break, press together to patch.) Trim edges as desired. Prick bottom at 1-inch intervals. Bake in preheated 375° oven for 20 minutes or until slightly browned. Cool in pan on rack.

Filling:

⅓ cup sugar	1½ teaspoons vanilla extract
¼ cup cornstarch	1 16-ounce can sliced cling peaches, well drained
Salt	
1¾ cups milk	1 16-ounce can sliced Bartlett pears, well drained
2 eggs, beaten	
½ cup apple or peach jelly, melted	

In medium saucepan, mix sugar, cornstarch, and salt. Gradually stir in milk over medium heat until boiling. Boil for 1 minute, reduce heat to low. Remove about ¼ cup of milk mixture, stir into eggs, and return to saucepan. Cook and stir for 2 minutes. Remove from heat and stir in vanilla. Cover surface with wax paper or plastic wrap to avoid forming skin. Let cool 30 minutes to 1 hour. Pour into cooled crust. Cover surface and refrigerate at least 2 hours. Arrange fruit over custard and refrigerate. Just before serving, brush or spoon jelly over fruit to glaze. Serve immediately.

Note: Pastry and custard can be made a day in advance and fruit and glaze added just before serving.

Chocolate Chip Pie

½ cup all-purpose flour
1 cup sugar
2 eggs, lightly beaten
¼ pound butter, melted and
   cooled (no substitute)

1 teaspoon vanilla extract
1 cup chopped walnuts or pecans
1 cup chocolate chips
1 9-inch pie shell

Mix flour and sugar, add eggs and cooled butter. Add vanilla and mix well. Fold in nuts and chocolate chips. Pour into prepared pie shell. Bake for 30 to 35 minutes in a preheated 350° oven. (Test center of pie for firmness.)

Dinner for the Boss

Scrumptious Shrimp Mold
Chicken Dijon
Baked Cherry Tomatoes and Basil
Pasta Broccoli
Sesame Seed Cheese Bread
Cassata alla Siciliana

PREVIOUS DAY	EARLY MORNING	FREEZER
Shrimp Mold	*Chicken Dijon*	*Shrimp Mold*
Pasta Broccoli		*Cheese Bread*
Cassata		

Scrumptious Shrimp Mold

¼ pound softened butter
8 ounces cream cheese
Juice of 1 lemon
2 tablespoons mayonnaise
1 scallion, chopped
½ teaspoon salt

¼ teaspoon pepper
¼ teaspoon garlic powder
¼ teaspoon Worcestershire
   sauce
½ cup finely chopped celery
2 cups chopped shrimp

Blend butter and next 8 ingredients. Stir in celery and shrimp. Place in oiled 3- or 4-cup mold. Chill until set. Remove from mold an hour before serving and refrigerate until serving time to firm edges. Freezes well. Defrost 1 day in refrigerator before serving.

Chicken Dijon

4 whole chicken breasts, split, center breast bone only removed	½ to ¾ cup Dijon mustard

Dry the chicken breasts. Divide the mustard equally over the skin side of the breasts, spread smoothly.

Crumb Topping:

¼ pound butter or margarine	½ cup teaspoon salt
2 cloves garlic, finely minced	¼ teaspoon freshly ground
2 cups fresh bread crumbs	black pepper
¾ cup minced fresh parsley	

Melt butter in a large frying pan, add the garlic, and sauté until soft. Do not allow butter or garlic to turn brown. Add the bread crumbs and sauté until golden brown. Remove from heat and toss in the parsley, salt, and pepper. Turn the crumbs out on a large sheet of wax paper and spread into an even layer.

Press mustard-coated side of the chicken into the crumb coating. Line a 10-by-15-inch jelly-roll pan with foil. Place chicken, crumb side up, in the pan. Bake chicken on center rack of preheated 425° oven for 10 minutes. Dot chicken with additional butter and reduce heat to 375° for additional 25 minutes.

Baked Cherry Tomatoes and Basil

1 quart cherry tomatoes	⅛ cup melted butter (no substitute)
1 tablespoon olive oil	
Salt and pepper, to taste	1½ teaspoons fresh chopped
¼ cup bread crumbs	basil (or ½ teaspoon dried)
1 clove garlic, minced	

Cut off tomato stems. Brush bottom of 1½-quart baking dish with olive oil. Arrange tomatoes cut side up in dish. Sprinkle with salt and pepper. Mix bread crumbs, garlic, melted butter, and basil. Crumble over tomatoes. Bake in preheated 400° oven about 10 minutes, until slightly brown.

Pasta Broccoli

1 16-ounce package linguini	1 cup grated Parmesan
2 16-ounce cans stewed sliced tomatoes	2 cloves garlic, minced
	2 cups sour cream
3 tablespoons ketchup	1 teaspoon nutmeg
½ cup melted butter	2 heaping tablespoons spaghetti
3 4-ounce cans sliced mushrooms	sauce seasoning
1 large bunch broccoli, flowerets only	

Cook linguini lightly. Mix all remaining ingredients and uncooked broccoli flowerets, reserving ½ cup Parmesan. Put into two well-greased flat 8-by-10-inch casseroles. Cover and bake in preheated 350° oven for 30 minutes. Do not overcook. Serve sprinkled with remaining cheese. Can be prepared a day in advance up to baking stage.

Sesame Seed Cheese Bread

1 envelope active dry yeast	1 large egg, lightly beaten
¼ cup warm water (100° to 115° F)	½ pound sharp Cheddar, shredded
1 teaspoon sugar	⅓ cup, plus 2 tablespoons toasted sesame seeds
1 cup water	
¼ cup sugar	4 to 5 cups sifted all-purpose flour
2 tablespoons shortening	
2 teaspoons salt	1 egg white, beaten, for glaze

Soften yeast in ¼ cup warm water containing the teaspoon of sugar. Combine remaining water and the next 3 ingredients. Cool to luke-warm. Add yeast mixture, egg, cheese, and ⅓ cup sesame seeds. Gradually stir in 3½ cups of the flour. Turn onto lightly floured board. Gradually knead in the remaining flour. Knead gently 2 to 3 minutes. Place in a large greased bowl, turning to coat all sides. Cover and let rise in a warm place until doubled in size. Punch down dough. Form into 2 loaves. Place in two greased 9-by-5-by-3-inch loaf pans. Cover and let rise until doubled in bulk. Glaze with beaten egg white and sprinkle the remaining 2 tablespoons of sesame seeds on top. Bake in preheated 375° oven for 40 minutes or until browned.

Cassata alla Siciliana (Sicilian Cake)

1 fresh 9-by-3-inch pound cake
1 pound ricotta cheese
2 tablespoons heavy cream
¼ cup sugar
4 tablespoons Strega, Grand Marnier, or other orange-flavored liqueur

3 tablespoons coarsely chopped mixed candied fruit (or use 2 tablespoons orange bits from strained marmalade)
3 ounces semisweet mini chocolate morsels

Slice the end crusts off the pound cake and level the top if rounded. Cut the cake horizontally into ½- to ¾-inch-thick slabs. Put the ricotta through a coarse sieve and then beat with rotary beater until smooth. Beating constantly, add the cream, sugar, and liqueur. With rubber spatula fold in fruit and chocolate bits.

Center bottom slab of cake on a plate and spread generously with the ricotta mixture. Do the same as you build up all slabs. Gently press the loaf to make it compact. Do not worry if it feels wobbly; chilling will firm it up. Refrigerate 2 hours or until ricotta is firm.

Chocolate Frosting:

12 ounces semisweet chocolate, cut in small pieces
¾ cup strong black coffee

11 tablespoons unsalted butter, cut into ½-inch pieces and chilled

Chopped nuts, to sprinkle over top (optional)

Melt chocolate in the coffee in a small heavy saucepan over low heat, stirring constantly until completely dissolved. Remove from heat and beat in butter, 1 piece at a time. Beat until mixture is smooth; chill until thickened to spreading consistency. With a metal spatula, spread the frosting evenly over the top, sides, and end of the Cassata, swirling it decoratively. Garnish with nuts if desired. Cover loosely with plastic wrap and refrigerate at least 24 hours before serving.

Black Tie Dinner

Baked Brie
Beet Salad Dijon
Stuffed Trout with Cucumber Sauce
Lemon-Parsley Rice
Baked Zucchini
Ivory Mousse with Ebony Sauce

PREVIOUS DAY	EARLY MORNING	FREEZER
Baked Zucchini	*Salad dressing*	
Ivory Mousse	*Ebony Sauce*	

Baked Brie

1 2.2-kilo wheel of Brie cheese, ½ package (1 sheet) frozen
   not overly ripe   puff pastry, thawed
1 12-ounce jar apricot preserves

Spread top of Brie with preserves. Place in center of puff pastry and wrap it well. Any leftover pastry may be cut into shapes and used to decorate top. Place wrapped Brie on greased cookie sheet and bake in preheated 425° oven for 20 to 25 minutes. Let stand several minutes before cutting into small wedges. A smaller piece of Brie can be used, with only enough of the puff pastry to wrap it. Does not freeze successfully.

Beet Salad Dijon

1 16-ounce can whole beets, ¼ cup olive oil
   drained, *or* 4 large beets, 3 scallions, chopped
   cooked, drained, and peeled 1 large clove garlic, minced
1 tablespoon white vinegar 3 ribs celery, diced
1 tablespoon red wine vinegar Salt and freshly ground black
2 teaspoons Dijon mustard   pepper, to taste
¼ cup vegetable oil

Cut beets into ¼-inch-thick slices. Mix vinegars and mustard in medium bowl. Gradually whisk in both oils until smooth and thickened. Stir in scallions and garlic. Add celery and stir to coat. Toss in beets. Season to taste and serve immediately.

Stuffed Trout

1 5- to 6-pound lake trout, 1 walleye pike, or 2 3-pound fish
1 cup seasoned stuffing mix
½ cup hot water
2 tablespoons capers, drained and chopped
2 tablespoons chopped fresh parsley

3 strips bacon, minced
¼ cup finely chopped onion
½ cup melted butter
½ teaspoon salt
¼ teaspoon finely ground pepper
Lemon slices, for garnish
Parsley sprigs, for garnish
Cucumber Sauce

Rinse and thoroughly dry fish inside and out. In large mixing bowl combine stuffing mix, hot water, capers, and parsley. Toss lightly until blended and well moistened. Place bacon in heavy 12-inch skillet and sauté for 4 to 6 minutes. Add onion and sauté for 3 to 5 minutes more until bacon is crisp, stirring frequently. Add the bacon-onion mixture to stuffing, with pan drippings. Toss lightly to combine. Brush inside of fish with melted butter and sprinkle with salt and pepper. Fill fish loosely with stuffing mixture. Skewer or sew opening shut.

With heavy foil, line a shallow baking dish or pan large enough to accommodate the fish. Place fish in pan and bake in preheated 425° oven for 25 minutes or until it flakes easily when tested with a fork. Remove from oven and keep warm. When ready to serve, the skin can be removed, leaving head and tail intact. Garnish with lemon slices and parsley and serve with Cucumber Sauce (see Index).

Lemon-Parsley Rice

4 tablespoons butter
1½ cups rice
1 cup dry vermouth
2 cups chicken broth

1 teaspoon salt
½ teaspoon pepper
Grated rind of 1 lemon
⅛ cup minced fresh parsley

Melt butter in a skillet, add rice, and sauté a few minutes. Add vermouth, broth, salt, and pepper and bring to a boil. Add lemon rind and parsley. Pour into an ovenproof 10-by-6-inch casserole. Cover and bake until all liquid is absorbed, approximately 50 minutes to 1 hour, at 350°. The parsley rises to the top, for an interesting effect.

⚜ ⚜ ⚜

Baked Zucchini

4 eggs
1 cup biscuit mix
3 cups chopped zucchini
½ cup chopped onion

½ cup grated Parmesan
1 tablespoon chopped parsley
½ teaspoon each salt, dried
oregano, and garlic powder

¼ cup oil

Beat eggs and add biscuit mix. Drain and squeeze juice from zucchini. Add all ingredients to egg mixture. Pour mixture into greased 8-inch-square pan and bake in preheated 350° oven for 30 to 35 minutes. Cut into squares. Can be cut into small squares and served as hors d'oeuvres.

Note: Can be prepared a day in advance. Cover with foil and reheat before serving.

Ivory Mousse with Ebony Sauce

Mousse:

½ cup cold milk
1⅛ teaspoons unflavored
gelatin
6 ounces white chocolate
1 teaspoon vanilla extract
1 cup whipping cream

¼ teaspoon lemon juice
Salt
2 egg whites
Dark semisweet chocolate
shavings, for garnish

Place milk in top of double boiler and sprinkle with gelatin. After gelatin has softened, turn on heat and dissolve gelatin, stir, and add chocolate. Stir until melted. Add vanilla and remove from heat. Let cool for ½ hour. Beat cream until soft peaks form and fold, one-half at a time, into chocolate mixture. Mix lemon juice and salt into egg whites. Beat until stiff. Fold whites into chocolate mixture. Chill.

Ebony Sauce:

2 tablespoons unsalted butter	½ cup unsweetened cocoa,
½ cup sugar	Dutch or Belgian
	2 cups heavy cream

Melt butter in a small saucepan, add sugar, beat; add cocoa, and whisk all together. Add cream and heat thoroughly without boiling. Remove from heat and refrigerate. Put plastic wrap over top to avoid skin formation.

To serve, place 3 tablespoons sauce on plate, and, with heated spoon, scoop 2 spoonfuls of mousse onto plate. Dark chocolate shavings can be sprinkled on top of scoops.

Chamber Music Supper

Chutney-Cheese Rounds
Mixed Green Salad with Celery Seed Dressing
Broiled Rock Cornish Hens à l'Orange
Confetti Wild Rice
Sautéed Julienne Vegetables
Frozen Lemon Crumb Dessert
Chocolate Crunch Cookies

PREVIOUS DAY	EARLY MORNING	FREEZER
Celery Seed Dressing	Prepare vegetables	Chutney Rounds
Confetti Rice		Lemon Crumb Dessert
Chocolate Crunch Cookies		

Chutney-Cheese Rounds
(Makes 40)

40 rounds of white bread	½ scant teaspoon salt
4 tablespoons melted butter	8 ounces sharp Cheddar cheese
4 ounces cream cheese	⅓ cup chutney
½ of 1 beaten egg	3 to 4 tablespoons ground
1 tablespoon flour	pecans or bread crumbs

Cut white bread rounds 1¾ inch in diameter. Melt butter, brush lightly on both sides, and toast until golden. Soften cream cheese, add egg, flour, and salt. Grate Cheddar into mixture and stir until combined. Should be stiff. Empty chutney onto cutting board and chop until it is in very small pieces. Add chopped nuts or bread crumbs until all the juice of the chutney is absorbed. On toasted round, place chutney in center, then build cheese around sides, allowing chutney to show in center. Can be frozen at this stage. Freeze on cookie sheet and then store flat in plastic freezer bag. When ready to serve, broil for 5 minutes.

Celery Seed Dressing

½ cup sugar, more or less, to taste	1 tablespoon onion, finely grated
1 teaspoon paprika	½ cup ketchup
1 teaspoon salt	1 cup wine vinegar
1 teaspoon celery seeds	1½ cups salad oil
	Garlic powder (optional)

Combine all ingredients. Mix well in tightly lidded jar. Keep in refrigerator. Serve over fresh assortment of at least 3 kinds of greens.

Broiled Rock Cornish Hens à l'Orange

3 hens, about 1¾ pounds each	6 tablespoons butter or
1¾ teaspoons salt	margarine
⅓ teaspoon freshly ground black pepper	2 tablespoons lemon juice
	1½ tablespoons soy sauce
¾ cup orange marmalade	

Remove giblets, necks, etc., from hens (can use another time for soup or stock). Rinse hens in running cold water, pat dry. Cut in half and sprinkle with salt and pepper. Place hen halves skin side down in broiler pan, put 1 tablespoon butter in each cavity, and pour 1 teaspoon of lemon juice over each half.

Place hen halves about 7 to 9 inches from broiler flame and broil 20 to 25 minutes. As soon as butter melts, brush lemon juice and butter over all of hen. Turn hen over, brushing skin, and broil until fork tender. Brush occasionally with pan drippings. During last 5 minutes, brush with soy sauce. Just before hen is done, brush with marmalade.

Confetti Wild Rice

1 cup processed American
cheese, cut in cubes
1 cup ripe olives, chopped
1 1-pound, 4-ounce can
tomatoes
½ cup chopped onions
¼ cup chopped green pepper

1 4-ounce jar mushroom stems
and pieces, drained
½ cup wild rice, washed
½ cup olive oil
1 teaspoon salt
¼ teaspoon freshly ground
black pepper

1½ cups boiling water

Mix all ingredients except water in a 2-quart round casserole and refrigerate for 24 hours. Add boiling water when ready to bake. Bake in preheated 350° oven for 1½ hours, or until all liquid is absorbed.

Note: If recipe is increased for a larger crowd, it should be made in separate 2-quart casseroles.

Sautéed Julienne Vegetables

1 large bunch fresh broccoli
3 large carrots, peeled
1 medium onion, sliced thin
4 tablespoons butter or
margarine (or less)

Salt and freshly ground black
pepper, to taste
2 tablespoons fresh chopped
parsley

Trim broccoli stems, reserving flowerets for another use. Julienne broccoli stems, carrots, and onion and steam until barely tender. Refresh in cold water. (Can be prepared in advance up to this point and refrigerated, well covered.) Melt butter and toss in vegetables to coat well. Season with salt, pepper, and parsley and cook and stir for 3 to 4 minutes to heat through.

Frozen Lemon Crumb Dessert

½ cup flour
2 tablespoons brown sugar
4 tablespoons butter or
margarine
¼ cup finely chopped pecans

2 eggs, separated
1 14-ounce can condensed milk
1½ teaspoons grated lemon
peel
⅓ cup lemon juice

3 tablespoons granulated sugar

Mix flour, brown sugar, butter, and nuts until crumbly. Spread on foil-lined baking sheet or in bottom of 2 9-by-5-inch loaf pans. Bake in 350° oven for 13 to 15 minutes or until golden. Cool. Break apart into crumbs. Line loaf pans with foil, leaving a 1½-inch collar around top. Spread ⅔ of crumb mixture in bottom.

Beat egg yolks until lemon-colored and thick. Blend in condensed milk, add lemon peel and juice, and stir until thickened. Beat egg whites until foamy. Gradually add sugar and continue beating until stiff peaks form. Fold into lemon mixture, pour into prepared pans, and sprinkle remaining crumbs on top.

Freeze until firm, then cover each with a piece of foil slightly larger than top of cake. Press foil directly onto cake, smoothing over to eliminate air. Fold collar edges up and over, and overturn cake to release from pan. Return to freezer until ready to slice.

To defrost, put into refrigerator 1 hour before serving.

Chocolate Crunch Cookies

3 ounces semisweet chocolate	⅓ cup firmly packed brown
1 ounce unsweetened chocolate	sugar
1 tablespoon butter	2 tablespoons flour, sifted
1 teaspoon vanilla extract	⅛ teaspoon baking powder
1 tablespoon water	1 cup semisweet chocolate chips
1 egg	1 cup chopped pecans

Pecan halves, to top cookies

Melt chocolate (except chips) with butter in top of double boiler. Stir until smooth and thoroughly mixed. Remove from heat and let cool to the touch. Stir in vanilla, water, egg, sugar, and other dry ingredients. Mix in chocolate chips and chopped pecans. Drop by the tablespoonful onto nonstick cookie sheet, about 2 inches apart. Press pecan halves into centers of cookies. Bake in preheated 350° oven for 12 minutes.

December Dinner

Alsatian Onion Tart
Shrimp-stuffed Eggplant
Roast Marinated Tenderloin of Beef
Double-baked Potatoes
Brown Velvet Cordial Pie

PREVIOUS DAY	EARLY MORNING	FREEZER
Marinate beef	*Eggplant*	*Cordial Pie*

Alsatian Onion Tart

Pastry:

3 cups flour
1½ teaspoons salt
Pinch of sugar
¼ cup sour cream
¼ cup cold water, or more

12 tablespoons cold, unsalted
    butter in ½-inch pieces
½ cup solid shortening, well
    chilled

Mix flour, salt, and sugar in large bowl. Mix sour cream and cold water in a measuring cup. Cut butter and shortening into flour mixture with two knives or pastry blender until coarse crumbs form. Blend in liquid and mix until pastry dough can be gathered into a ball. More cold water may be necessary. On a floured board, roll dough into an 8-by-10-inch rectangle. Fold the bottom to center and top to bottom, turn and roll again, then repeat the folding. Wrap in foil and chill 2 hours. (Pastry can be refrigerated up to 2 days or frozen, well wrapped. Thaw overnight in refrigerator.)

Roll dough to fit a 10-by-15-inch jelly-roll pan. Crimp edge and prick the surface with a fork. Refrigerate 30 minutes. Line pastry with foil filled with rice or dried beans to hold it flat. Bake in preheated 300° oven for 8 minutes. Remove weights and foil, prick pastry again, and return to oven for 10 minutes longer, or until golden.

Filling:

½ pound thick-sliced bacon in ½-inch pieces

2 tablespoons unsalted butter

2½ pounds onions, halved lengthwise and cut into ¼-inch slices

¼ cup flour (leveled)

Salt and freshly ground black pepper, to taste

1¼ cups milk

4 eggs

¾ cup whipping cream

⅛ teaspoon nutmeg

⅛ teaspoon red pepper

Cook bacon, drain on paper towels, and discard bacon grease. Add butter to the skillet, add onions, and cook over medium heat. Cover and stir until cooked but not brown, about 30 minutes. Sprinkle flour over the onions and cook, stirring, for 3 or 4 minutes. Add bacon and season with salt and pepper to taste. (Can be done 6 or 8 hours ahead.) Spread onion and bacon mixture on crust. Whisk milk, eggs, cream, nutmeg, and pepper until blended. Pour over onion mixture. Bake in preheated 375° oven for 30 to 35 minutes or until set and golden. Cut into squares to serve as appetizer or main course.

Shrimp-stuffed Eggplant

3 medium eggplants, halved

Salt

1 cup chopped scallions

1 cup chopped celery

½ cup chopped onion

1 cup chopped green pepper

½ cup olive oil

2 tablespoons chicken bouillon granules

Butter

1½ cups Italian seasoned bread crumbs

2 cups peeled raw shrimp

2 cloves garlic, pressed

1 cup peeled chopped tomatoes

1 teaspoon Tabasco sauce

Scoop pulp out of eggplant halves and dice. Wash and lightly salt shells. Drain. Steam pulp and other vegetables in oil and butter until tender (about 30 minutes). Stir in 1 cup of the crumbs, the shrimp, and other ingredients. Cook until shrimp are pink, stirring constantly, about 5 minutes. Stuff lightly into shells or lightly greased casserole and sprinkle with remaining crumbs. Bake at 350° for 30 minutes.

Note: It is easier to scoop eggplants if they have been split and baked at 300° for a few minutes.

Vegetables can be chopped ahead of time. Whole casserole can be prepared early in morning if eggplant shells are not being used. Crabmeat or ham can be substituted for shrimp.

Roast Marinated Tenderloin of Beef

1 5- to 6-pound beef tenderloin, trimmed and tied into a neat cylinder
½ cup red wine
2 tablespoons brandy
⅔ cup oil
1½ garlic cloves, slivered

3 teaspoons green peppercorns, drained and crushed
1 bay leaf, broken in half
2 shallots, chopped
½ teaspoon crushed dried thyme
Salt

Place meat in a glass bowl or large plastic bag. Combine all other ingredients into a marinade and pour over the beef. Cover or close bag and refrigerate for 24 to 30 hours. Turn bag or meat several times during marinating.

Butter bottom of shallow roasting pan. Remove meat from the bag or bowl. Remove bay leaf and garlic pieces from marinade. Season roast with salt just before cooking and place in shallow pan. Roast in preheated 425° oven for 30 to 35 minutes, basting several times with reserved marinade. Meat at thickest part should register 125° for rare or 120° for very rare. Let meat rest 20 minutes before carving.

Double-baked Potatoes

6 large baking potatoes
12 tablespoons butter (1½ sticks)
6 ounces chopped onions

3 ounces chopped chives
¾ to 1 cup dry cottage cheese
Nutmeg

Salt and freshly ground black pepper, to taste

Bake potatoes, cut in half lengthwise, and remove pulp. Blend together butter, onions, chives, cottage cheese, and seasonings. Mix with potato pulp and refill shells. Rebake in preheated 350° oven for 20 minutes.

Brown Velvet Cordial Pie

1½ cups chocolate wafer crumbs
¼ cup melted butter
½ cup cold water
1 envelope unflavored gelatin
⅔ cup sugar
⅛ teaspoon salt

3 eggs, separated
¼ cup Triple Sec
¼ cup crème de cacao
1 cup heavy cream
Food coloring (optional)
Bittersweet chocolate curls (optional garnish)

Combine crumbs with butter. Press into a 9-inch pie tin and bake in preheated 350° oven for 10 minutes. Cool.

Pour water into a saucepan and sprinkle gelatin over it. Add ⅓ cup of the sugar, salt, and egg yolks. Stir to blend. Place over low heat and stir until gelatin dissolves and mixture thickens. Do *not* boil! It is more important that gelatin dissolves than that mixture thickens over heat. Stir the liqueurs into mixture. Chill until mixture starts to mound slightly when dropped from spoon. For fluffier pie, whip the mixture when chilled.

Beat egg whites until stiff, add remaining sugar and beat until peaks are firm. Fold meringue into thickened gelatin mixture. Whip the cream and fold into mixture. Add food coloring if desired. Turn mixture into prebaked crust. Garnish, if desired, with chocolate curls.

Freezes well. Defrosting time is 1 hour.

Variations:
1. Substitute white crème de menthe for the Triple Sec.
2. Change liqueurs to chocolate mint and vodka.

Ice-Skating Party

Raw Mushrooms Stuffed with Brie and Roquefort
Shrimp Gumbo with White Rice
Chicken Breasts Creole
Marbleized Cauliflower and Broccoli Mold
Apple Crisp

PREVIOUS DAY	EARLY MORNING	FREEZER
	Stuffed mushrooms	*Shrimp Gumbo*
	Vegetable mold	*Chicken sauce*
	Apple Crisp	

Raw Mushrooms Stuffed with Brie and Roquefort

24 large mushrooms
2 ounces Roquefort
5 ounces Brie, rind removed
2 tablespoons unsalted butter
1 tablespoon chopped chives
¼ cup light cream
Freshly ground black pepper, to taste
1 tablespoon chopped parsley

Clean mushrooms and remove stems (reserve for another use). Process cheeses and butter with cream until smooth. Add pepper to taste. Fill mushroom caps with cheese mixture, sprinkle with parsley and chives.

Shrimp Gumbo

1½ tablespoons flour
1½ tablespoons butter or
   margarine
1 large onion, chopped
4 tablespoons chopped parsley
3 ribs celery, chopped
1½ teaspoons garlic powder
1½ teaspoons salt
¾ teaspoon freshly ground
   black pepper

4 teaspoons horseradish
½ teaspoon concentrated
   brown seasoning sauce
¾ teaspoon dry mustard
1 15-ounce can tomato sauce
1 15-ounce can water
3 chicken bouillon cubes
1½ pounds shrimp, shelled
   and cleaned
½ to 1 10-ounce package
   frozen cut okra

In a 3-quart pot, make a roux of flour, butter, and onion. Add all ingredients except shrimp and okra. Simmer about ½ hour until thickened. Add shrimp and okra and simmer 10 minutes. Serve over white rice, cooked according to package directions.

Note: Sauce can be made 2 or 3 days in advance or frozen without shrimp and okra. Add these two ingredients when reheated, 10 minutes before serving.

Chicken Breasts Creole

½ cup flour
½ cup corn oil
1 cup chopped scallions
3 tablespoons chopped parsley
½ cup chopped green pepper
1 clove garlic, pressed
16 ounces tomato sauce
½ cup white wine

⅓ cup water
1 tablespoon freshly ground
   black pepper
½ teaspoon cayenne
Salt, to taste
6 whole chicken breasts, boned
   and skinned
4 tablespoons butter

Garlic salt, to taste

Make a roux by browning flour in oil over low heat, stirring constantly until dark brown. Add remaining ingredients except chicken, butter, and garlic salt. Pepper and cayenne can be reduced to taste. Stir all together and simmer 30 minutes. Freezes well.

Sauté chicken breasts in butter and garlic salt until cooked, several minutes on each side. Serve sauce over cooked chicken breasts.

Variation:

Replace chicken with 1 pound shrimp, peeled and cleaned and cooked in sauce until done, and 1 pound scallops for a shrimp creole dinner to be served with white rice.

Note: The sauce in this recipe makes enough for approximately 2 pounds of fish or chicken pieces.

Marbleized Cauliflower and Broccoli Mold

1½ to 2 pounds cauliflower	1½ cups milk
1½ to 2 pounds broccoli	Salt and freshly ground black
4 tablespoons butter	pepper or nutmeg, to taste
4 tablespoons flour	6 eggs
¾ cup grated Cheddar cheese	

Steam cauliflower and broccoli separately until tender and purée each, placing 2 cups of each in separate bowls. Melt butter in saucepan, stir in flour, and cook 2 to 3 minutes. Whisk in milk. Season with salt and pepper or nutmeg, and simmer for 5 minutes longer. Beat 3 eggs and mix in cauliflower. Beat remaining eggs and add to broccoli. Divide sauce and cheese between the two purées. Season both mixtures.

Butter a 2-quart mold. Add cauliflower, then cover with broccoli. With a flat knife, swirl the mixtures together to give a marbleized appearance. Mold can be covered with plastic wrap or foil at this stage and refrigerated. Cover with buttered wax paper and place in deep baking pan when ready to cook. Pour in boiling water around mold, at least halfway up the sides. Bake in preheated 375° oven for 40 to 50 minutes, or until mixture is lightly browned on edges and is set in the center.

Apple Crisp

5 large tart apples, peeled, cored,   ½ cup sugar
and chopped into big pieces   3 teaspoons vanilla extract
1½ teaspoons cinnamon

Combine apples with remaining ingredients and place in a lightly greased 2-quart soufflé dish.

Topping:

½ cup chopped walnuts   ¼ pound butter
¾ cup flour   ¼ cup rolled oats
¾ cup dark brown sugar   ¼ teaspoon salt

Mix ingredients and pour over apples. Bake in preheated 350° oven for 1 hour. Serve with vanilla ice cream. Can be baked in morning and reheated before serving.

Celebration

White Wine Punch
Cheese Ring
Antipasto
Veal Chops Orloff
Angel Hair Pasta
Vegetables Provençal
Uncle Albert's Something Special Cake

PREVIOUS DAY	EARLY MORNING	FREEZER
Antipasto dressing	Punch	Ice Ring
Vegetables Provençal	Something Special Cake	

White Wine Punch
(Makes about 25 ½-cup servings)

½ gallon Chablis or Chenin
  Blanc
½ cup sugar, or to taste
3 6-ounce cans frozen lemon-
  limeade concentrate, thawed

1 6-ounce can frozen orange
  juice concentrate, thawed
Ice Ring
2 cups club soda

In large punch bowl, stir together wine, sugar, and fruit juice concentrates and let blend. Shortly before serving, add Ice Ring and club soda.

Ice Ring:

Clarify 2 quarts water by bringing it to a boil and letting cool. In bottom of ring mold, overlap slices of citrus fruits. Pour about ¼ inch of cooled water over fruit, and freeze until solid. Fill mold with remaining water and freeze. Unmold and float, fruit side up, in punch bowl.

Cheese Ring

1½ cups water
9 tablespoons butter
2 teaspoons salt

1½ cups sifted flour
7 eggs, beaten
2 cups grated Gruyère or other
  Swiss cheese

Bring water, butter, and salt to boil in a saucepan. When butter has melted, remove pan from heat and vigorously beat in the flour, all at once. Beat until flour is totally incorporated. Return saucepan to moderate heat and beat constantly with wooden spoon until dough forms a ball and comes away from sides of the pan, about 2 minutes. Remove from heat.

Beat in 6 eggs a little at a time, making sure each addition is well incorporated before adding more. Gradually beat in the grated cheese. Spoon dough onto greased cookie sheet by spoonfuls to form a ring and brush top and sides with last egg. Bake in preheated 400° oven for 20 minutes, until golden brown and puffed up. Do not open oven door until end of baking time. Slice and serve immediately.

Antipasto

2 6-ounce jars marinated
  artichoke hearts
½ cup garlic red wine vinegar
4 teaspoons chopped chives or
  onions
1 teaspoon garlic salt
½ teaspoon dry mustard
½ teaspoon dried oregano
½ teaspoon paprika
1 head Boston lettuce
2 cups cherry tomatoes
1 6-ounce jar stuffed green olives
1 cup sliced fresh mushrooms
12 ounces small salami slices

Drain artichoke hearts. Reserve liquid and mix with next 6 ingredients for dressing. Heat well. Arrange lettuce leaves on a platter, and arrange artichoke hearts and other vegetables on top, with salami. Just before serving, reheat dressing and pour over salad.

Veal Chops Orloff
(Serves 8)

8 rib veal chops, about 1 inch
  thick
Salt, freshly ground black
  pepper, and flour, for
  dredging
¼ cup melted butter or
  margarine
1 cup minced onion
1 pound mushrooms, minced
1¼ teaspoons salt
Freshly ground black pepper, to
  taste
1 tablespoon lemon juice
4 tablespoons butter
6 tablespoons flour
2 cups light cream
¾ cup grated Parmesan or
  Swiss cheese
Watercress, for garnish

Sprinkle chops with salt and pepper. Dredge in flour and shake off excess. Brown chops over medium heat 10 to 12 minutes on each side in melted butter. Remove from skillet and keep warm. Add onion to fat left in skillet, scraping bottom with wooden spoon. Add mushrooms, sprinkle with 1 teaspoon salt, dash of pepper, and lemon juice, and cook 5 to 6 minutes, stirring occasionally. Melt 4 tablespoons butter in small saucepan and stir in 6 tablespoons flour. Cook 1 minute, stirring constantly. Add cream, ¼ teaspoon salt, and dash of pepper. Cook over medium heat, stirring rapidly with wooden spoon or wire whisk until sauce bubbles. Remove from heat. Stir sauce into mushroom mixture and mix well. Correct seasoning. Place chops in shallow roasting pan. Top each chop with mushroom mixture, dividing it evenly among chops. Sprinkle with grated cheese. Place chops under broiler for a few minutes, until cheese melts and is lightly browned. Arrange chops on heated serving platter. Garnish with parsley or watercress, if desired.

Angel Hair Pasta

1 pound angel hair pasta (found in specialty food stores)	3 tablespoons melted butter
	¼ teaspoon salt
¼ cup fresh chopped parsley	

Bring 3 quarts of water to a boil, add 1 teaspoon salt along with pasta to boiling water. Cook al dente, 2 to 3 minutes. Drain and toss with melted butter, salt, and parsley.

Vegetables Provençal

2 to 3 tablespoons corn oil	1 tablespoon thyme
3 medium-size baking potatoes	Garlic powder, to taste
1 large onion	1 tablespoon sweet basil
1 large green pepper	3 tablespoons chopped fresh
½ pound mushrooms	parsley
2 16-ounce cans stewed tomatoes	½ cup chopped celery
Freshly ground white pepper, to taste	(optional)

In large nonstick skillet, pour 2 tablespoons corn oil. Peel and cube potatoes and dice onion. Cut green pepper into small pieces and slice mushrooms.

Cook potatoes in oil over medium heat. Add mushrooms. When slightly done, add green pepper. Do not overcook. Add onion when other vegetables are tender. Cook only until transparent. Add tomatoes. Add seasonings, simmer for 5 to 10 minutes, and sprinkle with fresh parsley when serving. For stronger garlic flavor, crush 2 whole garlic cloves into the oil just before adding the potatoes. Celery may be added.

Uncle Albert's Something Special Cake

8 egg whites
1¾ cups granulated sugar
1 teaspoon vanilla extract

3 cups finely chopped sweetened
  coconut
2 tablespoons cake flour

Line three well-buttered 8-inch cake pans with wax paper and sweet butter. Beat egg whites until just stiff, gradually add ¾ cup sugar and vanilla, and beat until soft peaks form. Mix together 1 cup sugar, coconut, and cake flour and fold into beaten egg whites. Pour into prepared pans.

Bake in preheated 350° oven for 20 minutes or until lightly browned and firm to touch. Cool on cake racks. Remove wax paper while layers are warm.

Filling:

3 cups heavy cream
3 tablespoons confectioners'
  sugar
1 tablespoon instant coffee

12 ounces apricot jam
Unblanched almonds, toasted,
  for garnish

Whip 3 cups of heavy cream and fold in sugar and instant coffee dissolved in 1 tablespoon hot water. Cover first layer of cake with apricot jam, spread ⅓ of whipped cream over jam. Repeat on second layer. Repeat on top layer and frost sides of cake also. Decorate top with lots of toasted, unblanched almonds.

Club Dinner

Mushroom Salad
Steak Beaujolais
Spicy Lima Beans
Golden Potato Casserole
Creamy Coleslaw
Blueberry Cheesecake

Mushroom Salad

1½ pounds fresh mushrooms, halved or sliced thick
Juice of 1 lemon
2 tablespoons mayonnaise
1 clove garlic, minced

½ cup bottled Italian dressing
1 tablespoon Dijon mustard
2 tablespoons grated Parmesan
½ head romaine lettuce
Chopped parsley

12 cherry tomatoes

Sprinkle sliced mushrooms with lemon juice. Mix next 5 ingredients and toss with mushrooms. Chill at least 2 hours, tossing lightly several times. Serve on a bed of romaine lettuce leaves, garnished with chopped parsley and cherry tomatoes.

Steak Beaujolais

4 cups Beaujolais
24 shallots, finely minced (approximately 1½ cups)
3 cloves garlic, finely minced
½ teaspoon salt

Freshly ground black pepper
4 tablespoons clarified unsalted butter
8 rib-eye steaks (approximately 8 ounces each)

¼ pound unsalted butter

Heat 3 cups of the wine, shallots, garlic, salt, and pepper in a heavy medium-size saucepan over high heat. Bring to boil and cook, uncovered, until reduced by half—about 15 minutes.

In a heavy skillet (or 2 skillets, so that steaks fit easily), heat the clarified butter. When butter is sizzling, add steaks and pan-fry, 2 minutes per side for rare, 3 minutes on 1 side and 2 minutes on the other for medium-rare.

Remove steaks and keep warm. Season with salt and pepper. Add remaining cup of wine to the skillet or skillets. Heat to boiling over high heat. With a wooden spoon, scrape browned bits from skillet.

Add reduced wine-shallot mixture to skillet and heat to boiling. Remove from heat and add ¼ pound butter, stirring to blend. Pour over steaks and serve immediately.

Spicy Lima Beans

2 10-ounce packages frozen baby
   lima beans
3 small bay leaves
2 teaspoons minced onion
½ teaspoon freshly ground
   black pepper

2 tablespoons butter
2 teaspoons salt
½ teaspoon dried basil
½ cup water

Combine all ingredients in pot, cover, and bring to a boil. Reduce heat and cook 15 minutes. Remove bay leaves. Refrigerate. Reheat when ready to serve.

Golden Potato Casserole

6 medium potatoes
1 pint sour cream
10 ounces sharp Cheddar cheese,
   grated
5 scallions, chopped

3 tablespoons milk
1 teaspoon salt
½ teaspoon pepper
⅓ cup bread crumbs
2 tablespoons melted butter

Scrub potatoes and cook in boiling water until tender. Cool, after draining. Peel potatoes and grate coarsely. Combine with next 6 ingredients. Turn into well-buttered 9-by-13-inch baking dish. Smooth top, sprinkle with bread crumbs which have been combined with melted butter. Bake in preheated 300° oven for 40 minutes, or until very hot. Cut into squares.

Creamy Coleslaw

6 cups shredded cabbage (3
   white and 3 red is pretty)
½ cup thinly sliced scallions
2 carrots, shredded

1½ cups mayonnaise
2 tablespoons sugar
3 tablespoons white vinegar,
   more or less, to taste

2 teaspoons celery seed

Combine chilled vegetables in a large bowl. Combine remaining ingredients until sugar is dissolved. Pour over the vegetables and toss well. Chill at least 1 hour.

Blueberry Cheesecake

Crust:

1½ cups graham cracker crumbs

½ cup finely chopped walnuts
½ cup melted butter
⅓ cup sugar

Combine ingredients and pat into greased 9-inch springform pan. Freeze while preparing filling.

Filling:

1 pound cream cheese, softened
3 jumbo eggs
1 cup sugar
¼ teaspoon salt

1 teaspoon vanilla extract
1 teaspoon lemon extract
½ teaspoon almond extract
3 tablespoons flour

1 pint sour cream, at room temperature

Mix all ingredients on low speed until blended. Turn mixer to high speed and mix for a full 5 minutes. Mixture will be very smooth. Pour over crumb crust. Bake in preheated 350° oven for 45 minutes. When time is up, turn off heat and let cake remain in closed oven for an additional half-hour, without opening oven door. Cool thoroughly.

Glaze:

2 cups fresh blueberries
¾ cup cold water

½ cup sugar
1 tablespoon cornstarch

1 teaspoon grated fresh lemon rind

Combine blueberries and water in 1½-quart saucepan. Bring to a boil over moderate heat, remove from heat at once, and strain, reserving liquid. Mix sugar and cornstarch and stir into the blueberry liquid. Cook over medium heat, add lemon rind, and stir constantly until mixture thickens. Add to the berries and mix together. Cool and spoon over cheesecake.

Holiday Buffets

All recipes serve six unless otherwise indicated.

Holidays offer a perfect occasion for entertaining family and friends, whether for an informal Fourth of July picnic or an elegant New Year's Eve dinner party. Traditional fare is wonderful, but don't hesitate to try something new now and then. The following pages contain innovative ideas as well as old favorites.

New Year's Eve (Serves 8)

Shrimp Merlin
Onion and Tomato Tart
Hearts of Palm Salad with Watercress Dressing
Chateaubriand with Madeira Sauce
Roquefort-stuffed Potatoes
Artichokes Mornay
French Apple Tart with La Tarte Crust
Chocolate Truffles

PREVIOUS DAY

Shrimp Merlin
Salad dressing

EARLY MORNING

Tart shell
Madeira Sauce
Artichokes Mornay
French Apple Tart

FREEZER

Stuffed Potatoes
Apple Tart crust
Truffles

Shrimp Merlin

1 tablespoon dried thyme
½ teaspoon dried basil
2 pounds large shrimp, shelled
  and deveined
2 cups mayonnaise-style salad
  dressing

1 4-ounce jar capers, with juice
2 medium onions, sliced thin
1 teaspoon dry mustard
¼ teaspoon freshly ground
  black pepper
1 head romaine lettuce

In large pot bring 3 quarts water to a boil. Add thyme and basil, drop in the shrimp, and bring to a boil again. Reduce heat and simmer 3 minutes or until shrimp turn pink. Drain and cool shrimp completely. Combine salad dressing with capers and their juice, onions, mustard, and pepper. Add the shrimp. Blend well and refrigerate for 24 hours. Serve on lettuce.

Onion and Tomato Tart

4 tablespoons butter
2 pounds onions, to make 6 cups
  finely chopped
2 or 3 cloves garlic, finely
  chopped
3 tablespoons olive oil
2 pounds fresh ripe tomatoes,
  peeled, seeded, and chopped
1 teaspoon dried oregano
2 tablespoons dried basil
1 tablespoon tomato paste

1 teaspoon salt
Freshly ground black pepper, to
  taste
1 partially baked 10-inch pastry
  shell
1 tablespoon dry bread crumbs
24 flat anchovy fillets, drained
24 black olives
1 tablespoon finely chopped
  fresh Italian parsley

Melt butter in 10- to 12-inch skillet over moderate heat. Stir in onions and sauté for 10 minutes, stirring occasionally. Uncover and add garlic and cook for 30 minutes over low heat, stirring occasionally, until all liquid is evaporated and onions are translucent. Put 2 tablespoons of the olive oil in another pan and set over high heat. Add chopped tomatoes and bring to a boil. Stir frequently and let boil until all liquid is gone. Remove from heat and stir in oregano, basil, and tomato paste. Combine onions and tomatoes and add salt and pepper. Correct seasoning.

Place the partially cooked pastry shell, still in its pan, on a cookie sheet. Spread bread crumbs on bottom to absorb any excess liquid and prevent a soggy shell. Spoon in onion and tomato mixture and smooth to edges of crust. Make a latticework of the anchovies across top. Place an olive in each resulting square. Dribble remaining tablespoon olive oil on top. Bake in center of preheated 375° oven for 30 to 40 minutes or until onion and tomato mixture is lightly browned.

Serve either hot or at room temperature. Sprinkle with chopped parsley just before serving.

Hearts of Palm Salad

4 small heads Bibb lettuce	3 tomatoes, sliced thick
1 14-ounce can hearts of palm	

Arrange Bibb lettuce on individual dishes and top with slices of tomato and hearts of palm. Top with Watercress Dressing.

Watercress Dressing:

1 large bunch watercress	½ 12-ounce bottle chili sauce
¾ cup oil	2 tablespoons sugar
⅓ cup vinegar	Garlic powder, to taste
Salt, to taste	

Put cleaned watercress leaves in food processor with metal blade. Add remaining ingredients and process until all is liquified. Refrigerate overnight.

Chateaubriand with Madeira Sauce

1 5-pound beef tenderloin	½ teaspoon flour
¼ pound fresh mushrooms, chopped	2 tablespoons brandy
½ small onion, finely chopped	⅔ pound bacon, or strips of fat prepared by butcher
3 tablespoons butter	

Make a 1½-inch-deep slash on top of meat lengthwise to form a pocket. Do not cut through to the two ends. In skillet, sauté the mushrooms and onion in butter over medium heat for 4 to 5 minutes. Sprinkle flour over mixture and add brandy. Heat and mix for 5 minutes, stirring constantly. Remove from heat and cool slightly.

Stuff mushroom mixture into pocket of meat. Layer strips of bacon or fat lengthwise over top and bottom of meat. Tie securely every few inches so mushroom mixture will remain intact. Bake in preheated oven at 350° for 45 minutes. Slice thin and serve immediately, with Madeira Sauce.

Madeira Sauce:

3 tablespoons butter	1 teaspoon gravy thickener
1½ tablespoons flour	¼ cup Madeira
¾ cup beef stock	1 teaspoon Worcestershire sauce

½ cup minced mushrooms, sautéed

In heavy saucepan, melt butter over medium heat. Add flour, stir well, and cook for about 5 minutes. Add stock, thickener, Madeira, and Worcestershire and cook a few minutes. Stir in the mushrooms and serve with meat.

Note: Can be made early in the day and reheated.

Roquefort-stuffed Potatoes

4 large baking potatoes	3 tablespoons cream, hot
6 tablespoons butter	Salt and freshly ground black
3 ounces Roquefort cheese, crumbled	pepper, to taste

Bake potatoes. Cut in half lengthwise and scoop out pulp. Mix pulp with other ingredients. Refill potato shells. Heat in 450° oven to brown along with roast. These freeze well after refilling. Bring to room temperature before placing in oven.

Artichokes Mornay

5 tablespoons butter
4½ tablespoons flour
1¾ cups milk
Salt and freshly ground black
   pepper, to taste
1 teaspoon grated nutmeg
⅛ teaspoon cayenne

½ cup grated Gruyère
1 egg yolk
½ pound mushrooms sliced
   thin
3 10-ounce bags spinach,
   cooked, drained, and chopped
8 artichoke bottoms

3 tablespoons grated Parmesan

Melt 3 tablespoons butter in saucepan and add flour. When blended, add the milk, stirring rapidly with whisk. Add salt, pepper, ½ teaspoon nutmeg, and cayenne. Stir in cheese and heat until melted and blended. Adjust seasonings. Remove from heat and add yolk, stirring vigorously. Set aside. Sauté mushrooms in remaining butter and sprinkle with salt and pepper. Add spinach and remaining nutmeg. Toss to blend and heat thoroughly.

Spoon a little cheese sauce into a flat dish. Place artichoke bottoms on top of sauce and cover with spinach filling. Spoon remaining cheese sauce over all and top with Parmesan cheese. Bake at 400° until hot throughout and bubbling on top. To glaze, run briefly under broiler.

Note: Can be prepared in morning and heated before serving.

French Apple Tart

3½ pounds (9 to 10) Granny
   Smith or other crisp apples
Lemon juice
12 tablespoons unsalted butter
1 1-inch piece vanilla bean
1 La Tarte Crust

¼ cup confectioners' sugar
¼ cup apricot jam
2 tablespoons water
2 tablespoons Grand Marnier
¼ cup slivered almonds,
   toasted

Peel, core, and cut apples in half. Set aside 10 best-looking halves, sprinkled with lemon juice to prevent browning. Slice remaining halves into thin slices, and sprinkle with lemon juice. Melt butter and vanilla bean, add sliced apples, and cook until dry and brown, about 30 to 35 minutes. Remove vanilla bean. Put apples into tart shell. Slice remaining apple halves and arrange in attractive overlapping pattern over cooked apples. Sprinkle confectioners' sugar over all. Bake in preheated 400° oven for 1 hour.

Melt together jam, water, and Grand Marnier. Paint this heated mixture over cooked tart. Top with toasted almonds. Must be prepared same day.

La Tarte Crust:

1¾ cups flour	¼ pound plus 2 tablespoons
¼ teaspoon salt	unsalted butter, cut into pieces
½ teaspoon sugar	and chilled
4 to 6 tablespoons ice water	

Mix all together with pastry blender. Roll out three times as long as wide. Fold both ends to middle and then fold in half. Can now be refrigerated. If using immediately, roll out to fit a 9- or 10-inch pan. Refrigerate while filling is being prepared. Freezes well.

Chocolate Truffles
(Makes 18 to 20)

4 ounces semisweet chocolate	3 tablespoons unsalted butter
1 tablespoon sugar	1 egg yolk
1 tablespoon water or cream	Unsweetened Dutch cocoa

Put chocolate, sugar, and water or cream in double boiler, and stir to dissolve sugar. Add butter and stir until all is melted. Cool slightly, add yolk, and refrigerate until it holds its shape. Roll into small balls. Roll balls in Dutch cocoa. Keep cool. Freezes well.

Super Bowl Sunday

Baked Clams
Poor Boy Sandwich
Chili
Creamy-Crunch Salad
Cherry Strudel Rolls
Caramel Cookies

PREVIOUS DAY	EARLY MORNING	FREEZER
Cherry Strudel Rolls	*Creamy-Crunch Salad*	*Baked Clams*
		Chili
		Caramel Cookies

Baked Clams

2 6½-ounce cans clams and the water they are packed in	**⅛ teaspoon Worcestershire sauce**
Juice of 1 large lemon	**1 cup seasoned bread crumbs**
¼ pound butter or margarine	**Grated Parmesan**
⅛ teaspoon hot pepper sauce	**Lemon wedges, for garnish**

Sauté clams, clam juice, and lemon juice for 10 minutes. Add butter and sauté 10 minutes more. Add seasonings and 1 cup of bread crumbs.

May be refrigerated at this point. Spread mixture into a 7- or 8-inch pie pan. Sprinkle with cheese.

Freezes well. If frozen, bring to room temperature. Bake for 20 minutes in preheated 350° oven. Serve garnished with lemon wedges.

Poor Boy Sandwich (Giant Sub)

1 long loaf unsliced Italian bread	**½ pound thinly sliced provolone cheese**
4 tablespoons bottled Italian dressing	**3 large tomatoes, sliced thin**
½ pound thinly sliced Italian salami	**1 Bermuda onion, sliced thin**
½ pound thinly sliced ham or prosciutto	**2 cups shredded lettuce**
½ pound thinly sliced turkey	**Hot peppers, for garnish (optional)**

Slice bread lengthwise. Brush cut sides with the Italian dressing. Arrange meat slices and cheese on bread. Add tomatoes, onion, and lettuce and fold sandwich closed. Cut into 6 thick sandwiches. Garnish with bottled hot peppers if desired.

Chili

2 pounds ground round steak	3 tablespoons chili powder
Salt and freshly ground black pepper, to taste	1 teaspoon paprika
	2 tablespoons garlic powder
1 large onion, chopped	1 tablespoon cayenne pepper
2 large cloves garlic, minced	1 16-ounce can tomato sauce
2 tablespoons dried oregano	2 cups water
1 16-ounce can kidney beans	

Season ground beef with salt and pepper. Brown in large frying pan with chopped onion and garlic. Pour off fat. Place beef in large saucepan and add seasonings, tomato sauce, and water. Simmer for 20 minutes. Add beans and simmer for another 20 minutes. Freezes well.

Note: Can be made 2 days in advance and refrigerated.

Creamy-Crunch Salad

1 small bunch broccoli, cut into flowerets	1 pint mushrooms, quartered
1 small head cauliflower, cut into flowerets	1 8-ounce can water chestnuts, drained and sliced thin
3 carrots, sliced into ¼-inch rounds	¼ pound green beans, trimmed and cut in ½-inch pieces
1 pint cherry tomatoes, for garnish	

Combine vegetables, except tomatoes, with dressing and refrigerate combined salad for 8 to 14 hours. Garnish with cherry tomatoes.

Dressing:

1 package garlic dressing mix	½ cup white vinegar
1 package onion dressing mix	1 cup sour cream
1 package blue cheese dressing mix	¼ to ½ cup grated Parmesan
1⅓ cups vegetable oil	1 egg
1 teaspoon dry mustard	

Combine dressing ingredients and blend thoroughly. Refrigerate for 2 days before serving.

Note: Dressing must be made 2 days in advance. Salad can be combined in morning.

Cherry Strudel Rolls

1 package active dry yeast	1 teaspoon vanilla extract
½ cup lukewarm water	Melted butter
¼ cup sugar	2 12-ounce jars cherry preserves
3 cups flour	1 cup chopped nuts (almonds or
½ pound soft butter or	pecans)
margarine	1 cup sugar
3 egg yolks, beaten	2 teaspoons cinnamon (or more)

In small bowl, mix yeast and water, adding 1 teaspoon of sugar. Set in warm place to proof. Sift flour and remaining sugar and cut in butter. Make a well in dry ingredients. When yeast mixture is bubbling strongly, add to beaten egg yolks and vanilla. Add this to dry ingredients. Mix well, knead, and divide into 4 pieces. Let rest, covered, for 10 minutes, then roll out each piece into a very thin rectangle. Combine butter, preserves, nuts, sugar, and cinnamon and spread on dough. Roll each piece up as you would a jelly roll. Sprinkle outsides of rolls with sugar and cinnamon. Bake in preheated 350° oven for 30 to 45 minutes on a cookie sheet. Slice to desired width, right out of the oven. Cool.

Note: Can use apricot or apple preserves in place of cherry preserves.

Caramel Cookies
(Makes about 40)

7 ⅞-ounce Heath bars	5 tablespoons vegetable
¾ cup flour	shortening, room temperature
¾ cup oatmeal	6 tablespoons light brown sugar
½ teaspoon salt	6 tablespoons granulated sugar
½ teaspoon baking soda	1 egg
5 tablespoons butter, room	2 teaspoons vanilla extract
temperature	

Chop the candy bars into coarse pieces. Combine the flour, oatmeal, salt, and soda. Beat the butter, shortening, and sugars until creamy. Add the egg and vanilla and beat to combine. Turn mixer to low and blend in the dry ingredients, then stir in the chopped candy. Drop batter by teaspoons on greased baking sheets, about 1 inch apart. Bake in preheated 375° oven until golden brown, about 8 minutes. Cool on rack and store the cooled cookies in an airtight container or well-sealed bag.

Presidents' Day Dinner

Meatballs in Sauerkraut
Cumberland Chicken Wings
Endive, Grapefruit, and Orange Salad with Honey-Lemon Dressing
Grilled Swordfish with Ginger-flavored Sauce
Zubriak
Southern Pecan Tart

PREVIOUS DAY	EARLY MORNING	FREEZER
Chicken Wings	*Southern Pecan Tart*	*Meatballs*
Honey-Lemon Dressing		*Zubriak*

Meatballs in Sauerkraut

2 eggs	2 tablespoons grated onion
2 pounds ground round	1 teaspoon salt
½ cup cornflake crumbs	¼ teaspoon freshly ground
½ cup milk	black pepper

Beat eggs and mix thoroughly with remaining ingredients. Shape in balls about 1¼ inches in diameter and place in shallow baking pan. Bake in preheated 300° oven, shaking pan often or turning meatballs with slotted spoon to brown on all sides. Will take about 30 minutes. Remove meatballs with slotted spoon and add to Sauerkraut Sauce.

Sauerkraut Sauce:

1 cup applesauce	2 cups tomato sauce
1 cup sauerkraut	1 cup brown sugar
	Juice of ½ lemon

Mix all together and add meatballs. Simmer for 1 hour and 30 minutes. If freezing, simmer for only 1 hour, then reheat for 30 minutes or until hot, when thawed. Freezes well.

Cumberland Chicken Wings

24 chicken wings, approximately 4½ pounds	Salt and freshly ground black pepper
	Cumberland Sauce

Preheat broiler. Clip off chicken wing tips with shears. Arrange wings on broiler pan with outside of wings down. Sprinkle with salt and pepper. Broil, about 5 inches from heat, until skins begin to lightly brown, about 5 minutes. Turn wings over and sprinkle with salt and pepper. Broil again until skin is light brown.

Transfer wings to large bowl and pour Cumberland Sauce over them. Cover and refrigerate overnight, turning occasionally.

Position rack in center of oven. Line large jelly-roll pan with heavy-duty foil. Arrange wings on pan with outside of wings down and pour sauce over. Bake in preheated 450° oven until browned, about 35 to 40 minutes. Turn wings over, using tongs, and brush with sauce. Continue baking 8 to 10 minutes, watching carefully to prevent burning. Transfer to serving platter immediately.

Cumberland Sauce:

Peel of 1 large orange	1 teaspoon salt
3 large shallots	¼ teaspoon ground red
1½ cups red currant jelly	pepper
2 tablespoons red wine vinegar	Freshly ground black pepper, to
1 tablespoon dry mustard	taste
2 teaspoons ground ginger	

Place orange peel in processor bowl. With processor running, drop shallots through feed tube and mince, about 3 seconds. Add jelly, vinegar, mustard, ginger, salt, ground red pepper, and ground black pepper and mix for 5 seconds.

Endive, Grapefruit, and Orange Salad

6 Belgian endives	18 orange sections
18 grapefruit sections	6 strips of pimento

Cut each endive lengthwise into quarters. Line 4 quarters of endive, cut sides up, on each salad plate and lay alternate grapefruit and orange sections, 3 of each, across endive. Lay pimento strip across citrus sections.

Note: Can be arranged on a platter for buffet serving.

Honey-Lemon Dressing:

3 tablespoons honey
4½ tablespoons lemon juice
1½ teaspoons sesame seeds, lightly toasted in oven

¾ teaspoon salt
¾ teaspoon ginger

In small bowl, mix together all ingredients. Chill. Pour over individual salads and serve cold.

Grilled Swordfish with Ginger-flavored Sauce

3 swordfish steaks, about 1 inch thick, each about 2¼ pounds

Salt and freshly ground black pepper, to taste
3 tablespoons cooking oil
Basil leaves, for garnish

Sprinkle swordfish on all sides with salt and pepper. Brush all over with oil. Brush broiler rack with oil. Place swordfish on rack; broil 2 to 3 inches from heat source with door partly open for 7 minutes. Carefully turn with spatula. Broil about 3 minutes on second side. Transfer fish to warm serving platter. Garnish with basil leaves and serve with Ginger-flavored Sauce.

Ginger-flavored Sauce:

⅓ cup finely diced tomatoes
⅓ cup finely chopped shallots
3 tablespoons finely chopped
  fresh ginger
⅓ cup dry white wine

⅓ cup white vinegar
⅓ cup whipping cream
9 tablespoons cold butter, cut
  into small cubes

Peel and seed tomatoes before dicing. Mix shallots, ginger, wine, and vinegar in heavy saucepan. Cook over medium-high heat until liquid is almost completely reduced. Add cream, cooking 1 minute. Gradually add butter, stirring constantly. Cook only until sauce is thickened and butter totally melted. Strain through a fine sieve. Return to saucepan, add tomatoes, and reheat gently.

Zubriak

9 lasagna strips (½ pound)
2 10-ounce packages frozen
   chopped spinach, cooked and
   drained
4 tablespoons butter
1 egg, beaten
1 pint small curd cottage cheese
1 6-ounce package sliced
   Monterey Jack cheese
1 6-ounce package grated
   Monterey Jack cheese with
   jalapeño peppers
½ teaspoon nutmeg
1 teaspoon salt
1 teaspoon garlic powder

Cook noodles while steaming spinach. Melt butter. Beat egg, cottage cheese, and grated cheese together, then add spinach and spices. Put a little of the melted butter into a 7-by-11-inch glass baking dish and lay 3 strips of lasagna on the bottom. Layer in half the cheese mixture, then noodles, butter, and mixture again. Put on last layer of noodles. Dot with butter and put sliced cheese on last. Cover with foil. Bake in preheated 325° oven for ½ hour covered, then ½ hour uncovered.

Southern Pecan Tart

Shell:

2 cups sifted all-purpose flour
2 tablespoons sugar
½ teaspoon salt
7 tablespoons butter, chilled
4 tablespoons solid vegetable
   shortening, chilled
5 tablespoons cold water

Place flour, sugar, and salt in food processor. Add butter and shortening and turn on-off to make coarse crumbs. Add water while machine is running. Stop as soon as a mass begins to form. Press dough into a ball. Wrap and refrigerate until well chilled. Roll dough out on floured board or between pieces of wax paper. Roll into circle about ⅛-inch thick and 2 inches larger than an 11-inch tart pan. Butter the tart pan shell and removable bottom. Press dough lightly into pan. It is best to make sides of pastry shell a little thicker than bottom.

Filling:

4 large eggs
1⅓ cups brown sugar
¼ teaspoon salt
1½ teaspoons vanilla extract
4 tablespoons melted butter
1 cup pecan halves
Confectioners' sugar

Beat eggs well, add rest of ingredients, and blend. Pour into tart shell and bake in preheated 400° oven for 10 minutes. Reduce heat to 325° and bake for 40 minutes or until set.

Remove from oven, let sit for 5 minutes, then remove outer tart pan ring and place tart on baking rack. Allow to cool. Sift confectioners' sugar over top

☙ ☙ ☙

Easter Dinner

Spicy Crabmeat Spread
Spinach Hors d'Oeuvres
Eggplant Salad
Leg of Lamb with Mustard and Herbs
Potatoes Dauphinois
Strawberries Romanoff
Chocolate Pecan Pie

PREVIOUS DAY	EARLY MORNING	FREEZER
Spicy Crabmeat Spread	*Leg of Lamb*	*Spinach Hors d'Oeurves*
Eggplant Salad	*Strawberries Romanoff*	

Spicy Crabmeat Spread

1 8-ounce package cream cheese
3 tablespoons sour cream
2 tablespoons horseradish
5 drops Worcestershire sauce
5 drops hot pepper sauce
Garlic salt
Onion salt
6 to 7 ounces crabmeat, frozen
  or canned
Small rye bread or pumpernickel
  squares

Mix cream cheese, sour cream, and seasonings in processor until creamy. Stir in crabmeat. Refrigerate several hours or overnight. Serve with small rye bread or pumpernickel squares.

Spinach Hors d'Oeuvres

5 slices home-style white bread,
   cut into 2-inch rounds
8 tablespoons butter
1 10-ounce package frozen
   chopped spinach, thawed

⅛ teaspoon salt, for spinach
⅓ cup bread crumbs
4 ounces aged Swiss cheese,
   grated

Fry bread in skillet with 4 tablespoons of the butter, until brown on both sides. Squeeze moisture from spinach and add salt. Mix bread crumbs, cheese, and remaining butter, melted. Mix one-half of the mixture into spinach. Mound spinach mixture on bread rounds, put remaining bread-crumb mixture on top of each round. Place rounds on cookie sheet and broil until brown. Serve immediately. Can be frozen before broiling.

Note: Do not overbroil or hold in warm oven, as they will dry out.

Eggplant Salad

1½ pounds eggplant, trimmed
   and peeled
Salt
¾ cup olive oil
1 clove garlic, minced
¼ cup red wine vinegar
1½ tablespoons fresh lemon
   juice
1½ tablespoons dry red wine
½ teaspoon dried basil
¼ teaspoon dried oregano
¼ teaspoon dried thyme
2 bell peppers (red, green, or
   combined)

2 tomatoes, diced
1 small cucumber, peeled,
   seeded, and chopped
2 scallions, chopped
2 tablespoons chopped fresh
   parsley
⅛ teaspoon freshly ground
   black pepper, or to taste
Lettuce leaves
Scallions, cucumbers, tomato
   wedges, and parsley, for
   garnish

Cut eggplant into ½-inch slices and sprinkle liberally with salt. Place slices between several layers of paper towels and top with a weight for 1 hour to extract bitter juices. Sauté in large skillet in ¼ to ½ cup olive oil over medium heat, about 1 minute per side. Do not overcook. Add more oil as necessary. Combine next 7 ingredients into a marinade in a bowl. Set aside. Cut eggplant slices to ½-inch cubes, put in a nonaluminum bowl, and pour marinade over. Chill at least 3 hours. Add peppers, tomatoes, cucumber, scallions, and parsley and stir to mix. Season to taste with salt and pepper. Serve in bowl or platter lined with lettuce leaves and garnish with scallions, sliced cucumbers, tomato wedges, and parsley.

Leg of Lamb with Mustard and Herbs

1 clove garlic, crushed	2 teaspoons dried rosemary,
½ cup Dijon mustard	crushed
2 tablespoons soy sauce	2 tablespoons vegetable or olive
¼ teaspoon ground ginger	oil

1 leg of lamb, about 6 pounds

Whisk the garlic, mustard, soy sauce, ginger, and rosemary in a bowl, blender, or processor. Slowly pour in the oil, whisking or blending as you do. Mixture will resemble mayonnaise in consistency.

Early in the day, place the lamb on a rack in a shallow roasting pan. Spread the mustard and herb mixture over the meat, coating it on all sides. Refrigerate, but bring to room temperature before roasting the lamb. Roast the lamb in preheated 350° oven for 2 to 2½ hours, or about 20 minutes per pound. A meat thermometer inserted in the thickest part of the leg should register 140° for medium rare or 150° for medium well done. Remove the meat to a carving board, cover very loosely with foil, and allow to rest for 15 minutes before carving.

Potatoes Dauphinois

2½ cups heavy cream	½ cup grated Swiss cheese
2 tablespoons butter	¼ cup grated Parmesan cheese
1 clove garlic, crushed	½ teaspoon salt
Pinch of nutmeg	Freshly ground black pepper
6 Idaho potatoes, peeled and thinly sliced	

Simmer cream, butter, garlic, and nutmeg in small saucepan over low heat for 10 minutes, until cream is reduced to 2 cups and has thickened slightly. Butter a small casserole and arrange a layer of one-third of the potatoes in bottom of the dish. Add one-third of the combined cheeses, season with salt and pepper, and repeat until 3 layers of potatoes and cheese have been made. Dot top with butter. Add cream mixture—there should be enough to cover potatoes. Cover casserole and cook in preheated 300° oven for 1 hour.

Strawberries Romanoff

1 quart fresh strawberries	1 cup whipping cream
¼ cup orange juice	2 tablespoons sugar
¼ cup curaçao	1 teaspoon vanilla extract

Wash and hull strawberries. Marinate in mixture of juice and curaçao for several hours, stirring occasionally. Place strawberries in stemmed sherbet glasses.

Whip cream, folding in sugar and vanilla. Spoon over strawberries.

Chocolate Pecan Pie

2 eggs	1 cup chocolate chips
¼ pound butter	1½ cups coarsely chopped
½ teaspoon salt	pecans
½ cup granulated sugar	1 tablespoon bourbon
½ cup brown sugar	1 tablespoon flour, to thicken

1 unbaked 9-inch pie shell

Beat eggs slightly. Melt butter, then cool. Mix all ingredients except pie shell, in order. Pour into unbaked pie shell. Bake in preheated 350° oven for 30 minutes.

Passover Dinner

Charoset
Gefilte Fish Mold
Chicken Soup with Matzo Balls
Capon with Orange Stuffing and Apricot Glaze
Steamed Asparagus in Scallion Bundles
Matzo Farfel
Wine Cake
Frozen Chocolate Crepes
Raspberry Ribbons

Charoset

6 apples, peeled and coarsely chopped	½ cup chopped dates (optional)
⅓ cup chopped almonds	½ teaspoon cinnamon
2 tablespoons sugar	Grated rind of 1 lemon

1 tablespoon sweet red wine, more as needed

Combine all ingredients, mixing thoroughly. Can be blended in processor for even texture. Add more wine to taste or to improve texture.

Gefilte Fish Mold

1 pound ground whitefish	1 cup cream
1 pound ground pike	1½ tablespoons salt, or more to taste
1 pound ground trout	½ tablespoon freshly ground black pepper
1 large onion, grated	
4 egg yolks, slightly beaten	

4 egg whites, stiffly beaten

Combine fish in large bowl. Add onion, then yolks, then cream and seasonings. Fold in stiffly beaten egg whites. Grease a large fish-shaped mold with mayonnaise. Pour fish mixture into mold and cover entirely and tightly with foil.

Bake mold in a pan of hot water in 350° oven for 1 hour and 15 minutes. Remove from oven and cool. Refrigerate overnight, keeping foil cover in place. Unmold and serve with red and white horseradish and lemon wedges.

Chicken Soup with Matzo Balls

1 large, fresh kosher chicken
Water to cover
3 carrots, sliced
1 parsley root, chopped
1 parsnip, peeled and cut in
　pieces
1 turnip, peeled and cubed

3 ribs celery, with leaves,
　chopped
1 whole onion, scored with fork
Salt and freshly ground white
　pepper, to taste
1 stalk fresh dill (or 2 teaspoons
　dried)

2 sprigs parsley

Place chicken in large pot, cover with water. Bring to a boil and skim off foam. Add remaining ingredients, cover, and simmer 3 hours. Strain. Pick out a few tablespoons carrots and turnip pieces, place in strainer, and mash with back of spoon into soup. Refrigerate overnight. Before reheating, remove all congealed fat from top.

Matzo Balls:

2 eggs, slightly beaten
2 tablespoons chicken fat
½ cup matzo meal
½ teaspoon salt

Parsley
2 tablespoons soup stock or
　water

Mix eggs and fat and add matzo meal, salt, and parsley. When well blended, add soup or water. Cover bowl and put in refrigerator for at least 30 minutes. Roll spoonfuls of mixture into balls and boil in salted water or bouillon, covered, for 1 hour or longer. Drain and add to chicken soup.

Capon with Orange Stuffing

1 capon (approximately 8
　pounds)
½ teaspoon each salt, freshly
　ground pepper, garlic powder,
　and onion powder

2 oranges, with juice
2 tablespoons melted butter or
　margarine

Sprinkle neck and body cavity with salt, pepper, garlic powder, and onion powder. Cut the oranges into halves and squeeze juice into cavity and over outside of capon. Place orange halves into cavity. Set bird in shallow roasting pan, breast side up. Sprinkle additional salt and pepper on top. Spread 2 tablespoons butter on top.

Apricot Glaze:

¾ cup apricot jam   6 tablespoons orange juice
2 tablespoons brandy

Combine glaze ingredients and mix well. Brush capon with glaze. Roast in preheated 350° oven for 2 hours 30 minutes, basting with glaze every half-hour. Combine pan drippings with any remaining glaze and skim off fat. Serve capon with this sauce.

Steamed Asparagus in Scallion Bundles

2 pounds fresh asparagus   Salt and freshly ground black
2 bunches scallions   pepper, to taste
4 tablespoons butter, melted

Clean asparagus and peel bottoms with potato peeler. Steam asparagus in a large glass pan in microwave oven for 6 minutes. Clean scallions. Use green part as a string to tie 4 or 5 asparagus spears together. Pour butter over all and season to taste.

Note: If cooking on stove, tie asparagus into serving bunches with white string. Stand upright in deep pan with ½ cup boiling water; cover and steam 7 to 10 minutes, until desired tenderness is reached. Proceed with recipe, replacing string with scallions.

Matzo Farfel

1 cup minced onion   ¼ teaspoon freshly ground
1 cup diced celery   black pepper
½ pound mushrooms, sliced   2 teaspoons paprika
6 tablespoons chicken fat   2 eggs, beaten
3½ cups matzo farfel (½   1 10½-ounce can condensed
    pound)   chicken soup
1 teaspoon seasoned salt   1¼ cups hot water

Sauté vegetables in chicken fat until tender. Add farfel. Combine remaining ingredients in separate bowl and add to matzo mixture. Add hot water last. Bake in preheated 375° oven for 30 minutes, or until firm.

Note: Can be assembled early in day. Add eggs, chicken soup, and water just before baking.

Wine Cake

6 or 7 eggs, separated	Juice and grated rind of ½
1½ cups sugar	lemon or orange
¼ cup sweet red wine, or a	1 cup finely chopped walnuts
little more	½ cup matzo cake meal

Pinch of salt (optional)

Beat yolks until light and thick, add half of sugar, and beat well until thoroughly mixed. Add wine and juice and rind (on blending speed). Mix nuts and meal and pour into mixed liquids. When thoroughly blended, fold into egg whites, which have been beaten until stiff with remaining sugar (add pinch of salt for stiffness). Pour batter into tube pan and bake in preheated 350° oven for approximately 1 hour. Cake is done when it springs back to touch.

Frozen Chocolate Crepes

½ cup, less 1 tablespoon, potato starch	6 eggs
½ cup, less 1 tablespoon, matzo cake meal	1½ cups water
	1 tablespoon butter or margarine, melted
½ teaspoon salt	White grapes or strawberries, for
¼ cup sugar	garnish
3 tablespoons unsweetened cocoa	Nuts, for garnish

Sift together dry ingredients. Beat eggs until light. Add ½ cup water and beat again. Gradually add remaining cup water, beating until smooth. Add melted butter and beaten eggs to the batter, a small amount at a time, stirring each time until smooth. In a food processor or blender combine all ingredients until smooth. Let batter stand for 1 hour before making crepes.

Place 8-inch crepe pan over medium-high heat and brush lightly with butter. When butter is sizzling but not brown, pour scant

¼ cup batter into pan. Quickly lift pan off heat and swirl to coat bottom and sides, pouring excess batter back into bowl. Loosen sides of crepe with spatula. Return to heat and cook 1 minute or until bottom darkens slightly and looks dry. Watch carefully, because both cocoa and sugar can cause crepes to burn easily. Turn crepes onto paper towel or wax paper. Continue until all batter is used, brushing pan with butter as needed. When crepes are cooled place 2 tablespoons of Chocolate Mousse Filling on each and roll up cigar fashion. Place seam side down on baking sheet and freeze. When firm, wrap carefully and keep in freezer until ready to serve.

Remove crepes 10 minutes before serving. Pour a small amount of hot Chocolate Sauce over and around crepes and sprinkle nuts over top. Garnish plate with small cluster of grapes or strawberries.

Chocolate Mousse Filling:

9 ounces semisweet chocolate	2 tablespoons brandy
9 egg yolks	9 egg whites, stiffly beaten

Melt chocolate over hot, not boiling water, in top of double boiler. When smooth, remove from heat. Add small amount of chocolate to yolks, stirring constantly. Add yolks to chocolate and heat thoroughly. Cool, stirring occasionally. Blend in brandy and fold in egg whites. Chill thoroughly overnight in refrigerator before filling crepes.

Chocolate Sauce:

6 ounces semisweet chocolate	6 tablespoons black coffee
3 tablespoons butter or margarine	1 to 2 tablespoons brandy

Combine first 3 ingredients in top of double boiler over hot water. When very warm, remove from heat and add brandy.

Raspberry Ribbons
(Makes 20)

8 ounces shelled walnuts	Matzo cake meal
⅔ cup sugar	⅔ cup raspberry preserves
2 egg whites, slightly beaten, until foamy	

Grate walnuts in processor or blender. Nuts should be dry and powdery. (Do not grind or nuts will be oily.) Stir sugar into grated walnuts. Add egg whites, a small amount at a time, until mixture forms a paste that can be kneaded. Shape paste into 2 rolls, 10 inches long and ¾ inch in diameter. Put rolls on cookie sheets that have been greased and lightly dusted with cake meal. With a finger, make a channel about ½ inch deep down center of each roll, leaving ¼ inch intact at each end. Bake at 350° for 20 to 25 minutes or until golden. Meanwhile, heat preserves until syrupy in a saucepan. Remove rolls from oven and fill channels with hot preserves. When cool, cut rolls into crosswise slices, ¾-inch thick.

Mother's Day

Gouda en Croute
Marinated Mushrooms
Asparagus Salad with Continental Dressing
Chicken Breasts Piquant
Herbed Green Beans
Rice Potpourri
Flan
Peachy Keen Meringue

PREVIOUS DAY	EARLY MORNING	FREEZER
Marinated Mushrooms	*Meringue*	
Continental Dressing		
Flan		

Gouda en Croute

1 package refrigerator crescent rolls	1 8-ounce Gouda cheese (wax cover removed)

Remove and unroll dough. Lay flat on board and pinch edges to make a square. Place cheese on dough and cover completely, making design on top if desired. Chill until ready to bake. Bake in preheated oven at temperature on package for 30 to 35 minutes. Check for golden color after 30 minutes of baking. Cut in wedges and serve.

Marinated Mushrooms

4 tablespoons water
6 tablespoons lemon juice or
  vinegar
3 cloves garlic, minced
6 tablespoons salad oil
½ teaspoon salt

⅓ teaspoon freshly ground
  black pepper
3 bay leaves
1 pound mushrooms, brushed
  and trimmed

Combine all ingredients, except mushrooms, in saucepan and heat for a few minutes. Pour marinade over raw mushrooms and marinate for 1 day. Serve on toothpicks.

Asparagus Salad

1½ pounds fresh asparagus or
  2 cans asparagus spears
1 head Bibb lettuce
1 head curly red lettuce

2 14-ounce cans hearts of palm
1 can artichoke hearts
1 cup cherry tomatoes
Pimentos, for garnish

Steam asparagus for 5 minutes, then chill. Arrange lettuce on individual salad plates and place several stalks of asparagus, one stalk heart of palm (sliced in half if very thick), and an artichoke heart on each. Garnish with cherry tomatoes and/or several small pimentos. Drizzle Continental Dressing over each salad.

Continental Dressing:

½ cup salad oil
¼ cup lemon juice
½ teaspoon salt
½ teaspoon sugar
½ teaspoon paprika

1 tablespoon finely minced celery
2 tablespoons minced pimento-
  stuffed green olives
2 tablespoons finely minced
  scallions, including tops

Combine all ingredients 1 day in advance to allow flavors to blend.

Chicken Breasts Piquant
Crumb Mixture:

½ cup grated Parmesan   2 cups seasoned bread crumbs
              3 tablespoons sesame seeds

Mix all ingredients and spread on big plate or flat pan.

Sauce:

1 10-ounce jar currant jelly   1 teaspoon dry mustard
1 6-ounce can frozen orange   ¼ cup sherry
  juice concentrate

Combine and heat ingredients in small saucepan.

6 boneless, skinless chicken   4 tablespoons butter or
  breasts, cut in half   margarine, melted

Dip chicken breasts in melted butter and then crumb mixture. Shape
into ball and place on buttered glass pan. Bake in preheated 350° oven
for 1 hour and 15 minutes. Pour sauce over chicken just before serving.
  Note: Chicken can be prepared up to baking step in morning.

Herbed Green Beans

2 pounds young, tender green   1¼ teaspoons chopped mint
  beans, snapped   2½ tablespoons minced
6 tablespoons olive oil   parsley
2 cloves garlic   2½ cups peeled and chopped
2½ tablespoons chopped fresh   tomatoes
  basil   Salt, to taste

Soak beans for 15 minutes in water to cover and then drain. Cook
remaining ingredients together for 5 minutes. Blanch beans in boiling
salted water about 1 minute, drain, and plunge into cold water. Drain.
Add herbs and tomatoes and cook for 10 minutes.

Rice Potpourri

1 medium onion, chopped	¼ teaspoon curry
1½ cups long grain white rice	½ teaspoon dried sage
3 tablespoons butter	1 teaspoon salt
¾ teaspoon each dried basil, marjoram, and thyme	3 cups chicken broth

Sauté onion and rice for about 5 minutes in butter. Add remaining ingredients and heat to boil. Cover and cook about 30 minutes. Fluff before serving.

Flan

8 eggs	¼ teaspoon cinnamon
1 8-ounce package cream cheese at room temperature	1½ cups sugar
2 13-ounce cans evaporated milk	3 tablespoons water, approximately
2 14-ounce cans condensed milk	Fresh fruit, for topping and garnish
2 tablespoons vanilla extract	

Place large frying pan half filled with water into preheated 350° oven (use pan with ovenproof handle, large enough to hold 10- or 11-cup ring mold).

In large bowl, beat eggs together. In smaller bowl, mix softened cream cheese with small amount of evaporated milk until cream cheese is smooth. Add this to eggs along with remaining milk, vanilla, and cinnamon. Mix well.

Put sugar in a saucepan and add water. Over high heat, mix sugar and water until smooth, stirring constantly with wooden spoon. The sugar will first harden and turn crumbly but continue stirring. Once it begins to caramelize, it will liquefy quickly. Do not let it turn too dark, as it will burn quickly and it continues to cook even after removal from heat. When it is runny and light brown (some lumps may still be present) pour into a lightly oiled 10- or 11-cup ring mold. (Be sure to hold mold with potholders.) Swirl the sugar around the bottom of the pan until it is evenly distributed.

Place mold in water bath in oven. Pour mixed egg mixture into mold. Bake at 350° for 1 hour and 20 minutes. Check after about 1 hour and 10 minutes and test for doneness with a toothpick or knife. Let cool and then refrigerate overnight. Unmold onto serving platter. Fill center with fresh strawberries and decorate top with sliced kiwi, blueberries, or other available fresh fruit.

Hints:

1. Do not submerge saucepan from sugar in water until it is completely cooled—it can explode. The hardened sugar will come off if you run the pot under hot water.
2. Make sure potholders are on hand, since the ring mold will become very hot once the sugar is in it.
3. Pour the custard into the ring mold after it is in the oven to avoid spilling when you transfer the mold into the water.

Peachy Keen Meringue

3 egg whites	2 cups sour cream
¼ teaspoon cream of tartar	5 large, ripe peaches, *or* 1 20-
¼ teaspoon salt	ounce package frozen sliced
1 cup firmly packed brown sugar	peaches, defrosted and drained

In large bowl of electric mixer, let egg whites come to room temperature, about 1 hour. Cover a large cookie sheet with foil. Draw around the edge of a bowl or pie plate to make a 10-inch circle. Lightly butter the circle.

At high speed, beat egg whites with cream of tartar and salt until soft peaks form. Gradually beat in brown sugar, 2 tablespoons at a time, beating well after each addition. Continue beating until very stiff peaks form. Meringue should be shiny and moist.

Spread three-quarters of meringue to cover circle. Build up sides about 1 inch with remaining meringue by shaping with 2 tablespoons. Bake in preheated 275° oven for 1 hour. Remove from oven, cool for 30 minutes, then peel foil from bottom and place meringue on serving dish. Just before serving, spread sour cream over meringue and top with sliced peaches arranged decoratively.

Father's Day

Avocado-Grapefruit Salad with Honey and Poppy Seed Dressing
Family Chicken
Asparagus with Parmesan Brown Butter
White and Wild Rice Casserole
Michigan Blueberry Dessert

PREVIOUS DAY   EARLY MORNING   FREEZER

Salad dressing   *Rice Casserole*

Avocado-Grapefruit Salad

3 heads Boston lettuce or a
   mixture of romaine and
   iceberg lettuces
2 avocados, peeled and sliced,
   sprinkled with lemon juice

2 pink grapefruit, peeled and
   sectioned
¼ cup black or stuffed green
   olives (optional)
Pomegranate seeds, for garnish

Honey and Poppy Seed Dressing

Line salad bowl with lettuce torn into bite-sized pieces. Arrange avocados, grapefruit, and optional olives on top. Serve garnished with
pomegranate seeds and with Honey and Poppy Seed Dressing (see
Index).

Family Chicken

2 3-pound chickens, cut up
½ cup soy sauce
¼ cup granulated sugar
¼ cup brown sugar

3 tablespoons Hoisin sauce
¼ teaspoon garlic salt
½ cup sherry (optional)
Paprika, for color

In shallow pan, place chicken skin side up. Mix together remaining
ingredients, except for paprika. Spread mix on chicken. Bake in preheated 375° oven for 30 minutes. Turn chicken and baste with remaining sauce. Cook 20 minutes longer. Sprinkle with paprika and
broil for 2 to 3 minutes before serving.

Asparagus with Parmesan Brown Butter

1½ pounds asparagus   4 tablespoons butter
          3 tablespoons freshly grated Parmesan

Steam asparagus for 7 minutes and drain. Melt butter until it begins to brown. Pour over asparagus in serving dish. Sprinkle with Parmesan.

White and Wild Rice Casserole

½ cup wild rice
½ cup long grain white rice
1 10½-ounce can consommé
1 10½-ounce can onion soup
1 8-ounce can water chestnuts,
  drained and sliced thin

1 4½-ounce jar mushroom
  pieces, drained
1 ounce sliced almonds
4 tablespoons butter or
  margarine, cut up

Combine wild rice, white rice, consommé, and onion soup in a 2-quart covered casserole. Add water chestnuts, mushroom pieces, almonds, and butter. Mix well. Cover casserole and bake for 1 hour in preheated 350° oven. Check after 45 minutes to see if all liquid is absorbed.

Michigan Blueberry Dessert

¼ cup butter
2 eggs, beaten well
¾ cup sugar
1 cup flour

¼ cup solid vegetable
  shortening, melted
½ cup chopped pecans
2 pints fresh blueberries

Butter a 9-inch pie plate. Beat eggs, add sugar, flour, and melted shortening, then nuts. Place blueberries in pie tin and pour batter over berries. Bake in preheated 350° oven for 1 hour.

Fourth of July

Texas Torte
Gourmet Cheeseburgers with Barbecue Sauce
Baked Onions Gratinée
Potato Skins
Blueberry Lattice Pie à la Mode
Strawberry Torte

PREVIOUS DAY	EARLY MORNING	FREEZER
Blueberry Pie	Bake potatoes	
Strawberry Torte		

Texas Torte

2 eggs, beaten	½ pound sharp Cheddar
2 tablespoons flour	cheese, grated
½ teaspoon salt	½ pound Monterey Jack
⅓ cup milk	cheese, grated
1 4-ounce can chopped green	Red taco sauce (optional)
chilies	

Beat eggs, add flour, salt, and milk. Beat well. Add remaining ingredients except taco sauce and mix well. Pour into a flat, well-greased 8-by-12-inch glass baking dish. Bake in preheated 350° oven for 35 minutes. Cut into small squares and serve as an hors d'oeuvre. Can be sliced in wedges and served with bottled red taco sauce.

Gourmet Cheeseburgers

½ pound Roquefort cheese	½ pound Gouda cheese
2½ pounds ground beef	

Cut cheese into 1-ounce chunks, about ⅓-inch thick, in a rectangular shape. Mold the ground beef around the cheese so that it is completely enclosed. Hamburgers should be very thick. Barbecue a few minutes on each side, basting frequently with Barbecue Sauce.

Barbecue Sauce:

6 ounces ketchup
4 ounces bottled barbecue sauce
¼ cup light brown sugar
2 tablespoons lemon juice

1½ teaspoons Worcestershire
   sauce
½ cup pineapple juice
1 tablespoon steak sauce

¼ cup white vinegar

Combine all ingredients.

Baked Onions Gratinée
(Serves 8)

4 tablespoons unsalted butter
8 large sweet onions, cut into
   chunks

½ cup long grain white rice
1½ cups shredded Jarlsberg
   cheese

1 cup half-and-half

Melt butter in large skillet over medium heat. Sauté onions until transparent and remove from heat. Cook rice in 3 cups salted boiling water for 5 minutes and drain well. Blend in onions, cheese, and half-and-half. Turn mixture into 2-quart casserole and bake for 1 hour at 325°. Serve hot.

Potato Skins

6 large potatoes
4 tablespoons oil
2 tablespoons grated Parmesan
½ teaspoon salt

½ teaspoon paprika
¼ teaspoon freshly ground
   black pepper

Scrub potatoes and bake in preheated 400° oven for 1 to 1¼ hours. Cut baked potatoes in sixths, removing white potato pulp from skins. Mix remaining ingredients and toss potato skins in mixture. Place on baking sheet and bake in 475° oven for 8 minutes. Turn once during cooking.

Blueberry Lattice Pie à la Mode

Pastry for 2-crust 9-inch pie
6½ cups blueberries, fresh or
   frozen, thawed
1 cup sugar
4 tablespoons flour
1½ tablespoons quick-cooking
   tapioca

Pinch of salt
Pinch of cinnamon
Juice of 1 large lemon
1½ to 2 tablespoons butter
Vanilla ice cream

Line 9½-inch deep pie dish with pastry. Combine berries and dry ingredients. Allow to stand 5 minutes. Add lemon juice and toss gently. Pour into crust and dot with butter. Place lattice crust over top. Make circle of foil and place over rim of crust. Bake in preheated 450° oven for 10 minutes, then reduce heat to 350° and bake 10 minutes. Remove the foil and bake 20 minutes longer, or until bubbly.

Top with vanilla ice cream.

Strawberry Torte

3 eggs, separated
1 cup sugar
3 tablespoons water
1 teaspoon vanilla extract
1 cup chopped nuts
1¼ cups graham cracker
   crumbs

2 teaspoons baking powder
2 cups whipping cream
3 tablespoons confectioners'
   sugar
1 quart strawberries

Beat egg whites until stiff. Beat yolks until thick and add sugar, water, and vanilla. Combine nuts, cracker crumbs, and baking powder and add to batter. This will be thick. Fold in egg whites. Line two 8-inch layer-cake pans with wax paper. Pour batter into prepared pans. Bake in preheated 350° oven for 25 minutes. Remove from pans immediately. Peel off wax paper and place on rack to cool.

Whip cream with confectioners' sugar. Clean and slice strawberries. Place one-third of sliced berries on 1 layer of cake. Cover with whipped cream. Repeat with second layer. Decorate top with sliced berries. Refrigerate.

Labor Day Supper

Zucchini Soup
Pasta and Artichoke Salad with Lemon-Tarragon Dressing
Chicken in Hearty Tomato Sauce
Dill Bread
Peanut Brittle
Pumpkin Cake

PREVIOUS DAY	EARLY MORNING	FREEZER
Zucchini Soup	*Pasta and Artichoke*	*Pumpkin Cake*
Tarragon Dressing	*Salad*	
Dill Bread	*Chicken*	
Peanut Brittle		

Zucchini Soup

1½ pounds zucchini
3 tablespoons butter
3 tablespoons finely chopped onion
1 large clove garlic
2¾ cups chicken stock
¾ cup heavy cream
1 teaspoon curry, or more, to taste
¾ teaspoon salt
Minced chives, for garnish

Wash and slice zucchini, but do not peel. Melt butter in large skillet. Add onion, garlic, and zucchini. Sauté 10 minutes or until tender. Do not let brown. Put into blender or processor and process until thoroughly liquefied. Add stock, cream, and seasonings and process. Serve sprinkled with minced chives.

Note: Delicious hot or cold.

Pasta and Artichoke Salad

1 pound pasta shells
2 14-ounce cans artichokes in water
1 bunch scallions, chopped small
1 large red pepper, chopped
1 large green pepper, chopped
¾ pound Asiago cheese, coarsely grated (for milder taste, use Swiss or Provolone)
½ red onion, chopped
½ pound dry cured ham, julienned

Cook pasta 5 minutes and drain. Drain artichokes and quarter. Combine all ingredients and toss with Lemon-Tarragon Dressing.

Lemon-Tarragon Dressing:

1 cup olive oil	1 teaspoon lemon pepper
¼ cup red wine vinegar	Juice of ½ lemon
2 tablespoons tarragon vinegar	Salt, to taste

Combine all ingredients in jar with tight-fitting lid. Shake well and chill. Shake before pouring over salad.

Chicken in Hearty Tomato Sauce

1 pound ground sirloin	2 cloves garlic, minced
¼ cup plus 1 tablespoon safflower oil	¾ teaspoon each dried sweet basil and oregano
Salt and pepper, to taste	8 whole, skinless, boned chicken breasts
2 1-pound, 13-ounce cans plum tomatoes, in purée	Seasoned flour, for dredging
1 12-ounce can tomato paste	4 tablespoons melted butter or margarine, or more, if needed
1 12-ounce can water, plus ¼ cup water	1 pound mozzarella, shredded
1 teaspoon sugar	½ cup grated Parmesan

Sauté ground sirloin in 1 tablespoon safflower oil and season with salt and pepper. Drain off fat when browned and set meat aside. Put tomatoes through sieve, removing all seeds. Simmer the tomatoes and seasonings for 2½ hours; add sirloin for the last 30 minutes.

Dredge chicken breasts in seasoned flour and sauté in melted butter and ¼ cup safflower oil. Sauté until lightly browned. More butter and oil may be added as needed. In 9-inch-by-13-inch baking dish, layer sauce, chicken, and shredded mozzarella; top with grated Parmesan. Bake in 350° oven for 45 minutes.

Note: Sauce can be made in advance and frozen.

Dill Bread
(Makes 1 loaf)

1 package active dry yeast	2 teaspoons dill weed
2 tablespoons sugar	1 teaspoon salt
¼ cup warm water	¼ teaspoon baking soda
1 cup cottage cheese	1 egg
4 tablespoons butter	2½ cups flour
1 tablespoon minced onion	Dill seed (optional)

Dissolve yeast with 1 tablespoon of the sugar in warm water and let proof about 10 minutes or until yeast bubbles up in the cup. Place cottage cheese, butter, remaining sugar, onion, dill weed, salt, and baking soda in saucepan and heat slowly until just warm. Beat the egg well in a large bowl and stir the yeast mixture into it. Beat in the cottage cheese mixture and enough flour to make a soft dough. Turn dough out onto lightly floured surface and knead 10 minutes or until it is smooth and springs back when indented with fingers. Place in a buttered bowl, turning to coat all over, and cover with a damp towel. Let rise in warm place for 1 hour or until doubled in bulk.

Punch dough down and shape into a loaf. Place in buttered 8-by-5-by-3-inch loaf pan or a 1½-quart round casserole. Cover with a damp towel and let rise in warm, draft-free place for 30 to 40 minutes. Bake in preheated 350° oven for about 30 minutes or until loaf is golden brown and sounds hollow when tapped on bottom. Turn out of pan and cool on rack. While still warm, if desired, brush with melted butter and sprinkle with dill seed.

Peanut Brittle

2 cups sugar	2 cups Spanish peanuts
1 cup light corn syrup	½ teaspoon soda
	1 tablespoon butter

Put sugar and syrup in a 2-quart micro-safe bowl. Cook on high power for 9 minutes, stirring with a wooden or micro spoon every 3 minutes. Add the peanuts and cook on high for 10 minutes, stirring every 3 minutes, until the mixture is golden brown. It may take a few minutes more or less. Remove from the oven, stir in the soda and butter, and blend well. *Carefully* pour mixture on greased cookie sheet with sides, spreading into a thin layer with a wooden spoon. This mixture is very hot—don't get burned!

Pumpkin Cake

3 cups all-purpose flour	1¼ cups cooking oil
1 teaspoon salt	2 cups canned pumpkin
2 teaspoons baking powder	2 cups sugar
2 teaspoons baking soda	4 eggs, well beaten
2 teaspoons pumpkin pie spice	¾ cup chopped nuts

Sift flour, salt, baking powder and soda, and pie spice. Combine oil, pumpkin, sugar, and eggs. Mix dry ingredients into pumpkin mixture. Add nuts. Pour mixture into 13-by-9-by-2-inch pan. Bake in preheated 350° oven for 45 minutes. Cool in pan. Frost cake before cutting into squares.

Icing:

1 tablespoon butter   2 cups confectioners' sugar
Strong black coffee (enough to make very thin)

Cream butter and sugar and thin with coffee.

Columbus Day

White Sangria
Turkey Sabers
Honeydew with Lime and Coriander
Jimmy's Place Salad with Jimmy's Quick Dressing
Sesame Sea Bass
Paillason
Eclair Ring

PREVIOUS DAY	EARLY MORNING	FREEZER
Salad dressing	*Sangria*	
	Melon with Lime and Coriander	
	Marinate bass	
	Paillason	
	Eclair Ring	

White Sangria

2 bottles white wine, chilled
½ orange, thinly sliced
½ lemon, thinly sliced
1 kiwi fruit, peeled and sliced

2 ounces cognac
8 teaspoons sugar
½ cup fresh blackberries
Club soda, to taste

Pour wine into glass pitcher and add fruit slices, cognac, and sugar. Stir until sugar dissolves. Add blackberries. Chill several hours. Add ice cubes and club soda to taste.

Turkey Sabers

1 pound turkey breast
2 egg whites, from extra-large
eggs
Salt and freshly ground pepper,
to taste
Dash of Tabasco sauce
¼ teaspoon each fresh chervil,
tarragon, and chives

1 cup fine bread crumbs
6 tablespoons salad oil
6 tablespoons unsalted butter
Capers and lemon wedges, for
garnish

Cut turkey into slices about ⅛-inch thick, then into strips 3 inches long and about 1 inch wide. Beat the egg whites until frothy. Season with salt, pepper, and Tabasco. Add the finely minced herbs and beat well. Set bread crumbs in dish. Melt the oil and butter in a large skillet. Dip the turkey sabers first into the egg-white mixture, then coat lightly with bread crumbs. Sauté over medium heat in the oil-butter mixture for 1 to 2 minutes, turning once, until crisp and golden. Transfer to a heated oven and keep warm or serve at once on a warmed platter. Garnish with cluster of tiny capers and lemon wedges.

Honeydew with Lime and Coriander

1 medium-size honeydew melon
1 medium-size cantaloupe
2 tablespoons fresh lime juice
⅔ cup chopped fresh coriander leaves (approximately)

1½ tablespoons honey
½ teaspoon ground coriander
⅛ teaspoon ground nutmeg

Halve and seed the melons. Scoop out with a melon ball cutter and put the melon balls and their juices in a large bowl. Set aside. Mix

lime juice, honey, coriander, and nutmeg together in a separate bowl,
then pour over melon. Toss to coat and chill about 2 hours to blend
flavors. When serving, sprinkle generously with fresh coriander.

Jimmy's Place Salad

6 ounces fresh spinach	12 tomato wedges
¼ head iceberg lettuce	6 lemon wedges
1 head Boston lettuce	6 slices bacon, cubed and fried
½ romaine, small	crisp
1 2½-ounce package Enoki	6 radishes, sliced
Japanese mushrooms	1 cup croutons

Freshly ground black pepper (optional)

Clean spinach and lettuce separately. Break lettuce into bite-size pieces
and mix in bowl with half of the dressing. Arrange lettuce neatly on
large plates. Break spinach leaves and mix in bowl with remaining
dressing. Arrange spinach neatly on top of lettuce. Garnish sides of
each plate with Japanese mushrooms, two tomato wedges, and 1 lemon
wedge. Sprinkle top of salad with bacon bits, radish slices, and croutons. Top with freshly ground pepper, if desired.

Note: If you cannot get Japanese mushrooms, substitute fresh raw
mushrooms, sliced.

Jimmy's Quick Dressing:

¼ cup fresh lemon juice	Pinch of freshly ground white
¼ cup Dijon mustard	pepper
Pinch of salt	1½ cups pure vegetable oil

Put lemon juice and mustard in blender. Add salt and pepper and mix
well. While mixer is running, very slowly add vegetable oil. Do not
let dressing separate. Refrigerate.

Sesame Sea Bass

2½ pounds fresh sea bass	¾ teaspoon each salt, dried
fillets	crushed rosemary, dried
Juice of 3 limes	tarragon, and pepper
1 cup toasted sesame seeds	Salad oil for frying
¾ cup flour	Lemon wedges, for garnish

Parsley or watercress, for garnish

Marinate fillets in lime juice at least 1 hour; preferably all day. Mix seeds, flour, and seasonings in pie pan. Dip moist fillets in mixture and fry in oil until brown on all sides. Serve with lemon wedges dipped in paprika on a bed of parsley or watercress.

Note: Can be made 1 hour in advance, put on cookie sheet, and heated in oven for a few minutes.

Paillason

3 cups julienned potatoes	⅓ cups melted butter
1½ cup julienned turnips,	¾ teaspoon salt
blanched	⅓ teaspoon freshly ground
1½ cups julienned carrots	pepper

⅛ teaspoon freshly ground nutmeg

Combine all ingredients and mix well. Turn into a 10-inch or larger nonstick skillet that can be placed in the oven. Press down with the back of a spoon. Brown vegetables over medium heat on one side (about 10 minutes). Bake in preheated 450° oven until tender, about 30 to 40 minutes. Cut into wedges or squares and serve very hot.

Note: A metal casserole dish can be used instead of the frying pan. Vegetables can be prepared a few hours ahead. Keep potatoes in cold water to prevent darkening. Dry well before cooking.

Eclair Ring

Pastry:

¾ cup water	⅛ teaspoon salt
⅓ cup butter	¾ cup sifted flour

3 eggs

In saucepan, bring water, butter, and salt to boil. Remove and quickly add flour, all at once. Beat constantly over low heat with wooden spoon until mixture forms into ball and then remove from heat. Beat in eggs one at a time until glossy. Drop dough onto ungreased cookie sheet and form into a ring about 7 inches in diameter, with a small hole in center. Bake in preheated 400° oven for 40 minutes. Ring should be golden brown. Remove from oven. When cool, slice horizontally and scoop out uncooked center. Reserve top slice and replace after filling.

Filling:

2 pints whipping cream
⅞ cup cold milk

2 3¾-ounce boxes vanilla
instant pudding

2 tablespoons Grand Marnier or rum

Whip cream. Mix milk, pudding, and liqueur and fold into whipped cream. Fill shell.

Frosting:

1 cup chocolate chips
2 tablespoons butter

2 tablespoons corn syrup
3 tablespoons milk

Melt ingredients in double boiler. Dribble across top of filled ring.

Jack-O'-Lantern Eve

Spinach Balls with Mustard Sauce
Chick Pea and Sesame Dip
Lamb Curry
Mock Wild Rice Ring
Steamed Fresh Broccoli and Carrots
Cinnamon Cake
Lemony Apples

PREVIOUS DAY	EARLY MORNING	FREEZER
Chick Pea and Sesame Dip	*Mustard Sauce*	*Spinach Balls*
Mock Wild Rice Ring	*Lemony Apples*	*Lamb Curry*
		Cinnamon Cake

Spinach Balls
(Makes 10 dozen)

2 10-ounce boxes frozen
chopped spinach, cooked and
well drained
2 cups herb-seasoned stuffing
mix
2 onions, chopped finely

6 eggs, beaten
¾ cup butter, melted
½ cup grated Parmesan
1 tablespoon garlic salt
½ teaspoon thyme

Mix all well and form walnut-sized balls, using 1 teaspoon of the mixture per ball. Place on lightly greased cookie sheet and bake in preheated 350° oven for 20 minutes. Freezes well.

Mustard Sauce #1:

½ cup dry mustard	¼ cup sugar
½ cup white vinegar	1 egg yolk

Mix mustard and vinegar in a small bowl, cover, and let stand, not refrigerated, 4 to 5 hours. Combine sugar and egg yolk in small saucepan, add mustard mixture, and cook over low heat until slightly thickened. Stir constantly.

Remove from heat, cover, and chill until 1 hour before serving. Serve at room temperature with Spinach Balls.

Chick Pea and Sesame Dip

1 20-ounce can chick peas, including the liquid, or 1 cup dried chick peas	Cayenne, to taste
	½ teaspoon black pepper
	1 teaspoon salt
3 cloves garlic, minced or crushed	10 ounces tahini (sesame paste)
	Small amount of olive oil
Juice of 3 lemons	
Pita bread and/or raw vegetables cut for dipping	

If dried chick peas are used, cover with boiling water and soak in a covered pan for at least an hour, then cook for 2 to 3 hours until the skins separate. Strain the chick peas from the cooking liquid, but reserve the liquid.

Put chick peas, garlic, lemon juice, cayenne, black pepper, and salt into a blender or food processor. If dried chick peas are used, add ½ cup of the cooking liquid. Blend until puréed and fairly smooth. Add the tahini and continue blending until it is well mixed. Do not overmix. Mixture should be the consistency of a dip and it will get thicker with additional mixing. If mixture gets too thick, add water or more cooking liquid, one or two tablespoons at a time, until it is the right consistency. Adjust seasoning.

Mound dip in a bowl and make a depression in the middle. Pour a small amount of olive oil in this depression. Sprinkle ground cayenne around the outside of the depression, not too heavily. Serve with wedges of pita and raw vegetables.

Note: Can be made 2 or 3 days in advance.

Lamb Curry

2 pounds lean lamb, cubed	2½ cups beef stock
4 tablespoons butter	1 teaspoon freshly grated lemon
¼ cup all-purpose flour	rind
½ teaspoon thyme	Salt and freshly ground black
¼ teaspoon ginger	pepper, to taste
2 tablespoons curry powder	½ cup currants or raisins,
1 cup chopped onions	plumped in red wine to cover
2 cloves garlic, minced	Chutney
6 ounces mixed dried fruit,	Chopped hard-cooked eggs
chopped	Shredded coconut

Brown meat in butter in a skillet and sprinkle with flour, thyme, ginger, and curry powder. Stir well and add onions, garlic, and dried fruit bits. Cook and stir about 5 minutes. Gradually add 2 cups of the stock. Cook, stirring occasionally, until slightly thickened and smooth. Add lemon rind, salt, and pepper. Cover and simmer for 1 hour, adding more stock if needed. Test meat for tenderness. Stir in raisins and wine. Simmer for 30 minutes longer. Serve with side dishes of chutney, chopped hard-cooked egg, and coconut.

Mock Wild Rice Ring
(Serves 10 to 12)

2¼ cups long grain white rice	7 tablespoons butter or 4
(not instant)	tablespoons butter and 3
2 large onions, chopped	tablespoons chicken fat
1 pound fresh mushrooms	Salt, to taste
¼ teaspoon freshly ground black pepper	

Cook rice according to the directions on the package. Do not overcook.

Sauté onions and mushrooms in 4 tablespoons butter in large frying pan, about 3 or 4 minutes, until onions are transparent. Chop mushrooms and onions fine. Add salt, pepper, and remaining butter and toss with cooked rice to blend. Turn mixture into a well-buttered 3-quart ring mold and set in pan of hot water.

Place in preheated 350° oven and bake for 1 hour. When ready to serve, unmold onto warmed platter and fill center of ring with Steamed Fresh Broccoli and Carrots or any desired vegetable. Freezes well. If frozen, defrosts in 1 hour. Reheat at 350° for 30 minutes.

Steamed Fresh Broccoli and Carrots

2 pounds fresh broccoli,
    julienned
2 pounds fresh carrots, julienned

3 tablespoons butter
Salt and freshly ground black
    pepper, to taste

Steam broccoli for 5 to 10 minutes, until tender. Steam carrots for approximately 10 to 15 minutes or until tender. Toss both lightly with butter and seasonings and place in center of Mock Wild Rice Ring.

Cinnamon Cake

½ pound butter
2½ cups sugar
4 eggs
4 cups flour

4 teaspoons baking powder
1 pint vanilla ice cream, softened
2 to 3 teaspoons cinnamon
1 cup chopped walnuts

Cream butter and 2 cups of the sugar and add eggs, flour, baking powder, and softened vanilla ice cream. Separately mix remaining ½ cup sugar, cinnamon, and chopped nuts. Grease a 9-by-13-inch pan. Pour half of batter into baking pan, sprinkle half of chopped nut mixture on batter, add another layer of batter, and top with remaining nuts. Bake in preheated 350° oven for 40 minutes. Use cake tester to make certain cake is done.

Lemony Apples

6 apples: Jonathan or Granny
    Smith
1½ teaspoons lemon juice

⅓ cup sugar
6 tablespoons unsalted butter
⅓ cup heavy cream

Peel, core, and quarter apples. Cut each quarter into ⅓-inch slices and sprinkle with lemon juice. Butter generously a 1½-quart baking dish and lay overlapping slices of apple in dish. Sprinkle with sugar and add butter cut into very thin slices. (Can be prepared to this stage early in day.) Bake in preheated 400° oven for 30 minutes. Turn oven up to 500°. Spread cream over apples and bake 5 minutes more or until apples are slightly golden on top. Serve hot as a side dish with Cinnamon Cake.

🐚 🐚 🐚

Thanksgiving

Wintry Punch
Harvest Cheese Dip with Crudités
Grav Lax with Mustard Sauce
Roast Turkey with Corn Bread Dressing
Marbled Mashed Potatoes
Squash-Apple Casserole
Broccoli with White Lemon Butter
Cranberry-Grape Mold
Pecan Rum Cake
Pumpkin Flan
Hopscotch Chocolate Cake

PREVIOUS DAY	EARLY MORNING	FREEZER
Wintry Punch	*Squash-Apple Casserole*	*Corn Bread*
Harvest Cheese Dip	*Pumpkin Flan*	*Marbled Mashed*
Grav Lax		*Potatoes*
Cranberry Grape Mold		*Squash-Apple Casserole*
Pecan Rum Cake		
Hopscotch Cake		

Wintry Punch

6 cloves	1 lemon, sliced
3 cardamom seeds	1 navel orange, sliced
2 cinnamon sticks	1 bottle red wine
⅓ to ½ cup superfine sugar	½ cup cognac
3 cups cranberry juice	¼ cup Cointreau

Tie spices in cheesecloth and place in large saucepan with sugar and cranberry juice. Cook until sugar dissolves. Add lemon, orange, and rest of ingredients. Simmer over low heat for 15 minutes. Chill punch overnight to mellow flavors. Reheat and remove fruit slices and spices before serving.

Harvest Cheese Dip with Crudités

1 8-ounce package cream cheese, room temperature	1 teaspoon paprika
	1 teaspoon chopped chives
¼ cup milk	1 teaspoon grated onion
1 teaspoon anchovy paste	½ teaspoon caraway seeds
1 teaspoon capers	

Combine softened cream cheese and remaining ingredients. Blend well. Serve with crackers and Crudités (see Index) for dipping.

Grav Lax

3-pound piece fresh Red Pacific salmon, taken from middle and filleted into 2 pieces	4 tablespoons salt
	2 teaspoons white peppercorns
	1 4-ounce bunch fresh dill, or
1 teaspoon sugar	more
Small rye or pumpernickel bread	

Remove bones, not skin, from salmon fillets. Mix sugar, salt, and peppercorns. Rub salmon with this mixture. Scatter one-third of the dill in a shallow buttered dish and place one fillet on top, skin side down. Cover with the next one-third of the dill, and place the second fillet on this first, skin side up. Cover with the rest of the dill. Cover with plastic wrap, place a lightweight object on top, and refrigerate for 2 days, turning twice. Scrape spices off when ready to serve and slice, cutting slantwise across the grain as you would a Scotch salmon. Serve on small rye or pumpernickel bread with Mustard Sauce #2.

Mustard Sauce #2:

2 tablespoons sweet mustard
1 tablespoon sugar
1 tablespoon vinegar

6 tablespoons oil
6 tablespoons fermented cream
or yogurt
¼ cup minced fresh dill

Process first 4 ingredients in blender or food processor. Then add cream or yogurt and ¼ cup of dill.

Roast Turkey

1 turkey (1 pound per person)
Garlic powder
Onion powder
Salt
Apples or oranges, quartered
(optional)

Chicken fat or butter
Paprika
Garlic cloves (optional)
Salad oil

Clean turkey thoroughly inside and out. Sprinkle garlic powder, onion powder, and salt inside. Fill cavity loosely with quartered apples or oranges, or stuff with Corn Bread Dressing. Lace cavity closed. Spread chicken fat or butter generously over entire turkey and season with garlic powder, onion powder, and paprika. If desired, place garlic cloves beneath skin in legs and wings.

Slip turkey into large brown paper bag and staple closed. Brush top of bag liberally with salad oil. Bake in preheated 325° oven for 20 minutes per pound.

One hour before estimated finish of roasting, remove turkey from brown bag. If not done, return to oven for remaining time. If ready, remove from oven and allow to set 30 to 50 minutes before carving.

Corn Bread Dressing

Corn Bread:

1 cup yellow cornmeal	½ teaspoon salt
1 cup all-purpose flour	1 cup milk
¼ cup sugar	1 egg
4 teaspoons baking powder	¼ cup vegetable shortening

Combine cornmeal, flour, sugar, baking powder, and salt. Add milk, egg, and shortening. Beat until fairly smooth, about 1 minute. Bake in greased 8-inch-square pan in preheated 425° oven for 20 to 25 minutes.

Stuffing:
(Makes 3 quarts, for 16- to 18-pound bird)

¼ cup butter	2 eggs, beaten
1 cup chopped onion	4 teaspoons salt
2 cups chopped celery	1¼ teaspoons freshly ground
3 cups fresh mushroom slices	white pepper, *or* 4 teaspoons
6 cups egg bread, toasted and	poultry seasoning plus ½
made into crumbs	teaspoon salt
2 to 2½ cups chicken broth	

Melt the butter in a large skillet. Sauté onion for one minute, add the celery, and cook 1 to 1½ minutes longer. Celery should be softening but still crisp. Crumble the corn bread and add to mixture with remaining ingredients in a large bowl and mix well, then put into a 3-quart buttered casserole and dot with 1 tablespoon additional butter. Cover with a lid or foil. Dressing can be made early in the day, refrigerated immediately, and lightly stuffed into the body and neck cavities of a turkey. *Do not* stuff the bird until you are ready to roast it. If you don't want to stuff turkey, roast dressing in casserole at 325° about 1 hour. Baste with ½ cup of turkey drippings after 30 minutes. Foil can then be removed if a crisp top is desired.

  Note: All dressing must be removed from the bird and refrigerated in a separate container if there are any leftovers.

Marbled Mashed Potatoes

1½ pounds medium red
   potatoes, halved
3 large sweet potatoes, quartered
4 tablespoons butter
4 large shallots, minced

1 cup sour cream
1 cup whipping cream, whipped
½ teaspoon salt
¼ teaspoon freshly ground
   white pepper

⅛ teaspoon ground nutmeg

Cook potatoes separately in boiling water for 30 minutes or until tender. Drain, cool, and peel. Rice potatoes into separate bowls. Melt butter; add shallots, and sauté until they are tender. Stir half the shallot mixture into each potato mixture. Whisk sour cream into whipped cream and gently fold half of cream mixture into each potato mixture. Combine seasonings and add half to each potato mixture; taste, and adjust.

Put half of the sweet potatoes into a 2-quart baking or soufflé dish and top with half the white potatoes. Repeat. Swirl potatoes with a metal spatula to give a marbled effect. (Can be frozen at this point and topping added right before baking.)

Topping:

½ cup fresh bread crumbs
¼ cup minced parsley

6 tablespoons melted butter

Mix all ingredients and sprinkle over potatoes. Bake in preheated 350° oven for 30 to 35 minutes, until topping is golden and potatoes are heated throughout.

Squash-Apple Casserole

Squash Purée:

4 acorn squash, 2 pounds each
¼ pound butter

2 tablespoons brown sugar
½ teaspoon salt

Wash squash, puncture, and wrap in foil. Bake in foil in preheated 400° oven for 2 hours until soft. Remove from oven and cool slightly. Process pulp with butter, sugar, and salt until mixture is smooth, using metal blade.

Apple Layer:

4 pounds tart apples   ⅔ cup sugar
¼ pound butter   ½ teaspoon cinnamon
            1 cup raisins (optional)

Peel apples, cut into halves lengthwise, remove core, and slice. In skillet, melt butter, add sliced apples, sugar, cinnamon, and raisins. Sauté until tender, about 10 minutes.

Spoon puréed squash into 14-by-12-inch baking dish. Spread cooled apple mixture over squash. Cover top with aluminum foil. (Can be refrigerated at this stage for 1 day in advance of cooking, or frozen up to 4 months.)

Topping:

6 cups cornflakes   1 cup brown sugar
1 cup chopped pecans   4 tablespoons butter

Place ingredients in processor with steel blade. Combine, but don't chop too fine.

Bring casserole to room temperature. Spread topping evenly over casserole and bake in preheated 350° oven for 20 to 30 minutes or until lightly browned.

Broccoli with White Lemon Butter

3½ pounds broccoli   ⅛ teaspoon freshly grated
⅓ cup dry white wine or   nutmeg
   vermouth   Salt and freshly ground white
2 tablespoons fresh lemon juice   pepper, to taste
¼ pound chilled, unsalted
   butter, cut in ½-inch pieces

Steam broccoli in a basket over boiling water for 14 to 20 minutes, or until tender.

Combine wine and lemon juice in a heavy, small saucepan over medium heat and cook until reduced to 2 tablespoons, about 5 minutes. Remove from heat and whisk in 2 tablespoons of the butter until just blended. Place over very low heat and whisk in the remaining butter, one small piece at a time. If sauce begins to melt and separate instead of thickening, remove from the heat and whisk in two pieces of butter. Whisk in the seasonings.

Sauce can be made up to 2 hours ahead. Keep it warm in a water bath or vacuum bottle. Serve over hot broccoli.

Cranberry-Grape Mold

1 pound cranberries	½ cup sugar
1¾ cups water	2 cups red grapes, cut and
2 3-ounce packages cherry	seeded, *or* 2 cups Bing cherries
gelatin	1 cup chopped celery or nuts

1 20-ounce can crushed pineapple, undrained

Boil cranberries in water until they finish popping and cook 5 minutes longer. When done, beat to break up berries, add gelatin and sugar, and stir. Let stand to cool, stirring occasionally. Add grapes or cherries, celery or nuts, and pineapple. Put into 1½-quart ring mold and refrigerate overnight.

Dressing:

3 ounces cream cheese, softened	1 cup whipping cream
16 large marshmallows (or 1 cup small)	

Mash cheese and marshmallows together and add whipping cream. Refrigerate overnight, and before serving whip until stiff.

Pecan Rum Cake

1½ cups all-purpose flour	1½ cups sugar
½ cup yellow cornmeal	4 eggs
½ teaspoon salt	⅓ cup milk
2 teaspoons baking powder	¼ cup dark rum
12 tablespoons butter (1½ sticks), softened	½ cup pecan halves

Combine first 7 ingredients in a large mixing bowl and beat until light and smooth. Slowly add milk and rum and blend well. Stir in the pecans. Spoon the batter into a buttered, lightly floured 9-by-5-inch loaf pan. Bake in preheated 350° oven for 1 hour and 10 minutes, or until toothpick inserted in the center comes out clean. Cool in the pan for 15 minutes and then cool on a rack.

Pumpkin Flan

1 cup sugar   1 teaspoon water

Melt sugar and water over medium high heat until it forms a golden syrup, stirring constantly to prevent burning. Pour immediately into 8-inch-square pan, flan pan, or ring mold, turning and rolling from side to side to coat with caramel. Set aside.

¾ cup sugar
½ teaspoon salt
1 teaspoon cinnamon
1 cup mashed cooked pumpkin
5 large eggs, lightly beaten
1½ cups undiluted evaporated
  milk

⅓ cup water
1½ teaspoons vanilla extract
½ cup heavy cream, whipped
1 tablespoon sugar
¼ teaspoon ground ginger

Combine ¾ cup sugar, salt, and cinnamon and add pumpkin and eggs. Mix well. Stir in next 3 ingredients, mix well, and turn into caramel-coated pan. Place in pan of hot water in preheated 350° oven and bake for 1 hour and 20 minutes, or until knife inserted in the center comes out clean. Remove from oven; cool, then chill. To serve, run spatula around the sides of pan, turn out onto a serving plate, and cut into squares or slices. Top with whipped cream flavored with sugar and ginger.

Hint: Place pan of hot water on shelf of oven before placing flan into it. This will eliminate spills.

Hopscotch Chocolate Cake

½ cup raisins
½ cup Scotch
14 ounces semisweet chocolate
¼ cup water
½ pound unsalted butter

6 eggs, separated
1⅓ cups sugar
9 tablespoons cake flour
1⅓ cups finely ground
  almonds

Pinch of salt

Soak raisins overnight in Scotch. Butter a 10-inch or 12-inch cake pan and line bottom with buttered wax paper.

Melt chocolate in water and stir in butter until smooth. Beat egg yolks with sugar until creamy and stir into chocolate mixture. Add flour and almonds and then raisins and whisky. Mix gently. Beat egg whites with salt until stiff, not dry. Fold into chocolate mixture carefully. Do not overmix. Pour into prepared pan and bake in preheated 350° oven for 30 minutes. Cake will be moist in center. Cool, remove paper, and place cake flat side down on plate.

Easy Icing:

8 ounces semisweet chocolate   1 cup heavy cream

Melt chocolate in cream, whisking until smooth. Pour over cake.

Christmas Eve Feast

Curry Dip
Sweet and Sour Meatballs
Harvest Soup
Spanish Orange Salad
Flounder Grenoble
Gruyère Baked Noodles
Spinach with Sesame Seeds
Strawberry Pecan Torte
Fruit Cake

PREVIOUS DAY	EARLY MORNING	FREEZER
Curry Dip	*Spanish Orange Salad*	
Meatballs	*Gruyère Baked Noodles*	
Fruit Cake	*Strawberry Pecan Torte*	
Harvest Soup		

Curry Dip

1 cup mayonnaise
1 teaspoon curry powder
2 teaspoons tarragon vinegar

½ tablespoon grated onion (or
1 tablespoon dry minced
onion)

Mix all ingredients together. Make several hours in advance for best flavor. Serve with Crudités (see Index) for dipping.

Sweet and Sour Meatballs

1½ pounds ground chuck or
round beef
1 12-ounce bottle chili sauce

1 12-ounce bottle water
1 tablespoon lemon juice
1 tablespoon brown sugar

Shape meat into 1-inch balls or smaller and brown in skillet. Drain fat and add rest of ingredients. Simmer 1 hour. If served for main course, serve over rice. Can be refrigerated in sauce overnight and reheated gently.

Harvest Soup

2 medium onions, chopped
1 large garlic clove, crushed
½ cup olive oil
2 medium eggplants (2 pounds in
all), peeled and cubed
6 tablespoons flour
2 10½-ounce cans condensed
beef broth
6 cups water
1 5-ounce jar sliced mushrooms,
undrained
4 cups shredded zucchini (2
medium)

3 teaspoons salt
½ teaspoon rosemary
½ teaspoon thyme
2 teaspoons sugar
1 small piece dried hot chili
pepper, or ⅓ to ½
teaspoon crumbled red pepper
flakes
2 tablespoons lemon juice
⅓ cup Madeira wine
½ cup chopped parsley

In a large heavy pot or Dutch oven, sauté onion and garlic in oil until tender. Add eggplant and sauté 5 minutes. Stir in flour, add broth, water, mushrooms, zucchini, salt, herbs, and sugar. Remove seeds from pepper, crumble, and add to soup, with lemon juice. Bring to a boil and simmer, uncovered, stirring occasionally, about 30 minutes. Can be prepared in advance to this point. Add Madeira to soup and stir. Sprinkle with parsley when serving.

Spanish Orange Salad

1 large onion, thinly sliced,
  separated into rings
3 oranges, peeled, thinly sliced
6 tablespoons olive oil
3 tablespoons red wine vinegar

⅓ teaspoon salt
Freshly ground black pepper
Salad greens
½ cup salad olives (or pitted
  black olives)

Marinate onion and oranges in oil, vinegar, salt, and pepper for 15 minutes to 1 hour. Add to salad greens, and toss with olives.

Flounder Grenoble

2 pounds flounder or fillet of
  sole
Pinch of salt
Pinch of freshly ground white
  pepper
1 cup milk
1 beaten egg

Flour, for dredging
¼ pound butter or margarine
Juice of 2 lemons
1 tablespoon Worcestershire
  sauce
1 tablespoon chopped parsley
¼ cup capers

Sprinkle fish with salt and white pepper. Make batter of milk and egg. Dip fish in batter and dredge in flour. Melt 5 tablespoons of the butter in heavy skillet. Sauté fish until golden.

Remove fish to heated platter, keep warm. Add remaining butter, lemon juice, and all other ingredients to skillet. Heat through and pour sauce over fish.

Gruyère Baked Noodles

1 pound fine noodles
Salt and freshly ground black
  pepper, to taste
¼ teaspoon dried thyme

¼ teaspoon dried dill
1 cup heavy cream
2 cups grated Gruyère
4 tablespoons butter

½ cup milk

Butter a 9-by-13-inch baking dish. Cook noodles in boiling water until barely tender. Drain well and put into baking dish. Season with salt, pepper, and herbs. Pour cream over and sprinkle with 1 cup of the cheese. Blend and sprinkle with remaining cheese. Dot with butter and sprinkle milk all over. Bake in preheated 450° oven for 20 minutes. Place baking dish under broiler for a few minutes to glaze.

Note: Can be prepared in morning, up to baking.

Spinach with Sesame Seeds

2 pounds fresh spinach
¼ cup sesame seeds
3 tablespoons soy sauce
4 tablespoons butter

Juice of ½ lemon
Salt and freshly ground pepper,
 to taste

Wash spinach and break off any tough stems. Put in a saucepan, adding no more water than whatever remains on washed leaves. Cook, covered, until wilted. Drain and return to pot to keep warm. In another small pan, lightly brown sesame seeds. Add soy sauce, butter, lemon juice, salt, and pepper to sesame seeds and cook until butter is melted. Place spinach in serving bowl, and pour sesame butter on top. Serve at once.

Strawberry Pecan Torte

1 18¼-ounce box yellow cake
 mix
4 eggs, separated
¾ cup sugar
1 cup chopped pecans

2 cups heavy cream, whipped
 and slightly sweetened
1 10-ounce package frozen
 strawberries, partially thawed
Pecan halves, for garnish

Whole strawberries, for garnish

Make cake as directed on package, substituting the egg yolks for eggs required. Spoon cake batter into 3 buttered and floured 9-inch cake pans.

Beat egg whites until almost stiff, then gradually add sugar and beat until stiff. Divide in thirds and spread evenly over cake batter. Sprinkle each layer with ⅓ cup chopped pecans.

Bake layers in preheated 350° oven for 25 to 30 minutes. Cool 10 minutes in pan on rack and then turn out right side up on rack. Cool completely.

Assemble cake shortly before serving. Spread first layer with one-half of whipped cream and top with one-half partially thawed strawberries. Repeat with second layer. Top with third layer and decorate top of cake with pecan halves and whole strawberries.

Fruit Cake

1 cup seedless raisins	¼ pound butter
1 pound mixed glazed fruit	1 cup sugar
1 cup chopped nuts	3 eggs
2 cups sifted flour	½ teaspoon lemon flavoring
¼ teaspoon salt	¼ cup orange juice or sweet
1 teaspoon baking powder	wine

Cinnamon and ginger (optional)

Combine fruits and nuts. Sift flour, salt, and baking powder together over fruit and blend with fingers. Cream butter and add sugar gradually until all is combined. Beat in eggs, one at a time. Add flavoring. Stir this into floured fruit and add juice last. Line one large loaf pan with greased wax paper. Bake loaf in preheated 300° oven for 1½ hours. Place pan filled with hot water on lowest rack of oven during baking time.

Summer Buffets and Barbecues

Each recipe serves six unless otherwise indicated.

Common wisdom has it that everything tastes better outdoors. This is true for a beach picnic as well as an elegant supper on the patio. Barbecuing offers a special opportunity for guests to pitch in and help with the preparation and cooking and is a foolproof ice breaker. Be flexible in your arrangements, though, since you never know when darkening skies may force the party indoors.

Garden Supper

Cold Marinated Shrimp
Tossed Salad with Walnut Oil Dressing
Barbecued Turkey
Baked Sweet Potatoes
Spinach Bread
Ice Cream Bombe
Toffee Fudge Brownies

PREVIOUS DAY	EARLY MORNING	FREEZER
Marinate shrimp	*Salad dressing*	*Spinach Bread*
	Toffee Fudge Brownies	*Ice Cream Bombe*

Cold Marinated Shrimp

3 11-ounce cans mandarin
  oranges, or sections of fresh
  oranges
4 medium Bermuda onions,
  sliced and separated into rings
2½ pounds large shrimp,
  cooked and shelled
¼ cup sugar
2 teaspoons salt, or to taste
½ teaspoon freshly ground
  black pepper

2 teaspoons mustard seed
1 teaspoon celery seed
½ teaspoon crushed red
  pepper
2 tablespoons bell pepper flakes
2 tablespoons snipped parsley
2 cloves garlic, crushed or
  minced
1½ cups cider vinegar
1 cup salad oil
⅔ cup fresh lemon juice

½ cup ketchup

Layer oranges, onions, and shrimp in bowl. Mix remaining ingredients and pour over shrimp. Marinate 1 to 2 days in refrigerator, stirring twice a day. Drain and serve.

Tossed Salad

2 or 3 heads Bibb lettuce
3 ribs chopped celery

12 sliced radishes

Clean lettuce and break into bite-size portions. Toss with radishes and celery. Serve with Walnut Oil Dressing.

Walnut Oil Dressing:

1 small clove garlic, peeled
¼ cup raspberry, honey, or
  other fruit or herb vinegar
Pinch of salt (optional)

3 tablespoons walnut oil
½ cup olive, safflower, or
  vegetable oil

Chop garlic in processor, using metal blade. Add vinegar within 15 seconds, then scrape down container sides. Add salt and with machine running pour oils through chute in steady stream within 40 seconds. Process additional 5 seconds.

Barbecued Turkey

1 12- to 15-pound turkey	Seasoned salt and freshly ground
Peanut oil	black pepper
1 fresh orange	½ teaspoon rosemary

Brush turkey with peanut oil. Squeeze orange juice into cavity of turkey and leave orange inside bird. Season outside of turkey and cook on barbecue indirectly, for 11 minutes a pound. Baste every 30 minutes with peanut oil. Let turkey stand for about 15 minutes before carving.

Note: Indirect cooking on a barbecue means that the hot coals are not directly underneath the meat being cooked, but mounded on the sides of the barbecue. This works best in a rounded or bubble-shaped barbecue.

Baked Sweet Potatoes

6 medium sweet potatoes	Corn oil
	Butter

Scrub potatoes, prick with fork, and rub with oil. Bake in preheated 425° oven for 50 minutes. Split and serve with butter.

Spinach Bread

Bread Dough:

1 package active dry yeast	1 teaspoon salt
1 teaspoon sugar	1 tablespoon oil
7 ounces warm water	
2¼ cups unbleached all-purpose flour	

Mix yeast and sugar with warm water and allow to stand for 15 minutes. It should be foamy. Put flour and salt in bowl of processor. Process and add yeast mixture while machine is running. Process until dough forms a ball. Add the oil and process for another minute. Place the dough in an oiled bowl and turn dough to coat entire surface with oil. Allow dough to rise for 1 hour or until doubled in size.

Spinach Filling:

2 10-ounce packages frozen
    chopped spinach, drained
Pinch of salt

2 cloves garlic, minced
4 ounces shredded mozzarella
¾ cup grated Parmesan

Roll dough with rolling pin into rectangle approximately 24 by 10 inches. Brush dough lightly with oil. Combine spinach, salt, and garlic and spread on dough. Spread mozzarella and ½ cup of the Parmesan over spinach. Sprinkle a few drops of oil on filling and roll up like a jelly roll. Pinch ends together and tuck under roll. Place on lightly oiled cookie sheet. Bake in preheated 450° oven for 25 minutes. Allow bread to stand at least 20 minutes. Slice and return to cookie sheet. Brush lightly with oil and sprinkle with remaining 1 cup Parmesan. Broil 3 minutes or until lightly browned.

Ice Cream Bombe

1 quart vanilla ice cream,
    softened
½ pound seedless grapes,
    halved

¼ to ½ cup eau-de-vie,
    mirabelle, or kirsch
1 12-ounce jar apricot jam

Fill a quart mold with vanilla ice cream. Freeze until hard. Marinate the grape halves in the liqueur for 15 minutes. When ice cream is hard, hollow out the center and fill with lightly drained grapes, reserving the liqueur. Cover grapes with ice cream and freeze until serving (2 or 3 days). Just before serving, melt the jam over low heat and dilute with the liqueur, to taste. Unmold bombe onto a platter and pour hot apricot sauce over and around ice cream.

Toffee Fudge Brownies
(Makes about 25)

1 cup walnut pieces
6 chocolate-covered toffee bars
    (6⅔ ounces total), broken
    into pieces
5 ounces unsweetened chocolate,
    broken into pieces
1¼ cups sugar

¼ pound unsalted butter,
    quartered
4 large eggs
¼ teaspoon salt
1 tablespoon pure vanilla extract
⅔ cup unbleached all-purpose
    flour

Grease a 9- or 10-inch-square baking pan and coat with flour.

Chop walnuts and toffee bars coarsely in processor by pulsing 6 to 8 times. Remove from work bowl. Add chocolate and sugar to work bowl with metal blade and pulse 6 times. Process until chocolate is as fine as the sugar. Add the butter and process for 1 minute. Add eggs, salt, and vanilla and process for 40 seconds, or until fluffy. Add the flour, nuts, and toffee. Combine batter by pulsing 4 or 5 times, until flour has disappeared. Do not overprocess.

Pour batter into prepared baking pan and spread evenly. Bake in preheated 325° oven for 45 minutes, or until toothpick inserted in center comes out with some moist crumbs clinging to it. (Toothpick should not be wet.) Baking for 45 minutes produces fudgelike brownies—bake for 3 to 5 minutes longer for cakelike brownies. Let brownies cool in the pan on a rack and then cut into ¾-inch squares.

Summer Dinner

Cold Spinach Soup
Artichoke Squares
Fillet of Sole Français
Rice with Zucchini
Sautéed Cherry Tomatoes
Strawberry Tart in Sabayon Cream

PREVIOUS DAY	EARLY MORNING	FREEZER
Spinach Soup	Sole Français	Artichoke Squares
	Strawberry Tart	

Cold Spinach Soup

2 tablespoons butter
¼ cup chopped onion
2 chicken bouillon cubes
1 cup boiling water
1 strip lemon peel
1 teaspoon salt
2 cups peeled, diced potatoes

½ pound fresh spinach, washed and cut up
2 cups milk
¼ cup lemon juice
1 cup sour cream
Additional sour cream, for garnish

Grated lemon peel, for garnish

In a 3-quart saucepan, melt butter and sauté onion until just tender. Dissolve bouillon cubes in boiling water and add to pan, along with the lemon peel, salt, and potatoes.

Cover and bring to a boil. Cook about 15 minutes or until potatoes are nearly tender. Add spinach and cook 5 minutes. Purée in processor or blender. Stir in milk and lemon juice. (Can be frozen at this stage.) Add sour cream. Cover and chill until very cold and serve in chilled bowls. Garnish with a dollop of sour cream and a sprinkling of grated lemon peel, if desired.

Artichoke Squares

2 6-ounce jars marinated artichokes	⅛ teaspoon freshly ground black pepper
1 clove garlic, minced, or more, to taste	⅛ teaspoon oregano
1 small onion, chopped	⅛ teaspoon Tabasco sauce
4 eggs	½ pound shredded Cheddar cheese
¼ cup bread crumbs	2 tablespoons minced parsley
¼ teaspoon salt	Onion salt

Drain 1 jar of artichoke marinade into frying pan. Sauté garlic and onion for 5 minutes. Drain second jar of artichokes and discard marinade. Mix all other ingredients with onion and garlic. Spread mixture into 7-by-11-inch pan. Bake in preheated 325° oven for 30 minutes. Freezes well.

Fillet of Sole Français

12 medium sole fillets	2 10-ounce cans cream of mushroom soup
Freshly ground black pepper	
Dash of lemon juice	1 4- to 6-ounce jar whole mushrooms
1 6- or 7-ounce can medium shrimp	Chopped parsley
1 cup white wine	1 tablespoon paprika

Butter large oval glass baking dish. Wipe sole with damp paper towel. Season with pepper and dash of lemon juice. Place fillets in baking dish and scatter half of shrimp over all. Combine wine with mushroom soup and spread over fillets. Scatter mushrooms around fish. Put rest of shrimp on top, in a straight line. Dust with parsley flakes and paprika. Broil for 8 minutes.

Rice with Zucchini

1½ pounds zucchini, unpeeled
¼ cup olive oil
3 cups coarsely chopped onions
3 sprigs fresh thyme (or ½ teaspoon dried)

1 bay leaf
Salt and freshly ground black pepper, to taste
1 cup long grain white rice
1 cup chicken broth

Cut zucchini into 1½-inch cubes. Set aside. In large, heavy casserole, heat the oil and add the onions and seasonings. Cover tightly. Cook until the onions are tender but not brown. Add zucchini, rice, and broth and bring to boil on top of stove. Cover and bake in preheated 400° oven for 20 minutes. Remove bay leaf before serving.

Sautéed Cherry Tomatoes

2 tablespoons butter
2 quarts ripe, firm cherry tomatoes (approximately 40)
Salt and freshly ground black pepper, to taste

1 tablespoon finely chopped shallots
1 tablespoon finely chopped parsley

Heat butter in a large skillet and when quite hot, but not brown, add the tomatoes, salt, and pepper. Cook about 2 minutes, shaking the skillet so that the tomatoes cook evenly. Tomatoes should just be heated through; they will collapse if overcooked. Add shallots and parsley and cook, shaking the skillet, about 15 seconds. Serve immediately.

Strawberry Tart in Sabayon Cream

Crust:

6 tablespoons unsalted butter, at room temperature
2 tablespoons sugar
1 egg yolk
1 teaspoon grated lemon peel

½ teaspoon vanilla extract
3 drops almond extract
Pinch of salt
¾ cup, plus 2 tablespoons all-purpose flour

¼ cup very finely chopped blanched almonds

Cream butter, sugar, egg yolk, lemon peel, vanilla, almond extract, and salt in large bowl. Add flour and almonds and mix until smooth. Press crust evenly into 9-inch tart pan with removable bottom, dusting hands with flour as necessary. (Crust can be frozen at this point.) Refrigerate at least 6 hours before using. Preheat oven to 375°. Bake pastry shell until brown, 15 to 20 minutes. You may have to pierce pastry with fork if bubbles form.

Strawberry Glaze:

⅓ cup strawberry jam 1½ tablespoons water
1 tablespoon orange liqueur

Melt jam with water in small saucepan over medium heat. Strain. Blend in liqueur and set aside.

Sabayon Cream Filling:

½ teaspoon unflavored gelatin   Pinch of salt
½ cup sherry   ⅓ cup whipping cream, at
½ cup sugar   room temperature
2 egg yolks, at room temperature   1 tablespoon orange liqueur
1 pint fresh strawberries

Sprinkle gelatin over wine in large metal bowl and let stand several minutes until soft. Whisk in sugar, yolks, and salt, using circular motion, until top is foamy. Place bowl over large saucepan of hot water, set over low heat, and continue whisking until egg mix is thick and foamy, about 15 minutes. Cool to room temperature, stirring occasionally. Meanwhile, brush surface of pastry shell with Strawberry Glaze, reserving some. Whip cream in large bowl to soft peaks. Stir liqueur into cooled sabayon. Gently fold whipped cream into sabayon. Pour into pastry shell and refrigerate several hours. Halve strawberries vertically and arrange on sabayon, cut side down. Brush remaining glaze over berries.

Barbecue

Spring Lettuce Soup
Sesame Cheese Sticks
Tomato-Cucumber Salad with Sauce Vinaigrette
Barbecued Steak
Western Fried Potatoes
Curried Cauliflower
Glazed Chocolate Squares
Raspberry Ice Cream

PREVIOUS DAY	EARLY MORNING	FREEZER
Sesame Cheese Sticks	*Curried Cauliflower*	*Chocolate Squares*
Sauce Vinaigrette		*Raspberry Ice Cream*
Barbecued Steak		

Spring Lettuce Soup

2 medium heads iceberg lettuce, *or* 1 large head romaine, shredded (about 8 cups)	4 tablespoons butter or margarine
1½ cups chicken broth	1 teaspoon sugar
1½ cups light cream	½ teaspoon salt
	⅛ teaspoon nutmeg

Freshly ground black pepper

In 4-quart kettle, combine lettuce and chicken broth. Bring to boil over medium heat. Reduce heat and simmer covered for 10 minutes, or until lettuce is soft.

Place half of the lettuce and liquid in an electric blender, cover, and blend at high speed for 1 minute. Pour into bowl and repeat with remaining lettuce and broth. Pour all back into kettle. Add cream, butter, and rest of ingredients. Cook over medium heat, stirring, until butter is melted and soup is hot. Beat with rotary beater until very smooth. Serve soup at once.

Sesame Cheese Sticks
(Makes 40)

1 cup sifted all-purpose flour
½ teaspoon salt
¹⁄₁₆ teaspoon cayenne
½ teaspoon powdered
   mustard
½ teaspoon ground ginger
½ teaspoon sugar

½ cup grated sharp Cheddar
   cheese
⅓ cup toasted sesame seeds
1 large egg yolk, lightly beaten
⅓ cup melted butter or
   margarine
1 tablespoon water

Stir first 6 ingredients together. Stir in the cheese and sesame seeds. Combine remaining ingredients. Add to first mixture and stir, forming a ball. Wrap in wax paper and chill. Pat to ⅛-inch thickness on a lightly floured board. Cut into 1-by-2-inch strips. Place on ungreased baking sheet and bake in preheated 350° oven for 15 minutes. Cool.

To Toast Sesame Seeds:

Spread on a shallow baking pan in a preheated 350° oven for 20 to 22 minutes, shaking 2 or 3 times to obtain uniform toasting.

Tomato-Cucumber Salad

4 large tomatoes

2 large cucumbers

Slice tomatoes and cucumbers thin. Arrange in overlapping circles on platter. Serve with Sauce Vinaigrette (see Index).

Barbecued Steak

2 top sirloin steaks or flank
   steaks, about 3 to 4 pounds
   total
¾ cup ketchup
¾ cup chili sauce
1½ tablespoons soy sauce
3 tablespoons honey

3 tablespoons Hoisin sauce
   (optional)
3 tablespoons minced scallions
3 cloves garlic, crushed
½ teaspoon salt
⅛ teaspoon freshly ground
   black pepper

If using flank steak, score diagonally on both sides. Place steak in plastic bag or in shallow pan. Mix other ingredients in small bowl. Pour mixture over steak and fasten bag or cover pan with foil. Marinate in refrigerator for 24 hours, turning occasionally.

Lift steak out of marinade and barbecue, basting several times with remaining marinade.

Western Fried Potatoes

6 large potatoes	½ teaspoon white pepper, or
1 teaspoon garlic powder	to taste
1 teaspoon seasoned salt, or to	1 teaspoon grated Parmesan
taste	Oil

Cut potatoes in wedges, but do not remove skin. Mix all dry ingredients, being sure to use equal parts garlic powder and Parmesan cheese. Shake potatoes in mixture and spread on well-oiled cookie sheet. Bake in preheated 400° oven for 1 hour.

Curried Cauliflower

1 large cauliflower, broken into	1 teaspoon powdered chicken
flowerets	broth
¾ cup cream of chicken soup	⅓ cup mayonnaise
1 cup grated Cheddar cheese	¾ teaspoon curry powder

Cook flowerets in salted water for 10 minutes. Drain. Mix cauliflower, soup, cheese, and balance of ingredients together. Place in greased casserole. Bake 30 minutes in preheated 350° oven.

Glazed Chocolate Squares

Cake Bars:

2 cups flour	1 cup water
2 cups sugar	¼ pound butter or margarine
1 teaspoon baking soda	¼ pound shortening (butter or
⅛ teaspoon salt	margarine may be substituted)
½ cup unsweetened cocoa	2 eggs
powder	½ cup buttermilk
1 teaspoon vanilla extract	

Grease and flour a 15-by-10-by-1-inch pan. Sift flour, sugar, baking soda, and salt together. Bring the cocoa, water, butter, and shortening to a boil in a small saucepan, stirring to blend. Pour over the dry ingredients and combine well. Beat in the eggs, buttermilk, and vanilla. Pour into pan, spread evenly, and bake in preheated 350° oven for 25 minutes. Cool and turn out on a cake rack.

Glaze:

2 ounces unsweetened chocolate	2 cups confectioners' sugar
2 tablespoons butter	1 teaspoon vanilla extract
2 tablespoons boiling water	

Melt the chocolate and butter over low heat. Stir in the sugar and vanilla. Stir in the boiling water to make a smooth glaze. A little more water can be added to give the glaze a pouring consistency. Cut the cooled cake into 3-by-2-inch servings, place them on the cake rack, and drip the glaze over them with a spoon, allowing the glaze to drip down the sides of each piece.

Raspberry Ice Cream
(Makes about 2 quarts)

2 cups mashed raspberries	2 tablespoons lemon juice
3 cups sugar	4 cups whipping cream
Pinch of salt	

Mash berries well, then mix with all other ingredients. Freeze in ice cream machine according to directions. Pour into smaller containers and freeze.

🐚 🐚 🐚

Evening Entertaining

Shrimp de Jonghe
Vegetable Dip
Spinach Salad with Mustard Dressing
Chicken Premier
Pasta Salad
Caraway Bread
Raspberry Crunch Squares
Lemon Pudding

PREVIOUS DAY	EARLY MORNING	FREEZER
Mustard Dressing	*Vegetable Dip*	*Caraway Bread*
Chicken Premier	*Lemon Pudding*	*Raspberry Squares*
Pasta Salad		

Shrimp de Jonghe

½ cup butter
2 cloves garlic
1 teaspoon salt
1 cup bread crumbs, plus
    more for topping

1 cup chopped parsley
1 cup sherry
White pepper
Paprika
3 pounds cooked shrimp

Soften butter in processor. While machine is running, drop in garlic and salt. Mix in bread crumbs, parsley, sherry, pepper, and paprika. Butter a casserole and layer sauce with shrimp. Top the casserole with additional bread crumbs. Bake 12 to 15 minutes in preheated 400° oven.

Vegetable Dip

½ small onion, grated
1 cup mayonnaise
2 teaspoons tarragon vinegar
Freshly ground black pepper
¼ teaspoon salt

½ teaspoon curry powder
⅛ teaspoon thyme
2 tablespoons sweet pickle relish
    or chili sauce

Combine all ingredients. Chill. Serve with Crudités (see Index).

Spinach Salad

2 12-ounce bags fresh spinach, thoroughly washed and drained
3 hard-cooked eggs, crumbled
½ pound fresh mushrooms, sliced

6 strips bacon, cooked and crumbled
3 to 5 scallions, chopped
Mustard Dressing

Combine all salad ingredients. Toss with Mustard Dressing immediately before serving.

Mustard Dressing:

½ cup mayonnaise
½ cup oil
2 teaspoons mustard
1 teaspoon sugar

Salt and freshly ground black pepper, to taste
Garlic powder, to taste
1 teaspoon red wine vinegar

Italian seasoning, to taste (optional)

Combine all ingredients, adjust seasonings, and refrigerate. Dressing can be prepared day before using.

Chicken Premier

3 cups seasoned bread crumbs
1 cup grated Parmesan

2 broilers, cut into serving pieces
¾ cup melted butter

Combine crumbs and cheese. Dip chicken first into melted butter and then into crumb mixture. Arrange in shallow baking pan. (At this stage, can be refrigerated for baking later.) When ready to bake, dot generously with butter and bake in preheated 350° oven for about 1 hour or until chicken is tender. Cover loosely with foil if it browns too quickly.

Pasta Salad

12 ounces spiral or shell pasta
1¼ cups pitted black olives, sliced
1 cup chopped red or green pepper, or a combination for color
1 small red onion, sliced thin
½ cup grated Parmesan
¼ cup chopped parsley
¾ cup Italian or other hearty oil and vinegar dressing, or more, to taste
1 tablespoon capers (optional)
1 2-ounce jar pimento, chopped (optional)

Cook pasta according to package directions. Drain well. In large bowl, combine olives, pepper, and other ingredients. Mix with pasta. Serve at room temperature or chilled.

Caraway Bread

3 cups flour
3 teaspoons baking powder
1 teaspoon baking soda
1 teaspoon salt
2 tablespoons sugar
1 cup seedless raisins
2 tablespoons caraway seeds
2 cups buttermilk

Mix all ingredients together with wooden spoon until moist. Turn into 9-inch round pan sprayed with noncaloric shortening. Bake in preheated 350° oven for 45 minutes. Rather than slicing, cut into large chunks to serve.

Raspberry Crunch Squares

Crust:

2 cups flour
½ cup sugar
Pinch of salt
½ pound cold butter
1 cup red raspberry preserves

In processor, mix 2 cups flour, sugar, salt, and butter (in pieces). Blend on-off a few times until coarsely crumbed. Take out of processor bowl and lightly knead, until butter is evenly incorporated. Pat dough in an even layer in an ungreased jelly-roll pan (15½-by-10¼-by-1-inch). Bake 15 to 18 minutes on centered rack of preheated 350° oven until light brown. Cool on wire rack, about 15 minutes. Spread preserves over warm crust.

Topping:

1½ cups firmly packed brown sugar

3 large eggs

½ teaspoon vanilla extract

1½ cups chopped nuts

¾ cup sweetened shredded coconut

4½ tablespoons flour

¾ teaspoon baking powder

Pinch of salt

Beat brown sugar, eggs, and vanilla at high speed in mixer until light and fluffy, 2 to 4 minutes. Add nuts, coconut, flour, baking powder, and salt. Stir, then spread batter evenly over preserves. Bake in preheated 325° oven on centered rack until top is brown and center is firm to touch (about 35 minutes). Cool thoroughly, about 25 minutes. Cut with sharp knife into 2-inch squares or triangles.

Note: Also good made with apricot preserves.

Lemon Pudding
(Serves 8)

3 eggs, separated

2 teaspoons grated lemon peel

⅓ cup lemon juice

1¼ cups milk

1 cup sugar

⅓ cup flour

¼ teaspoon salt

2 tablespoons butter or margarine, melted

In large bowl slightly beat egg yolks with lemon peel and juice. Stir in remaining ingredients except egg whites and mix well. Beat egg whites until stiff but not dry and fold into yolk mixture until just blended. Turn into ungreased 1½-quart casserole. Place in pan of hot water. Bake in preheated 350° oven for 45 minutes or until brown (knife inserted in center should come out clean). Serve warm or cold.

Supper on the Patio

Clam Dip

Dutch Slaw

Meatless Spaghetti Casserole

Baked Fish Fillets

Amish Sugar Cookies

Vanilla Ice Cream with Nutty Fruit Topping

PREVIOUS DAY	EARLY MORNING	FREEZER
Clam Dip	*Dutch Slaw*	*Amish Cookies*
Nutty Fruit Topping	*Spaghetti Casserole*	

Clam Dip

1 8-ounce can minced clams and juice	½ cup bread crumbs
6 tablespoons butter	2 cloves garlic, minced
1 cup shredded mozzarella	½ teaspoon each dried parsley and oregano

Mix all ingredients together in casserole. Bake in preheated 350° oven for 15 to 20 minutes, until bubbling. Serve with crackers.

Dutch Slaw

5 cups finely shredded red cabbage	⅔ cup oil
1 cup diagonally sliced celery	⅓ cup vinegar
1 to 2 tablespoons salt, to taste, plus additional ½ teaspoon	⅓ cup sugar
¼ pound mushrooms, thinly sliced	1 teaspoon dry mustard
	¼ teaspoon hot pepper sauce
	1 to 1½ tablespoons poppy seeds

Combine cabbage and celery in large bowl. Sprinkle with 1 to 2 tablespoons of salt and refrigerate 30 minutes. Rinse cabbage and celery to remove salt, drain well, and add mushrooms. For dressing, combine remaining ingredients. Beat until thick and creamy. Pour over cabbage mixture and toss gently.

Meatless Spaghetti Casserole

1 pound vermicelli	1 pound sliced mushrooms, sautéed (or 3 4½-ounce jars)
2 bunches scallions, chopped	
2 green peppers, chopped	Grated Parmesan
¼ pound butter	1 cup milk (approximately)
1 1-pound can tomatoes	
3 8-ounce packages Cheddar cheese slices	

Boil vermicelli for 10 minutes or according to package directions and drain in cold water. Sauté scallions and green peppers in butter in large pan. Add tomatoes and 2 packages Cheddar. When cheese has melted, add mushrooms and juice from mushrooms. In 13-by-15-inch greased casserole pan (paella pan works very well) layer spaghetti, then sauce. Continue layers and put third package of sliced cheese across top of casserole. Sprinkle generously with freshly grated Parmesan cheese. (Can be made early in day, up to this stage.) Before baking, bring to room temperature. Pour on milk to barely cover layers. Bake in preheated 350° oven for 1 hour.

Baked Fish Fillets

6 fillets	Paprika, lemon pepper, thyme,
½ cup white wine	salt, freshly ground black
Mayonnaise	pepper

Marinate fish in white wine for 1 hour. Spread mayonnaise to cover top of fillets and sprinkle with paprika and other seasonings. Bake fish for 40 minutes in preheated 350° oven.

Amish Sugar Cookies
(Makes about 6 dozen)

½ pound butter or margarine	1 teaspoon vanilla extract
1 cup vegetable oil	1 teaspoon cream of tartar
1 cup confectioners' sugar	1 teaspoon baking soda
1 cup granulated sugar	1 teaspoon salt
2 eggs	4½ cups all-purpose flour

Cream the butter, oil, and sugars. Add eggs and vanilla and then blend in the combined dry ingredients with mixer on low speed. Roll teaspoonfuls of dough into balls. Roll the balls in additional granulated sugar. Place the balls on greased cookie sheets. Flatten them with a flat-bottomed glass that has been lightly oiled and dipped in sugar. Bake in preheated 350° oven for 8 to 10 minutes until lightly browned. Cool on racks. Cookies freeze well.

Note: These cookies are very delicate; they do *not* travel well.

Nutty Fruit Topping

1½ 16-ounce cans pineapple chunks, drained (approximately 3 cups)
1½ 16-ounce cans sliced peaches, drained (approximately 3 cups)
1½ tablespoons lemon juice

1⅓ cups firmly packed brown sugar
¾ cup coarsely chopped pecans
¾ teaspoon pumpkin pie spice
8 tablespoons melted butter or margarine

Turn drained fruit into a 9-by-13-inch flameproof baking dish, add lemon juice, and mix gently. Mix brown sugar, pecans, spice, and melted butter and spread evenly over fruit. Broil 6 inches from heat for 3 minutes or until sugar melts and bubbles. Cool for a few minutes or until melted sugar forms a crust. Break crust by tapping with back of spoon. Serve over vanilla ice cream. If topping is made in advance, keep in airtight container.

Summer Splendor

Pink Carnation Beverage
Cheese and Spinach Puffs
Cold Crab and Cucumber Soup
Green Bean and Onion Salad
Curried Chicken Salad
Banana Tea Bread
Chocolate Velvet Cream
Frosted Almonds

PREVIOUS DAY	EARLY MORNING	FREEZER
Crab and Cucumber Soup	Marinate strawberries	Ice Ring
Bean and Onion Salad	Chicken Salad	Cheese and Spinach Puffs
Frosted Almonds	Chocolate Velvet	Banana Bread

Pink Carnation Beverage
(Serves 12)

2 quarts strawberries, sprinkled
with sugar, if desired

3 bottles white German wine
5 bottles sparkling wine
1 bottle claret

Sugar berries and soak in white wine in refrigerator. When ready to serve, put berries and wine into bowl and add remaining well-chilled ingredients. Add Ice Ring (see Index).

Cheese and Spinach Puffs

1 10-ounce package frozen
chopped spinach
½ cup chopped onion
2 slightly beaten eggs
½ cup Parmesan
½ cup shredded Cheddar
cheese

½ cup blue cheese salad
dressing
4 tablespoons butter or
margarine
⅛ teaspoon garlic powder
1 package corn muffin mix
(approximately 8 ounces)

Combine spinach and onion and cook according to package directions. Drain well, pressing out excess liquid. Combine eggs, cheeses, salad dressing, butter, and garlic powder. Add spinach mix and muffin mix and combine well. Cover and chill. When chilled, shape into 1-inch balls. Refrigerate until ready to use. (Can be frozen at this stage.) To serve, place chilled or frozen puffs on a baking sheet. Bake in preheated 350° oven until light brown. For chilled puffs, about 10 to 12 minutes. For frozen puffs, about 12 to 15 minutes. Serve warm.

Cold Crab and Cucumber Soup

6 ounces crabmeat
2 cups plain yogurt
1 cup chicken broth
½ cup white wine
½ teaspoon dill weed

½ teaspoon salt
⅛ teaspoon freshly ground
black pepper
2 cups diced cucumber
½ cup chopped scallions
¼ cup snipped parsley

Thaw crab, if frozen. Combine yogurt, broth, and wine. Blend in dill weed, salt, and pepper. Add remaining ingredients, stir, and chill at least 3 hours.

Green Bean and Onion Salad

2 pounds small green beans	⅛ teaspoon dried savory
1 tablespoon prepared mustard	1 medium onion, chopped fine
1 tablespoon olive oil	6 slices bacon, cooked crisp,
½ tablespoon wine vinegar	drained, and chopped
½ teaspoon each salt and freshly ground black pepper	

Trim ends of beans and blanch in boiling salted water to cover, about 2 to 3 minutes. Drain, immerse in cold water, drain, and set aside. Mix together remaining ingredients, except bacon, and pour dressing over beans. Refrigerate overnight. Just before serving, add the bacon.

Curried Chicken Salad

3 cups diced cooked chicken	⅓ cup chopped dates
1½ apples, peeled and diced	3 tablespoons chopped chutney
1½ cups diced fresh pineapple	with syrup
⅓ cup white raisins	¾ teaspoon salt

Combine all ingredients.

Curry Dressing:

1 to 1½ tablespoons curry powder	1½ cups mayonnaise
3 tablespoons chicken consommé	¾ cup shredded, canned coconut, for garnish

Simmer curry powder in consommé for 2 minutes, stirring to a smooth paste. Cool the paste and add to mayonnaise, combining well. Stir dressing into the previously combined salad ingredients and chill thoroughly. Sprinkle coconut on top of salad when serving.

Note: Can be made up to 3 hours in advance.

Banana Tea Bread

2 ripe medium bananas	1 teaspoon baking soda
2 eggs	1 teaspoon vanilla extract
1¾ cups flour	½ teaspoon salt
1 cup sugar	1 cup chopped walnuts
½ cup vegetable oil	(optional)
¼ cup buttermilk, plus 1 tablespoon	

Grease one 9-by-5-inch loaf pan. In a large bowl, mash the bananas with the eggs until blended. Add the remaining ingredients and stir to mix well. Pour into prepared pan and bake in preheated 325° oven for 1 hour and 20 minutes, or until golden brown and the top splits slightly.

Note: Can be frozen. Cannot be doubled successfully.

Chocolate Velvet Cream

1½ cups chocolate wafers, crumbled	2 eggs, separated
⅓ cup butter or margarine, melted	1 6-ounce package semisweet chocolate pieces, melted
1 8-ounce package cream cheese	2 cups heavy cream
½ cup sugar	2 tablespoons confectioners' sugar
1 teaspoon vanilla extract	¾ cup chopped pecans

Unsweetened shaved chocolate, for garnish

Combine crumbs and butter and press into 9-inch springform pan. Bake in preheated 350° oven for 10 minutes. Combine softened cream cheese, ¼ cup of the sugar, and vanilla. Mix until well blended. Stir in beaten egg yolks and melted chocolate. Beat egg whites until soft peaks form and gradually beat in remaining sugar. Fold egg whites into chocolate mixture. Whip 1 cup cream with confectioners' sugar and nuts and fold into chocolate mixture as well. Pour the mixture into cooled crust and refrigerate for 6 to 8 hours. Garnish with second cup cream, whipped, and unsweetened shaved chocolate before serving.

Frosted Almonds

1 egg white, plus 2 teaspoons water	½ cup brown sugar
1 pound almonds	1 teaspoon cinnamon
1 cup sugar	½ teaspoon nutmeg
	½ teaspoon salt

In large bowl, beat egg white and water until frothy and add nuts. In a separate bowl combine the rest of the ingredients. Pour over nuts and mix until all nuts are coated. Place on ungreased cookie sheet and bake in preheated 250° oven, approximately 45 minutes. When cool, break nuts apart. Store in airtight container.

Sunday Night Barbecue

Vodka Bog
Taco Dip
Barbecued Skirt Steak
Fantastic Potato Salad
Spinach Casserole
Divine Mocha-Chip Cheesecake
Fresh Berries with Sour Cream

PREVIOUS DAY	EARLY MORNING	FREEZER
Cheesecake	*Taco Dip*	*Ice Ring*
	Marinate steaks	
	Potato Salad	

Vodka Bog
(Serves 15 to 20)

1 fifth vodka
4 ounces cranberry liqueur
2 quarts cranberry juice
1 6-ounce can frozen
  concentrated orange juice,
  undiluted

2 or 3 bottles club soda, or to
  taste
Orange slices, for garnish

Put vodka, liqueur, and fruit juices in punch bowl with Ice Ring (see Index) or serve in individual glasses. Add soda just before serving; garnish with thin orange slices.

Taco Dip

1 8-ounce package cream cheese
2 cups cottage cheese
1 1¼-ounce package taco
  seasoning mix
⅔ cup sour cream (or sour
  half-and-half)
Chopped lettuce

4 ounces sharp Cheddar cheese
3 dozen ripe pitted black olives,
  sliced
1 medium tomato, chopped
1 avocado, diced
1 small onion, chopped
Taco chips

In food processor, blend cream cheese, cottage cheese, and taco seasoning mix. Spread mixture on round platter, about 12 to 14 inches in diameter. Refrigerate for 1 hour. Cover cheese mixture with sour cream. Garnish with remaining ingredients, starting with shredded lettuce. Sprinkle grated Cheddar and other ingredients in concentric circles. Serve with plain, salted taco chips.

Barbecued Skirt Steak

3 cups bottled onion-flavored
   barbecue sauce
1 large onion, sliced
1 green pepper, cubed
1 red pepper, cubed
2 or 3 cloves garlic, diced
¼ cup ketchup
¼ cup chili sauce
   (approximately)

3 tablespoons soy sauce
   (approximately)
2 tablespoons mustard
   (approximately)
3 pounds skirt steak
Freshly ground black pepper, to
   taste
Seasoned salt, to taste

Mix all marinade ingredients together in deep container. Score and season each steak with pepper and seasoned salt. Place steaks in container with marinade. Be sure to cover completely with sauce. Marinate 3 or 4 hours. Barbecue meat. Heat marinade and serve as sauce.

Fantastic Potato Salad

8 medium-size potatoes
2 tablespoons cider vinegar
2 tablespoons butter or
   margarine, melted
2 tablespoons sugar
2 teaspoons salt

6 ribs celery, chopped
6 hard-cooked eggs, sliced
½ cup minced fresh parsley
1 4-ounce jar chopped pimento
½ cup minced onion
½ cup sweet pickle relish

Boil potatoes in skins until tender. While hot, peel and cube potatoes and toss with the vinegar, butter, sugar, salt. Refrigerate until chilled. Add balance of salad ingredients and chill to blend the flavors. About 1 hour before serving, fold in enough dressing to moisten.

Dressing:

2 cups Homemade Mayonnaise (see Index)	4 tablespoons prepared horseradish

Combine dressing ingredients.

Note: Leftover dressing makes an excellent sauce for roast beef.

Spinach Casserole

5 eggs	1 pound cottage cheese
5 tablespoons flour	9 slices American cheese
6 tablespoons butter or margarine	Garlic powder, to taste
1 10-ounce package frozen chopped spinach, drained	Salt and freshly ground black pepper, to taste

Butter a 2-quart soufflé dish. Mix all ingredients. Pour into soufflé dish and bake in preheated 350° oven for 1 hour. Let set 5 to 10 minutes before serving.

Note: Casserole can be assembled in morning and baked just before serving.

Divine Mocha-Chip Cheesecake

Crust:

1½ cups graham cracker crumbs	2 tablespoons sugar
	3 tablespoons unsweetened cocoa
4 tablespoons butter, melted	

Mix crust ingredients together and press firmly into 9-inch springform pan. Bake in preheated 350° oven for 5 to 7 minutes until crisp and toasted. Remove from oven and cool completely.

Filling:

3 8-ounce packages cream cheese, at room temperature	⅓ cup crème de cacao
1 cup (scant) sugar	2 generous tablespoons instant coffee
2 tablespoons all-purpose flour	1 teaspoon vanilla extract
¼ teaspoon salt	½ to ¾ cup miniature semisweet chocolate chips
3 extra large or jumbo eggs, at room temperature	

In large bowl of electric mixer, whip cream cheese until fluffy and gradually beat in sugar, flour, and salt. Beat in eggs, one at a time, beating well after each addition. Add liqueur mixed with instant coffee and vanilla. Carefully mix in chocolate chips and pour filling into baked, cooled crust. Bake in preheated 250° oven for approximately 1 hour or until center of cake feels firm to touch. Remove from oven and allow to cool on rack in draft-free place. When cake is completely cool, chill in refrigerator for several hours until firm and completely cold.

Topping:

Whipped cream   **Instant coffee or cocoa powder**

Decorate top of cake with rosettes of sweetened whipped cream, dusted with instant coffee or cocoa powder.

Topping (Optional):

1 cup sour cream   **Semisweet chocolate bits or**
1 cup confectioners' sugar   **grated chocolate**
2 teaspoons instant coffee

Mix together ingredients and chill in refrigerator for several hours. Before serving, spread over top of cold cake and scatter a few small chocolate bits or grated chocolate over top.

Fresh Berries with Sour Cream

2 cups sour cream   **2 quarts strawberries or**
¼ cup brown sugar   **blueberries**

Spread sour cream in an even layer over the fresh, prepared fruit. Sprinkle with the brown sugar about 10 minutes before serving.

Tropical Memories

Crab Puffs with Mustard Dip
Honeymooners' Salad
Curried Chicken
Cracked Wheat with Pine Nuts
Pecan Balls
Orange Liqueur Freeze

PREVIOUS DAY	EARLY MORNING	FREEZER
Salad dressing	*Curried Chicken*	*Crab Puffs*
Vegetables for salad		*Pecan Balls*
Cracked Wheat with		*Orange Liqueur Freeze*
Pine Nuts		

Crab Puffs

1½ cups biscuit mix
⅓ cup grated Parmesan
¼ cup finely chopped
   scallions, including some tops
8 ounces crabmeat

1 egg, slightly beaten
⅓ cup water
1 teaspoon Worcestershire sauce
¼ teaspoon liquid hot pepper
   seasoning

Salad oil, for frying

Combine biscuit mix, cheese, and scallions. Shred crabmeat and add to cheese mixture. Combine egg, water, Worcestershire, and hot pepper seasoning. Stir into crab mixture until just blended. Heat about 1½ inches of oil in a deep frying pan, electric frying pan, or wok. Fry 3 or 4 puffs at a time by dropping batter from a teaspoon into hot oil. Turn until golden on all sides (about 1½ to 2 minutes). Lift out with slotted spoon, drain. Keep warm until all are fried; or cool, wrap in foil, and freeze. Serve with Mustard Dip. Reheat frozen puffs in preheated 350° oven for 12 to 15 minutes to heat through.

Mustard Dip:

½ cup sour cream

2 tablespoons Dijon mustard
1 teaspoon lemon juice

Combine all ingredients.

Honeymooners' Salad

1 pound spinach or leaf lettuce, torn	1 8-ounce can water chestnuts, sliced thin
¾ pound fresh bean sprouts, or 1 15-ounce can bean sprouts, drained	3 or 4 hard-cooked eggs, diced 6 to 8 slices bacon, fried crisp and crumbled

Toss all together in salad bowl.

Dressing:

1 cup oil	1 tablespoon Worcestershire
⅓ cup sugar	sauce
⅓ cup ketchup	1 onion, grated
¼ cup vinegar	½ teaspoon salt

Combine well and chill before serving. Add to salad and toss immediately before serving.

Curried Chicken

2 chickens, cut up	1½ tablespoons freshly
4 tablespoons sugar	ground black pepper
4 tablespoons butter	1 teaspoon salt
1 large onion, chopped	1 cup pineapple juice
3 large cloves garlic, chopped	1 cup white raisins
3 tablespoons curry powder (or	2 tablespoons grated orange peel
more, to taste)	½ cup sherry

Slivered almonds, chutney, unsweetened coconut,
raisins, pineapple

Parbroil chicken on both sides until brown. Cook sugar and butter until brown, add ingredients through salt quickly, and cook until onion is soft, stirring occasionally. Add remainder of measured ingredients and cook a few minutes more. Place chicken in roasting pan and pour sauce over it. Bake in preheated 325° oven for approximately 1 hour. This is best if made in morning, so that chicken sits all day in sauce. Finish cooking before serving. Serve with side dishes of slivered almonds, chutney, coconut, raisins, and pineapple as desired.

Cracked Wheat with Pine Nuts

2 tablespoons butter	2 tablespoons chopped parsley
¼ cup chopped onion	½ teaspoon powdered
2 garlic cloves, minced	oregano
2 cups cracked wheat (bulgar)	4 cups chicken broth

½ cup pine nuts

Melt butter in casserole and sauté onion and garlic until transparent.
Add cracked wheat and stir. Add parsley and oregano and simmer for
5 minutes, stirring occasionally. Add chicken broth and cover casserole. Refrigerate until liquid has been absorbed. Bring casserole to
room temperature, sprinkle with pine nuts, and bake at 350° for
40 minutes, or until well heated.

Pecan Balls

½ pound butter	2 teaspoons vanilla extract
½ teaspoon salt	2½ cups cake flour
6 tablespoons sugar	2 cups chopped pecans

2 cups confectioners' sugar

Cream butter, salt, and sugar together. When light and fluffy, add
vanilla, flour, and nuts. Roll into 1-inch balls, roll in confectioners'
sugar, and place on ungreased cookie sheet. Bake in preheated
325° oven for 15 to 20 minutes. Roll in confectioners' sugar again
after baking. Freezes well.

Orange Liqueur Freeze

1 quart vanilla ice cream,	6 ounces frozen orange juice,
softened	undiluted

¼ to ½ cup Grand Marnier or other orange liqueur

Mix all ingredients until well distributed but not totally blended. Place
in individual glass serving dishes and freeze.

Summer Sensation

Borscht
Rye Wafers
Avocado and Bacon Salad with Lime Dressing
Cold Fillet of Sole Romanoff
Baked Sliced Tomatoes
Herbed Potato Salad
Cappuccino Ice Cream
Coconut Dream Bars

PREVIOUS DAY	EARLY MORNING	FREEZER
Poach sole	*Borscht*	*Cappuccino*
	Lime Dressing	*Ice Cream*
	Fish sauce	*Coconut Dream Bars*
	Baked Sliced Tomatoes	
	Potato Salad	

Borscht

1 pound beets, cooked until
  tender
2 teaspoons vinegar
4 teaspoons lemon juice
3 citric acid (sour salt) crystals
  (each about ¼ teaspoon)
9 tablespoons sugar

1½ teaspoons coarse salt
½ cup sour cream
⅔ cup heavy cream
Chopped onion, cucumber, dill,
  lemon wedges, sour cream,
  heavy cream, reserved grated
  beets, for garnish

Drain beets, reserving cooking liquid. Run beets under cold water; when cool enough to handle, peel them. Grate beets in food processor with grating disc. Return half the grated beets to liquid. Reserve rest for garnish or other use. Season warm liquid with vinegar and next 6 ingredients. Serve cold with assorted garnishes.

Rye Wafers

24 slices cocktail rye bread   4 tablespoons butter, melted

Brush bread with butter. Put on cookie sheet. Bake in preheated 350° oven until curled and crisp.

Avocado and Bacon Salad

8 strips bacon, diced   1 large head Boston lettuce
2 small avocados, cubed

Cook bacon until crisp and drain well. Right before serving, combine lettuce, bacon, and cubed avocado. Pour Lime Dressing over and gently toss.

Lime Dressing:

Juice of 2 limes   Salt and coarsely ground pepper,
¼ cup olive oil   to taste
½ cup sour cream   2 cloves garlic, minced
¼ cup mayonnaise

Combine the ingredients, blend thoroughly, and pour over salad.

Cold Fillet of Sole Romanoff

12 small (or 6 medium) halved   1 3-ounce jar red caviar
   fillets of sole or flounder

Roll up fish fillets and stick a toothpick through each. Barely simmer fish in Court Bouillon #1 (see Index) for about 4 or 5 minutes or until it flakes when pierced with a fork. Drain well and then chill thoroughly. Put chilled fillets on serving platter and cover each with sauce. Place dollop of caviar on each piece.

Sauce:

¾ cup sour cream   1 clove garlic, crushed
¾ cup mayonnaise   1 shallot, finely minced
4 teaspoons Dijon mustard   Salt and freshly ground white
1½ teaspoons lemon juice   pepper, to taste
                    ¼ cup vodka

Whisk sour cream with all remaining ingredients. Chill for at least 5 to 6 hours before serving.

Baked Sliced Tomatoes

4 tablespoons butter or margarine
¼ cup chopped scallions or shallots
1½ cups fresh bread crumbs (3 slices)

2 tablespoons chopped parsley
1 teaspoon salt
Dash of freshly ground black pepper
6 large, firm, ripe tomatoes
3 teaspoons sugar

Melt butter in saucepan over medium heat. Sauté scallions or shallots until tender. Stir in bread crumbs, parsley, salt, and pepper. Remove from heat. Dip tomatoes in boiling water for 30 to 40 seconds and then remove skins. Core tomatoes, cut into ½-inch slices. Arrange some slices around sides of a buttered 1½-quart ovenproof dish. Put layer of slices in bottom of dish. Sprinkle with sugar and crumb mixture. Repeat layering two more times, ending with crumbs. Cover dish with foil. Refrigerate until ready to bake. Bake in preheated 350° oven for 25 minutes, or until bubbly.

Herbed Potato Salad

2 pounds new potatoes, boiled
¼ cup finely chopped shallots
1 clove finely minced garlic
2 tablespoons chopped fresh chives
3 tablespoons finely chopped parsley
1 tablespoon chopped fresh tarragon (or 1 teaspoon dried)
Lettuce leaves (optional)

¼ cup dry white wine
1 teaspoon red wine vinegar
3 tablespoons walnut oil (preferably), or peanut, vegetable, or corn oil
Salt and freshly ground black pepper, to taste
½ cup walnut halves, toasted (optional)

Peel potatoes when cooled and cut into ¼-inch slices. Place in bowl. Add shallots, garlic, chives, parsley, tarragon, wine, vinegar, oil, and salt and pepper to taste. Add toasted walnuts. Toss very well. Serve on lettuce leaves if desired.

Cappuccino Ice Cream

5 ounces bittersweet chocolate	1½ to 2 cups whipping cream
¾ cup espresso or French roast coffee, freshly brewed	3 to 4 ounces chocolate-covered, nut-sprinkled toffee (Heath
3 large egg yolks, lightly beaten	bars, or similar), chopped
⅔ cup sugar	

Chop bittersweet chocolate into small pieces and place in small bowl. Pour hot coffee over chocolate and let sit until melted. Put egg yolks into medium bowl and beat well. Put sugar and 1 cup of the cream into a small saucepan and stir well. Heat to a simmer. Remove from heat and pour sugar/cream mixture into beaten egg yolks, whisking vigorously.

Return custard to saucepan and warm over medium-low heat until mixture reaches 180° and thickens. Sieve the custard into the bowl filled with chocolate/coffee mixture and stir well. If bits of chocolate remain unmelted, sieve again into clean bowl. Let custard cool to room temperature and taste. Add ½ to 1 cup of the remaining cream to mixture, depending on how bitter or sweet you want it to taste (the less cream you use, the more bitter it will be). Chill custard thoroughly. Then process custard in your ice cream machine according to manufacturer's directions. When ice cream is made but is still soft, fold in the toffee pieces. Transfer ice cream to a small container with a cover and put into freezer. Allow to ripen and semifreeze for 2 to 4 hours, depending on the consistency you like. Serve immediately.

Coconut Dream Bars
(Makes 24)

Base:

1 cup all-purpose flour	¼ cup brown sugar
	½ cup butter

Sift flour, add brown sugar, and cut chilled butter into mixture until it resembles coarse meal. Pat into ungreased 9-inch-square pan and bake in a preheated 350° oven for 15 minutes. Cool.

Filling:

1 cup sweetened coconut	½ teaspoon baking powder
1 cup coarsely chopped walnuts	¼ teaspoon salt
1 cup chopped maraschino	2 eggs
cherries	1 cup brown sugar
2 tablespoons flour	1 teaspoon vanilla extract

Mix coconut, walnuts, and cherries in a large bowl. Combine flour, baking powder, and salt and sift over the fruit. Mix well.

In a second large bowl, beat eggs, add brown sugar gradually, and beat until light and thick. Add vanilla. Fold in fruit and dry ingredients. Pour over cooled base and bake in preheated 350° oven for 30 to 35 minutes. When cool, cut into bars.

🌱 🌱 🌱

August Supper

Horseradish Beet Ring with Seafood-filled Avocados
and Russian Dressing
Chicken Breasts Mousseline
Vermicelli Vinaigrette
Pink Raspberry Mold
Oat Carmelitas

PREVIOUS DAY	EARLY MORNING	FREEZER
Beet Ring	*Chicken*	
Russian Dressing	*Mousseline sauce*	
Pink Raspberry Mold	*Vermicelli Vinaigrette*	
Oat Carmelitas		

Horseradish Beet Ring with Seafood-filled Avocados and Russian Dressing

2 15-ounce cans beets, drained,
    with juice reserved, and riced
Juice of 1 lemon
2 packages lemon gelatin

Salt, to taste
4 heaping tablespoons prepared
    red horseradish
Watercress, for garnish

Heat 2 cups beet juice (add water to make measure) and lemon juice and dissolve gelatin in mixture. Chill. Allow to set partially; add beets, salt, and horseradish. Pour into oiled ring mold and chill until firm.

Russian Dressing:

1 cup mayonnaise
½ cup ketchup
½ cup chili sauce
½ pimento, minced
2 tablespoons chopped chives

1 tablespoon minced parsley
1 hard-cooked egg, chopped
½ tablespoon fresh caviar
Salt, to taste
Dash of cayenne pepper
Paprika

Mix all ingredients and chill.

Seafood-filled Avocado:

½ pound each crabmeat and
    baby shrimp

3 avocados, halved
Fresh caviar, for garnish
Watercress, for garnish

Combine seafood with Russian Dressing. Stuff avocado halves with mixture and top with caviar.

Unmold ring on platter. Surround with Seafood-filled Avocados. Serve additional Russian Dressing in center of ring. Garnish platter with watercress.

Chicken Breasts Mousseline

Six-Minute Chicken:

6 halved chicken breasts, skinned and boned

Place chicken in deep soup kettle. Cover with cold water to depth of 3 inches. Bring to a boil over high heat, uncovered. Boil for 6 minutes. Remove kettle from heat. Cover with tight-fitting lid. Let sit in pot for 3 or 4 hours. Remove chicken after this time and reserve broth for sauce. Slice the meat.

Mousseline Sauce:

1 cup chicken broth	1 to 2 tablespoons lemon juice,
½ cup dry white wine	to taste
2 tablespoons chopped fresh	Freshly ground black pepper, to
tarragon (or 2 teaspoons	taste
dried)	1 large cucumber, thinly sliced,
1 tablespoon chopped fresh	for garnish
parsley	2 lemons, thinly sliced, for
4 egg yolks	garnish
½ cup heavy cream or crème	Watercress, for garnish
fraîche	

Combine first 4 sauce ingredients in small saucepan. Simmer until reduced to approximately ½ cup. In top of double-boiler combine egg yolks and cream. Mix well. Stir in ½ cup reduced liquid. Cook, stirring, until sauce is thick and creamy. Stir in lemon juice and pepper. Pour sauce in bowl. Refrigerate, covered, to chill.

To serve, arrange cooked chicken slices on platter. Spoon some of sauce over each chicken piece, reserving remaining sauce to pass in gravy boat. Garnish platter with cucumber, lemon, and watercress. Can be made 4 to 8 hours before serving, but cover chicken with foil or plastic to lock in moisture.

Vermicelli Vinaigrette

4 ounces vermicelli or spaghetti,	1 6-ounce jar marinated
broken into small pieces	artichoke hearts, drained and
½ cup salad oil	chopped
¼ cup wine vinegar	1 cup sliced fresh mushrooms
1 large clove garlic, minced	2 tomatoes, peeled, seeded, and
¼ teaspoon salt	chopped
¼ teaspoon basil	½ cup chopped walnuts
½ teaspoon freshly ground	2 tablespoons chopped parsley
black pepper	Lettuce

Cook pasta in boiling, salted water. Rinse and drain. Combine oil, vinegar, garlic, salt, basil, and pepper and mix well. Toss about ½ cup of this dressing with pasta and cover. Chill. Toss remaining dressing with artichokes and mushrooms and cover and chill. To serve, toss pasta, artichokes, mushrooms, tomatoes, walnuts, and parsley together. Serve over lettuce leaves.

Note: Can be prepared in morning. Do *not* mix all parts together until ready to serve.

Pink Raspberry Mold

1 10-ounce package frozen red raspberries, thawed
2 3-ounce packages raspberry gelatin
2 cups boiling water

1 pint vanilla ice cream
1 6-ounce can frozen pink lemonade, thawed and undiluted

Drain raspberries and reserve syrup. Dissolve gelatin in boiling water. Add ice cream by spoonfuls, and stir until melted. Stir in lemonade and raspberry syrup. Chill in large bowl until partially set. Fold in raspberries and turn mixture into an oiled 6-cup mold (Teflon-lined Bundt pan works well). Chill until firm. Do *not* freeze.

Oat Carmelitas

1 cup flour
½ teaspoon baking soda
¼ teaspoon salt
1 cup oatmeal
¾ cup brown sugar
12 tablespoons butter, melted

1 cup chocolate chips
½ cup ground pecans
32 small square caramels, melted together with
5 tablespoons half-and-half or evaporated milk

Combine flour, soda, salt, oatmeal, and sugar. Add butter and stir. Press one-half of the mixture into greased 11-by-7-inch pan. Bake in preheated 350° oven for 10 minutes. Sprinkle with chocolate, pecans, and melted caramel mixture. Top with remaining crumb mixture. Bake for 25 minutes longer. Cool and cut. Do not overbake.

Grilled Hamburger Dinner

Burgers with Mustard Herb Sauce
Onion Rings
Baked Beans
Coleslaw
Sliced Tomato and Onion Platter
Fruity Streusel Bars
Assorted Sherbets

PREVIOUS DAY	EARLY MORNING	FREEZER
Coleslaw	*Mustard Herb Sauce*	*Sherbets*
	Baked Beans	

Burgers

2 to 3 pounds ground beef
1 egg
¼ cup bread crumbs

Salt and freshly ground black
 pepper, to taste
Garlic powder, to taste

Mix all ingredients together and form into 6 to 8 patties. Grill or broil and serve with Mustard Herb Sauce.

Mustard Herb Sauce:

2 teaspoons dried tarragon
¼ cup finely chopped parsley
1 tablespoon lemon juice

4 teaspoons white wine Dijon
 mustard
4 tablespoons unsalted butter

Mix the herbs in a bowl with the lemon juice, mustard, and butter. Cover and set aside in a warm place until butter is soft.
Note: Also good on steak.

Onion Rings

⅔ cup all-purpose flour
⅓ cup cornstarch
¼ teaspoon salt

1 cup ice water
Oil for frying
½ teaspoon baking soda

2 large onions, sliced and separated into rings

Sift flour and cornstarch into a medium bowl. Add salt and ice water. Beat until smooth, cover with plastic wrap, and refrigerate a minimum of 1 hour.

In a deep fryer or heavy saucepan, heat oil to 375°. Oil should be at least 3 inches deep.

Whisk the baking soda into the cold batter and dip several onion rings at a time into the batter. Fry quickly until light brown. Remove with a slotted spoon and drain on paper towels. The onion rings can be kept warm in a 250° oven until all are ready.

Baked Beans

4 1- pound, 12-ounce cans pork and beans	1 teaspoon dry mustard
	2 tablespoons vinegar
¾ pound dark brown sugar	1 large onion, grated
1 14-ounce bottle ketchup	3 bacon strips, halved

Mix first 6 ingredients, place in bean pot or casserole, and cover with strips of bacon. Cover and bake in preheated 300° oven for 4 to 5 hours. Stir frequently.

Coleslaw

1 small head cabbage	⅓ cup cooking oil
1 small onion, freshly grated	½ cup white vinegar
1 tablespoon ground celery seed	1 teaspoon sugar
⅛ teaspoon pepper	Salt, to taste

Shred cabbage and mix with onion, celery seed, and pepper. Combine the oil, vinegar, and sugar and mix into the cabbage. Toss lightly. Salt to taste. Chill and serve.

Sliced Tomato and Onion Platter

Several leaves romaine lettuce	Olive oil
3 or 4 Beefsteak tomatoes, sliced	Italian seasoning
2 medium-size red onions, sliced	Freshly ground black pepper

Line platter with romaine leaves. Alternate sliced tomatoes and onions over leaves. Sprinkle with olive oil and 1 to 2 teaspoons of Italian seasoning and freshly ground pepper.

Fruity Streusel Bars

Crust:

2 cups flour
¾ cup confectioners' sugar
½ teaspoon salt
¼ teaspoon baking powder
½ pound butter or margarine

Mix dry ingredients in a processor or bowl. Cut in butter with a pastry blender or steel blade of processor, using several on-off pulses. If using processor, pulse only until the mixture is crumbly. Do *not* allow a ball to form. Press dough into 12-by-9-inch glass pan. Bake in preheated 350° oven for 30 minutes.

Filling:

½ cup red raspberry jam
½ cup apricot jam
3 tablespoons orange marmalade
½ cup golden raisins

Combine filling ingredients and spread over partially baked crust.

Topping:

½ cup sugar
½ cup flour
1 tablespoon cinnamon
½ cup chopped pecans
6 tablespoons (scant) butter or
  margarine

Blend ingredients together until crumbly and sprinkle over filling in the pan.

Return to oven for 30 to 35 minutes. Cool and cut into bars.

Assorted Sherbets

1 pint raspberry sherbet
1 pint orange sherbet
1 pint pineapple sherbet

Scoop sherbet into balls and serve on glass plate.

Family Buffets

<hr style="width:15%" />

Each recipe serves six unless otherwise indicated.

The current life-style of the American family often makes it difficult for everyone to sit down at the same time. Buffet service allows for a family meal to be enjoyed in a civilized, intimate way despite busy individual schedules. With all the modern kitchen helpers—microwave ovens, blenders, food processors, bread and pasta makers—it is easier than ever to dress up family meals.

Family Gathering

Cucumber Dip
Mushroom Rounds
Baked Chicken
Vegetable Soufflé
Mixed Grain Pilaf
Challah
Clafouti

PREVIOUS DAY   EARLY MORNING   FREEZER

Baked Chicken   *Cucumber Dip*   *Challah dough*
                           Mushroom Rounds
                           Prepare fruit for
                             Clafouti

Cucumber Dip

1 small or ½ large cucumber,
  peeled and grated
1 small onion, grated
8 ounces cream cheese, room
  temperature

Salt and freshly ground black
  pepper, to taste
Potato chips, crackers, or
  Crudités

Mix grated cucumber and onion with softened cream cheese. Salt and pepper to taste. Serve with potato chips, crackers, or Crudités (see Index).

Mushroom Rounds

1 cup chopped mushrooms
1 cup shredded Cheddar cheese
1 cup shredded Monterey Jack
  cheese
1 7-ounce jar black olives,
  chopped

1 small onion, chopped
1 cup mayonnaise, more if
  needed
1 loaf party rye bread rounds,
  toasted on one side

Mix all ingredients except bread. Blend well. Spread on untoasted side of rye bread rounds. Bake in preheated 375° oven for approximately 20 minutes, or until cheese melts.

Baked Chicken

½ pound mushrooms, sliced
2 medium onions, sliced,
  separated into rings
2 green peppers, cubed
2 chickens, quartered
Seasoned salt, to taste

Paprika, to taste
1 cup dry white wine
½ 12-ounce bottle chili sauce
1 10-ounce package frozen
  artichoke hearts, drained
  (optional)

Line bottom of large baking pan with mushrooms, onions, and green peppers. Place chicken on top of vegetables. Season chicken with seasoned salt and paprika. Bake uncovered for 1 hour in preheated 350° oven. Remove chicken but keep warm. Mix the wine and chili sauce into the vegetables. Add artichokes for more festive look, if desired. Cook for 20 minutes more. Arrange vegetables around chicken on serving platter.

Note: If you make one day in advance, add wine, chili sauce, and reheat chicken and vegetables all together.

Vegetable Soufflé

1 10-ounce package frozen cauliflower	½ cup grated Parmesan
2 10-ounce packages frozen broccoli	1 tablespoon chopped fresh parsley
3 tablespoons butter	1 tablespoon chopped chives
3 tablespoons flour	1 clove garlic, finely chopped
1 cup milk, hot	Freshly ground white pepper
3 eggs, separated	¼ teaspoon salt
	Pinch of nutmeg

Thaw, drain, and chop vegetables. In 4-quart pot melt butter, add flour slowly, mixing until smooth, and then slowly add milk, stirring constantly to make white sauce. When slightly thickened, remove from heat and cool. Beat egg yolks and fold into cooled sauce. Add Parmesan cheese and mix. Add cauliflower, broccoli, parsley, chives, garlic, pepper, salt, and nutmeg. Beat egg whites until stiff and fold into vegetable mixture. Pour into buttered soufflé dish and bake at 350° for 1 hour and 10 minutes, or until firm in center. Do not open oven until near end of cooking time.

Mixed Grain Pilaf
(Serves 6 to 8)

5 tablespoons butter	½ cup bulgar wheat or kasha
½ cup chopped walnuts	3¾ cups chicken broth
1 large onion, chopped	¼ cup sherry
1 large carrot, shredded	¾ teaspoon oregano
1 clove garlic, minced	¾ teaspoon dried basil
⅓ cup chopped parsley	Salt and freshly ground black pepper, to taste
½ cup barley	
½ cup brown rice	

In a 4-quart pan over medium heat, melt butter. Add nuts and stir until toasted. Then remove nuts with a slotted spoon and reserve.

Increase heat to medium-high and sauté the onion, carrot, garlic, and parsley until the vegetables are soft. Stir in the barley, rice, and bulgar and stir-fry until the grains are lightly browned.

Stir in the broth, wine, oregano, and basil. Bring to a boil, cover, and reduce the heat. Simmer until the grains are tender, about 45 minutes. Let stand, covered, for 10 minutes. Season to taste with salt and pepper. Garnish with nuts.

Challah (Egg Bread)

2 packages active dry yeast	1 teaspoon salt
1½ cups warm water	¼ pound softened butter or
½ cup plus 1 tablespoon	margarine
sugar	4 eggs, well beaten
7½ cups flour	Sesame or poppy seeds (optional)

Dissolve yeast in ½ cup of the warm water with 1 tablespoon of the sugar. Set aside. Put 6 cups of the unsifted flour, ½ cup of the sugar, and 1 teaspoon salt in large mixer bowl. With dough hook, mix on low speed. Gradually add yeast mixture, butter, 3 well-beaten eggs, and remaining 1 cup warm water. Continue mixing on low speed until thick batter is formed. Gradually add remaining flour and continue mixing at high speed for 4 to 6 minutes or until dough is satiny smooth.

Put dough in greased bowl and turn to oil entire surface. Cover with plastic wrap and allow to rise in warm, draft-free place, until doubled, about 2 hours. On a well-floured surface, punch dough down and divide into 3 equal pieces. Divide each piece into 3 parts. Roll each part into a rope and braid the 3 strands together, securely tucking in ends. Repeat for each third of dough. Place on ungreased cookie sheets and let rise again, until doubled, about 1 hour. Brush tops of loaves with remaining beaten egg and sprinkle with sesame or poppy seeds, if desired.

Bake loaves in preheated 350° oven for 20 to 25 minutes or until golden brown.

Note: Raw dough freezes well after first rising and shaping. Bring to room temperature, let rise the second time, and bake.

Clafouti

3 cups fruit: peaches, nectarines, strawberries, raspberries, blueberries, etc.	2 tablespoons rum or cognac
2 tablespoons lemon juice	1 tablespoon confectioners' sugar, plus more for garnish

Combine all ingredients and place in a buttered 9-by-10-inch baking dish.

Batter:

3 eggs	1¼ cups milk
⅔ cup flour	1 tablespoon vanilla extract,
¼ cup sugar	rum, or cognac
Pinch of salt	

In blender or processor, whirl batter ingredients until very smooth. Pour batter over fruit. Bake in preheated 350° oven for 50 minutes to 1 hour until it is puffed and browned. Sprinkle with confectioners' sugar and serve warm.

Americana Dinner

Artichokes with Lemon Sauce
Raw Vegetable Salad in Marinade
Apple Butter Grilled Chicken
Crispy Potato-Onion Bake
Golden Cordial Dream Pie

PREVIOUS DAY	EARLY MORNING	FREEZER
Artichokes with sauce	Vegetable Salad	Cordial Pie
	Marinate chicken	
	Potato-Onion Bake	

Artichokes with Lemon Sauce

6 artichokes	Lemon juice
3 teaspoons salt	

Trim stems from artichokes so they stand upright. Cut off tips of leaves with scissors and wash artichokes under cold running water. Spread leaves and remove purple choke with sharp spoon. Roll artichokes between hands to original shape. Put in boiling water with 3 teaspoons salt and lemon juice. Cover and cook until tender, about 40 minutes. Drain artichokes well. Serve warm or chilled with Lemon Sauce.

Lemon Sauce:
(Makes 1⅔ cups)

1 cup mayonnaise	½ teaspoon salt
3 tablespoons lemon juice	½ teaspoon dry mustard
2 eggs	

Whisk all ingredients together in a small saucepan until they are smooth. Cook over low heat until thickened (*do not boil*). Serve as a dipping sauce.

Raw Vegetable Salad in Marinade

¼ cup canned tomato sauce	¼ teaspoon pepper
⅓ cup red wine vinegar	⅛ teaspoon Tabasco sauce
1 cup salad oil	1 clove garlic
1 tablespoon sugar	Green pepper rings
1 teaspoon salt	Chopped celery and carrots
1 teaspoon dried basil	Sliced mushrooms, zucchini, and
1 teaspoon Worcestershire sauce	tomatoes
¼ teaspoon dry mustard	Any others that taste good raw

Blend all marinade ingredients and pour over vegetables. Marinate at least 6 hours.

Apple Butter Grilled Chicken

1 cup apple butter	1 medium onion, minced
3 tablespoons prepared mustard	4 to 8 chicken breasts
1 teaspoon celery seed	¾ teaspoon salt, or to taste
½ cup apple cider vinegar	⅓ teaspoon freshly ground
2 tablespoons butter	black pepper, or to taste
2 tablespoons brown sugar	

Mix apple butter, mustard, celery seed, vinegar, butter, brown sugar, and onion in saucepan. Heat to boil. Pour over chicken. Marinate and chill at least 1 hour. Reserve sauce. Grill chicken for 1 hour, turning every 15 minutes. Brush with sauce and season to taste.

Crispy Potato-Onion Bake

4 pounds red boiling potatoes, washed and sliced thin in machine (don't peel)
1 large sweet onion, sliced thin
8 to 10 ounces Swiss cheese

Salt and freshly ground black pepper, to taste
¼ pound unsalted butter
1 cup beef broth

Grease a 9-by-13-inch pan. Layer in potatoes, onion, and half the cheese, and season. Add half the butter, cut up and dotted on evenly. Repeat second layer of all ingredients. Pour beef broth over all. Cover and bake in preheated 400° oven for about 40 minutes. Uncover for last 10 minutes of baking time so that potatoes will brown.

Golden Dream Cordial Pie

Crust:

1½ cups graham cracker crumbs

⅓ cup melted butter

Combine crumbs with butter. Press into a 9-inch pie plate and bake 20 minutes in preheated 350° oven. Cool.

Filling:

¾ cup orange juice
1 envelope unflavored gelatin
⅔ cup sugar
⅛ teaspoon salt
3 eggs, separated

2 tablespoons grated orange peel
¼ cup Galliano
¼ cup Cointreau
1 cup heavy cream
Food coloring (optional)

Toasted sweetened coconut, for garnish

Pour juice into a saucepan and sprinkle gelatin over it. Add ⅓ cup of the sugar, salt, egg yolks, and orange peel. Stir to blend. Place over low heat and stir until gelatin dissolves and mixture thickens. Do not boil! Remove from heat.

Stir the liqueurs into the mixture and chill until mixture mounds slightly when dropped from a spoon.

Beat egg whites until stiff, then add remaining sugar and beat until peaks are firm. Gelatin mixture can also be whipped for a higher, fluffier pie. Fold meringue into gelatin mixture. Whip the cream and fold in. Add food coloring, if desired. Turn mixture into prepared crust. Add garnish, if desired. Chill overnight or several hours. Freezes well. Allow 30 minutes for defrosting.

Variations:

Brandy Alexander Pie: Change orange juice to ½ cup cold water; liqueurs to ¼ cup cognac and ¼ cup brown crème de cacao.

Blackberry Alexander Pie: Change orange juice to ½ cup cold water, liqueurs to 3 ounces blackberry brandy and 1 ounce white crème de cacao.

🌿 🌿 🌿

Sloppy Joe Dinner

Crudités with Summer Dip
CCC Slaw
Herbed Potato Salad (see Index)
Sloppy Joes on Overnight Buns
Ice Cream and Peaches
Chocolate Chunk Cookies

PREVIOUS DAY	EARLY MORNING	FREEZER
Summer Dip	*CCC Slaw*	*Sloppy Joes*
Sloppy Joes	*Potato Salad*	*Cookies*
Overnight Buns		

Summer Dip

¾ cup sour cream
¾ cup mayonnaise
1 2-ounce can anchovy fillets
⅓ cup chopped parsley
3 tablespoons snipped chives
3 tablespoons white vinegar
1 clove garlic, crushed

¼ teaspoon salt, or more, to
  taste
⅛ teaspoon freshly ground
  black pepper
Tabasco, red pepper, and
  Worcestershire sauce, to taste

Mix all ingredients together. Let sit overnight. Serve with Crudités (see Index).

CCC Slaw (Cabbage, Caraway, and Cucumber)

¼ cup each oil and white
  vinegar
1 tablespoon sugar
½ teaspoon salt, or to taste

½ cup sour cream
2 teaspoons caraway seed
1 large cucumber (about 10
  ounces)

6 cups shredded cabbage (about 1 pound)

In large bowl mix oil, vinegar, sugar, and salt. Stir in sour cream and caraway seed. Peel and seed cucumber and chop into dressing. Add cabbage and toss to mix well.

Sloppy Joes

3 pounds ground beef
¾ cup chopped onion
1½ cups chopped celery
¾ cup chopped green pepper
1½ 10½-ounce cans
  condensed tomato soup

18 ounces ketchup
¾ cup brown sugar
1½ tablespoons
  Worcestershire sauce
Salt and freshly ground black
  pepper, to taste

Brown meat, breaking apart, and drain fat. Add rest of ingredients, cook 40 minutes to 1 hour. Serve on Overnight Buns. Freezes well.
  Note: Can be prepared 2 days in advance.

Overnight Buns:

4 cups water
1½ cups sugar
1 cup oil
1 package active dry yeast
  (1 tablespoon)

4 beaten eggs
2 tablespoons salt
12 cups flour (approximately)

At about 1:00 P.M., boil water and sugar for 5 minutes. Add oil and cool to lukewarm. Mix yeast with this mixture until yeast starts to work. Add eggs, salt, and a little flour. Gradually mix in rest of flour. Turn out onto floured board and knead until elastic. Put into large greased bowl and let rise until about 5:00 P.M. Knead down, let rise again until about 9:00 to 9:30 P.M. Shape into hamburger buns, set in greased pans on kitchen table or in cupboard. *Do not refrigerate!* Cover with towel and bake in morning. Bake in preheated 350° oven for about 18 minutes or until lightly browned. Brush lightly with oil to keep tops from getting too hard.

Note: Great dinner rolls too.

Ice Cream and Peaches

1 tablespoon dark rum	4 peaches, sliced
1 tablespoon brandy	1 pint vanilla ice cream, softened
1 tablespoon honey	Whipped cream
1 teaspoon grated orange peel	

Combine rum, brandy, and honey. Heat through. Sprinkle over sliced peaches. Fold into the softened ice cream and place in individual dessert dishes. (Can be returned to freezer at this stage.) Top with whipped cream flavored with the orange peel.

Chocolate Chunk Cookies
(Makes 50 cookies)

1 cup raisins	2 cups flour
½ pound unsalted butter	1 teaspoon salt
1 cup firmly packed brown sugar	1 teaspoon baking soda
½ cup granulated sugar	8 ounces semisweet chocolate,
1 teaspoon vanilla extract	coarsely chopped
2 large eggs	

Cover raisins with boiling water and allow to plump for 15 minutes. Pat dry on paper towels.

Beat butter until creamy. Add sugars slowly, beating until fluffy. Add the vanilla and eggs, beating well. Combine the flour, salt, and soda. Add to butter and egg mixture one-third at a time. Beat after each addition. Stir in the drained raisins and chocolate pieces. Chill the dough until it is firm, 30 to 45 minutes. Drop rounded teaspoonfuls, 3 inches apart, on ungreased cookie sheets. Bake in preheated 375° oven for 8 to 10 minutes or until edges are golden brown. Cool on racks.

Spring Supper

Herbed Cheese Spread
Spinach and Romaine Salad with Poppy Seed Dressing
Slim-Style Chicken
Steamed Fresh Broccoli
Carrot Mold
Strawberry-Rhubarb Compote
Company Oatmeal Cookies

PREVIOUS DAY	EARLY MORNING	FREEZER
Cheese Spread	Poppy Seed Dressing	
Strawberry-Rhubarb	Carrot Mold	
Compote		
Oatmeal Cookies		

Herbed Cheese Spread

8 ounces cream cheese, softened	1 teaspoon dried dill weed
1 clove garlic, minced	1 teaspoon chopped chives
1 teaspoon caraway seed	Lemon-pepper seasoning
1 teaspoon dried basil	Wheat crackers

Soften cheese and mix with all herbs but lemon pepper. Shape cheese into a flattened circle, sprinkle top with lemon pepper, and flip to other side. Season other side with lemon pepper. Serve with wheat crackers.

Note: Flavor is enhanced if made a day in advance.

Spinach and Romaine Salad

10 ounces fresh spinach, washed,   1 large head romaine, thoroughly
   cleaned, and trimmed   washed
              4 large tomatoes, quartered

In large salad bowl, arrange bite-size pieces of the greens. Just before
serving, toss with Poppy Seed Dressing. Arrange tomato wedges across
top.

Poppy Seed Dressing:
(Makes about 1 pint)

1½ cups sugar   ⅔ cup tarragon vinegar
2 teaspoons salt   3 tablespoons onion juice
Freshly ground black pepper   3 tablespoons poppy seed
2 teaspoons dry mustard   2 cups salad oil

Mix first 7 ingredients, then slowly beat in oil.

Slim-Style Chicken

3 chicken breasts, split (or other   1½ tablespoons dry white
   chicken parts)   wine (optional)
6 tablespoons plain low-fat   ⅓ teaspoon dried tarragon
   yogurt   Salt and freshly ground pepper,
3 tablespoons Dijon mustard   to taste

Trim fat from chicken and remove as much skin as possible. Blend
remaining ingredients together and spread over chicken. Arrange
chicken, meat side up, on shallow pan sprayed with noncaloric cooking
spray. Bake uncovered in preheated 350° oven for 45 to 50 minutes.
May be placed under broiler for 5 minutes if more browning is desired.

Steamed Fresh Broccoli

2 pounds fresh broccoli   ½ teaspoon dill weed
              Lemon juice

Wash broccoli and trim. Cut into 2-inch lengths and julienne stems.
Place in steamer and sprinkle with dill weed. Steam 15 to 20 minutes
or until stems are tender. Sprinkle with lemon juice and serve.

Carrot Mold

¼ pound unsalted butter	1 teaspoon baking soda
½ cup brown sugar	½ teaspoon baking powder
1 cup grated carrot	Pinch of salt
2 eggs	1 teaspoon nutmeg
1¼ cups sifted flour	½ teaspoon cinnamon

Cream butter. Add sugar, carrot, and eggs. Combine flour with baking soda, powder, and salt. Fold flour into egg mixture and add nutmeg and cinnamon. Place mixture in buttered ring mold. Set mold in pan of warm water and bake in preheated 350° oven for 30 to 35 minutes or until it tests done.

Strawberry-Rhubarb Compote

1 pound fresh strawberries	1 pound fresh rhubarb, as red as possible

¾ cup sugar, divided

Wash, hull, and cut strawberries in half. Wash rhubarb and cut crosswise into 2- to 3-inch sections. Layer the strawberries and ¼ cup sugar in a bowl. Layer rhubarb and ½ cup sugar in second bowl. Cover and refrigerate both bowls for several hours or overnight. Pour off the accumulated fruit juices into a 4-quart saucepan and bring the liquid to a boil. Add the rhubarb and simmer for 20 minutes or until it softens. Add the strawberries and simmer until the berries are softened. Chill for several hours before serving.

Note: Can be made 2 to 3 days in advance.

Company Oatmeal Cookies
(Makes about 4 dozen)

½ pound butter or margarine	1 teaspoon cream of tartar
1 cup granulated sugar	1 teaspoon baking soda
1 cup brown sugar	1 teaspoon salt
2 eggs	3 cups old-fashioned or quick oats
1 teaspoon vanilla extract	½ cup raisins (optional)
1½ cups flour	

1 cup chopped nuts

Cream butter and sugars until light and fluffy. Blend in eggs and vanilla. Combine flour, cream of tartar, soda, and salt. Add to creamed mixture, blending well. Stir in oats, raisins, and nuts and roll dough into sausage shape, approximately 1½ inches in diameter. Wrap in wax paper and place in freezer a minimum of 2 hours. Cut dough into ¼-inch slices and bake in preheated 350° oven on ungreased baking sheet for 12 to 15 minutes or until lightly browned.

Note: Place cookies at least 2 inches apart on cookie sheet, as they spread.

After the Movies   (Serves 4)

Taco Pizza
Orange and Cucumber Green Salad with Chili Dressing
Jumbo Chocolate Chip Cookies
Peppermint Ice Cream

PREVIOUS DAY	EARLY MORNING	FREEZER
Salad dressing	*Taco Pizza*	*Jumbo Chip Cookies*
		Peppermint Ice Cream

Taco Pizza

1½ pounds ground beef	1 11-ounce package hot roll mix
1 onion, grated	Salad oil
1 1¼-ounce envelope taco seasoning	1 8-ounce can enchilada sauce, mild or hot
1 cup water	2 cups grated Cheddar cheese

Brown ground beef and onion until crumbly and drain fat. Add taco seasoning and water and stir and bring to boil. Reduce heat and simmer for 15 to 20 minutes, stirring occasionally. Meanwhile prepare the dough according to package directions, but *do not* allow to rise. Roll the dough to fit a greased 17-by-12-inch baking sheet (or use two smaller baking sheets).

Leaving 1-inch border around sides of pan, brush dough with salad oil, and spread taco meat over dough. Then spread enchilada sauce over meat. Top with cheese. Bake in preheated 400° oven on bottom shelf for 15 to 20 minutes. Cut in squares. (Don't let enchilada sauce drip over sides as it will smoke up oven.) Can be prepared a couple of hours in advance and baked at last minute.

Orange and Cucumber Green Salad

2 heads Boston or butter lettuce
3 large oranges, peeled and sliced
  with membrane removed
1 small cucumber, sliced, and
  peeled if desired

½ red onion, sliced thin,
  separated into rings

Arrange lettuce in a large shallow bowl or on a rimmed platter. Garnish with oranges, cucumber, and onion slices. Sprinkle Chili Dressing on salad just before serving.

Chili Dressing:

½ cup salad oil
3 tablespoons wine vinegar
¼ teaspoon chili powder

Salt and freshly ground black
  pepper, to taste.

Combine all ingredients in blender or shake in jar.

Jumbo Chocolate Chip Cookies
(Makes 2 dozen large cookies)

¼ pound butter
¼ pound unsalted margarine
¾ cup granulated sugar
¾ cup brown sugar
1 teaspoon vanilla extract
2 eggs
2¼ cups plus 4 heaping
  tablespoons flour

½ teaspoon salt
1 teaspoon baking soda, plus a
  pinch
1¾ 12-ounce packages semisweet chocolate chips

Cream butter, margarine, and sugars. Add vanilla and eggs, beating well. Combine dry ingredients and add slowly to creamed mixture. Stir chocolate chips into mix. Use a tablespoon to spoon mixture onto ungreased cookie sheet. Leave 2 inches between each. Bake in preheated 375° oven for 10 to 12 minutes.

Peppermint Ice Cream

6 ounces crushed peppermint candy	1 quart vanilla ice cream, softened

Mint leaves, for garnish

Mix crushed candy into softened ice cream, blending well. Spoon into glass ice cream dishes and freeze until ready to serve. Garnish with mint leaves.

Great Lakes Event

Spinach Dip
Barbecued Chicken Wings
Zucchini Salad with Garlic Scallion Dressing
Whitefish Livornese
Potato and Onion Pie
Ice Cream Fudge Pie

PREVIOUS DAY	EARLY MORNING	FREEZER
Spinach Dip *Chicken Wings*	*Garlic Scallion Dressing*	*Ice Cream Pie*

Spinach Dip

1 10-ounce package frozen chopped spinach, thawed and drained	1¼ cups sour cream or sour half-and-half
1 2¼-ounce package dry vegetable soup mix	1 bunch scallions, chopped
1 8-ounce can water chestnuts, chopped	¾ cup mayonnaise Crudités or sesame crackers

Combine all dip ingredients 24 hours in advance of serving. Serve with Crudités (see Index) or sesame crackers.

Barbecued Chicken Wings

3 pounds chicken wings (about 16)	¼ cup vegetable oil
¼ teaspoon salt	1 cup ketchup
⅛ teaspoon pepper	½ cup apricot preserves
1 cup chopped onion	1 tablespoon Worcestershire sauce
1 clove garlic, crushed	¼ teaspoon hot pepper sauce

Remove tips of wings and discard. Cut each wing into two pieces. Sprinkle with salt and pepper. Place in single layer in shallow glass dish. Sauté onion and garlic in hot oil about 3 minutes, or until golden brown. Stir in remaining ingredients and simmer 5 minutes. Cool, pour over chicken wings, cover, and chill several hours or overnight. Bake in preheated 350° oven for 40 minutes or until tender.

Zucchini Salad

1 small head romaine lettuce	1 cup sliced radishes
1 head Boston lettuce	½ cup sliced cauliflower
2 medium zucchini	

Tear lettuces into bite-size pieces. Slice vegetables and spread over greens. Serve with Garlic Scallion Dressing.

Garlic Scallion Dressing:

3 tablespoons chopped scallions	2½ teaspoons salt
⅓ cup salad oil	1 clove garlic, crushed
3½ tablespoons tarragon vinegar	¼ teaspoon freshly ground black pepper

Place steel cutting blade into processor bowl. Add scallions and process thoroughly. Add salad oil, vinegar, and seasonings and mix thoroughly. Chill for 30 minutes. Pour over Zucchini Salad and toss until all is well coated.

Whitefish Livornese

3 pounds whitefish 2 tablespoons butter
Salt and white pepper, to taste

Oil a large, shallow broiler pan. Place fillets in pan, skin side down.
Dot with 2 tablespoons of butter and sprinkle with salt and white
pepper to taste. Broil in a preheated broiler for 5 to 8 minutes, depending on thickness of fish. Baste once, halfway through cooking
time. Do not turn fillets.

Sauce:
(Makes about 3 cups)

24 ounces canned tomatoes in 4½ tablespoons white wine
purée 4 anchovy fillets, chopped
1 tablespoon capers ⅓ cup sliced green olives

Combine all ingredients in saucepan and simmer about 15 minutes.
Pour over broiled fish.

Potato and Onion Pie

4 pounds baking potatoes, peeled ¼ pound butter
and sliced thin (about 8 cups) ½ cup freshly grated
2 large onions, peeled and sliced Parmesan
thin (about 3 cups) Paprika
Salt and freshly ground black
pepper, to taste

Butter a 13-by-9-inch baking dish. Layer one-third of potatoes, then
one-third onions. Season with salt and pepper. Dot with one-third
of the butter. Continue layering twice more. Cover and bake for
45 minutes in preheated 400° oven or until potatoes test tender. Remove from oven and allow to rest at room temperature for 5 minutes.

Loosen with a knife and turn out onto an ovenproof platter. Sprinkle
with cheese and paprika. Return to oven to brown cheese. Watch
carefully. Serve very hot, cutting into squares.

Note: Can also be kept in baking dish after first baking. Sprinkle
cheese and paprika on top and put under broiler for 3 to 4 minutes
to brown.

Ice Cream Fudge Pie

Crust:

18 Oreo cookies, crushed
4 tablespoons butter or
　margarine

1 quart vanilla or coffee ice
　cream, softened

Combine cookie crumbs and butter. Press into pie plate. Freeze. When set, add softened ice cream, refreeze.

Fudge Sauce:

2½ squares unsweetened
　chocolate
4 tablespoons butter

1½ cups unsifted
　confectioners' sugar
7¼ ounces evaporated milk

⅔ teaspoon vanilla extract

Melt chocolate and butter. Remove from heat. Mix in sugar alternately with milk. Place pan on heat and bring to boil, stirring constantly. Cook and stir for 8 minutes or until thick and creamy. Remove from heat and stir in vanilla. Let fudge cool, then pour over pie and serve.

Teen Get-Together

Appetizer Pizzas
Do-It-Yourself Salad with Anchovy Dressing
Rotini with Tomato Meat Sauce
Ranger Cookies
Assorted Ice Creams

PREVIOUS DAY	EARLY MORNING	FREEZER
Tomato Meat Sauce	*Appetizer Pizzas*	*Ranger Cookies* *Ice Creams*

Appetizer Pizzas

1 loaf sliced party rye bread
1 8-ounce can tomato paste
1 pound thinly sliced salami or
　pepperoni

1 pound thinly sliced mozzarella
　cheese
Oregano

Spread individual slices of rye bread with tomato paste. Place salami or pepperoni on top, layer on a slice of cheese, sprinkle with oregano, and broil. Watch carefully to prevent burning.

Do-It-Yourself Salad

1 head iceberg lettuce, shredded
2 2½-ounce cans sliced black olives
2 red peppers, diced
1 cup sliced radishes
1 12-ounce jar pepperoncini
1 cup crumbled cheese-flavored crackers

Place each ingredient in a separate container. Serve with bowl of Anchovy Dressing.

Anchovy Dressing:

⅓ cup wine vinegar
1 clove garlic
1 teaspoon salt
¼ teaspoon freshly ground black pepper
1 cup olive oil or salad oil
3 or 4 anchovy fillets

Place vinegar, garlic, salt, and pepper in blender and blend until garlic is finely chopped. Add oil and anchovy and blend until smooth.

Rotini with Tomato Meat Sauce

2 tablespoons olive oil
1 cup diced onion
2 cloves garlic, minced
1½ cups grated carrots
1 pound lean ground beef
1 28-ounce can tomato purée or Italian plum tomatoes
1 6-ounce can tomato paste
1 10¾-ounce can tomato soup, undiluted
½ pound fresh mushrooms, sliced
½ cup chopped green pepper
1 tablespoon chopped parsley
1 tablespoon brown sugar
1 teaspoon granulated sugar
½ teaspoon beef base or 1 beef bouillon cube
1 teaspoon each salt, dried oregano, and dried basil
1 bay leaf
½ teaspoon pepper
½ teaspoon allspice
⅛ teaspoon crushed red pepper
½ cup red wine
1 1-pound box rotini

Heat oil in 5-quart saucepan over medium-high heat. Add onion and garlic and sauté until lightly browned. Reduce heat to medium, add carrots, and cook until softened. Add meat and cook until crumbly and liquid has evaporated. If oily, skim.

Reduce heat to low. Add remaining ingredients except wine and rotini and simmer uncovered for 1½ hours. Add wine and cook 30 minutes more. Adjust seasonings if necessary.

Cook rotini according to directions on package. Serve with sauce. *Note:* Can be served over any pasta.

Ranger Cookies
(Makes 5 dozen)

1 cup shortening	2 cups flour
1 cup granulated sugar	1 teaspoon baking soda
1 cup brown sugar	½ teaspoon baking powder
2 eggs	½ teaspoon salt
1 teaspoon vanilla extract	2½ cups quick oatmeal

2½ cups Rice Krispies

Beat shortening and sugars until fluffy and then blend in eggs and vanilla. Combine with flour, soda, baking powder, and salt, adding slowly and blending well. Mix in the cereals. The dough will appear crumbly. Drop by tablespoonfuls on ungreased cookie sheets. Bake in preheated 350° oven for 8 to 10 minutes or until golden brown. Cool cookies on a rack.

Tradition Updated

Marinated Herring
Brisket with Fruit
Potato Kugel
Zucchini Soufflé
Braided Sesame Ring
Triple-Treat Bars
Pears in Caramel Pecan Sauce over Coffee Ice Cream

Marinated Herring

1 12-ounce jar herring in wine	½ green pepper, chopped fine
½ cup mayonnaise	1 apple, chopped (optional)
½ pint sour cream	1 tablespoon sugar
1 tablespoon lemon juice	1 tablespoon celery seed
2 scallions, cut fine	Cocktail rye or pumpernickel bread

Drain herring, rinse, and cut up fillets. Add remaining ingredients except bread and refrigerate overnight. Serve with cocktail rye or pumpernickel bread.

Brisket with Fruit

1 large onion, sliced	Juice and peel of 1 large lemon
1 first cut brisket of beef	¾ teaspoon ginger
1 12-ounce can beer	½ teaspoon cinnamon
1 cup dried, pitted prunes	1 teaspoon Worcestershire sauce
1 cup dried apricots	½ teaspoon freshly ground black pepper
3 tablespoons brown sugar	
2 tablespoons orange marmalade	

Put half of the sliced onion under and half over the brisket in a large shallow pan. Brown in preheated 350° oven for 30 minutes and then cover with foil, sealing it tightly, and continue roasting for 3 hours. Bring all of the remaining ingredients to a quick boil in a large saucepan. Reduce oven temperature to 300°, uncover the meat, and pour the fruit mixture on top of the brisket. Cover the pan and continue roasting for 1 hour. Add more beer if the sauce appears dry. Freezes well. If frozen, defrost overnight in refrigerator.

Note: Can be made a day ahead of serving.

Potato Kugel

6 medium-size potatoes, grated
3 eggs
4 tablespoons flour

1 teaspoon baking powder
Salt and freshly ground black
    pepper, to taste

2 tablespoons melted butter

Mix all ingredients except butter. Grease muffin tins and fill three-quarters full. Brush tops with melted butter. Bake in preheated 350° oven for 45 minutes to 1 hour. Potato mixture should be crisp and brown.

Zucchini Soufflé

2 pounds cottage cheese
6 eggs, lightly beaten
4 tablespoons melted butter
3 cups shredded and well
    drained zucchini

8 ounces shredded mozzarella
6 tablespoons flour
¼ cup grated Parmesan

Mix all ingredients together. Pour into 9-by-13-inch greased pan. Bake in preheated 350° oven for 1 hour or until it tests set (with knife).

Braided Sesame Ring

1 package active dry yeast
1¼ cups lukewarm water
4 to 4½ cups white flour
1 tablespoon sugar

2 eggs
2 teaspoons salt
2 tablespoons melted butter
Sesame seeds

Dissolve yeast in ¼ cup of warm water. Put 4 cups of flour into bowl. Add sugar, 1 egg, yeast, remaining water, salt, and butter. Stir, adding enough flour to make a stiff dough. Knead dough until smooth and elastic. Put dough into an oiled bowl and cover with a towel. Let rise until doubled (approximately 1 hour). Punch down dough. Make 2 ropes and twist, shaping into circle. Place braid on buttered cookie sheet. Cover with a towel and let rise until doubled. Beat second egg with 1 tablespoon water, brush loaf, and sprinkle with sesame seeds. Bake in preheated 375° oven for about 50 minutes.

Triple-Treat Bars

Oatmeal Base:

2 cups quick-cooking rolled oats
1 cup flour
1 cup brown sugar
½ teaspoon baking soda
½ teaspoon salt
12 tablespoons butter or
   margarine, melted

Stir together oats, flour, sugar, soda, and salt. Add melted butter. Pat into bottom of greased 9-by-13-inch pan. Bake in preheated 350° oven for 10 minutes.

Chocolate Layer:

4 squares unsweetened chocolate
½ pound butter
2 cups sugar
4 eggs
1 cup flour
1 teaspoon vanilla or rum
   extract

Melt chocolate and butter. Mix sugar and eggs. Add chocolate to mixture and add flour and vanilla. Pour over baked crust. Bake 25 minutes at 350°. Cool.

Frosting:

2 squares unsweetened baking
   chocolate
4 tablespoons butter
3 cups confectioners' sugar
1 teaspoon vanilla or rum
   extract
4 tablespoons *hot* water

Melt chocolate and butter. Remove from heat and stir in confectioners' sugar and vanilla. Blend in enough hot water to make mixture of almost pourable consistency. Spread over cooled chocolate layer and refrigerate until serving. Cut into bars. Freezes well. Defrosting time, 3 hours.

Note: Can be made 2 days in advance.

Pears in Caramel Pecan Sauce

¼ cup golden raisins
¼ to ⅓ cup golden rum
4 tablespoons unsalted butter
6 semi-ripe pears, peeled and
　quartered
½ cup plus 3 tablespoons
　sugar

½ teaspoon cinnamon
Grated nutmeg
2 tablespoons water
½ pint warm whipping cream
6 scoops coffee ice cream

Place raisins in a small bowl. Pour in enough rum to cover and reserve
overnight. In a heavy 12-inch skillet, melt the butter and add the pears,
3 tablespoons sugar, cinnamon, and nutmeg. Sauté gently for 25 to
30 minutes over low flame until pears are golden.

Mix ½ cup sugar with water in small saucepan. Do not stir at
all. Cook until sugar turns deep brown. Add warmed whipping cream
immediately. Stir until sauce is smooth. Add raisins which have been
drained. Pour sauce over pears and heat through for 2 to 3 minutes.
Put into a pretty glass bowl and serve with coffee ice cream.

Mom's Birthday

Black Bean Soup
Tossed Green Salad with Tarragon-Shallot Dressing
Chicken with Shrimp
Easy Flavored Rice
Mushrooms Bordelaise
White Chocolate Cake with Buttercream Frosting
Ice Cream

PREVIOUS DAY	EARLY MORNING	FREEZER
Tarragon-Shallot 　*Dressing* *White Chocolate Cake*	*Chicken* *Prepare shrimp*	*Bean Soup* *Ice cream*

Black Bean Soup

2½ cups dried black beans
10 cups water, or more
2 tablespoons butter
1 cup chopped onion
½ cup chopped celery
10 cups beef stock
1 piece sausage, about ½ pound
1 teaspoon chopped garlic

½ cup sherry or Madeira
1 teaspoon salt
½ teaspoon freshly ground black pepper
2 hard-cooked eggs, chopped
1 or 2 lemons, sliced thin and dipped in minced fresh parsley, for garnish

Soak beans in 10 cups water for at least 12 hours in refrigerator. Drain well. Heat butter in large Dutch oven over medium-high heat. Add onion and celery and sauté until tender. Add beans, stock, sausage, and garlic and simmer, uncovered, stirring occasionally, until tender, about 2½ hours. Add additional water, if needed, to keep beans covered. Transfer to blender in batches and purée roughly.

Turn into large saucepan and stir in sherry or Madeira, salt, and pepper. Place over medium heat and bring to serving temperature. Gently blend in chopped eggs. Ladle into bowls and garnish with lemon slices dipped in parsley.

Tossed Green Salad with Tarragon-Shallot Dressing

½ head each iceberg and Bibb lettuce
2 tomatoes, quartered, for garnish

2 hard-cooked eggs, quartered, for garnish

Toss lettuce with dressing. Garnish with tomatoes and eggs.

Dressing:

¾ cup olive oil
¼ cup tarragon wine vinegar
1 tablespoon minced fresh parsley
2 shallots, finely minced

1 scallion, minced
1 teaspoon salt
½ teaspoon freshly ground pepper
1 teaspoon Dijon mustard

⅓ cup chili sauce

Blend all ingredients in a blender. Taste improves if made 1 or 2 days ahead of serving.

Chicken with Shrimp

3 pounds chicken pieces
Salt and freshly ground black
  pepper, to taste
¼ pound plus 3 tablespoons
  butter
2 tablespoons corn or peanut oil
2 tablespoons finely chopped
  shallots
⅔ cup diced carrots
⅔ cup finely chopped onion
2 or 3 cloves garlic, peeled and
  minced
2 tablespoons cognac

⅔ cup dry white wine
5 tablespoons tomato paste
2 teaspoons loosely packed stem
  saffron
18 raw shrimp
1 bay leaf
½ teaspoon dried thyme
6 tablespoons heavy cream
2 teaspoons finely chopped fresh
  tarragon (or 1 teaspoon dried)
¼ to ½ teaspoon cayenne
  pepper (or more, to taste)

Sprinkle chicken with salt and pepper to taste. Heat 3 tablespoons butter and 2 tablespoons oil in heavy skillet and add chicken pieces, skin side down. Cook until nicely browned. Turn and cook on second side, also until nicely browned. Remove chicken, set aside, and pour off fat from skillet.

Add remaining butter to skillet and then add shallots, carrots, onion, and garlic. Cook over low heat, stirring, about 10 minutes. Add cognac and wine and bring to a boil, stirring to dissolve the brown particles that cling to pan. Add tomato paste, chicken, saffron, salt and pepper to taste, and stir. Cover closely and cook over very low heat for 30 minutes. (This much can be done early in the day. Refrigerate chicken and then bring to room temperature before final cooking.)

Put shrimp in saucepan, cover with water, and add salt and pepper to taste, bay leaf, and thyme. Bring to boil and let simmer 2 minutes. Let stand briefly; drain, peel, and devein shrimp. Set aside.

When chicken is cooked, add cream, tarragon, and cayenne and stir. Add shrimp, bring to boil, and heat thoroughly.

Easy Flavored Rice

2 cups long grain white rice
4 cups chicken broth

1 teaspoon salt
1 tablespoon cooking oil

Combine all in 2-quart saucepan. Bring to rolling boil, stirring a little. Lower heat to simmer, cover, and cook 20 minutes or until rice is fluffy. Try not to take lid off until cooking time is complete.

Mushrooms Bordelaise

1½ pounds mushrooms
3 tablespoons butter
3 tablespoons olive oil
5 scallions, chopped fine
3 cloves garlic, crushed
4 tablespoons finely chopped
 parsley

½ scant teaspoon salt
Freshly ground black pepper
3 tablespoons lemon juice
⅓ cup heavy cream
⅓ cup fine bread crumbs

Remove mushroom stems from caps and sauté caps in hot butter up to 2 minutes on each side, until lightly browned. Place caps in buttered baking dish, hollow side up. Add oil to the skillet. Chop mushroom stems finely and combine with scallions, garlic, and parsley. Season with salt and pepper. Sauté stem mixture in hot oil and butter for 5 minutes. Add lemon juice and cream and simmer 5 minutes. Fill caps with this mixture and top with bread crumbs. Bake 5 minutes in preheated 400° oven. Serve immediately.

White Chocolate Cake with Buttercream Frosting

Cake:

⅓ pound white chocolate
½ cup water
½ pound butter or margarine
2 cups sugar
4 eggs, separated
2½ cups sifted cake flour
1½ teaspoons baking powder

½ teaspoon salt
1 cup buttermilk
1 teaspoon vanilla extract
1 cup chopped pecans or
 almonds
1 3½-ounce can flaked
 coconut

Melt white chocolate in water in top of double boiler. Beat with whisk until blended. Cool.

Cream butter and 1½ cups of the sugar until light and fluffy. Add egg yolks and beat thoroughly. Sift flour with baking powder and salt. Add to creamed mixture in thirds, alternately with buttermilk, vanilla, and chocolate. Beat until smooth after each addition.

Beat egg whites until soft peaks form. Gradually add remaining ½ cup sugar, continuing to beat until stiff but not dry. Fold into batter. Gently fold in pecans or almonds and coconut. Turn into three 9-inch-round greased cake pans lined with greased wax paper. Bake in preheated 350° oven for 35 minutes. Let cakes cool on racks, then remove from pans.

Frosting:

5 tablespoons butter or margarine, softened	3 tablespoons cream
3 cups confectioners' sugar	1 teaspoon vanilla extract
	Pecans, for garnish

Cream butter until light and fluffy. Add 1 cup sugar and beat until well blended. Add cream, vanilla, and remaining sugar. Beat until thick and smooth and of spreading consistency. Frost cake layers with Buttercream Frosting and sprinkle with pecans—leaving room for birthday decorations and candles!

Serve with Mom's choice of ice creams.

Dad's Birthday

Hot and Creamy Crabmeat Spread
Salad with Green Goddess Dressing
Chicken with Orange
Cheesy Zucchini Bake
Mushroom-Rice Casserole
Old-Fashioned Oatmeal Cake with Broiled Frosting

PREVIOUS DAY	EARLY MORNING	FREEZER
Crabmeat Spread	*Chicken with Orange*	*Cake*
Salad dressing	*Zucchini Bake*	
Mushroom-Rice Casserole		

Hot and Creamy Crabmeat Spread

8 ounces cream cheese, softened	2 teaspoons cream-style horseradish
1 tablespoon milk	¼ teaspoon salt
1 6½-ounce can crabmeat	Freshly ground black pepper
2 tablespoons minced onion	

1 cup almonds (optional)

Cream softened cream cheese with milk. Add other ingredients except almonds and mix well. Put into small baking dish. Top with almonds and bake in preheated 375° oven approximately 15 minutes, until bubbly. Serve with crackers.

Salad with Green Goddess Dressing

½ clove garlic
½ teaspoon salt
½ cup mayonnaise
½ cup sour cream
4 tablespoons tarragon vinegar

15 to 20 anchovies, chopped
4 tablespoons minced parsley
½ teaspoon freshly ground
black pepper
1 head Boston lettuce
2 heads Bibb lettuce

Mash garlic with salt. Blend with remaining ingredients, except greens. Toss lightly with greens in salad bowl. Serve immediately.

Chicken with Orange

6 whole chicken breasts, boned,
skinned, and split, or 2
chickens
1½ cups flour, seasoned with
salt and freshly ground black
pepper

½ to 1 cup oil
1 onion, chopped
2 12-ounce cans orange juice
concentrate, defrosted
1 cup white wine
1 5-ounce can mandarin oranges

Coat chicken in seasoned flour and brown in heated oil. Remove chicken to large casserole or pan. Chop and sauté onion until soft. Add orange juice and wine and cook for a few minutes. Pour over chicken. Bake uncovered in preheated 350° oven for 1 hour. Add mandarin oranges and put under broiler for a few minutes.

Note: Can be assembled in the morning and baked 1 hour before serving.

Cheesy Zucchini Bake

4 medium zucchini, sliced
1 cup grated Cheddar cheese
2 eggs, beaten
¾ cup plain yogurt

1¼ cups slightly crushed
garlic- or onion-flavored
croutons
½ teaspoon salt

Freshly ground pepper
Margarine

Cook zucchini in boiling water until tender. Drain and mash coarsely. Blend in cheese, eggs, yogurt, 1 cup of the crushed croutons, and seasonings, mixing lightly but thoroughly. Sprinkle remaining croutons on top and dot with margarine. Bake in preheated 350° oven for 25 to 30 minutes, until bubbly and lightly browned.

Mushroom-Rice Casserole

½ pound butter or margarine	½ cup canned mushrooms,
1 large onion, chopped	whole or sliced, undrained
3 ribs celery, chopped	2 10½-ounce cans chicken
1 small package slivered almonds	bouillon
1½ cups long grain white rice	Salt to taste

In deep 2½-quart casserole dish or large skillet, melt butter, add onion and celery, and sauté about 2 minutes. Stir in almonds and sauté another 2 minutes, stirring. Add rice and mushrooms and cook 1 minute. Add bouillon and salt and stir. Cook covered in preheated 350° oven for 1 hour.

Old-Fashioned Oatmeal Cake

1¼ cups boiling water	¾ teaspoon ground cinnamon
1 cup uncooked oats (quick or old-fashioned)	¼ teaspoon ground nutmeg
1½ cups sifted all-purpose flour	½ cup butter or margarine
	1 cup granulated sugar
1 teaspoon baking soda	1 cup firmly packed brown sugar
½ teaspoon salt	2 eggs, slightly beaten
	1 teaspoon vanilla extract

Pour boiling water over oats in medium bowl, cover, and let stand 20 minutes. Grease and flour a 9-by-9-by-2-inch baking pan.

Sift flour, baking soda, salt, cinnamon, and nutmeg onto wax paper. Beat butter and both sugars in a large bowl with electric mixer until light and fluffy. Stir in eggs and vanilla. Add oats and mix well. Stir flour into butter mixture until well mixed. Pour batter into prepared pan and bake in preheated 350° oven for 50 minutes or until top springs back when lightly pressed with fingertip.

Broiled Frosting:

¼ cup melted butter
½ cup firmly packed brown
   sugar
3 tablespoons light cream

½ cup chopped walnuts
¾ cup flaked sweetened
   coconut

Combine all frosting ingredients in small bowl and spread evenly over warm cake. Place into broiler with top of cake about 4 to 5 inches from heat and broil until topping is bubbly. Watch carefully to prevent burning. Serve warm or cold.

Friday Dinner by the Lake

Vegetable Jardine with Red Wine Vinaigrette
Stuffed Fish
Orange Rye Bread
Pea-Rice-Tomato
Apricot Velvet
Cary's Turtle Brownies

PREVIOUS DAY	EARLY MORNING	FREEZER
Vegetable Jardine	*Pea-Rice-Tomato*	*Turtle Brownies*
Orange Rye Bread		
Apricot Velvet		

Vegetable Jardine

¾ pound carrots, roll cut
1 to 1½ pounds broccoli,
   stems trimmed to 2 inches
   long
1 to 1½ pounds cauliflower,
   cored, stems trimmed to 2
   inches long
2 tablespoons white wine vinegar
2 tablespoons cold water
¼ pound red cabbage,
   shredded

3 medium-size red bell peppers,
   blistered over gas stove flame
   or under broiler and peeled
3 small zucchini, scored and
   sliced into ¼-inch slices
¾ pound celery (4 large ribs),
   cut in wide julienne strips
¼ medium bulb fresh fennel,
   thinly sliced (optional)
¼ pound olives

On day before serving, steam carrots 8 to 10 minutes, remove, and refresh in cold water. Drain well. Steam broccoli 6 to 8 minutes and cauliflower 10 to 11 minutes. Refresh each in cold water. Set vegetables aside in individual dishes. Bring vinegar and water to boil in small pan. Pour hot mixture over cabbage and toss well. Cool, squeeze gently to remove excess vinegar, and set cabbage aside separately. Scrape blistered skin off peppers and cut into 1-inch squares, reserving any juices. Add peppers and their juice to carrots. Add zucchini to same dish, along with celery, fennel, if used, and olives.

Red Wine Vinaigrette:

3 medium cloves garlic, peeled	2 tablespoons fresh parsley,
¼ cup red wine vinegar	chopped
¼ teaspoon salt	1 teaspoon dried oregano
Freshly ground black pepper, to	1 teaspoon dried basil
taste	½ teaspoon dried thyme

½ cup Italian olive oil

Press garlic into small bowl or jar and add vinegar, salt, pepper, and herbs. Mix in oil. Stir well or cover and shake vigorously before using.

Pour half the vinaigrette into bowl with mixed vegetables and toss well. Pour remaining vinaigrette over broccoli and cauliflower. Set all vegetables aside at room temperature to marinate for several hours. Cover and refrigerate overnight.

Bring vegetables to room temperature. Just before serving, add cabbage to vegetable mixture and adjust seasonings. Spoon the mixed vegetables and their marinade into large serving dish. Arrange broccoli and cauliflower around edge of dish in a border. Spoon remaining vinaigrette over mixed vegetables. Serve.

Stuffed Fish

5 tablespoons butter	14 ounces frozen shrimp,
4 slices bread, soaked in water	defrosted and raw
2 cloves garlic, chopped	Salt and freshly ground black
4 large shallots, chopped	pepper, to taste
6 medium sprigs parsley,	2 white fish or red snapper,
chopped	approximately 4 pounds,
1 teaspoon tarragon	boned but retaining head and
2 tablespoons white wine	tail
12 large mushrooms, sliced	Lemon slices, for garnish
12 ounces frozen crabmeat,	Chopped parsley, for garnish
defrosted	

Melt butter in skillet; squeeze water out of bread, and cut into pieces.
Add bread and all other ingredients, except fish and garnishes, to
skillet and slowly sauté for about 15 minutes. Stuff the fish with this
mixture and season. Put a little butter on the fish if using red snapper,
but not if using white fish. Bake in preheated 400° oven for about 30
to 45 minutes. Baking pan can be lined with aluminum foil, oiled.
Garnish fish with lemon slices and chopped parsley.

Orange Rye Bread
(Makes 3 loaves)

2½ to 3 cups all-purpose flour	¼ cup water plus 2
2½ cups rye flour	tablespoons
2 tablespoons grated orange rind	¼ cup light molasses
1 package active dry yeast (1	¼ cup firmly packed brown
tablespoon)	sugar
1 10½-ounce can condensed	1 tablespoon shortening
beef broth	1 teaspoon salt
	1 egg white

In large bowl, combine 1 cup of the all-purpose flour, all of rye flour,
orange rind, and yeast. In saucepan, heat broth, ¼ cup of the water,
molasses, sugar, shortening, and salt to lukewarm. Add to dry ingredients. Beat at low speed on electric mixer for 30 seconds, scraping
sides of bowl often. Beat at high speed for 3 minutes. Stir in enough
remaining all-purpose flour to make a stiff dough. On lightly floured

surface, knead dough until smooth. Place in greased bowl, turning once. Cover and let rise in warm place until doubled (about 30 minutes). Punch dough down, cover, and let rest 10 minutes. Shape dough into 3 round loaves. Place on greased cookie sheet. Cover and let rise until doubled (about an hour and a half). Beat egg white and remaining 2 tablespoons water together until blended. Brush glaze over loaves. Bake in preheated 375° oven for 25 minutes or until done. Serve warm.

Pea-Rice-Tomato

5 tablespoons salad or olive oil	1 cup chopped parsley
3 onions, sliced	2 eggs, beaten lightly
2 10-ounce boxes frozen peas	Salt and freshly ground black
1 cup cooked rice	pepper, to taste
¾ cup grated Swiss or	4 tomatoes, sliced thick
Parmesan cheese	3 tablespoons bread crumbs

Heat 3 tablespoons of the oil in large skillet. Add onions and cook until they are soft and translucent. Add peas and cook 4 minutes longer over low heat, stirring once or twice. Blend rice, cheese, half the parsley, the eggs, and seasonings. Stir in peas and onions. Spread mixture in shallow ovenproof serving dish (about 8-by-11-inch). Place tomatoes on top and sprinkle with remaining 2 tablespoons oil and bread crumbs mixed with remaining parsley. Sprinkle with salt to taste. (Can be prepared in morning up to baking stage.) Bake in preheated 375° oven for 20 minutes.

Apricot Velvet
(Serves 8)

1 6-ounce package dried	Pinch of salt
apricots, about 1¼ cups	3 egg whites, at room
½ teaspoon grated lemon peel	temperature
¾ cup sugar	1 cup heavy cream

Place apricots in small saucepan with enough water to cover. Simmer for 20 to 25 minutes or until tender. Drain, reserving liquid. If necessary, add water to make 1 cup liquid. Press apricots through sieve or purée in blender or processor. Add peel, cover, and chill. In medium saucepan, combine apricot liquid, sugar, and salt. Cook over low-medium heat to 230° on candy thermometer, or to thread stage. In large bowl, beat egg whites until stiff, beating constantly. Very slowly pour hot syrup over egg whites. Continue beating until mixture is cool. In medium bowl, beat cream until stiff and gently fold in puréed apricots. Fold apricot mixture by thirds into egg-white mixture. Turn into 9-by-5-by-3-inch loaf pan lined with wax paper. Freeze until firm. Unmold onto serving dish, remove wax paper, and slice to serve.

Cary's Turtle Brownies

¼ pound butter	Dash of vanilla
3 squares unsweetened chocolate	1 pound (20 to 25) caramels
2 eggs, well beaten	⅓ cup milk
1 cup sugar	1 6-ounce bag chocolate chips
½ cup all-purpose flour	⅓ cup chopped pecans

Melt butter and chocolate in double boiler or microwave oven. Cool. Cream eggs and sugar and add to chocolate mixture; add flour and vanilla. Blend well and pour half the mixture into greased 8-inch-square pan. Bake in preheated 350° oven for 15 minutes.

Melt caramels with ⅓ cup milk. Spread caramel mixture over baked brownie mixture. Add chocolate chips to remaining unbaked brownie mixture and pour over caramel layer. Sprinkle chopped pecans over top and return to oven for 20 minutes longer.

After the Ball Game   (Serves 4)

Cream of Tomato Soup
Corn-Zucchini Salad
Sweet-and-Sour Meat Loaf
Potato Puff
Quick Creamed Spinach
Macaroon Ice Cream Pie

PREVIOUS DAY	EARLY MORNING	FREEZER
Cream of Tomato Soup	Meat Loaf	Macaroon Pie
Salad dressing		

Cream of Tomato Soup

2½ pounds fresh tomatoes (or
  2 28-ounce cans pear
  tomatoes, drained)
2 tablespoons safflower oil
1 small onion, chopped
2 cloves garlic, minced
4 teaspoons tomato paste

3 cups chicken broth
1 teaspoon sugar
Salt and freshly ground black
  pepper, to taste
3 tablespoons chopped fresh
  basil (or 2 teaspoons dried)
3 to 4 teaspoons Crème Fraîche

Peel, seed, and chop tomatoes. Sear oil in a 4-quart pot and add chopped onion. Sauté 5 minutes, but do not brown. Add garlic, sauté 1 minute; add tomatoes, tomato paste, chicken broth, sugar, salt and pepper to taste, and basil. Bring to a boil, cover, and reduce to low heat. Simmer for ½ hour. Cool and purée in the blender or processor.

Reheat, adding Crème Fraîche, and stir thoroughly. Heat and serve. *Note:* Also delicious cold.

Crème Fraîche:

¼ cup sour cream   ¼ cup whipping cream

Mix the two creams together thoroughly. Let mixture sit at room temperature overnight. Refrigerate thickened Crème Fraîche until needed.

Corn-Zucchini Salad
(Serves 10 to 12)

2 cups fresh or frozen corn,
  cooked
2 cups thinly sliced zucchini
1 cup diced red or green peppers

1 cup shredded red cabbage
  (optional)
½ cup finely diced red onion
Large zucchini or bed of lettuce
  (optional)

Combine vegetables in bowl and toss to mix. Pour dressing over vegetables and toss to coat. Serve at once or cover and refrigerate several hours before serving. Serve in the shell of a large zucchini or on a bed of lettuce.

Dressing:

⅓ cup vegetable oil
⅓ cup brown rice vinegar or
    cider vinegar
½ teaspoon salt

¾ teaspoon sugar
¼ teaspoon freshly ground
    black pepper

Combine ingredients in a small screw-top jar. Cover and shake well to blend.

Sweet-and-Sour Meat Loaf

1 15-ounce can herbed tomato
    sauce
½ cup brown sugar
¼ cup vinegar
2 teaspoons dry mustard
2½ pounds ground chuck

1 medium onion, minced
½ cup crushed saltines
1 egg
Salt and freshly ground black
    pepper, to taste

Mix together first 4 ingredients on low heat for sauce. Mix together balance of ingredients. Add ¾ cup of tomato sauce mix to meat. Mix well. Arrange meat in greased meat-loaf pan. Pour rest of sauce over. Bake in preheated 350° oven for 1 hour. Baste often. Serve sauce from pan at table.

Potato Puff

5 tablespoons freshly grated
    Parmesan
2 cups cooked mashed potatoes
1 teaspoon salt

¼ teaspoon black pepper
⅛ teaspoon nutmeg
½ cup half-and-half
4 eggs, separated

In a buttered 6-cup soufflé dish, sprinkle 2 tablespoons of the cheese and coat bottom and sides of the dish. Remove excess. Refrigerate dish.

In a large bowl, combine potatoes, salt, pepper, and nutmeg. Beat in the half-and-half and blend well. Stir in the remaining 3 tablespoons of cheese. Add the egg yolks, one at a time, beating constantly.

Beat the egg whites until stiff but not dry. Stir one-quarter of the beaten egg whites in the potato mixture. Carefully fold in the remaining whites. Scrape the mixture into the prepared soufflé dish and level the top. Put the dish in a baking pan that has been filled with enough hot water to reach ½-inch up the side of the soufflé dish.

Place the pan in the middle of the oven and bake in preheated 325° oven for 1½ hours or until the potatoes are golden brown on top.

Quick Creamed Spinach

2 10-ounce packages frozen chopped spinach, cooked and drained
Minced dried onions, to taste (optional)

1 10¾-ounce can cream of mushroom soup, undiluted
1 2.8-ounce can French-fried onions

Combine cooked spinach, dried onions, and undiluted can of soup and place in casserole. Bake in preheated 325° oven until almost warmed through, then sprinkle canned onions on top and finish cooking until warmed through, about ½ hour in all.

Macaroon Ice Cream Pie

1 10-ounce package almond macaroons
¾ cup coffee liqueur or rum
1 quart coffee ice cream, softened

1 12-ounce jar chocolate or fudge sauce (see Index)
1 pint whipped cream

Put macaroons on the bottom of a pie dish. Dribble liqueur or rum over macaroons. Spread ice cream over macaroons. Pour chocolate or fudge sauce over ice cream and freeze. Serve with whipped cream.

Sunday Dinner

Broccoli Soup
Beet and Onion Salad
Red Snapper Supreme
Noodle Pudding
Okra Caribe
Banana Cake with Chocolate Frosting

Broccoli Soup

12 ounces fresh broccoli   5 cups chicken bouillon
¼ teaspoon freshly ground white pepper

Clean broccoli and cut into small pieces. Bring chicken bouillon to boil and add broccoli and pepper. Bring back to a boil and cook until broccoli is tender. Cool slightly and purée in blender. Reheat before serving. Serve in heated bouillon cups.

Beet and Onion Salad

2 1-pound cans sliced beets   3 tablespoons cider vinegar, or
1 large onion, sliced thin   more, to taste
1 teaspoon sugar, or more, to   ¼ cup olive oil
     taste   3 whole cloves (optional)
Salt and freshly ground black pepper, to taste

Drain beets well. Separate onion slices into rings. Combine all ingredients and adjust seasonings to taste. Refrigerate for several hours or overnight.

Red Snapper Supreme

2 to 3 pounds red snapper, whole or fillets

Red Wine Marinade:

½ cup finely chopped onions   1 teaspoon dried thyme
½ cup red wine   ½ teaspoon freshly ground
¼ cup soy sauce   white pepper
1 cup orange juice

Mix all marinade ingredients. Marinate fish fillets for 2 hours at room temperature. If using a whole fish make 3 or 4 slits on each side down to bone. Turn approximately every half-hour. Grill or broil.

Noodle Pudding

16 ounces cream cheese	1 16-ounce package wide
½ pound butter or margarine	noodles, cooked and drained
3 cups milk	Cornflake crumbs, for topping
½ cup sugar	Cinnamon and sugar, for
2 eggs, beaten well	topping
2 teaspoons vanilla extract	

Melt cream cheese and butter in large saucepan. Add milk and sugar and continue to stir until all is dissolved. Should be a light custard consistency. Remove from stove. Add eggs and vanilla. Mix with cooked noodles and pour into buttered 9-by-12-inch casserole sprinkled with light coating of cornflakes to provide good crust. Bake any leftover mixture in small pan. Refrigerate pudding until ready to bake.

Before baking, sprinkle top with crumbs, cinnamon, and sugar. Bake in preheated 400° oven for 15 minutes. Reduce heat to 375° and bake 30 minutes longer.

Note: Can be prepared a day in advance and refrigerated uncooked. Recipe can be halved by changing size of pan to 9-by-9-inch; bake at 400° for 10 minutes, and 375° for 20 minutes. If sweeter taste is desired, add up to 1 cup of sugar when combining ingredients.

Okra Caribe

3 tablespoons unsalted butter	3 1-pound cans whole, peeled
2 small onions, cut into ⅛-	tomatoes, drained and
inch slices	chopped with liquid reserved
3 dozen small fresh okra, stems	4 drops red pepper sauce
removed and cut into ¼-	Salt and freshly ground black
inch rounds	pepper, to taste

Melt butter in large, heavy skillet over medium-high heat. When foam subsides, add onions and okra. Sauté, stirring often, until onions are soft, about 5 minutes. Stir in drained tomatoes, pepper sauce, and salt and pepper to taste. Simmer, stirring occasionally, for 15 minutes. Add a few tablespoons of reserved tomato liquid if mixture seems dry.

Banana Cake with Chocolate Frosting

Cake:

2 cups flour	½ cup butter
¾ teaspoon baking powder	1¼ cups sugar
½ teaspoon salt	1 teaspoon vanilla extract
1 cup mashed bananas	2 eggs
½ cup sour cream or ¼ cup plain yogurt and ¼ cup sour cream	

Mix flour, baking powder, and salt in a small bowl. Combine mashed bananas and sour cream in another small bowl. Cream butter and sugar and add vanilla. Add eggs and beat for 2 minutes. With mixer on low speed, blend in half the dry ingredients, then the sour cream/banana mixture, and then the remaining flour mixture. Pour into 2 greased and floured 8-inch layer pans. Bake in preheated 350° oven for 25 to 30 minutes or until it tests done. Cool on rack. Frost with Chocolate Frosting.

Chocolate Frosting:

2 ounces unsweetened chocolate, melted	1 cup confectioners' sugar
½ pound unsalted butter	5 eggs, separated
	1 teaspoon vanilla extract
¾ cup chopped pecans	

Melt chocolate on very low heat. Cream the butter and sugar. Add the melted chocolate and blend. Beat in the egg yolks, one at a time, then add the vanilla. Beat egg whites until stiff peaks form. Fold whites into chocolate mixture. Spread the filling between the cake layers and frost the top and sides with the remaining frosting. Sprinkle with nuts. Chill for 24 hours before cutting. Cake must be served cold.

Autumn Dinner

Crudités with Herb Dip
Mock Caesar Salad
Lemon Grilled Veal Chops
Spinach Pasta with Stilton Cheese Sauce
Spicy Raisin Cake

PREVIOUS DAY	EARLY MORNING	FREEZER
Herb Dip	*Spicy Raisin Cake*	
	Salad dressing	

Herb Dip
(Makes about 1½ cups)

1 cup mayonnaise
½ tablespoon lemon juice
½ teaspoon salt
¼ teaspoon paprika
¼ cup chopped parsley
1 tablespoon grated onion
1 tablespoon chopped chives

⅛ teaspoon curry powder
½ teaspoon Worcestershire
  sauce
Garlic salt, to taste
1 tablespoon capers
½ cup sour cream

Blend all ingredients, folding in sour cream last. Serve with Crudités
(see Index).

Mock Caesar Salad

1 large head romaine
1 2¼-ounce can sliced, pitted
  ripe olives, drained
¼ cup salad oil
1 raw egg yolk
1½ teaspoons Worcestershire
  sauce
2 tablespoons lemon juice

¼ teaspoon freshly ground
  black pepper
2 tablespoons grated Parmesan
  cheese
1 clove garlic, minced or mashed
1 2-ounce can flat anchovy
  fillets, drained

In morning, wash the romaine, dry well, and refrigerate for several
hours until crisp and chilled. Just before serving, break the romaine

leaves into small pieces and put into salad bowl. Add the olives. In a glass jar with a tight-fitting lid, or in a blender, place salad oil, egg yolk, Worcestershire, lemon juice, pepper, Parmesan, and garlic. Shake ingredients well in jar or whirl in the blender. Chop drained anchovies well and stir into dressing. Just before serving, pour dressing over greens and mix lightly.

🐚 🐚 🐚

Lemon Grilled Veal Chops

3 tablespoons butter or
  margarine, melted
1 clove garlic, sliced in thirds
1½ teaspoons dried rosemary,
  or ½ teaspoon dried basil
6 large veal chops, rib or loin

¼ teaspoon salt, or less
Freshly ground black pepper, to
  taste
Juice of 2 lemons
Lemon wedges

Melt butter and add garlic pieces. Cook on low heat to flavor butter with garlic. Remove garlic from butter and discard. Add rosemary or basil. Season chops with salt and pepper, brush with butter, and broil 5 minutes. Squeeze fresh lemon on browned veal, turn, brush with butter, and continue grilling until done. Serve with lemon wedges.

Spinach Pasta with Stilton Cheese Sauce

¼ pound imported Stilton
  cheese, crumbled
½ cup milk
3 tablespoons butter
⅓ cup whipping cream

1 pound spinach pasta, cooked
  al dente
⅓ cup freshly grated
  Parmesan

Combine Stilton, milk, and butter in large nonaluminum skillet. Over low heat, stir until smooth. Add cream and blend well. Add pasta and Parmesan and toss until noodles are coated.

Note: Can be prepared about 1 hour before serving and gently reheated.

Spicy Raisin Cake

3 cups unsifted flour
2 cups sugar
1 cup mayonnaise
⅓ cup milk
2 eggs
2 teaspoons baking soda
1½ teaspoons ground
   cinnamon
½ teaspoon ground nutmeg

½ teaspoon salt
¼ teaspoon ground cloves
3 cups chopped and peeled
   apples
1 cup seedless raisins
½ cup coarsely chopped
   walnuts
1 cup cream for whipping
   (optional)

Confectioners' sugar (optional)

Grease and flour two 9-inch round baking pans. In large bowl, beat first 10 ingredients for 2 minutes at low speed, scraping bowl frequently, or vigorously 300 strokes by hand. (Batter will be very thick.) With spoon, stir in apples, raisins, and nuts. Spoon batter into pans. Bake for 45 minutes in preheated 350° oven or until tester inserted in center comes out clean. Cool in pans for 10 minutes. Remove and cool. Fill and frost with whipped cream, if desired, or serve sprinkled with confectioners' sugar.

Fall Dinner

Chutney Cheese Spread
Roast Half Breast of Turkey
Acorn Squash with Cranberry Relish
Green Beans à la Suisse
Chocolate Cream Pie

PREVIOUS DAY	EARLY MORNING	FREEZER
Chutney Cheese Spread	Acorn Squash	Chocolate Cream Pie
	Green bean casserole	

Chutney Cheese Spread

1 pound Cheddar cheese, grated
2 3-ounce packages chive cream
   cheese

2 teaspoons curry powder
1 cup chopped scallions
4 tablespoons mayonnaise

9 ounces chutney, chopped

Beat cheeses, curry, ¾ cup scallions, and mayonnaise very thoroughly. Line a 5-cup bowl with plastic wrap. Fill the bowl with the cheese mixture and press it down firmly. Refrigerate overnight or up to a week. Before serving, unmold onto a serving plate. Spread the chopped chutney over the molded cheese and sprinkle with remaining scallions for color. Serve close to room temperature with crackers.

Roast Half Breast of Turkey

1 half breast of turkey	½ to 1 teaspoon tarragon
5 tablespoons melted butter	½ teaspoon white pepper
½ teaspoon salt	½ cup dry white wine
½ teaspoon paprika	1 cup sliced fresh mushrooms
1 6-ounce package dry stuffing mix	

Place turkey breast in shallow baking pan. Combine 2 tablespoons melted butter, salt, paprika, tarragon, and pepper and spoon over turkey. Bake 10 minutes in preheated 450° oven. Combine wine and mushrooms and pour over turkey. Lower oven temperature to 325° and bake 1½ hours or until done, basting with liquid in pan.

Prepare stuffing mix as package directs, using drained drippings for part of liquid and adding remaining 3 tablespoons of butter. Recipe can also be used with turkey legs and thighs.

Acorn Squash with Cranberry Relish

3 acorn squash, halved lengthwise and seeded	3 tablespoons orange marmalade
3 tablespoons butter or margarine	1 10-ounce package frozen cranberry-orange relish, thawed
3 tablespoons brown sugar	Salt (optional)

Place squash, cut side down, in a buttered pan. Bake for 40 minutes in preheated 325° oven. Melt butter over low heat and stir in sugar, marmalade, and cranberry relish. Turn squash cut side up and salt, if desired. Fill each cavity with cranberry mixture. Bake 30 minutes or until tender and serve.

Note: Squash can be baked day before. Cranberry mixture can be made early in day, or day before. Combine right before heating to serve.

Green Beans à la Suisse

4 tablespoons butter, melted
2 tablespoons flour
1 teaspoon salt
Freshly ground black pepper, to
  taste
1 teaspoon sugar
½ teaspoon grated onion

1 cup sour cream (or more, to
  taste)
2 10-ounce packages frozen
  French-cut string beans,
  cooked
¼ pound Swiss cheese
2 cups cornflakes

Into 2 tablespoons of the melted butter stir flour, salt, pepper, sugar, and onion. Add sour cream gradually, stirring until thick. Fold in cooked beans and heat.

Put into greased 1½-quart casserole. Grate cheese and sprinkle over top. Crunch cornflakes and mix with second 2 tablespoons of melted butter. Put over cheese and bake casserole in preheated 400° oven at least 20 minutes. A little additional sour cream can be added, to taste.

Chocolate Cream Pie

Crust:

1½ cups chocolate wafer
  crumbs

¼ cup butter, melted

Mix crumbs and melted butter. Pat into a 9-inch pie pan and bake in preheated 350° oven for 10 minutes. Cool before adding filling.

Filling:

1 6-ounce package semisweet
  chocolate bits
¼ cup light corn syrup
½ cup sugar
¼ cup water
1 egg white, unbeaten

1½ teaspoons vanilla extract
1 teaspoon lemon juice
1 to 2 teaspoons instant coffee
⅓ cup toasted chopped
  almonds
1 cup whipping cream

Melt first 3 ingredients together over low heat. Cool. Combine next 6 ingredients in small bowl and beat with electric beater at highest speed until soft peaks form (3 to 5 minutes).

Fold chocolate mixture into egg-white mixture. Add almonds. Beat cream until thick. Fold in whipping cream. Spoon gently into prepared pie crust. Freeze until firm (4 to 6 hours). Cover.

Topping:

1 cup whipped cream   Semisweet chocolate shavings

To serve, defrost for 20 minutes and top with whipped cream and shaved chocolate.

October Bounty

Tapenade
Spinach and Cucumber Salad with Mustard–Red Wine Dressing
Osso Bucco with Gremolada
Saffron Rice
Tuscan Bread
Cannoli Cream
Strawberry Loaf

PREVIOUS DAY	EARLY MORNING	FREEZER
Tapenade	*Mustard–Red Wine*	*Osso Bucco to addition*
Strawberry Loaf	*Dressing*	*of Gremolada*
Osso Bucco	*Cannoli Cream*	*Tuscan Bread*
	Gremolada	

Tapenade
(Makes about 1½ cups)

1 16-ounce can pitted black olives, drained
1 7-ounce can tuna, drained
2 ounces flat anchovy fillets, drained
¼ cup capers, drained
⅓ cup lemon juice

2 tablespoons Dijon or similar mustard
1 small clove garlic, minced
¼ cup olive oil
1 tablespoon brandy
Salt and freshly ground black pepper, to taste

Crudités or French bread

Combine ingredients through garlic in blender or food processor bowl, using steel blade, and blend until smooth. With machine running, add oil in a slow, steady stream until mixture is thick and creamy. Blend in brandy and season to taste with salt and pepper. Chill, tightly covered, for several hours or several days. Serve with Crudités (see Index) or spread on crusty French bread.

Spinach and Cucumber Salad

16 ounces spinach, washed and cleaned
1 small cucumber, scored and sliced thin

1 small red onion, sliced thin
4 radishes, shredded
½ cup crumbled Gorgonzola

Wash greens and place in large salad bowl. Add cucumber and onion and toss. Sprinkle with shredded radish and Gorgonzola. Serve with Mustard–Red Wine Dressing.

Mustard–Red Wine Dressing:

3 tablespoons vegetable oil
¼ cup white vinegar
¼ cup water
½ cup dry red wine

2 teaspoons Dijon or similar mustard
Dash of Tabasco sauce
¼ teaspoon salt
Pinch of freshly ground pepper

Combine dressing ingredients in jar and shake well.

Osso Bucco

2 veal shanks, about 5 pounds, cut crosswise into 8 2-inch pieces
¼ cup flour, seasoned with salt and pepper
4 to 6 tablespoons oil
1 cup white wine
2 cups chicken stock
6 tablespoons butter

2 cups chopped onion
¼ cup minced shallots
2 large cloves garlic, minced
1 cup chopped carrots
3 cups chopped zucchini
2 cups canned Italian tomatoes, drained
Bouquet of dried herbs: parsley, bay leaf, and thyme

Dry shanks well and tie string around each so meat doesn't fall apart. Coat meat heavily with flour and sauté in oil until brown on all sides. Transfer veal to plate. Pour fat from skillet. Pour in wine and ½ cup of the stock to deglaze skillet, scraping up crusty bits. Reduce glaze until syrupy and transfer to bowl. Add butter to skillet and cook onion, shallots, and garlic over medium heat until translucent. Add carrots and zucchini and cook for 5 minutes. Add veal in 1 layer (you need a large skillet) and add the sauce, tomatoes, herbs, and remaining 1½ cups broth to bring liquid three-quarters of the way up the shanks. Heat to boiling. Bake, covered, in preheated 325° oven for 1½ hours, or until very tender. Uncover for last 20 minutes. Ten minutes before serving, remove strings, and mix the Gremolada. Then sprinkle over meat. Serve with Saffron Rice.

Gremolada:

Rind of 1 lemon, grated   2 tablespoons minced parsley
½ teaspoon finely minced garlic

Mix ingredients together and sprinkle over meat.

Saffron Rice

4½ cups water   6 tablespoons butter
2 cups long grain white rice   1 teaspoon salt
8 strands saffron

Place all ingredients in a buttered casserole. Bake covered in preheated 350° oven for 45 minutes.

Tuscan Bread

1½ packages active dry yeast   3 cups all-purpose flour
  (1½ tablespoons)   3 cups bread flour
2 cups warm water, 105° to 115°   3 tablespoons yellow cornmeal
1 tablespoon sugar   1 tablespoon egg white, for glaze
1 tablespoon salt   1 teaspoon cold water, for glaze

Proof the yeast in the warm water with added sugar until foamy. Mix salt and flours and add gradually to the yeast mixture until dough is stiff. Knead dough on a floured board, adding flour if necessary. Butter a bowl, add dough, and turn to coat. Cover dough and put in a warm place until doubled in bulk, 1½ to 3 hours. Punch dough down and shape into 2 loaves. Sprinkle baking sheet with cornmeal. Make knife slashes on top of each loaf and brush with combined glaze ingredients. Place in cold oven and bake at 400° for 30 to 35 minutes. Freezes well.

Cannoli Cream
(Makes 4 cups)

2 15-ounce containers ricotta
1 cup orange marmalade, or more, to taste

4 tablespoons orange liqueur
1 teaspoon vanilla extract
3 squares semisweet chocolate

Blend ricotta in food processor with on-off motion until smooth, or whisk by hand. Do not use a blender. Add the next 3 ingredients and process very briefly, just until blended. Add the chocolate squares. Process briefly with on-off motion until most of the chocolate is chopped rather fine. Chill about 1 hour before serving in sherbet cups.

Strawberry Loaf

1½ cups flour
½ teaspoon salt
1 cup sugar
½ teaspoon baking soda
2 teaspoons cinnamon, or more
2 eggs, well beaten

1 cup plus 1 tablespoon cooking oil
1 10-ounce package frozen strawberries in juice, thawed and crushed

Sift together all dry ingredients. Make a well in center and pour in mixed liquids. Stir until moistened through. Pour into a large greased and floured loaf pan. Bake in preheated 350° oven for 1 hour.

Supper for the Family

Avocado-Cheese Dip
Prosciutto with Melon or Figs
Herbed Tomatoes and Red Onion Salad
Easy Roast Chicken and Potatoes
Almond-Cranberry Relish
Cheesecake Squares

PREVIOUS DAY   EARLY MORNING   FREEZER

Avocado-Cheese Dip
Cranberry Relish
Cheesecake Squares

Avocado-Cheese Dip

1 large ripe avocado
3 ounces cream cheese, at room temperature
2 tablespoons sour cream or plain yogurt
1 tablespoon freshly squeezed lemon juice

1 finely chopped scallion
1 ounce Gorgonzola or other blue cheese
½ teaspoon Worcestershire sauce
Tabasco sauce, to taste

In processor, blend avocado. Add remaining 7 ingredients and mix until smooth. Cover and refrigerate until served. Serve with Crudités (see Index).

Note: If you put the avocado pit into the dip and remove it right before serving, dip will not discolor as much.

🌸 🌸 🌸

Prosciutto with Melon or Figs

1 medium cantaloupe or 6 fresh figs

12 thin slices prosciutto
Freshly ground black pepper
Lime wedges

Peel cantaloupe and cut into 12 long, thin slices. Arrange 2 slices of melon on each plate. Wrap 1 slice of prosciutto over each piece of melon, top with ground pepper, and add a lime wedge. Serve at room temperature.

To serve with figs, cut 6 figs in quarters. Cut slices of prosciutto in half across the middle. Wrap prosciutto around each fig piece. Fasten each roll with a toothpick, grind black pepper over them, place on platter, and serve with lime wedges.

Herbed Tomatoes and Red Onion Salad

3 medium tomatoes, sliced
1 medium red onion, sliced
1½ tablespoons chopped fresh
  parsley
1½ tablespoons chopped
  chives

1½ tablespoons chopped
  chervil
1 tablespoon chopped tarragon
Balsamic Vinaigrette

Arrange tomatoes and onion on individual salad plates. At least 30 minutes before serving, sprinkle with the herbs. Sprinkle with Balsamic Vinaigrette (see Index).

Easy Roast Chicken and Potatoes
(Serves 6 to 8)

2 2½-pound chickens,
  quartered
4 medium potatoes, peeled and
  quartered
1 medium clove garlic, crushed
⅓ cup salad or olive oil

1 teaspoon oregano
1 teaspoon salt
½ teaspoon pepper
½ teaspoon paprika
1½ medium green or red
  peppers, cut in 1-inch strips

Parsley, for garnish

Spray large, shallow baking pan with nonstick spray. Wipe chicken with damp paper towels and arrange (skin side up) with potatoes in single layer. Combine garlic, oil, and oregano. Mix well and drizzle over chicken and potatoes. Sprinkle all over with salt, pepper, and paprika. Bake uncovered in preheated 350° oven, basting every 15 minutes. After 30 minutes, sprinkle peppers over chicken. If chicken is not brown after 1 hour, increase temperature to 400° for an additional 15 minutes. Arrange attractively on warmed platter. Garnish with parsley.

Almond-Cranberry Relish

1 pound raw cranberries
2 cups sugar
1 cup cold water

½ cup apricot jam
Juice of 2 lemons
⅓ cup blanched almonds

Wash and pick over berries. Bring sugar and cold water to a boil without stirring. Cook for 5 minutes, then add cranberries. Cook 3 to 5 minutes or until berries burst and sauce becomes transparent.

Remove from heat and add jam. Stir well and add lemon juice. Chill. Add the almonds just before serving.

Cheesecake Squares
(Makes 16)

⅓ cup firmly packed brown sugar
½ cup chopped walnuts
1 cup flour
⅓ cup melted butter
1 8-ounce package cream cheese

¼ cup granulated sugar
1 egg
1 tablespoon lemon juice
2 tablespoons cream or milk
1 teaspoon vanilla extract

Mix brown sugar, nuts, and flour in large bowl. Stir in melted butter and mix with hands until crumbly. Remove 1 cup of mixture to be used as a topping. Place remainder in an 8-inch-square pan and press down firmly. Bake in preheated 350° oven for 12 to 15 minutes.

Beat cream cheese with granulated sugar until smooth. Beat in egg, lemon juice, cream, and vanilla. Pour into baked crust. Top with reserved crumbs. Return to 350° oven and bake 25 minutes. Cool thoroughly and then cut into 2-inch squares. Cover with plastic wrap and keep refrigerated.

Harvest Moon Dinner

Creamy Stuffed Mushrooms
Roast Pork with Currant Jelly
Zucchini Scramble
Crisp Potato Bake
Cranberry-Apple Mold
Chocolate Cake Supreme

PREVIOUS DAY

Pork Roast
Crisp Potatoes
Cranberry Mold

EARLY MORNING

Stuffed Mushrooms
Chocolate Cake
Supreme

FREEZER

Creamy Stuffed Mushrooms

1 pound fresh mushrooms
2 tablespoons butter, melted
8 ounces cream cheese, softened

2 ounces blue cheese, crumbled
2 tablespoons finely chopped
   scallion
Paprika

Remove mushroom stems and reserve caps. Finely chop enough stems to make ½ cup. Sauté caps in butter for 3 minutes. Combine cheeses by using 2 forks. Blend well. Stir in chopped mushroom stems and scallion. Fill mushroom caps with cheese mixture. Place in broiler-proof baking dish. (Can be refrigerated at this time until ready to serve.) Bring to room temperature and broil, approximately 4 inches from flame, for about 5 minutes, or until golden brown. Sprinkle with paprika and serve hot.

Roast Pork with Currant Jelly

1 5-pound pork roast
½ cup soy sauce
½ cup sherry

2 cloves garlic, minced
1 tablespoon dry mustard
1 teaspoon thyme
1 teaspoon ginger

In large plastic bag, marinate the roast overnight in the next 6 ingredients. Remove from bag and place on rack in roasting pan. Bake in preheated 325° oven for 30 to 35 minutes per pound.

Sauce:

10 ounces currant jelly, melted
2 tablespoons sherry
1 tablespoon soy sauce

Prepare sauce by combining all ingredients and serve on the side as gravy. If desired, fat may be skimmed from pan drippings, and drippings mixed with the sauce.

Zucchini Scramble

6 tablespoons butter
1 large onion, diced
3 medium zucchini, sliced
Garlic salt, to taste

Salt and freshly ground black
   pepper, to taste
2 medium tomatoes, diced
Grated Parmesan

Melt butter and sauté onions until transparent in large frying pan. Add zucchini and seasonings to taste. Cook about 10 minutes, until tender. Add tomatoes and sprinkle with Parmesan. Heat thoroughly and serve immediately.

Crisp Potato Bake

¼ pound butter or margarine
1 10½-ounce can condensed
  cream of chicken soup
1 pint sour cream
Salt and freshly ground pepper,
  to taste
10 ounces Cheddar cheese,
  grated

2 pounds frozen hash-brown
  potatoes, thawed and moisture
  pressed out
½ cup chopped onions
Crushed cornflakes mixed with
  melted butter or margarine,
  for topping

Grease 9-by-13-inch pan or large casserole. Melt butter. Mix all ingredients together except for topping. Put into prepared pan. Place cornflake mixture on top. Bake in preheated 350° oven for 45 minutes.
Note: Casserole can be assembled up to 2 days in advance and baked before serving.

Cranberry-Apple Mold

1 3-ounce package red gelatin
1 cup boiling water
¾ cup canned pineapple juice

1 8-ounce can whole berry
  cranberry sauce
1 cup diced apples

⅓ cup chopped nuts

Dissolve gelatin in boiling water. Add juice and cranberry sauce. Chill until slightly thickened and stir in remaining ingredients.
Note: If doubling recipe use only 1 cup of pineapple juice.

Chocolate Cake Supreme

¼ pound unsalted butter
1 cup hot water
4 squares unsweetened chocolate,
  melted
2 cups sifted flour

2 cups sugar
¼ teaspoon salt
1½ teaspoons baking soda
1 cup sour cream
1 teaspoon vanilla extract

2 eggs

Grease 13-by-9-inch baking pan. Melt butter in hot water, then bring to boil. Add melted chocolate. Sift flour, sugar, and salt. Pour liquid into flour mixed with sugar and salt. Blend well. Add baking soda to sour cream. Add sour cream and vanilla to batter. Add eggs, mix well, and pour into prepared pan. Bake in preheated 350° oven for 30 minutes.

Frosting:

4 squares unsweetened chocolate	Pinch of salt
7 tablespoons milk	1 teaspoon rum, liqueur, or
3 cups confectioners' sugar	vanilla extract
3 tablespoons butter	

Melt chocolate in double boiler. Mix milk with confectioners' sugar. Add salt and liquor or extract and mix. Add chocolate and melted butter. If frosting is too thick, add water, a tablespoon at a time. Frost warm cake and cool in pan.

🌿 🌿 🌿

Snowfall Supper

Vegetable Soup
Green Beans Grimaldi with Niçoise Dressing
Chicken and Spinach Lasagna
Parsley Garlic Bread
Lemon Cake

PREVIOUS DAY	EARLY MORNING	FREEZER
Soup	Green Beans	Lasagna
Niçoise dressing		
Garlic Bread		

Vegetable Soup

6 cups strong chicken stock
1 teaspoon salt, or to taste
2 medium tomatoes, cored and
  chopped into medium-size
  pieces
¼ cup chopped fresh parsley
⅓ cup barley
1 bay leaf
¼ teaspoon dried sage

1 teaspoon dried oregano
1 tablespoon olive oil
1 medium onion, chopped
1 carrot, sliced thin
1 celery rib, chopped thin
2 medium zucchini, shredded or
  sliced thin
½ teaspoon freshly ground
  pepper, or to taste

½ to 1 cup grated Parmesan

Bring stock to boil with salt in large saucepan or stock pot. Add next six ingredients. Reduce heat, cover saucepan, and simmer until barley is tender, about 30 minutes.

Meanwhile, heat olive oil in large skillet over medium heat. Add onion and cook 1 to 2 minutes. Stir in carrot and celery and continue cooking for 3 minutes. Add zucchini and cook another 2 to 3 minutes. Stir vegetables into barley mixture and season with pepper to taste. Cover and simmer about 10 minutes. Serve with Parmesan sprinkled on top.

Green Beans Grimaldi

2 10-ounce packages frozen
  Italian green beans

½ cup olives

Cook beans until tender but still crisp. Cool and toss with olives and Niçoise Dressing as desired.

Niçoise Dressing:

⅔ cup olive oil
1 tablespoon lemon juice
2 tablespoons wine vinegar
2 tablespoons Dijon mustard
1 clove garlic, diced

1 tablespoon chopped basil,
  parsley, or dill
1 teaspoon sugar
Salt and freshly ground black
  pepper, to taste

Combine all ingredients and mix in blender for 2 minutes. The longer this is blended, the thicker it gets. Cover and refrigerate. Will keep for several days.

Chicken and Spinach Lasagna
(Serves 8)

4 or 5 chicken breasts, split in half
6 tablespoons butter
8 tablespoons flour
1 cup buttermilk
1 cup half-and-half
Salt and freshly ground black pepper, to taste
½ cup chicken broth or bouillon

3 10-ounce packages frozen spinach, thawed and squeezed dry
4 ounces cream cheese, softened
4 to 6 ounces ricotta
6 to 8 ounces Jarlsberg cheese, grated
Dry white wine
Nutmeg, to taste
1 pound lasagna noodles, cooked al dente

½ cup grated Parmesan

Place chicken breast halves in small stock pot with enough water to cover. Bring to simmer and cook, covered, for 5 to 10 minutes. Melt butter in heavy-bottomed saucepan. Stir in flour and form stiff paste. Then add buttermilk, half-and-half, and salt and pepper to taste. Stir briskly over low heat until mix is smooth. Add chicken broth if mixture becomes too thick. Set aside.

Cool chicken until it is easy to handle. Remove skin and bones. Cut into small pieces. In large bowl, combine chicken, spinach, cheeses (except Parmesan), and small amount of wine to moisten. Stir well. Season to taste with salt, pepper, and nutmeg. Add small amount of cream sauce to moisten. Pour small amount of sauce into an 11-by-9-inch baking dish. Add a layer of cooked lasagna noodles. Sprinkle liberally with wine (but not enough to make noodles soggy). Add layer of filling, then another layer of sauce. Place another layer of noodles over sauce. Sprinkle with wine and top with more filling. End with layer of sauce. Sprinkle with about ½ cup Parmesan cheese. Bake in preheated 350° oven for about 1 hour.

Note: For a lower-calorie variation, substitute 2% milk for half-and-half. Omit wine.

Parsley Garlic Bread

1 clove garlic
4 tablespoons butter, or more, to taste

1 loaf French bread
Minced fresh parsley

Brown clove of garlic in butter until soft, but do not let butter turn brown. Discard garlic clove and cool butter. Spread on split French bread and sprinkle with minced parsley. Wrap in foil and refrigerate 1 day in advance. Broil until bread is brown.

Lemon Cake

1 large sponge cake, sliced into 3 layers

To slice cake evenly, insert toothpicks at desired levels and use them as a cutting guide.

Lemon Filling:

3 tablespoons cornstarch	1 tablespoon butter
1 cup plus 2 tablespoons sugar	3 egg yolks, beaten
4 tablespoons lemon juice	1½ cups boiling water

Combine cornstarch with sugar in top of a double boiler. Add lemon juice, butter, and eggs. Mix well. Add boiling water and cook over hot water, stirring continuously until thick. Cool and spread between layers of sponge cake.

Frosting:

1 cup sugar	1 teaspoon vanilla extract
1 egg white	2 cups shredded sweetened
½ teaspoon cream of tartar	coconut
½ cup boiling water	

Combine all ingredients, except coconut, in large bowl at high speed with electric mixer for 20 minutes. Spread frosting over cake and sprinkle coconut over top and sides.

Note: The lemon filling also makes a delicious pie filling.

Dinner for the Neighbors

Hot and Snappy Cheese Melt
Colorful Carrot Salad
Flank Steak with Spicy Onion Sauce
Hash-Brown Platter
Tomatoes Stuffed with Mushrooms
Peach Ice Cream
Sugar Cookies

PREVIOUS DAY	EARLY MORNING	FREEZER
Carrot Salad		*Ice Cream*
Sugar Cookies		

Hot and Snappy Cheese Melt

2 pounds processed cheese
1 10-ounce can Mexican
   tomatoes with green chilies

1 1½-pound bag taco chips

Melt first two ingredients in top half of double boiler. Stir frequently.
Serve with taco chips.

Note: To microwave, microwave uncovered for 5 minutes and stir.
Microwave 5 minutes more or until cheese is melted and mixture
blended.

Colorful Carrot Salad

2 pounds carrots, finely shredded
¼ cup lemon juice
1 cup chopped parsley leaves
½ small onion, diced
1 small dill pickle, diced
2 tablespoons capers, chopped
2 tablespoons Dijon mustard

½ teaspoon tarragon
1¼ cups mayonnaise
1 10-ounce package tiny frozen
   peas
2 hard-cooked eggs, chopped
Salt and freshly ground pepper,
   to taste

Mix everything but peas, eggs, and salt and pepper. Refrigerate overnight. Add peas, chopped eggs, salt, and pepper just before serving.

Flank Steak with Spicy Onion Sauce

2 1½-pound flank steaks
2 cups salad oil
2 cups dry red wine
½ cup soy sauce
½ teaspoon liquid hot pepper
  sauce
2 tablespoons Worcestershire
  sauce

4 or 5 cloves garlic, minced
1 tablespoon crushed rosemary
4 or 5 bay leaves, crushed
2 teaspoons thyme
2 teaspoons freshly ground black
  pepper
1 large onion, sliced

Score the steaks with a sharp knife and put them in a large glass container. Mix remaining ingredients and marinate steaks 2 to 3 hours. Turn 3 or 4 times. Broil the steaks in a preheated broiler for 12 minutes, turning once. Allow steaks to rest 5 minutes before slicing. Pour Spicy Onion Sauce over the sliced steak.

Spicy Onion Sauce:

1 small onion, chopped
2 small cloves garlic, chopped
½ cup whiskey
¼ cup Worcestershire sauce
1½ teaspoons dry mustard

2 drops liquid hot pepper sauce
¼ cup white wine vinegar
Salt, to taste
1 tablespoon freshly ground
  pepper

1 cup unsalted butter

In a medium saucepan, mix ingredients except butter. Bring to a boil over high heat and reduce to ¾ cup liquid. Takes about 8 to 10 minutes.

Over a low flame, whisk in ½ cup unsalted butter. Continue whisking and add another ½ cup of butter, 2 tablespoons at a time, until melted.

Hash-Brown Platter

3 tablespoons vegetable oil
4 or 5 tablespoons butter
5 or 6 medium baking potatoes,
  peeled and grated

Salt and freshly ground black
  pepper, to taste

Heat the oil and 3 tablespoons of the butter in large nonstick frying pan. Heat until hot but before browning occurs. Add potatoes, sprinkle with salt and pepper, and add 1 or 2 more tablespoons of butter. Press down with back of a spoon so that the potatoes stick together. Cook for 3 minutes and reduce heat to medium. Cover pan and cook 5 to 8 minutes. Potatoes should be soft on top. Either flip potatoes or slide onto another pan and turn back into original pan. Raise heat to medium-high and cook until browned on bottom. Put on platter and serve immediately.

Tomatoes Stuffed with Mushrooms

3 large, firm, ripe tomatoes	1 teaspoon chopped parsley
4 tablespoons butter	1 tablespoon dry sherry
½ pound mushrooms, sliced	Salt and freshly ground pepper,
¼ cup sour cream	to taste
1 tablespoon flour	Blanched almonds or sesame
1 ounce Roquefort cheese	seeds, for garnish
¼ teaspoon thyme	Paprika

Cut tomatoes in half and carefully scoop out seeds and pulp. Set upside down to drain. In skillet, melt butter and sauté sliced mushrooms until all moisture is evaporated. Combine sour cream and flour and blend into mushrooms. Cook on low heat until thick and bubbly. Add cheese, thyme, parsley, and sherry and blend until smooth. Remove from heat, add salt and pepper, and cool.

Stuff tomatoes loosely and sprinkle top with ground blanched almonds or sesame seeds and dusting of paprika. Bake in preheated 375° oven for 15 minutes or until bubbly. Serve.

Peach Ice Cream

2¼ cups mashed peaches	Juice of ½ lemon
1½ cups sugar	Pinch of salt
	3 cups whipping cream

Mix peaches, sugar, and lemon juice in bowl and refrigerate overnight. Divide peach mixture in half and purée one half. Combine mashed and puréed peaches with salt and cream in electric ice cream machine. When ice cream is ready, place in container in freezer.

Sugar Cookies

½ pound butter	1 teaspoon vanilla extract
1 cup sugar, plus more for rolling	2½ cups sifted flour
	½ teaspoon baking soda
2 egg yolks	½ teaspoon salt

Cream butter and sugar. Add egg yolks and vanilla. Combine flour, soda, and salt and add to mixture. Form into large balls and roll in additional sugar. Put on ungreased cookie sheet. Press lightly with glass bottom to flatten. Bake in preheated 350° oven for 10 minutes.

Note: These cookies are best when made rather large. They should turn out puffy and chewy, but not flat.

Winter Sunshine

Mushroom Soup
Baltic Vegetable Salad with Dill Mayonnaise
Fruit-Glazed Chicken
Tropical Rice
Marble Brownies
Vanilla Ice Cream with Caramel-Nut Sauce

PREVIOUS DAY	EARLY MORNING	FREEZER
Mushroom Soup	*Baltic Salad*	*Marble Brownies*
Salad dressing	*Caramel-Nut Sauce*	
Marinate chicken		
Tropical Rice		

Mushroom Soup

¼ pound butter	3 cups boiling water
1 pound fresh mushrooms, sliced	1½ cups sour cream or sour half-and-half
3 tablespoons fresh lemon juice	
3 tablespoons seasoned beef base, in paste form	¾ cup chopped fresh parsley

Melt butter over low heat in a 4-quart pot. Add sliced mushrooms and lemon juice and sauté 8 to 10 minutes, stirring frequently, until tender. In separate bowl, combine beef base and water, mixing well. Add this to mushrooms, blending well. Remove from heat and cool for 20 minutes. Slowly blend in sour cream, mixing thoroughly with a whisk. Reheat slowly, mixing in parsley. Serve.

Do not boil or sour cream will separate. Soup may be prepared 2 days in advance and refrigerated. If prepared in advance, do not add parsley until heating to serve.

Baltic Vegetable Salad

1½ cups green beans, steamed for 3 minutes (or 1 10-ounce package, frozen)
1 cup lima beans, steamed for 6 minutes (or 1 10-ounce package, frozen)
1 cup peas, steamed for 6 minutes (or 1 10-ounce package, frozen)

2 cups carrots, diced and steamed for 3 minutes
Large red cabbage leaves
1 large tomato, cut in wedges, or cherry tomatoes, for garnish

Combine steamed vegetables in bowl and mix gently. Pour Dill Mayonnaise over vegetables and toss. Cover and refrigerate 1 hour or longer before serving. To serve, shape several large red cabbage leaves together to form a cup and spoon in salad. Garnish with tomato wedges.

Dill Mayonnaise:

½ cup mayonnaise
½ cup sour cream
¾ cup fresh snipped dill

1 tablespoon Dijon mustard
½ cup diced onion

Combine dressing ingredients in small bowl and blend well. Store, tightly covered, in refrigerator.

Fruit-Glazed Chicken

1 12-ounce can frozen orange
   juice concentrate
¼ cup lemon juice
½ cup ketchup
2 tablespoons soy sauce
1 teaspoon allspice
½ teaspoon garlic powder
¼ teaspoon ginger
Salt and freshly ground pepper,
   to taste

6 whole chicken breasts, boned
   and skinned
1 11-ounce can mandarin
   oranges, drained
3 bananas, peeled and quartered
6 to 12 dried apricots, simmered
   in equal parts of water and
   Marsala wine to cover until
   soft (optional)

Combine juices, ketchup, soy sauce, and seasonings, blending well. Roll chicken breasts into small "packages"; if large, they can be cut in half. Arrange chicken in 9-by-13-inch greased baking dish. Pour sauce over, cover, and marinate for several hours (or overnight if convenient) in refrigerator.

Remove chicken from refrigerator and bring to room temperature. Bake, uncovered, in preheated 350° oven for 30 to 40 minutes. Baste frequently. After approximately 30 minutes, add oranges and bananas and place 1 or 2 apricot halves, drained, on each piece if desired. Baste with sauce in pan. Bake additional 35 minutes, basting frequently. Before serving, place under broiler for 2 to 3 minutes to brown thoroughly and glaze well.

Tropical Rice

3 cups water
1½ cups long grain converted
   rice
1 teaspoon curry powder
1 teaspoon salt

½ cup canned coconut milk
½ cup toasted coconut
¼ cup chopped scallions
2 tablespoons each dark and
   white raisins

2 tablespoons butter

In medium saucepan, boil water. Combine rice, curry, and salt in water. Then stir, cover, and reduce heat. Simmer 20 to 25 minutes until all water is absorbed and rice is tender. Add remaining ingredients by mixing with a fork. Heat and serve.

Note: Can be prepared in advance and refrigerated. Bring to room temperature before reheating.

Marble Brownies

1 8-ounce package cream cheese,
   room temperature
2⅓ cups sugar
3 eggs
¼ pound butter or margarine
1½ squares unsweetened
   chocolate

¾ cup water
1¾ cups flour
½ cup sour cream
1 teaspoon baking soda
½ teaspoon salt
1 6-ounce package semisweet
   chocolate chips

Preheat oven to 375°. Butter well and lightly flour a 15½-by-10½-inch jelly-roll pan.

Combine softened cream cheese and ⅓ cup of the sugar. Add 1 egg, mix well, and set aside. Combine butter, chocolate squares, and water in a small saucepan. Bring to boil and remove from heat. Stir flour, remaining 2 cups sugar, and chocolate mixture in a large bowl. Add 2 eggs, sour cream, soda, and salt. Mix well. Pour into prepared pan. Spoon cream cheese mixture over top and cut through batter with a knife for a marbled effect. Scatter chocolate chips over top. Bake in preheated 375° oven for 25 to 30 minutes or until wooden pick comes out clean.

Caramel-Nut Sauce

½ cup firmly packed brown
   sugar
1 tablespoon cornstarch
¼ teaspoon salt
¼ cup water
⅓ cup light cream

2 tablespoons light corn syrup
¼ cup coarsely chopped
   pecans
1 tablespoon butter
1 tablespoon rum

In a heavy saucepan, combine brown sugar, cornstarch, and salt. Stir in water. Stir in cream and corn syrup. Cook, stirring constantly, until thickened and bubbly. Mixture may curdle while cooking but will smooth out. Stir in nuts, butter, and rum. Cool, cover, and refrigerate. Warm before serving over vanilla ice cream.

Hearty Dinner

Red Peppers Napoli
Spinach Salad with Pine Nut Dressing
Oxtails Forestière
Mashed Potatoes
Whole Wheat Biscuits
Black and White Layered Brownies
Poached Peaches with Plum Sauce

PREVIOUS DAY	EARLY MORNING	FREEZER
Black and White Brownies	*Red Peppers*	*Biscuits*
Oxtails	*Peaches*	*Brownies*
Plum Sauce		

Red Peppers Napoli

3 red peppers   **Balsamic Vinaigrette**

Broil peppers 6 inches from heat, until charred all over. Keep turning to char evenly. Place in brown bag for 15 to 20 minutes. Peel and slice into ¼-inch strips. Marinate with Balsamic Vinaigrette. (See Index).

Spinach Salad with Pine Nut Dressing

1 10-ounce package fresh spinach   **1 head butter lettuce**

Arrange greens on individual salad plates. Top each with about 2 tablespoons of Pine Nut Dressing.

Pine Nut Dressing:

¾ cup toasted pine nuts, coarsely chopped
½ teaspoon dried tarragon
¼ teaspoon grated lemon peel

⅛ teaspoon nutmeg
½ cup salad oil or olive oil
⅓ cup vinegar
½ teaspoon salt

Blend nuts with tarragon, lemon peel, nutmeg, oil, vinegar, and salt. Mix well before using.

Note: To toast pine nuts, spread them in a single layer on a pan, bake in 350° oven for 5 minutes. Shake pan occasionally.

Oxtails Forestière

Salt and freshly ground black pepper, to taste	1 13-ounce can or 1 package dried oxtail soup
Flour	1 cup water, or to cover
3 pounds lean oxtails	1 10-ounce package frozen peas
¼ pound butter	1 10-ounce package frozen sliced carrots
1 12-ounce can tomatoes	

Add salt and pepper to flour and coat oxtails in this mixture. In heavy skillet melt butter and brown oxtails.

In 4-quart casserole place oxtails and next 3 ingredients. Bake in preheated 325° oven, covered, for 3½ hours. Remove oxtails from pan. Add water to gravy in pan if too thick, or thicken as needed. Cook peas and carrots for 7 minutes in gravy. Put oxtails back into gravy and heat thoroughly before serving.

Note: Beef shanks can be substituted. Change oxtail soup to onion soup and cook 3 hours and 15 minutes.

Mashed Potatoes

2 pounds potatoes	2 ounces cream cheese
3 tablespoons butter	¼ cup warmed milk
Salt, to taste	

Peel potatoes and boil, covered, until soft. Drain and mash. Add remaining ingredients and mix thoroughly.

Whole Wheat Biscuits

1 envelope active dry yeast (1 tablespoon)	¼ cup sour cream
1¼ cups warm water (105° to 115°)	2 teaspoons salt
	3 cups unsifted whole wheat flour
All-purpose flour	

Soften yeast in warm water in large bowl of electric mixer and stir to dissolve. Add sour cream, salt, and 2 cups of the whole wheat flour. Beat at high speed until smooth, 2 to 3 minutes. Gradually add remaining whole wheat flour. Continue beating, using a wooden spoon if dough is too stiff for mixer. Beat until dough is stiff and smooth and clears the side of the bowl.

Place dough in large oiled bowl and turn to oil top. Cover loosely with wax paper or foil. Set in warm place, free from drafts, until doubled in bulk, about 1 hour.

Turn dough out onto a lightly floured board and knead 2 minutes, or until smooth and shiny. Divide in half. Shape each half of dough into a smooth ball. Place a ball at each end of large greased cookie sheet and pat into a 7-inch round. With a sharp knife, cut the rounds into eighths. Cover loosely and let rise in warm place again until double in bulk, about 1 hour.

Bake biscuits in preheated 350° oven for 25 minutes or until deep golden-brown and hollow-sounding when tapped. Remove to cooling rack. Dust tops with all-purpose flour and serve warm.

Black and White Layered Brownies

First Layer:

¼ pound butter	1 teaspoon vanilla extract
½ cup sugar	1 egg
5 teaspoons unsweetened powdered cocoa	2 cups graham cracker crumbs
	1 cup sweetened coconut

Mix butter, sugar, cocoa, vanilla, and egg and stir over heat until just melted. Add graham cracker crumbs and coconut. Pat first layer into 7-by-11-inch pan.

Second Layer:

2 teaspoons milk	¼ pound butter
2 teaspoons dry vanilla pudding mix (*not* instant)	2 cups confectioners' sugar

Process ingredients until creamy and spread over first layer.

Third Layer:

4 ounces unsweetened chocolate   1 teaspoon butter

Melt the unsweetened chocolate with the butter and pour over second layer. Tilt pan to spread melted chocolate. Refrigerate for an hour before serving.

Note: Can be made a day ahead.

Poached Peaches with Plum Sauce

2 cups sugar	Whole cloves (optional)
½ cup white wine	12 fresh peaches
4 lemons, sliced	"Fruit Fresh" or lemon juice

Put sugar, wine, lemon slices, and cloves in large saucepan with 2 quarts water. Bring to a boil and let simmer while you peel the peaches. Combine "Fruit Fresh" or lemon juice with water in a large bowl. Add the peaches as you peel them and let them sit about 5 minutes to avoid discoloration. Drain peaches and put into simmering sugar syrup. Simmer gently 30 to 40 minutes, depending on size and ripeness. Cool peaches in poaching liquid and refrigerate until ready to serve.

Plum Sauce:

1 10- to 12-ounce jar damson plum jam	¼ cup water
2 tablespoons sugar	¼ cup cognac, kirsch, or eau-de-vie

Combine jam, sugar, and ¼ cup water in saucepan. Bring to a boil and simmer 5 to 6 minutes. Refrigerate until cool. Stir in the liqueur and serve with peaches.

Midwinter's Eve

Quick Antipasto
Stuffed Flank Steak
Eggplant Marinara
Potato Muffins
Chocolate Cheesecake

PREVIOUS DAY	EARLY MORNING	FREEZER
Antipasto		*Potato Muffins*
Chocolate Cheesecake		*Marinara Sauce*

Quick Antipasto

1 8-ounce jar giardiniera (Italian pickled vegetables), well drained	8 ounces large green olives, well drained
1 12-ounce jar artichoke hearts in oil	1 8-ounce can tomato sauce
½ pound fresh mushrooms	1 7½-ounce can water-packed tuna, drained
	4 tablespoons white wine vinegar

Combine all ingredients in large glass or ceramic bowl. Mix well, cover, and refrigerate for 24 hours. Mix occasionally.

Note: Giardiniera can be found in the pickle and relish department of the supermarket.

Stuffed Flank Steak

1 3-pound flank steak	¾ cup water
1 large onion, finely chopped	¼ cup diced celery
1½ cups soft bread crumbs	½ teaspoon ginger
2 tablespoons chopped parsley	2 tablespoons fat, for frying
1 teaspoon salt	2 tablespoons brown sugar
¼ teaspoon pepper	¼ cup vinegar or red wine

Score flank steak. Mix next 8 ingredients and spread over steak. Roll up steak and fasten with small skewers. Brown meat roll in hot fat. Add brown sugar, vinegar or wine, and water to thin. Cover and place in preheated 325° oven and bake for about 2 hours. Add more vinegar if more liquid is needed. Liquid may be thickened for gravy.

Eggplant Marinara

1 large eggplant	⅔ cup salad oil
Salt	Marinara Sauce
¼ cup flour	½ cup grated Parmesan cheese

Wash and peel eggplant. Cut into ¼-inch slices. Sprinkle heavily with salt and let drain for 45 minutes. Rinse off salt. Roll slices in flour. Sauté eggplant in hot oil in large skillet. Brown on each side. Layer half the slices in bottom of 2-quart casserole. Spoon half of Marinara Sauce over them and sprinkle with half of cheese. Repeat layers. Cover and bake in preheated 375° oven for 25 to 30 minutes, or until eggplant is tender and cheese bubbly.

Marinara Sauce:

½ cup olive oil	⅛ teaspoon cayenne pepper
3 cups chopped onions	1 tablespoon basil
1½ cups peeled and chopped carrots	1 tablespoon thyme
	1 teaspoon sugar
2 1-pound, 13-ounce cans Italian plum tomatoes, in purée, chopped	2 tablespoons tomato paste
	3 large garlic cloves, minced
	1 bay leaf
1 teaspoon salt	1 cup chopped parsley

1 to 2 tablespoons red wine

Heat the oil in a large pot, mix in onions and carrots and sauté slowly until soft, about 25 to 30 minutes. Add tomatoes, salt, pepper, basil, thyme, sugar, tomato paste, garlic, and bay leaf. Cook over low heat for 30 to 40 minutes. Remove bay leaf. Remove sauce from heat and cool. Purée in blender or food processor. Add chopped parsley and wine, heat briefly before serving. Freezes well.

Potato Muffins
(Makes 2 dozen)

1 tablespoon active dry yeast	2 cups bread flour
1 cup potato cooking water	1 cup all-purpose flour
2 teaspoons sugar	1½ teaspoons salt
1 small potato, boiled	1 egg, beaten, for glaze
2 tablespoons butter	Sesame seeds (optional)

Proof yeast with 1 cup potato water and 2 teaspoons sugar until it foams. Mash the potato and combine with the yeast mixture. In bowl of electric mixer add to the potato the butter, both flours, and the salt. Knead until dough is smooth and elastic. Place dough in an oiled bowl, cover, and store in warm place until doubled in bulk. Punch down on floured board and divide into two. Roll each piece out and divide into 12 pieces. Roll each piece into a small roll and place in greased muffin tin, cover, and let rise 1 hour. Brush egg over rolls, sprinkle sesame seeds on top, if desired, and bake in preheated 400° oven for 10 minutes. Turn oven down to 350° and bake for 10 to 12 minutes more, until lightly browned. Cool on a rack.

Chocolate Cheesecake

1 8½-ounce package chocolate
   wafers
⅓ cup melted butter
¼ teaspoon nutmeg
1¼ cups sugar
3 eggs
3 8-ounce packages cream
   cheese, softened

1 teaspoon vanilla extract
2 6-ounce packages semisweet
   chocolate chips, melted
1 cup sour cream
Whipped cream, for garnish
Shaved chocolate, for garnish

Make fine crumbs of wafers. Mix crumbs, butter, nutmeg, and ¼ cup of the sugar. Press over bottom and sides of 9-inch springform pan to within 1 inch of top. Refrigerate.

In large bowl, beat eggs and remaining cup sugar at high speed until very light. Beat in softened cream cheese until smooth. Add vanilla, melted chocolate chips, and sour cream. Beat until smooth and pour into unbaked crust.

Bake in preheated 350° oven for 1 hour. Cool and refrigerate. Garnish with whipped cream and shaved semisweet chocolate before serving. Remove from refrigerator about 1½ hours before serving.

Microwave Buffets

◆

Each recipe serves four unless otherwise noted.

For the cook who really likes last-minute gourmet meals, we offer a few samples. Because microwave ovens vary, we suggest you check your manual for specific operating procedures.

Summer Satisfaction Dinner

Spinach Puff Pie
Salmon Ring
Cucumber Dill Sauce
Cheddar Scalloped Potatoes
Two-Bean Tango
Fruit Crisp

PREVIOUS DAY	EARLY MORNING	FREEZER
	Prepare vegetables *Fruit Crisp*	

Spinach Puff Pie

1 9-inch deep-dish frozen pie
  shell
2 eggs, separated
2 10-ounce packages chopped
  spinach, defrosted and drained
2 tablespoons butter
Salt and freshly ground black
  pepper, to taste

1½ cups sour cream
2 tablespoons chives or scallions
2 tablespoons flour
2 tablespoons grated Parmesan
2 tablespoons seasoned bread
  crumbs

Prick pie shell and brush with beaten egg white. Place in a 9-inch glass or microwave-safe deep-dish pie plate. Cook in microwave on medium for 6 minutes, rotating midway.

Cook spinach 4 minutes with butter, salt, and pepper. Beat egg yolks, mix into sour cream; add chives and flour. Beat remaining egg whites until stiff and add to sour-cream mixture. Season to taste. Layer spinach and cream mixture in pie shell. Sprinkle cheese and bread crumbs on top. Bake 9 minutes on high, rotating once.

Salmon Ring

1 16-ounce can salmon, skin and
  bones removed
2 eggs, beaten
1 cup soft bread crumbs
¼ cup evaporated milk
¼ cup finely diced celery
2 tablespoons finely chopped
  onion

2 teaspoons lemon juice
1 2-ounce jar diced pimento
Salt and freshly ground black
  pepper, to taste
2 tablespoons chopped scallion
  or chives

Mix all ingredients except scallions and place in a 6-cup glass or microwave plastic ring dish. Sprinkle scallions on top. Cook in microwave on high for 4 minutes. Rotate dish and cook 5 minutes more. Serve with Cucumber Dill Sauce.

Cucumber Dill Sauce:
(Makes 1¼ cups)

½ cup sour cream
½ teaspoon dill
½ cup finely chopped
  cucumber (peeled)

2 whole scallions, chopped
2 tablespoons milk or light
  cream

Combine all ingredients in glass bowl. Cook in microwave 1 minute on high or serve at room temperature.

Cheddar Scalloped Potatoes

3 medium potatoes, peeled and very thinly sliced	1 teaspoon butter or margarine, cut in pieces
1 cup Cheddar White Sauce	

Layer half of potato slices in 1-quart glass casserole. Spread ½ cup of sauce over potatoes. Repeat with remaining potatoes and sauce. Dot with butter. Cook in microwave on medium or on 6 for 25 to 28 minutes. Let stand 5 minutes before serving.

Cheddar White Sauce:

2 tablespoons butter or margarine	1 cup milk
2 tablespoons flour	½ cup grated sharp Cheddar cheese
½ teaspoon salt	Pinch of cayenne

Melt butter in small glass cup on high about 1 minute or until melted. Blend in flour and salt to make smooth, loose paste. Set aside. In 4-cup glass bowl, heat milk on high for 30 seconds. Beat in butter-flour paste with a wire whisk. Heat in microwave on meduim or on 8 for 1 to 2 minutes or until thickened. Stir well, add grated cheese and cayenne, and stir until melted.

Two-Bean Tango

4 slices bacon	½ cup white wine vinegar
⅓ cup sugar	1 onion, sliced thin
1 tablespoon cornstarch	1 16-ounce can cut green beans, drained
1 teaspoon salt	1 16-ounce can kidney beans, drained
¼ teaspoon freshly ground black pepper	
1 hard-cooked egg, sliced	

Arrange bacon on microwave rack in glass dish. Cover with paper towel. Cook in microwave on high for 4 minutes. Set bacon aside. (It will crisp during standing.) Remove rack. Add sugar, cornstarch, salt, pepper, vinegar, and onion to bacon drippings. Cook on high 4 to 5 minutes, or until thick, stirring several times. Add beans, mixing well. Cover. Cook on high or 4 to 6 minutes, stirring once. Crumble bacon and sprinkle over top of beans. Garnish with sliced egg.

Fruit Crisp

4 medium crisp apples, peeled and sliced	¼ cup brown sugar, packed
⅔ cup flour	1 teaspoon cinnamon
½ cup rolled oats	Pinch of nutmeg
	5 tablespoons butter

Place apples in 8-inch glass pie plate. Mix rest of ingredients in food processor until crumbly. Sprinkle on top of apples. Cook in microwave 6 to 7 minutes until apples are soft. Rotate plate once during baking time.

Note: You can put this under the broiler to brown lightly.

Mexican Dinner Pronto

Nachos
Chili Mole
Mediterranean Fruit Salad
White Chocolate Pretzels
Lemon Squares
Chocolate Caliente

PREVIOUS DAY	EARLY MORNING	FREEZER
Pretzels	*Fruit Salad*	
	Lemon Squares	

Nachos

1 12-ounce package tacos chips	1 2-ounce can green chilies
3 scallions, chopped	1 7-ounce jar taco sauce
1 cup grated sharp Cheddar cheese	

Spread chips on large paper plate. Scatter scallions, cheese, and small amount of chilies on chips. Sprinkle taco sauce lightly over all. Place in microwave on high for 2½ minutes. Serve hot and bubbling.

Chili Mole

1½ pounds chopped beef
1 clove garlic
1 medium onion, chopped
½ green pepper, chopped
½ ounce unsweetened
    chocolate
3 15-ounce cans tomato sauce
1 16-ounce can Italian plum
    tomatoes, drained

1 16-ounce can red kidney
    beans, drained
1½ teaspoons dried oregano
1 teaspoon salt
2 teaspoons chili powder
½ teaspoon freshly ground
    black pepper
½ teaspoon dry mustard
Pinch of cayenne

½ pound Cheddar cheese, shredded

Crumble beef and combine with garlic, onion, green pepper, and chocolate in 3-quart glass bowl. Cover with plastic wrap and microwave on high for 6 minutes, stirring after 3 minutes. Drain off liquid and add tomato sauce, tomatoes, beans, oregano, salt, chili powder, ground pepper, mustard, and cayenne. Cover and return to microwave for 20 minutes, stirring every 5 minutes. Just before serving, sprinkle cheese on top and reheat in microwave for 1 minute.

Mediterranean Fruit Salad

1½ cups freshly squeezed
    orange juice
2 to 3 teaspoons fresh lemon
    juice
Grated peel of 1 lemon
2 apples, peeled, cored, and
    diced

2 pears, peeled, cored, and diced
2 bananas, peeled and sliced
1½ cups grapes, sliced in half
6 to 8 tablespoons sugar
½ cup kirsch (optional)

Mix juices and lemon peel in a large bowl. Add the fruits and mix well to prevent discoloring. Add the sugar and liqueur if desired. Mix thoroughly and cover. Refrigerate 3 to 5 hours or overnight. Mix well before serving.

White Chocolate Pretzels

1 16-ounce package white chocolate	2 teaspoons vegetable oil (or less)
	1 package salted pretzels

Melt chocolate in a glass bowl 3 to 4 minutes on high in microwave. Thin mixture with 1 to 2 teaspoons of vegetable oil. Dip pretzels into mixture and place on sheet of wax paper. These will harden in 10 to 15 minutes.

Lemon Squares

1 cup flour, plus 1 tablespoon	½ teaspoon baking powder
½ cup butter	1 cup granulated sugar
¼ cup confectioners' sugar	Grated rind and juice of 2
2 eggs	lemons

Blend 1 cup flour, butter, and confectioners' sugar together and press lightly over bottom of 8-inch-square glass baking dish. Cook in microwave 3 minutes on high.

Beat eggs until light. Stir in remaining tablespoon flour, baking powder, granulated sugar, lemon rind, and juice. Pour over baked layer. Cook 6 minutes on high or until top is set and custardlike.

Chocolate Caliente

2 squares semisweet chocolate	Pinch of nutmeg
2 tablespoons sugar	Pinch of salt
¼ teaspoon ground cinnamon	4 cups milk
¼ cup water	½ cup heavy cream, whipped

Combine chocolate, sugar, cinnamon, water, nutmeg, and salt in glass bowl. Cover and cook in microwave 3 minutes on high. Stir once. Add milk and cook uncovered for 6 minutes more. Beat with a whisk until frothy. Pour into mugs, adding a dollop of whipped cream to each.

Microwave Fish Dinner

Stuffed Artichoke Bottoms
Poached Fish with Wine Sauce or Tomato Sauce
Ratatouille
Pineapple Upside-Down Cake

Stuffed Artichoke Bottoms

2 4½-ounce cans artichoke bottoms

2 tablespoons butter, melted

½ pound fresh mushrooms, chopped

3 tablespoons chopped shallots

1 tablespoon flour

3 tablespoons Madeira

¼ cup whipping cream

Salt and freshly ground black pepper, to taste

¼ teaspoon tarragon

Grated Parmesan

Drain artichoke bottoms and place on a microwave-safe cookie sheet. Melt butter and sauté mushrooms and shallots 4 to 6 minutes in microwave on high, stirring once, until mushrooms have absorbed all moisture. Add flour, Madeira, whipping cream, and seasonings. Whisk to blend well. Cook in microwave 2 minutes, stirring once, until mixture thickens. Fill bottoms with mushroom mixture, top with grated Parmesan, and heat for 30 seconds.

Poached Fish with Wine Sauce or Tomato Sauce

4 fish fillets, 1 to 2 inches thick

Add fish to prepared Wine Sauce or Tomato Sauce as noted and spoon liquid over top. Cover and cook in microwave on high until fish just turns opaque, about 5 minutes.

Note: Do not overcook or fish will be tough.

Wine Sauce:

4 cups water
1 cup dry white wine
6 lemon slices
3 celery ribs, with leaves, cut up
2 carrots, sliced
1 medium onion, sliced and
  separated into rings

6 peppercorns
1 sprig parsley
1½ teaspoons salt
¼ teaspoon crumbled dried
  thyme

Combine all ingredients in 2-quart glass baking dish. Cover and cook in microwave on high for 15 minutes. Strain poaching liquid and return to dish, then add fish fillets, with thickest portion facing outside of dish, and proceed.

Tomato Sauce:

1 small onion
¼ cup parsley
2 cloves garlic

⅛ teaspoon oregano leaves
1 15-ounce can stewed tomato
  slices, drained
¼ cup hot water

Chop onion in food processor and, with motor running, add parsley and garlic. Chop fine. Place in glass baking dish and cook in microwave for 30 seconds on high. Place fish fillets in dish with thickest portion facing outside of dish. Sprinkle on seasonings and tomato slices and water. Cover with plastic wrap and microwave on high for about 5 minutes. Let rest 3 minutes, covered, before serving.

Ratatouille

1 small eggplant, peeled and
  diced
1 clove garlic, minced
1 medium onion, sliced
2 tablespoons olive oil
1 16-ounce can stewed tomatoes

1 green pepper, sliced
1 medium zucchini, sliced
Salt and freshly ground black
  pepper, to taste
½ teaspoon oregano

Place eggplant, garlic, onion, and oil in 2-quart covered glass casserole. Cook in microwave on high for 3½ minutes. Add green pepper and zucchini. Mix salt and pepper, oregano, and tomatoes. Pour over vegetables and cook 8 to 10 minutes longer, covered. Let rest 5 minutes before serving.

Pineapple Upside-Down Cake

2 tablespoons butter or
  margarine
½ cup firmly packed brown
  sugar

5 slices pineapple, with syrup
5 maraschino cherries
1 8½-ounce package yellow
  cake mix

In 8¼-inch round or 8-inch-square glass dish, melt butter on high for 30 seconds. Stir in brown sugar. Drain pineapple and reserve syrup. Arrange pineapple over brown sugar with cherries inside centers. Prepare cake mix according to package directions, substituting pineapple syrup for water. Spoon ½ of batter over pineapple. (Use the other half of batter for another cake or cupcakes.) Cook in microwave on medium for 8 to 9 minutes, turning dish several times. Cook on high for 3 to 4 more minutes. Let stand 1 minute. Turn cake onto serving dish. Serve warm or cold.

Fit & Trim Buffets

———◆———

Each recipe serves four unless otherwise noted.

Fashions in food change often, and that is never more evident than when we reread our old cookbooks. These days everybody is aware of how easily we gain too much weight. But even being on a diet can be a gourmet experience today.

Here are some favorite diet-aware recipes, though you will notice that throughout the book there is an accent on chicken, fish, and salads. We are eating more lightly than our parents and grandparents did, and, we hope, more healthfully.

Fit & Trim I

Vegetables with Low-Cal Spinach Dip
Mixed Greens with Diet Italian Dressing
Dijon Chicken Tarragon
Spaghetti Squash with Low-Cal Tomato Sauce
Frosty Fruit

PREVIOUS DAY	EARLY MORNING	FREEZER
Diet Italian Dressing	*Spinach Dip*	*Frosty Fruit*
Dijon Chicken	*Spaghetti Sauce*	

Low-Cal Spinach Dip

1 10-ounce package frozen
  chopped spinach, defrosted
  and drained
1 1-ounce package buttermilk
  salad dressing mix

2 cups yogurt
1 cup low-cal mayonnaise

Blend all ingredients together and chill. Serve with carrots, zucchini, and celery, cut into strips.

Mixed Greens with Diet Italian Dressing

Bibb lettuce
Endive

Romaine lettuce
Iceberg lettuce

Combine all ingredients. Serve with Diet Italian Dressing.

Dressing:

½ cup oil substitute (see
  below)
¼ cup red or white wine
  vinegar
1 teaspoon salt
¼ teaspoon minced fresh
  green pepper

1 clove garlic, minced
1 teaspoon chopped parsley
1 teaspoon Worcestershire sauce
1 teaspoon each dried oregano,
  sweet basil, and tarragon

Combine all ingredients in blender or jar and shake vigorously or process until well blended. Refrigerate. Makes 1 cup.

Oil Substitute:

1 tablespoon arrowroot   1 cup cold water

Stir the arrowroot into the cold water. Heat in saucepan over low heat, stirring constantly, until mixture thickens and becomes transparent, about 8 to 10 minutes. When cool add to dressings and sauces and shake vigorously. This has no flavor. Can be stored in tightly sealed jar in refrigerator for several days. Makes ¾ cup.

Dijon Chicken Tarragon

4 chicken breasts, split
Seasoned salt
¼ cup Dijon mustard
3 tablespoons chopped scallions
¼ teaspoon crushed tarragon
⅛ teaspoon Tabasco sauce
  (optional)
Italian bread crumbs
1 tablespoon melted butter

Season chicken with seasoned salt and refrigerate overnight. Mix mustard, scallions, tarragon, and Tabasco and spread over chicken. With crumbs, coat the chicken pieces. Place in a flat roasting pan. Drizzle with melted butter before baking. Bake in preheated 350° oven, uncovered, for 1 hour or until done.

Spaghetti Squash with Low-Cal Tomato Sauce

1 spaghetti squash

Wash squash and slice off end tips. Make a few puncture holes in squash. Bake in preheated 350° oven for about 1 hour. Let cool slightly. Slice lengthwise. Remove seeds. Scrape out insides into a lightly buttered casserole to make spaghetti. Cover with Low-Cal Tomato Sauce.

Low-Cal Tomato Sauce:

1 48-ounce can tomato juice
4 tablespoons vinegar
2 tablespoons chopped green
  pepper
4 teaspoons Worcestershire sauce
4 teaspoons sugar substitute
1 tablespoon salt
2 teaspoons dry mustard
2 cloves garlic, minced
2 teaspoons oregano
1 tablespoon dehydrated onion
  flakes
2 teaspoons basil

Combine all ingredients and simmer, uncovered, until thick, about 1 hour.

Frosty Fruit

1 fresh pineapple
½ medium honeydew melon
2 tablespoons honey
2 tablespoons lemon juice
½ pint large strawberries

Cut pineapple into wedges and then into ½-inch slices. Halve melon, cut into wedges, then halve each wedge. Mix honey and lemon juice in bowl and dip each piece of fruit. Thread pineapple, strawberries, and melon on 4 skewers and freeze until firm (about 3 hours). Let stand about 10 minutes at room temperature before serving.

Fit & Trim II

Snow Peas and Dip
Lettuce Wedges with Low-Cal Dressing
Scallops and Tomatoes
Onion and Parsley Rice
Apple Pie-Cake

PREVIOUS DAY	EARLY MORNING	FREEZER
Low-Cal Dressing	Dip for snow peas Apple Pie-Cake	

Snow Peas and Dip

1½ pounds snow peas
1 6½-ounce can water-packed
  tuna, drained
2 tablespoons lemon juice

1 2-ounce can anchovies, drained
½ teaspoon paprika
1 8-ounce carton plain yogurt
½ cup mayonnaise

1 tablespoon capers, for garnish

Trim snow peas and drop into boiling water for 1 to 2 minutes. Drain and rinse under cold water.

In processor, mix tuna, lemon juice, anchovies, and paprika until smooth. Put mixture into bowl and add yogurt and mayonnaise. Place in serving bowl, garnish with capers, and arrange snow peas spoke fashion around dip.

Lettuce Wedges with Low-Cal Dressing

½ onion
½ cucumber
¼ green pepper
¼ fresh lemon—pulp and
  rind
½ cup water
1 cup cider, wine, or rice vinegar
¼ teaspoon garlic powder

¼ teaspoon freshly ground
  black pepper
½ teaspoon celery seed
½ teaspoon dill weed
1½ tablespoons chopped
  parsley
½ teaspoon sugar substitute
1 6-ounce can V-8 Juice

1 small head iceberg lettuce

Blend first 5 ingredients in blender. Add rest of ingredients except lettuce and blend well. Refrigerate. Cut lettuce into wedges and serve with sauceboat of dressing.

Note: Can be prepared up to 2 days in advance.

Scallops and Tomatoes

3 tablespoons margarine
1 pound fresh sea scallops or
  frozen scallops, thawed
1 clove garlic, minced
2 tomatoes, peeled and chopped
3 tablespoons chopped fresh
  basil (or 1 tablespoon dried)

½ teaspoon salt
⅛ teaspoon freshly ground
  pepper
3 scallions, cut into matchstick-
  thin pieces

In large skillet, over medium-high heat, melt 2 tablespoons of the margarine. Pat scallops dry on paper towels. Cook scallops in hot margarine until opaque and lightly browned. Scallops will cook more evenly if pan is not crowded. Cook in several small batches, if necessary.

With slotted spoon, remove scallops to platter and keep warm.

Add remaining tablespoon margarine to skillet. When melted, add garlic and cook for 1 minute. Add tomatoes, basil, salt, and pepper. Cook until tomatoes render their juice but still retain their shape, about 3 to 5 minutes. Return scallops to skillet and add scallions. Cook to heat through.

Onion and Parsley Rice

1 cup long grain white rice	½ cup minced fresh parsley
2 cups water	¼ cup finely slivered scallions
½ teaspoon salt	2 teaspoons sesame oil

Grated peel of 1 large lime

Add rice to rapidly boiling water with salt. Lower heat, cover, and simmer about 20 minutes or until water is absorbed. Remove from heat and keep covered for 10 more minutes. Toss in remaining ingredients and serve.

Apple Pie-Cake

½ cup plus 2 tablespoons sugar	4 cups apples, pared and sliced
3 packages powdered sugar substitute	1 tablespoon diet margarine
	1 egg, slightly beaten
¼ teaspoon cinnamon	1 teaspoon vanilla extract
	½ cup flour

½ teaspoon baking powder

Combine 2 tablespoons of the sugar, sweetener, and cinnamon. Mix with sliced apples and place in 9-inch pie plate. Cover with foil and bake 20 minutes in preheated oven at 400°. Mix margarine and remaining ½ cup sugar well, then blend in egg and vanilla. Sift flour and baking powder into creamed margarine mixture. Remove foil from apples, spread batter over apples, and bake 20 minutes longer, or until golden brown.

Fit & Trim III

Spa Vegetable Soup
Mixed Greens with Diet Vinaigrette
Breast of Chicken with Zucchini and Mushrooms
Chive-dotted Potatoes
Fresh Berries with Yogurt Mousseline

Spa Vegetable Soup

1 pound low-calorie vegetables:
  cauliflower, spinach,
  mushrooms, broccoli,
  asparagus
2 cups unsalted chicken stock or
  unsalted instant chicken broth

¼ cup chopped onion
½ teaspoon white pepper
Garlic powder, to taste
Onion powder, to taste
Cornstarch (optional)
Skim milk (optional)

Steam vegetables until soft. Blend in blender with a small amount of the chicken stock. Add onion and spices. Thicken with a small amount of cornstarch, or thin with chicken broth or skim milk, if desired.

Diet Vinaigrette

Sugar substitute, to taste
¼ cup each chopped onion,
  green pepper, and pimento

1 teaspoon sweet pickle relish
  (optional)
¼ cup water
¾ cup white vinegar

Add first five ingredients to water and vinegar. When large amounts of pimento, peppers, and onions are used, dressing can be quite thick. Serve over fresh mixed greens.

Breast of Chicken with Zucchini and Mushrooms

1 medium onion, sliced
4 chicken breast halves, skinned
  and boned
Salt and freshly ground black
  pepper, to taste
2 tablespoons Dijon mustard
2 medium zucchini, sliced ¼-
  inch thick

½ pound mushrooms, sliced
3 tablespoons diet margarine
¾ teaspoon basil leaves
⅛ teaspoon garlic powder
⅛ teaspoon paprika
1 tablespoon grated Parmesan

Tear off 4 12-by-18-inch lengths of heavy-duty aluminum foil. Place onion slices in center of lower half of each piece of foil. Flatten each chicken breast to ¼-inch thickness. Place chicken over onions and season with salt, pepper, and mustard. Top with zucchini and mushrooms. Season vegetables with salt and pepper and dot with margarine. Sprinkle with basil, garlic, and paprika. Fold upper half of foil over ingredients, meeting bottom edge. Secure all edges. Place foil packets on large cookie sheet. Bake in preheated 450° oven for 25 minutes or until chicken tests done. To serve, cut "X" in top of foil packets, fold outward, and sprinkle with cheese.

Chive-dotted Potatoes

12 small red potatoes
3 tablespoons diet margarine, in chunks
1½ tablespoons chives

Salt and freshly ground black pepper, to taste
1 teaspoon sweet pickle relish (optional)

Dice potatoes. Cut 4 big squares of foil and divide potatoes evenly among them. Add remaining ingredients, wrap securely, and bake in a preheated 400° oven for 30 minutes.

Fresh Berries with Yogurt Mousseline

3 pints strawberries
16 ounces plain yogurt

2 tablespoons sugar substitute, or to taste
Juice of ½ lemon

Wash, hull, and slice strawberries. Set aside in bowl. Separate ½ cup strawberries and add to processor along with remaining ingredients. Process and serve over strawberries.

Fit & Trim IV

Tomato and Feta Salad
Shrimp Linguini with Vegetables
Cabbage and Green Beans Paprika
Berries in Orange Cups
Carob Chip Cookies

PREVIOUS DAY   EARLY MORNING   FREEZER

                             Tomato and Feta Salad   Carob Chip Cookies
                             Orange Cups and
                               dressing

Tomato and Feta Salad

½ pound feta cheese
3 tomatoes
4 ounces pitted black olives,
     sliced

2 tablespoons olive or salad oil
½ teaspoon dried oregano
⅛ teaspoon freshly ground
     black pepper

Cube cheese and tomatoes and combine with other ingredients. Marinate about 1 hour and serve at room temperature.

Shrimp Linguini with Vegetables

½ cup half-and-half
6 tablespoons diet margarine
½ cup grated Parmesan
¾ teaspoon salt
¼ teaspoon freshly ground
     black pepper
4 cups hot, cooked linguini
     noodles (8 ounces uncooked)

18 ounces medium-size shrimp,
     cooked
4 cups assorted vegetables,
     cooked and cubed (fresh
     cauliflower, broccoli, and
     carrots)

Heat half-and-half in small saucepan over medium heat with margarine and stir until margarine melts. Remove from heat and whisk in cheese, salt, and pepper. Combine all ingredients well in large bowl and then divide into individual ramekins. Bake 10 minutes in preheated 400° oven.

Cabbage and Green Beans Paprika

1½ tablespoons unsalted
     butter
1 medium onion
3 cups fresh green beans, cut
     into 1-inch pieces
1 or 2 garlic cloves, minced
1½ cup unsalted chicken
     stock, reduced to ¾ cup

2 teaspoons Hungarian sweet
     paprika
1½ teaspoons tomato paste
3 cups coarsely chopped cabbage
1 to 2 tablespoons fresh lemon
     juice
Freshly ground black pepper

In large sauté pan, melt butter over medium-high heat. Add onion and sauté until lightly brown. Add beans and garlic and sauté 1 to 2 minutes, stirring constantly. Add reduced chicken stock, paprika, and tomato paste. Cover and bring to boil. Reduce heat and simmer 5 to 6 minutes. Add cabbage, mix, re-cover, and cook 3 minutes. Remove cover and let cook until liquid is reduced to a glaze. Season with lemon juice and pepper.

Berries in Orange Cups
(Serves 6)

Dressing:

¾ cup plain yogurt
2 tablespoons honey
1½ teaspoons grated orange peel

1½ tablespoons fresh orange juice
¼ teaspoon grated nutmeg

Thoroughly blend all ingredients and refrigerate several hours.

Fruit:

3 large oranges
½ cup fresh blueberries
½ cup fresh raspberries

1 cup hulled and halved fresh strawberries
6 fresh mint sprigs

Cut each orange in half and remove pulp. Trim oranges so bottoms will be flat. Combine berries with as much orange pulp as desired and spoon mixture into orange shells.

Spoon dressing over berries when ready to serve and garnish each orange with a sprig of mint.

Carob Chip Cookies

1 cup malted barley syrup or honey
1 cup diet margarine
3 eggs
1 teaspoon soda

½ teaspoon cinnamon
2½ cups stone-ground whole wheat flour
⅓ cup evaporated milk
2 cups quick-cooking oatmeal

6 ounces carob chips (unsweetened or date sweetened)

In Food Processor:

Place barley syrup, softened margarine, and eggs in processor. Blend. Add soda, cinnamon. Add flour. As you process the flour into the first mixture, add the milk through the feed tube. Blend for at least 1 minute.

Add oatmeal all at once. Start processor. As soon as oatmeal is mixed in, transfer batter to a bowl, add carob chips.

Regular Method:

Cream syrup, margarine, eggs. Sift soda, cinnamon, and flour together. Add alternately with evaporated milk. Blend in oatmeal and carob chips.

Drop by teaspoonfuls onto greased cookie sheet. Bake in preheated 350° oven for 12 to 15 minutes.

Note: This is a soft cookie and keeps well in an airtight jar.

Note: Malted barley syrup can be used as a sweetener by people on sugar-restricted diets. Honey can be substituted by people able to tolerate sweeteners.

A DAY AT LA COSTA
(Serves 4; total calories: 1035 per person)

We have been fortunate indeed to obtain, through Dr. R. Philip Smith, Medical Director of La Costa Spa, a sample diet for one complete day. We hope this will provide you with a delicious and healthy way to begin a weight-loss program.

Breakfast   (Total calories per person: 264)

Cantaloupe or Strawberries
Cheese Omelets with Creole Sauce
Whole Wheat Toast
Diet Jam

PREVIOUS DAY   EARLY MORNING   FREEZER

Diet Jam

Fruit
(40 calories per serving)

¼ cantaloupe, *or* **½ cup strawberries**

Cheese Omelets with Creole Sauce
(146 calories per serving)

Each Omelet:

2 eggs
Pinch of salt substitute
Pinch of freshly ground white
pepper

½ teaspoon water
1 ounce Cheddar cheese, grated

Make omelets one at a time. Beat 2 eggs until frothy, adding a pinch of salt substitute, white pepper, and ½ teaspoon water. Cook the omelet in hot, nonstick pan over low heat until bottom is set and slightly brown. Sprinkle with the grated cheese. Place about one-quarter of the Creole Sauce in the center of the omelet, fold the omelet in half, and slide it onto a plate. Repeat until all 4 omelets are made.

Creole Sauce:

¼ small yellow onion, sliced
½ whole green pepper, seeded
and sliced

½ small tomato, peeled and
diced
1 tablespoon diet ketchup

Heat a heavy skillet sprayed with a noncaloric vegetable spray and sauté the sliced onion until done but not brown. Add the pepper, tomato, and ketchup. Simmer until the vegetables are done, approximately 10 to 15 minutes.

Whole Wheat Toast
(68 calories per slice)

Diet Jam
(10 calories per teaspoon)

1 quart unsweetened berries or cut-up fruit
Lemon juice, to taste

1 envelope plain gelatin, dissolved in a little water
Liquid sugar substitute, to taste

Use a fresh or frozen fruit of your choice. Combine fruit and lemon juice and cook, covered, about 20 minutes. Stir often.

Add softened gelatin and stir until dissolved. Add sweetener after the jam has cooled.

Note: Fruits like blueberries or boysenberries are nice kept whole.

Luncheon
(Total calories per person: 386)

Clam Chowder
Citrus Bouquet Salad with Spa French Dressing
Coq au Vin
Fresh Artichokes with Hot Dip
French Bread
Chocolate Mousse

PREVIOUS DAY	EARLY MORNING	FREEZER
French Dressing	Clam Chowder	
Artichoke dip	Chocolate Mousse	

Clam Chowder
(50 calories per serving)

6 ounces chopped clams, with juice
1 small tomato, seeded and chopped
8 ounces unsalted tomato juice
¼ green pepper, seeded and diced

1 teaspoon diced scallion
1 bay leaf
¼ teaspoon whole thyme
Juice of ¼ lemon
½ cup water

Drain clams, reserving juice, and set aside. Combine clam juice and remaining ingredients and simmer, covered, until vegetables are tender. Add the chopped clams and heat through. Serve very hot in boullion cups.

Citrus Bouquet Salad
(46 calories per serving)

12 grapefruit sections
12 orange sections

Crisp lettuce cups

Arrange grapefruit and orange sections alternately in the lettuce cups. Serve with Spa French Dressing.

Spa French Dressing:

2 rounded teaspoons vegetable gum
4 ounces white vinegar
1½ cups unsweetened pineapple juice

Juice of ½ lemon
¼ level teaspoon dry mustard
⅛ teaspoon white pepper
3 heaping teaspoons paprika
Pinch of celery seed

Dissolve the vegetable gum in a small amount of the vinegar, or sprinkle the powdered gum very lightly on the top of the liquids, to prevent lumping. Mix the remainder of the vinegar, pineapple juice, lemon juice, mustard, pepper, paprika, and celery seed. Blend lightly with a wire whisk or fork. Do not overbeat. (If the dressing is overbeaten, the air incorporated dilutes the color.) Place in a covered container and store in the refrigerator until served.

Note: There are many kinds of vegetable gum. They can be purchased from your pharmacist.

Coq au Vin
(146 calories per serving)

4 3½-ounce chicken breasts
1 cup dry white wine
1 cup salt-free chicken broth
Pinch of thyme

Freshly ground white pepper
½ cup julienned carrots
½ cup sliced fresh mushrooms
½ cup pearl onions

Brown the chicken in preheated 500° oven for 15 minutes. Drain off all excess fat. Heat the wine and chicken broth in a heavy skillet and simmer for 10 minutes, uncovered. Pour the wine and chicken broth over the chicken. Add the thyme, pepper, and carrots. Cover and cook until the chicken is done, 5 to 15 minutes. Remove chicken pieces. Add mushrooms and pearl onions and simmer the sauce to reduce by one-half. Glaze each chicken piece with some of the sauce.

Fresh Artichokes with Hot Dip
(36 calories per serving)

4 small artichokes	**4 thick slices lemon**

Wash artichokes and cut off the tip of each leaf. Place each artichoke on a slice of lemon in a large shallow skillet. Add enough boiling water to half fill the skillet. Cover and cook until tender, about 12 minutes. Take the skillet off the heat and allow the artichokes to steep for 2 to 3 minutes longer. Drain well.

Hot Dip:

1 cup salt-free chicken broth	**½ teaspoon chopped parsley,**
1 teaspoon lemon juice	**for garnish**
½ teaspoon dill	

Combine cold broth, lemon juice, and dill and garnish with parsley. Heat and serve with artichokes.

French Bread
(68 calories per ½-inch-thick-slice)

Chocolate Mousse
(40 calories per serving)

1 teaspoon plain gelatin (⅓ envelope)	**1 package low-calorie chocolate pudding mix**
½ cup cold water	**3 egg whites**
	½ cup shaved ice

Dissolve the gelatin in the cold water and add the pudding mix, blending well. Simmer the mixture slowly, stirring constantly until it thickens. Let the mixture cool to room temperature. Beat the egg whites until frothy and add the shaved ice slowly, beating. Continue beating until the egg whites hold a peak. Fold the egg whites gently into the pudding mix, combining well. Spoon into sherbet glasses and chill.

Dinner   (Total calories per person: 385)

Shrimp Cocktail with Spa Cocktail Sauce
Italian Salad Bowl with Spa Vinaigrette
Pepper Steak
Baked Potato
Baby Carrots à l'Orange
Coconut Custard

PREVIOUS DAY	EARLY MORNING	FREEZER
Spa Cocktail Sauce	Coconut Custard	
Spa Vinaigrette		

Shrimp Cocktail with Spa Cocktail Sauce
(60 calories per serving)

8 large shrimp, cooked and cooled

Shredded lettuce
4 thin lemon slices, for garnish

Slice each shrimp in half lengthwise. Place a little shredded lettuce in the bottom of 4 cocktail glasses, top with 4 shrimp halves per person, and garnish with a lemon slice. Serve with Spa Cocktail Sauce.

Spa Cocktail Sauce:

1 11-ounce bottle diet ketchup (no sugar or salt)
1 tablespoon freshly squeezed lemon juice

¼ cup freshly grated horseradish
¼ cup chopped chives (optional)

Mix the first 3 ingredients, adjusting horseradish and lemon to taste. Refrigerate, covered. Serve very cold or very hot. Add fresh chives just before serving if desired.

Italian Salad Bowl with Spa Vinaigrette
(35 calories per serving)

1 small head romaine, torn into bite-size pieces	1 large tomato, cut into quarters
1 zucchini, seeded and sliced	1 small red onion, sliced very thin and separated into rings

Pinch of dried oregano

Chill romaine and zucchini in crushed ice until very crisp. Fill small salad bowls and garnish with tomato and onion rings. Sprinkle with oregano. Serve with Spa Vinaigrette.

Spa Vinaigrette:

¼ cup white vinegar	Pinch of freshly ground white pepper
1 cup unsweetened pineapple juice	¼ cup finely chopped celery hearts
Juice of ½ lemon	¼ cup chives or scallion tops
¼ teaspoon dry mustard	¼ cup sweet red peppers
1 clove garlic, bruised	

Blend well all ingredients except the chopped vegetables. (The garlic should be bruised only, and removed before serving.) Add the chopped vegetables, place in a covered container, and refrigerate.

Pepper Steak
(146 calories per serving)

4 3-ounce portions lean New York steak	2 thin slices onion
½ cup unsalted, defatted beef broth	4 thin slices green pepper
	4 mushrooms, sliced
	Freshly ground black pepper

Flatten the steaks lightly with a meat mallet. Place them in a hot nonstick frying pan or use a noncaloric vegetable spray and brown quickly, turning once. Set aside. Deglaze the pan with the beef broth, stirring to loosen any particles of beef clinging to the pan. Add the remaining ingredients, stirring lightly. Cook only long enough for the vegetables to soften. They should still be crunchy. Garnish the top of each steak with a portion of the pepper sauce.

Baked Potato
(68 calories per serving)

Bake 1 small potato per person in preheated 350° to 375° oven for 45 to 60 minutes or until done.

Baby Carrots à l'Orange
(36 calories per serving)

1½ cups unsalted chicken broth	2 large carrots, peeled and sliced
	1 medium scallion, chopped
1 small orange, peeled and diced	

Heat the chicken broth to boiling. Add the carrots and scallion. Cover and cook until nearly tender, approximately 7 to 8 minutes. Add the diced orange and cook 4 to 5 minutes more. Serve hot.

Coconut Custard
(Serves 6; 40 calories per serving)

5 egg whites	Yellow food coloring (optional)
2 cups nonfat milk	1 tablespoon unsweetened
Liquid sugar substitute, to taste	coconut, toasted in the oven
½ teaspoon vanilla extract	

Blend the egg whites and 1 cup of the milk until just combined. Do not overmix. Add the remaining milk, sweetener, vanilla, and a few drops of food coloring. Blend just enough to combine the ingredients. Fill 6 warmed custard cups with the mixture, place them in a pan of hot water, and bake at 350° for 45 minutes or until set. Chill thoroughly. Just before serving, sprinkle with the toasted coconut.

Equivalents and Substitutions

Equivalents

Sizes of cans: 8-ounce can = 1 cup
No. 1 can = 1¼ cups = 10½ ounces
No. 2 can = 2½ cups = 1 pound, 4 ounces
No. 2½ can = 3½ cups = 1 pound, 13 ounces
No. 3 can = 4 cups = 2 pounds
No. 10 can = 12–13 cups = 6 pounds, 1 ounce

1 cup whole milk = ½ cup evaporated milk plus ½ cup water, *or* ½ cup reconstituted dry skim milk plus 2 teaspoons butter

1 8-ounce box of spaghetti = 4 cups cooked

1 pound carrots = 3 cups shredded or 2½ cups cut

1 medium onion = ½ cup chopped

1 pound cabbage = 5 cups shredded

Substitutions

Out of confectioners' sugar? Whir granulated sugar in blender with ⅛ teaspoon cornstarch per 1 cup granulated sugar until consistency of confectioners' sugar.

Do you need Parisienne spices, or quatr' épices?

Combine: 2 tablespoons ground ginger
    1 tablespoon ground cloves
    1 tablespoon freshly grated nutmeg
    2 teaspoons fresh white pepper

For 1 tablespoon cornstarch, substitute 1 tablespoon arrowroot plus 2 tablespoons flour.

For 1 cup cake flour, substitute 1 cup minus 2 tablespoons all-purpose flour.

For 1 cup corn syrup, substitute 1 cup granulated sugar plus ¼ cup liquid.

For 1 cup honey, substitute 1¼ cups granulated sugar plus ¼ cup liquid.

For 1 cup light cream, substitute 2 tablespoons butter plus 1 cup, less 1 tablespoon, milk.

For 1 cup tomato juice, substitute ½ cup tomato sauce plus ½ cup water.

For 2 cups tomato sauce, substitute ¾ cup tomato paste plus 1 cup water.

For 1 teaspoon dry mustard, substitute 1 tablespoon prepared mustard.

Do you need 1 cup sour cream? Use:
    1 cup plain yogurt, *or*
    1 cup evaporated milk plus 1 to 1½ tablespoons
     vinegar, *or*
    1 cup cottage cheese mixed in the blender with
     2 tablespoons milk, plus 1 teaspoon lemon juice, *or*
    6 ounces cream cheese whipped with enough milk to
     make 1 cup

Not enough raisins for the recipe? Substitute an equal amount of chopped, pitted prunes.

Substituting cocoa for chocolate in recipes is simple:

Unsweetened baking chocolate: Use 3 tablespoons unsweetened cocoa plus 1 tablespoon shortening or salad oil for each ounce of chocolate required.

Semisweet chocolate: Use 6 tablespoons unsweetened cocoa, 7 tablespoons sugar, and ¼ cup shortening for 6 ounces.

Sweet cooking chocolate: Use 4 tablespoons cocoa, ¼ cup plus 2 teaspoons sugar and 2 tablespoons plus 2 teaspoons shortening to equal 4 ounces.

Additional Thoughts

Sprinkle a cake plate lightly with granulated sugar before unmolding the warm cake to prevent slices from sticking to the plate when cooled cake is cut.

Use unwaxed dental floss to divide a cake into layers.

Unbaked pie crusts will not become soggy if they are brushed with lightly beaten egg white before filling. Try this when making custard pies.

To avoid messy spills, place pie shell on the oven rack *before* pouring in custard pie or quiche fillings.

Having trouble removing something from a cookie sheet? Run unwaxed dental floss underneath.

To keep meringues from weeping, use superfine sugar.

Test meringues by rubbing ½ teaspoon of whipped meringue between fingers. If it feels grainy, keep beating.

When baking meringues, bake on parchment paper. This will keep meringues from sticking to pan.

To test whether yeast dough is kneaded enough, make an indentation with two fingers. Dough should spring back to shape.

To test when dough is properly risen, make an indentation in it with two fingers. If it is ready, the indentation will remain.

Bread is baked and ready when loaf sounds hollow when lightly tapped on bottom or side.

Nuts and marshmallows freeze well, and stay fresh longer frozen.

For best results, always whip egg whites at room temperature in a metal bowl.

Freeze leftover egg whites in ice cube trays, then put into freezer bags to store.

You can whip up to 2 cups of whipping cream in your food processor. The whipped cream will be dense and is wonderful for frosting cakes.

Before measuring anything sticky, such as honey, coat the measuring cup with oil.

To clarify butter, melt unsalted butter over low heat and skim off the froth that rises to the top. The remainder is the clarified butter.

Partially freeze meats for easy slicing or grinding.

Truss poultry with unwaxed dental floss.

To freeze fish, place in a freezer bag and fill ¾ full with water. Seal and freeze.

Interesting containers for dips can be made from hollowed-out vegetables, such as green peppers, zucchini, small pumpkins, or cabbages.

To store fresh ginger root, peel, cover with sherry, and place in a glass jar in the refrigerator.

To chop hard-cooked eggs quickly, use a ricer or potato masher.

To facilitate the job of chopping garlic, rub the knife blade with a light coating of vegetable oil.

Use an ice cream scoop to fill muffin and cupcake pans. Cakes will be of equal size, and messy drips avoided. A small ice cream scoop is the perfect utensil for making drop cookies.

Needlepoint pliers or tweezers are perfect for removing small bones from fish before cooking.

Before baking beans or other oven-simmered foods, lightly grease the inside of the casserole lid to ease cleanup.

When browning hamburgers or bacon, use a metal bulb-baster to remove excess grease from the pan.

A dampened paper coffee filter makes an excellent substitute for cheesecloth when straining stocks.

Bake stuffed tomatoes, onions, or peppers in a muffin tin to keep them upright.

Recipes containing acidic ingredients such as tomatoes, wine, lemon juice, and vinegar should be cooked in stainless steel, glass, or enamel utensils.

To ripen any fruit or vegetable, put in a brown bag and place in a dark place for a day or two.

To peel garlic, place garlic flat on board and strike with flat side of a broad knife.

To rescue a curdled egg sauce, add a couple of ice cubes and whisk. If it is still not of the consistency desired, whip in processor.

Index